A Poetics of the Image
Paul Celan and André du Bouchet

LEGENDA

LEGENDA is the Modern Humanities Research Association's book imprint for new research in the Humanities. Founded in 1995 by Malcolm Bowie and others within the University of Oxford, Legenda has always been a collaborative publishing enterprise, directly governed by scholars. The Modern Humanities Research Association (MHRA) joined this collaboration in 1998, became half-owner in 2004, in partnership with Maney Publishing and then Routledge, and has since 2016 been sole owner. Titles range from medieval texts to contemporary cinema and form a widely comparative view of the modern humanities, including works on Arabic, Catalan, English, French, German, Greek, Italian, Portuguese, Russian, Spanish, and Yiddish literature. Editorial boards and committees of more than 60 leading academic specialists work in collaboration with bodies such as the Society for French Studies, the British Comparative Literature Association and the Association of Hispanists of Great Britain & Ireland.

The MHRA encourages and promotes advanced study and research in the field of the modern humanities, especially modern European languages and literature, including English, and also cinema. It aims to break down the barriers between scholars working in different disciplines and to maintain the unity of humanistic scholarship. The Association fulfils this purpose through the publication of journals, bibliographies, monographs, critical editions, and the MHRA Style Guide, and by making grants in support of research. Membership is open to all who work in the Humanities, whether independent or in a University post, and the participation of younger colleagues entering the field is especially welcomed.

ALSO PUBLISHED BY THE ASSOCIATION

Critical Texts
Tudor and Stuart Translations • *New Translations* • *European Translations*
MHRA Library of Medieval Welsh Literature

MHRA Bibliographies
Publications of the Modern Humanities Research Association

The Annual Bibliography of English Language & Literature
Austrian Studies
Modern Language Review
Portuguese Studies
The Slavonic and East European Review
Working Papers in the Humanities
The Yearbook of English Studies

www.mhra.org.uk
www.legendabooks.com

STUDIES IN COMPARATIVE LITERATURE

Editorial Committee
Chairs: Dr Emily Finer (University of St Andrews)
and Professor Wen-chin Ouyang (SOAS, London)

Dr Ross Forman (University of Warwick)
Professor Angus Nicholls (Queen Mary, University of London)
Dr Henriette Partzsch (University of Glasgow)
Dr Ranka Primorac (University of Southampton)

Studies in Comparative Literature are produced in close collaboration with the British Comparative Literature Association, and range widely across comparative and theoretical topics in literary and translation studies, accommodating research at the interface between different artistic media and between the humanities and the sciences.

ALSO PUBLISHED IN THIS SERIES

20. *Aestheticism and the Philosophy of Death: Walter Pater and Post-Hegelianism*, by Giles Whiteley
21. *Blake, Lavater and Physiognomy*, by Sibylle Erle
22. *Rethinking the Concept of the Grotesque: Crashaw, Baudelaire, Magritte*, by Shun-Liang Chao
23. *The Art of Comparison: How Novels and Critics Compare*, by Catherine Brown
24. *Borges and Joyce: An Infinite Conversation*, by Patricia Novillo-Corvalán
25. *Prometheus in the Nineteenth Century: From Myth to Symbol*, by Caroline Corbeau-Parsons
26. *Architecture, Travellers and Writers: Constructing Histories of Perception*, by Anne Hultzsch
27. *Comparative Literature in Britain: National Identities, Transnational Dynamics 1800-2000*, by Joep Leerssen
28. *The Realist Author and Sympathetic Imagination*, by Sotirios Paraschas
29. *Iris Murdoch and Elias Canetti: Intellectual Allies*, by Elaine Morley
30. *Likenesses: Translation, Illustration, Interpretation*, by Matthew Reynolds
31. *Exile and Nomadism in French and Hispanic Women's Writing*, by Kate Averis
32. *Samuel Butler against the Professionals: Rethinking Lamarckism 1860–1900*, by David Gillott
33. *Byron, Shelley, and Goethe's Faust: An Epic Connection*, by Ben Hewitt
34. *Leopardi and Shelley: Discovery, Translation and Reception*, by Daniela Cerimonia
35. *Oscar Wilde and the Simulacrum: The Truth of Masks*, by Giles Whiteley
36. *The Modern Culture of Reginald Farrer: Landscape, Literature and Buddhism*, by Michael Charlesworth
37. *Translating Myth*, edited by Ben Pestell, Pietra Palazzolo and Leon Burnett
38. *Encounters with Albion: Britain and the British in Texts by Jewish Refugees from Nazism*, by Anthony Grenville
39. *The Rhetoric of Exile: Duress and the Imagining of Force*, by Vladimir Zorić
40. *From Puppet to Cyborg: Pinocchio's Posthuman Journey*, by Georgia Panteli
41. *Utopian Identities: A Cognitive Approach to Literary Competitions*, by Clementina Osti
43. *Sublime Conclusions: Last Man Narratives from Apocalypse to Death of God*, by Robert K. Weninger
44. *Arthur Symons: Poet, Critic, Vagabond*, edited by Elisa Bizzotto and Stefano Evangelista
45. *Scenographies of Perception: Sensuousness in Hegel, Novalis, Rilke, and Proust*, by Christian Jany
46. *Reflections in the Library: Selected Literary Essays 1926–1944*, by Antal Szerb
47. *Depicting the Divine: Mikhail Bulgakov and Thomas Mann*, by Olga G. Voronina
48. *Samuel Butler and the Science of the Mind: Evolution, Heredity and Unconscious Memory*, by Cristiano Turbil
49. *Death Sentences: Literature and State Killing*, edited by Birte Christ and Ève Morisi
50. *Words Like Fire: Prophecy and Apocalypse in Apollinaire, Marinetti and Pound*, by James P. Leveque

A Poetics of the Image

Paul Celan and André du Bouchet

Julian J. I. Koch

Studies in Comparative Literature 52
Modern Humanities Research Association
2021

*Published by Legenda
an imprint of the Modern Humanities Research Association
Salisbury House, Station Road, Cambridge CB1 2LA*

*ISBN 978-1-78188-356-3 (HB)
ISBN 978-1-78188-359-4 (PB)*

First published 2021

All rights reserved. No part of this publication may be reproduced or disseminated or transmitted in any form or by any means, electronic, mechanical, photocopying, recording or otherwise, or stored in any retrieval system, or otherwise used in any manner whatsoever without written permission of the copyright owner, except in accordance with the provisions of the Copyright, Designs and Patents Act 1988, or under the terms of a licence permitting restricted copying issued in the UK by the Copyright Licensing Agency Ltd, Saffron House, 6–10 Kirby Street, London EC1N 8TS, England, or in the USA by the Copyright Clearance Center, 222 Rosewood Drive, Danvers MA 01923. Application for the written permission of the copyright owner to reproduce any part of this publication must be made by email to legenda@mhra.org.uk.

Disclaimer: Statements of fact and opinion contained in this book are those of the author and not of the editors or the Modern Humanities Research Association. The publisher makes no representation, express or implied, in respect of the accuracy of the material in this book and cannot accept any legal responsibility or liability for any errors or omissions that may be made.

Trademark notice: Product or corporate names may be trademarks or registered trademarks, and are used only for identification and explanation without intent to infringe.

© Modern Humanities Research Association 2021

Copy-Editor: Dr Marie Isabel Schlinzig-Matthews

CONTENTS

	Acknowledgements	ix
	Abbreviations	xi
	Introduction	1
1	Paul Celan's Early Conception of the Image	21
2	Du Bouchet's Early Essays on the Conception of the Image in his Poetic Predecessors	34
3	The Typified Image in 'Tenebrae'	53
4	Writing as *Typos* in Celan's 'Bei Wein und Verlorenheit'	66
5	Du Bouchet's Polychotomous Image	81
6	The Self-Surpassing Image in Celan's 'Halbzerfressener'	105
7	The Conception of Translation in Celan and Du Bouchet	118
8	The Image in Celan's and Du Bouchet's Reciprocal Translations	134
	Conclusion	157
	Bibliography	165
	Index	177

ACKNOWLEDGEMENTS

This study originated in my PhD research and I owe much to the tireless work of my supervisor Leonard Olschner, with whom I had so many fruitful conversations on- and off-topic. I am also very grateful to my external examiners Emma Wagstaff and Shane Weller who have supported me and my work greatly. I extend deep gratitude to Clément Layet who patiently answered my questions about du Bouchet and pointed me to exciting research material. I also owe thanks for feedback to a number of anonymous peer reviewers of my journal articles as well as to those who have read or listened to chapters or conference papers based on the research for this book, particularly Rüdiger Görner and Christine Ivanović. My work was enriched by the Celan seminars given by Bertrand Badiou and Jean-Pierre Lefebvre at the ENS in Paris, which I attended during my all too brief research stay in France. During my time there, I was fortunate to meet Philippe Blanc who manages du Bouchet's estate at the Bibliothèque Littéraire Jacques-Doucet and who was more than forthcoming in giving me an overview of du Bouchet's estate and pointing me to interesting manuscripts.

The beginnings of this study can be traced back to research interests developed during my Master's, and the scrupulous feedback from my then supervisors Katrin Kohl and Patrick McGuinness proved very helpful for my PhD research as well.

I was fortunate enough to have been granted a funded internship by the German Literary Archive in Marbach am Neckar where I had the opportunity to do research on Celan. I am also thankful to the German Academic Exchange Service for awarding me a generous scholarship that made the research for this book possible.

Further thanks go to my friend Oliver Kenny who read parts of my research and always provided helpful comments.

This study has also been nourished by interests, preferences, and preoccupations that ultimately go back to my upbringing. Thus, my thanks and gratitude are first and foremost to my parents without whom I would not be who I am and who have relentlessly supported me.

I owe a debt of gratitude to Robin Steedman for the many productive exchanges, ideas, and her scrupulous comments and feedback on my work as well as her tireless support.

Finally, I would like to thank the S. Fischer Verlag for allowing me to reproduce Celan's poems for free. Because Suhrkamp and Mercure de France were only able to provide me with time-limited reprint rights, it is with great regret that Celan's poems 'Halbzerfressener' and 'Erblinde' as well as du Bouchet's poem 'Peinture' and his translation of Celan's 'Erblinde' entitled 'Sois en ce jour aveugle' are not reprinted here.

Parts of this book were already published in journal articles. I thank *German Life and Letters* and Wiley for allowing me to reproduce portions of the following articles: 'The Image in Celan's Poetics' (2018) and 'Between "Urbild" and "Abbild": The Conception of the Image in Celan's "Bei Wein und Verlorenheit", "Tenebrae", and "Halbzerfressener"' (forthcoming). I also thank the *Modern Language Review* and the MHRA for giving me permission to reprint portions of the article 'Translation as Poetics in the Works of André du Bouchet' (2019).

J.J.I.K., August 2021

ABBREVIATIONS

GS   Benjamin, Walter, *Gesammelte Schriften*, I–VII, ed. by Rolf Tiedemann and Hermann Schweppenhäuser (Frankfurt a. M.: Suhrkamp, 1974–89)

AB   Du Bouchet, André, *Aveuglante ou banale: Essais sur la poésie, 1949–1959*, ed. by Clément Layet and François Tison (Paris: Le Bruit du temps, 2011)

CW   Celan, Paul, *Gesammelte Werke*, I–V, ed. by Beda Allemann and Stefan Reichert (Frankfurt a. M.: Suhrkamp, 1983)

HKA   Celan, Paul, *Historisch kritische Ausgabe*, I–XVI, ed. by Rolf Bücher and Axel Gellhaus (Frankfurt a. M.: Suhrkamp, 2003–17)

KG   Celan, Paul, *Kommentierte Gesamtausgabe*, ed. by Barbara Wiedemann (Frankfurt a. M.: Suhrkamp, 2005)

M   Celan, Paul, *Der Meridian: Endfassung — Entwürfe–Materialien*, ed. by Bernhard Böschenstein and Heino Schmull (Frankfurt a. M.: Suhrkamp, 1999) [=Tübinger Ausgabe]

Mikro   Celan, Paul, '*Mikrolithen sinds, Steinchen': Die Prosa aus dem Nachlass*, ed. by Barbara Wiedemann and Bertrand Badiou (Frankfurt a. M.: Suhrkamp, 2005)

SA   Hölderlin, Friedrich, *Sämtliche Werke*, I–VIII, ed. by Friedrich Beissner (Stuttgart: Kohlkammer, 1946–85) [= große Stuttgarter Ausgabe]

INTRODUCTION

The 'image' is a notoriously difficult term to render in sharp contours. Frequently, it is thought to be synonymous with metaphor. However,

> [t]here is something fundamentally awkward and strange in using the word 'image' as a substitute for 'metaphor' [...]. For the word 'image', unlike 'metaphor', seems to suggest that the end result of what the author is doing is a picture.[1]

Yet '[i]f you read John Milton's phrase "a Forest huge of Spears", the final result of your reading can't be a picture, since you cannot permanently present something to your mind's eye as being a forest and spears'.[2] The image understood as metaphor thus soon comes up against considerable obstacles.

The use of the word image becomes even more problematic if it is employed anachronistically. The word 'image' does not come into common usage in application to literature and is not treated as synonymous with metaphor based on sense impressions until the seventeenth and eighteenth centuries.[3] There is a long tradition of rhetoric and classic literary criticism on which this more recent notion of the image builds, resting on a conceptual background in which the rhetorician appeals to the imagination of her audience.[4] Nonetheless, the ubiquitous use of the word image by poets and literary critics is unique particularly to the eighteenth century in which it is integrated into a framework of (divine) inspiration and creative imagination.[5]

But the word 'image' is not only used as a synonym for metaphor. Perhaps even more frequently, literary critics use it to denote a concoction of sense impressions,[6] for instance a vividly visual scene, smells, sounds, or any other poetic appeal to the senses. Understood in this sense, the image can be virtually anything. The lack of a clearly defined meaning of 'image', in turn, voids the term of any explanatory and analytical power. In short, all too frequently, the use of 'image' to fix evasive literary meanings simply results in relegating the semantic evasiveness on the level of the poem to the level of the scholarly vocabulary employed.

The frequent inattention in the use of the word 'image' among critics is perhaps epitomized when as eminent a philosopher and literary critic as Hans-Georg Gadamer uses the word in his analyses of Paul Celan within the space of three pages in completely different contexts and without regard for conceptual coherence. Interpreting Celan's poem 'Die Zahlen', he initially sees 'Bilder' as the result of sensory perception in the 'Bewußtsein, in dem immer etwas sich abbildet'. This reading would make 'Bilder' a mental phenomenon. Yet somehow these images are also of a semantic nature, because he subsequently utilizes 'Bilder' in order to describe the textual and linguistic phenomenon of Celan describing apparently vivisected body parts in the poem 'Weißgrau'.[7] Eventually Gadamer's lack of a critical discussion of the term in his interpretation leads to a mingling of Celan's own use of the word 'Bilder' in the poem 'Die Zahlen' with Gadamer's employment of the term by which he denotes the poet's metaphors more generally.

It is necessary to further illuminate the extremely rich conceptual history of the image, because we see it reflected particularly powerfully in Celan's poetry, but also in André du Bouchet's early writings on other poets. Since both poets draw quite extensively on terminology and ideas developed over centuries of discourse about the image, this introduction will, in the following, outline some central concepts and historical moments in this discourse and supplement this general framework in the respective chapters where relevant for the focused analyses. Yet, neither Celan nor du Bouchet simply subscribe to any of these historical notions. Therefore, a second reason for discussing Celan and du Bouchet against an informed background of previous conceptions of the image is to understand where either poet departs from them. Knowledge of these discourses will therefore help us understand why Celan adheres more to the traditional, historical discourse on the image, despite his reservations; it will also allow us to understand how different du Bouchet's later notion of the image is compared to traditional thinking about it.

We should briefly point to some of the difficulties in defining the image in Celan and du Bouchet here. In his famous 'Meridian' speech, Celan seems to use the word 'Bild' synonymously with tropes, figures of speech, or simply metaphor (*M*, 10). His notes to his speech, however, reveal that the presumed parallels between 'Bild' and metaphor are actually much more problematic.[8] A similarly tricky relationship to image as metaphor, image as mental image, and the image as a concept which cannot be fully visually captured can be observed in du Bouchet's early writings.[9] The conception of the image becomes even more complex as the later du Bouchet regards the poetic image at least in part as a visual image when he deliberately inserts spaces or gaps into his poetic texts (see chapter 5). To disentangle these different aspects of the image upon which both authors draw and to distinguish more lucidly the developments in their conception of the image, let us first examine the most important strands in the history of the discourses on the image.

The Distinction between *Archetypos* and *Typos*

Before it was applied to literature, the image was part of a lively discussion in philosophy, theology, and the visual arts, particularly in Platonic and Neoplatonic contexts.[10] Some of the complexity of these discussions is owing to the Old Greek and Latin with their wide range of different terms for the visual or mental image.[11] We will encounter linguistic disparities and translational difficulties again when we come to Celan and du Bouchet. The German language provides Celan with a wider range of terms for 'image', including the distinction between the image of something or someone (*Abbild*) and that of which the image is an image (*Urbild*).

French and English on the other hand only render the former meaning in their word 'image'. Thus, whenever the distinction between 'Urbild' and 'Abbild' becomes relevant in the discussion here, I will use the Old Greek terms of *archetypos* and *typos*, respectively, and use the term 'image' as an umbrella term that encompasses both *archetypos* and *typos*. When it must be made especially clear that I speak of the image as a representation of something else, that is in the German sense of *Abbild*, I will call it *typos*-image.

This distinction between the image and the model which gives the image its appearance is of fundamental importance. Discussed in the biblical context of man as *imago Dei* in Western philosophy and theology, the distinction lies at the heart of nothing less than the very constitution of human nature. Particularly influential in this respect was Augustine's discussion of humankind as *imago Dei*, which we will visit in the context of Celan's poem 'Tenebrae' in chapter 3.[12] The conception of the distinction between *archetypos* and *typos* also goes to the core of the debates on the status of the visual arts, since another discourse on the image in Western theology and philosophy revolves around the second commandment 'Thou shalt not make unto thee any graven image, or any likeness of any thing that is in heaven above, or that is in the earth beneath, or that is in the water under the earth' (Exodus 20. 4).[13] Thus depending on the interpretation of the nature of this distinction between *typos* and *archetypos*, humankind was either closer to or further from God and the creation of artistic representations legitimate or not.

To familiarize ourselves with this distinction, let us retrace the arguments in some of the historical, philosophical, and theological debates. The rootedness of the image in the material present and its character as a sign referring to something other than itself are at the core of the Byzantine iconoclastic discussions (between 726 and 787 and again between 814 and 842). Iconophiles defended Christian icons by carefully situating the image (*typos*), semiotically and ontologically, at the boundary to the invisible, incorporeal original image of the divinity (*archetypos*) and its material embodiment.[14] Thus, the *typos*-image remained ontologically dependent on the *archetypos*, which it resembled and imitated. Precisely in this resemblance lies the crucial difference to the *archetypos*. It is due to its resembling the *archetypos* that the *typos* is different from the *archetypos*. The *typos* consequently embodies the difference to the *archetypos*, thereby referring *ex negativo* to the *archetypos* it portrays.[15] In the view of the iconophiles, it is the fact that the religious icon (that is a *typos*-image) is discrepant to the *archetypos* visualized by the icon which sets the icon apart from the pagan idol that feigns to be *typos* and *archetypos* at once in a material object. The fact that the representation of divinity and the very divinity itself pretend to coincide in the idol reveals its blasphemous character.[16] In the eyes of the iconophiles such an assumed coincidence of *typos* and *archetypos* in the idol denigrated the status of the divinity to that of a material object.

Forms of iconoclasm are just as pervasive in the centuries after the Byzantine discussions. Iconoclasts typically targeted the image's physicality and instead favoured an immaterial truth, an 'inner form'.[17] For instance, the perceived dual nature of the image is reflected in the Renaissance in the art theoretical debates about *perspectiva*. The word perspective literally means 'to look through' and hence implies that the viewer looks through the image, presumably onto some form of essence behind the image, as if the image were transparent, irrespective of its artistically shaped material nature.[18] In a similar manner, controversies between artistic schools were articulated in the distinction between *archetypos* and *typos*. Hence Giorgio Vasari opposed Michelangelo's art, which emphasized form and outline (*disegno*), to (mostly Venetian) schools focusing on *colore*. According to Vasari, only the *disegno* could properly render the immaterial *concetto* (concept) of the drawn objects, whereas the *colore* was bound in its materiality.[19] To give one last example for the pervasiveness of the *archetypos*–*typos* distinction we turn to Eckhart von Hochheim (*c.* 1260–1328), a German mystic who was an enormous influence on the subsequent development of the German meaning of 'Bild'. He conceived of the image of God in man (*imago Dei*) dialectically as a continuous process of 'Bildung', implying a progressing assimilation to the archetypal deity ('Einbildung' and 'Überbildung'), and a parallel process of 'Entbildung' in which man dismantles himself of his mortal body that is merely a typified representation of the *archetypos*.[20]

Such discourses on the artistic image and the image in relation to humankind fed into the debates on the imagination and artistic as well as poetic genius in the eighteenth century. The genius was conceived as a *poeta alter deus*, 'a second maker, a just Prometheus under Jove'.[21] Subsequently, the emphasis was increasingly placed on the creative individual rather than divine inspiration. Soon enough the *archetypos* providing the artistic creation that is the *typos*-image resided in the mind of the imaginative subject rather than an absolute, invisible, and unattainable divine being. Possibly nowhere is the notion of the imaginative poet-creator as pronounced as in F. W. J. Schelling's *System des transzendentalen Idealismus*, in which he elevates the 'Einbildung' to highest power, effectively forming the infinite *archetypos* into the finite artistic creation.[22] Although Celan's own declarations in his poems 'Bei Wein und Verlorenheit' or 'Halbzerfressener' (chapters 4 and 7) are not quite as confident as Schelling is of the poetic ability to embody or express the *archetypos*, Celan's conception of poetry as genuine, truthful expression echoes and is indebted to these debates on the image in intellectual history. Similarly, du Bouchet's discussion of the image in his poetic predecessors touches upon these debates of *archetypos* and *typos* (see chapter 2).

The Image as Natural Sign

Another strand of thought runs parallel to the rise of the conception of creative imagination with the image in its tow. In the eighteenth century, philosophers and critics were increasingly preoccupied with the nature of language and particularly wanted to root words in reality, that is, they conceived or hoped to conceive of words as natural signs.[23] One way of doing this was to link the word to the image.[24] The physical presence of visual artworks increasingly fascinated poets who were hoping to transfix words and their meanings into similarly self-expressing signs that were, in modern terminology, signifiers and signifieds in one.[25] Whereas the majority of linguistic signs are arbitrary, as already indicated by the many vastly different languages in the world, the image seems at least to some extent to be self-explicatory or self-expressing. There is no phenomenon in the visual arts similar to the phenomenon of translation across languages.

Certainly, there are crass differences between different epochs and painters. Some of the symbolism may also be lost on the modern contemplator of medieval art, and she may not know 'that representations of God the Father, God the Son, the angels and the apostles should have the feet bare, while there would be real impropriety in representing the Virgin and the saints with bare feet' or that '[l]ittle figures of nude and sexless children, ranged side by side in the folds of Abraham's mantle, signified the eternal rest of the life to come'.[26] Thus there is a certain arbitrariness at play in highly symbolic visual art such as medieval art. But these types of symbolism work more like arbitrary signs, such as words, rather than being constituted by the specific signifying visuality of the image. Hence, apart from the symbolism of the bare feet as a sign for a certain group of people in the Christian faith, we still have, fundamentally and visually, the bare feet which we recognize as bare feet. Similarly, we recognize the human shape in the figures of the saints, however rudimentary their form and even if we are ignorant of their iconographic meaning.

Linking word and image therefore seemed to salvage poetic language as self-expressing natural sign in eighteenth-century aesthetics. Even though Gotthold Ephraim Lessing had persuasively argued that the sign systems of writing (which consist of 'willkürliche[] Zeichen') and the visual arts (consisting of 'natürliche[] Zeichen') worked in different ways and made previously commonplace assumptions about their similarity impossible,[27] the hope to join language and image to create a form of natural sign was never fully extinguished. Wendy Steiner argues this history and idea of the image as natural sign ultimately culminated in the concrete poetry of modernism.[28]

In Celan's poetry we see clear vestiges of the desire for words to be natural signs that are meaningful in themselves independent of linguistic conventions. For Celan truthful poetic speech is not arbitrary, but a veridical expression of reality without recourse to convention.[29] Certainly, it is highly doubtful whether such pure poetic expression is attainable. Apart from perhaps in his early text 'Edgar Jené: Der Traum vom Traume' Celan does not claim that it is, and in his 'Meridian' speech he even unambiguously denies the possibility of such an absolute poetry (*M*, 10). Yet the demand of poetry to approximate it is perennially present (*M*, 10). However, unlike for instance the concrete poets, Celan's desire for truthful poetic speech in some form of self-expressing natural sign is not articulated by means of the image as a *visual* sign.[30] Rather when Celan expresses this ambition for poetry to speak truthfully through the image, it is the poetic image as a concept indebted to Platonic and Neoplatonic ideas of the image as *archetypos* or *Urbild* he has in mind and not the poetic image somehow conceived as visual image.

Du Bouchet's poetic image on the other hand is clearly also a visual one. Yet rather than desiring the status of the natural sign, his poetry constantly problematizes the idea that a poem's visuality and its semantic content can be unified into a self-expressing sign. Du Bouchet's poetic image is constituted precisely by the difference between the visuality and the semantics of his poetry (see chapter 5).

The Renewal of the Image Discourse in France

In France, various aspects of previous discussions of the image and its relation to the written word resurfaced at around the turn of the twentieth century, a development which already had some roots in the poetic movement of Symbolism in the late 1800s.[31] Perhaps the preoccupation with visuality in poetry was inevitable in an age when photography was distributed widely through newspapers and moving images were soon to captivate large audiences.[32] There seem to be three distinct but interrelated ways in which the image sparked fruitful and controversial debates in twentieth-century poetry and poetics from around 1900 until the 2000s in France, spanning movements such as futurism, cubism, Dadaism, surrealism, and the more loosely grouped writers of *L'Éphémère*, especially du Bouchet (1924 to 2001), Celan (1920 to 1970), and Bonnefoy (1923 to 2016). These ways differ with respect to what aspect of the image is focused on: (1) the image as a particular visual arrangement of text, (2) the image conjoining poetry and visual arts, and (3) the image as a poetic and painterly theoretical discourse. Let us briefly outline these three concurrent developments.

(1) Perhaps no single text had as much of an influence on the visual arrangement of poetry in the modern period as Stéphane Mallarmé's 'Un coup de dés' (1897). The poem was the first piece of modern visual poetry and proved a continuous source of inspiration for the following generation.[33] Although the visuality of his poem served more as a means to the end of 'metaphysical speculation' rather than as an end in itself,[34] Mallarmé's poem helped the coming generation to turn an eye to the visual and material aspect of poetry. Mallarmé thus explicated in a letter to Edgar Degas: '[c]e n'est point avec des idées que l'on fait des vers ... C'est avec des mots.'[35] Mallarmé's experiments with spacing and typography in his poem outlined a whole new set of instruments emphasizing the visual character of poetry, which were then to be used by the concrete poets, even if for a very different end. Guillaume Apollinaire's *Lettre-Océan* (1914) would conjoin Mallarmé's abstract visual experiments as well as figurative ones which could be found in religious Christian poetry.[36] Inspired by Pierre Reverdy's own adaptations of Mallarmé's revolution in spacing, du Bouchet's experiments with the space of the page can be traced back to Mallarmé's seminal poem.[37]

(2) Almost contemporaneous to Mallarmé's 'Un coup de dés', another revolution in the visualization of poetry took place. The twentieth century became the century of the *livres d'artistes*, books created in collaboration between poets and painters. Even though these types of books had a long and rich history especially in France, going back to medieval book illustrations, the development of the abstract visual arts would fundamentally change the way illustrations interact with the text. Instead of having self-contained images which would be kept spatially and visually separate from the text, text and illustration would merge and interact not only on the level of meaning but also visually.[38] Perhaps the earliest and one of the most impressive examples of such a collaboration between artist and author is *La Prose du transsibérien* by the poet Blaise Cendrars and the painter Sonia Delaunay (1913).[39]

(3) From around 1910 onward, a lively poetic discourse arose on the nature of the

image. The discourse had its roots in the increased engagement and interaction of poets and painters in the second half of the nineteenth century in France (perhaps beginning with Charles Baudelaire's *Salons*), and also in the more abstract idea of the poet as seer as poignantly formulated in Arthur Rimbaud's 'Lettres du voyant' (with Victor Hugo as a predecessor, amongst others).[40] France had not had discussions of *ut pictura poesis* and imagination on a scale similar to that in German-speaking lands or even Britain,[41] which perhaps explains why this field still seemed ripe for exploration and cultivation in the eyes of French poets. The temporal difference to the earlier debates in German-speaking lands and Britain and the different cultural context of nineteenth-century France reshaped and reinvigorated poetic conceptions of the image. At the very latest when the surrealist movement spread across Europe, discussions of the image were resparked beyond the borders of France.

A particularly influential early figure for the French poetic discourse on the image starting around 1910 was Remy de Gourmont, for whom the image seems to lie at the heart of all thought.[42] Gourmont reduces all ideas, even abstract ones, to sense impressions in his *Le Problème du style* (1902): '[u]ne idée n'est qu'une sensation défraîchie, une image effacée.'[43] What Gourmont appears to mean by 'effacée' here is less a complete obliteration of what originally constituted sensory content in our thoughts, but rather the fact that it has been forgotten that ideas are images or sense impressions ('dénuées de mémoire ou d'imagination visuelle').[44] Hence an idea appears to be nothing but a representation of which we have forgotten that it is derived from sensory content. If these ideas cannot be retranslated into images, they are deprived of any insight and are effectively blind ('[c]'est un aveugle mental').[45] If it is thus images that make us see in more than just the literal sense, then the arts and their shared roots in sense impressions, which Gourmont predominantly describes visually, using visual metaphors, let us engage with and experience reality:[46] '[l]a sensation se transforme en mots-images; ceux-ci en mots-idées; ceux-ci en mots-sentiments.'[47] This fundamental conception of the image, coupled with the idea propagated in *La Culture des idées* (1900) that no images are so different that they cannot be combined in thought,[48] became fundamentally influential for Apollinaire, Pierre Reverdy, and their contemporaries.[49]

In Reverdy's influential conception of the image we see that it has been accorded an even more privileged position compared to its place in Gourmont's thinking. The image is able to elicit the same effect in our mind as reality itself without our being required to make recourse to reality.[50] Furthermore in Reverdy, the image understood as synonymous with metaphor is combined with Gourmont's proclamation that any two images can be paired and his assumption that what underlies images is reality:

> L'Image est une création pure de l'esprit.
> Elle ne peut naître d'une comparaison mais du rapprochement de deux réalités plus ou moins éloignées. [...]
> Deux réalités qui n'ont aucun rapport ne peuvent se rapprocher utilement. Il n'y a pas création d'image.[51]

In Reverdy's conception, the image therefore unites what he calls two realities which are equal constituents of the image (unlike metaphor which grafts a term into a context alien to it). André Breton cited and transformed Reverdy's notion of the image in his first surrealist manifesto (1924), significantly amplifying its influence. Breton shapes Reverdy's conception of the image as comprising two distinct realities in accordance with Apollinaire's aesthetics of surprise.[52] Breton's image then, under the influence of Reverdy and Apollinaire, favoured the unforeseeable, shocking clash of the as yet unknown (to which Reverdy objected).[53] We will see an influence of Reverdy via Breton's surrealist image in Celan's 'Traum vom Traume' (chapter 1) but also in du Bouchet's later conception of the image (chapter 5).

The Image in Du Bouchet and Celan

Both Celan and du Bouchet are informed by Reverdy's and Breton's image as well as the wider historical and conceptual context of the image. They grew up in different contexts and traditions leading them to follow quite distinct paths in poetry — paths, however, that intersected in the Paris of the 1960s. As editors of the Parisian poetry journal *L'Éphémère*, they found a shared platform for their approaches to poetry and painting.

Paul Celan grew up as a German-speaking Jew in Bukovina in what today is Ukraine. During World War II, his parents were killed by the Nazis, while Celan survived forced labour. After the war he spent six months in Vienna (from 17 December 1947 until July 1948)[54] before moving permanently to Paris, eventually becoming a French citizen in 1955.[55] In Paris, Celan emerged as one of the foremost German-speaking poets and translators after the war, demonstrating most powerfully the possibilities but also the difficulty of writing after Auschwitz. In 1955, Celan met and, in 1966, befriended André du Bouchet,[56] child of a French-American father and a Russian-Jewish mother, who had returned to Paris almost at the same time as Celan arrived after having spent the war years in American exile. After a few years as a researcher at the Centre National de la Recherche Scientifique (CNRS), du Bouchet took the poetic stage by storm with the publication of his first full volume of poetry, *Dans la chaleur vacante* (1961), which Celan would translate in 1968. When Celan psychological health deteriorated in the sixties, he found in du Bouchet a close friend of similar mind in whom he could confide.[57] The most apparent testimony to their friendship and poetic engagement are their reciprocal translations. Du Bouchet would continue honouring his friend in translating his poetry until long after Celan had died by suicide in 1970.

As previously mentioned, France, and specifically French poetry from the turn to the twentieth century onwards, was the site of a resurgent urgency in discussing the meaning and significance of the image. As we have seen, the various implications of the term 'image' are vast and not mutually exclusive. It can be anything from metaphor to something visual or painterly in poetry, or be a more particular concept within a poetic movement. For instance, surrealism, which underwent a brief but powerful renaissance after World War II, combined several different conceptions of the image, with poets working together with painters and other artists and pursuing a variation on Reverdy's image at the heart of the movement's poetic programme. Celan would briefly, and never in an orthodox manner, engage with the surrealist conception of the image in his months in Vienna. But his poetry also revealed the presence of much earlier conceptions of the image between *archetypos* and *typos* (see chapter 1). In his later poetry, Celan's image increasingly moved away from surrealist or even French poetic discussions of the image (whether Mallarméan or Reverdian) and engaged with the theological and philosophical discourses around the image which underlie his conception of poetry and language as such.

Even though du Bouchet was more influenced by the specific Reverdian image than by its surrealist redefinition, he would encounter in the Paris of 1948 a discursive environment revolving around the image similar to the one Celan found in Vienna. As a researcher at the CNRS, du Bouchet examined via Friedrich Hölderlin, Maurice Scève, Hugo, and Baudelaire some of the philosophical and theological implications of the image which also interested Celan. Unlike Celan, however, du Bouchet would soon thereafter move away from a terminology and conception of the image imbued with the distinction between *archetypos* and *typos*. Rather, he embraced a radical and paradoxical interpretation of the image in which the visual interaction between black ink and white page gains as important a place as semantic meaning. The currency of particularly the French poetic discourse of the image in du Bouchet's thought is apparent. Du Bouchet's poetry and poetics unite the three French strands of thought about the image in poetry outlined above. Du Bouchet makes extreme use of the space of the page to express his poetry. He also carries on the tradition of the *livre d'artiste* in his many collaborations with painters such as Pierre Tal-Coat (*Sur le pas*, 1959; *Laisses*, 1975; *Sous le linteau en forme de joug*, 1978), Alberto Giacometti (*L'Inhabité*, 1967), Bram van Velde (*L'Unique*, 1973; *Dans leur voix les eaux*, 1980), Geneviève Asse (*Ici en deux*, 1982), Albert Ràfols-Casamada (*Le Surcroît*, 1989), and the photographer Francis Helgorsky (*Andains*, 1996).[58] Finally, du Bouchet puts forth his own conception of the image indebted to rich traditions of discourse on the image, from the image as constituted by *archetypos* and *typos* (see chapter 2)[59] to an image inspired by Reverdy as the juxtaposition of disjunct but equal entities (see chapter 5). The extremes to which du Bouchet carries his notion of the image establishes him as a singular and perhaps the most radical exponent in the centuries-old poetic discourse on the image.

The image in Celan's poetry would not reach similar extremes as du Bouchet's, which at least in part is due to the fact that his poetry shows more reservation to the heritage of 'Un coup de dés', to which Reverdy's and du Bouchet's conceptions of the image and the visuality of their poetry are clearly indebted. Having experienced the Holocaust much more closely than his friend, Celan must have felt in his poetry a greater urgency than du Bouchet to remain grounded in a reality that is clearly not only a poetic reality but shares the same discursive and historical realm as his listeners and readers.[60] This need articulates itself in his poetics of the image, for instance, by taking up in his poem 'Tenebrae' the discourse of the impossibility of the *imago Dei* after the Holocaust.

The poetics of the image of Celan and du Bouchet offer themselves up for comparison not only because they negotiate so fruitfully the many rich traditions of discourse revolving around the image, but also because their reciprocal translations allow for direct comparisons of how each transformed the poetry of the other in his own image. This study will not only seek to complement existing literature on Celan's and du Bouchet's conceptions of the image, but also hopes to illuminate some of the richness of previous thinking and writing about the image with which Celan and du Bouchet engaged in their different ways. We discover in Celan's and in du Bouchet's conceptions of the image many of the theological and philosophical debates we outlined before, whereas particularly the mature poetry of du Bouchet lets us appreciate the relation between word and image in a new way.

As we have seen, the image is often conflated with metaphor. It is thus perhaps not surprising that Celan's poetics of the image has been scrutinized under the rubric of metaphor.[61] Another well-established avenue of inquiry into Celan and the image is his relation to the visual arts,[62] with studies focusing on the concrete biographical contexts of Celan's surrealist period and his collaboration with Edgar Jené,[63] his translation of Pablo Picasso,[64] or the collaborations with his wife, Gisèle Celan-Lestrange, on the *livres d'artistes Atemkristall* (1965) and *Schwarzmaut* (1969).[65] The question of the poetic image as a poetological concept in Celan that is distinct from metaphor — 'das Bild ist nicht Metapher' (*M*, 69) — and distinct from the visual artifice — 'Bildhaftes, das ist keineswegs etwas Visuelles' (*M*, 107) — is thus overlooked in Celan research. Only Catherine Fournanty-Fabre's study tries to balance between these different poles, scrutinizing the relation of Celan's image to metaphor, other poetic forms (even sonic ones), and the visual arts, and tries to give the image a more fundamental conceptual underpinning.[66] However, she does not realize that Celan's conception of the image is profoundly informed by the long-standing philosophical discussions of *archetypos* and *typos* — discussions which are especially prevalent in the German context given that the German 'Bild' resonates in both 'Urbild' and 'Abbild'.

Because our focus will be on the underlying discursive context of *archetypos* and *typos* in Celan's conception of language, we will not closely consider Celan's and Celan-Lestrange's *livres d'artistes*. Studying the correspondence between poems and images in these works simply does not provide the most fertile ground for engaging with Celan's conception of the image, not least since Celan's artistic collaborations with Celan-Lestrange seem to be predominantly motivated by private and amorous concerns rather than poetological or art-theoretical ones.[67] Hugo Huppert's short transcript of a conversation with Celan, which is often cited when looking for a poetological reflection by Celan on the influence of the visual arts and particularly his wife's work on his poetics, does not yield much insight beyond a few metaphors taken from the visual arts:

> [d]as Zeichnerische liegt mir näher, nur schattiere ich mehr als Gisèle [Celan-Lestrange], ich verschatte absichtlich manche Kontur, um der Wahrheit der Nuance willen, getreu meinem Seelenrealismus. Und was meine angeblichen Verschlüsselungen anlangt, so würde ich eher sagen: Mehrdeutigkeit ohne Maske, so entspricht sie exakt meinem Gefühl für Begriffsüberschneidung

> [...]. Sie kennen doch auch die Erscheinung der Interferenz, Einwirkung
> zusammentreffender kohärenter Wellen aufeinander. [...] Dem entspricht meine
> [...] Mehrdeutigkeit.[68]

While Celan admits to feeling closer to the visual arts than he does to 'Tonkunst', the core passages revolving around the 'Wahrheit' and the 'Seelenrealismus' of his poetry are not described in painterly terms and soon he switches to a scientific metaphor from physics to delineate the polysemy of his poetry as working by interferences. Indeed, the poetologically more fruitful outcome of Celan's engagement with Celan-Lestrange's work is his translation of Jean Bazaine's *Notes sur la peinture d'aujourd'hui*, whose conception of the painted image shares much with Celan's poetic image and its implied distinction between *archetypos* and *typos* (see chapters 1 and 6).[69] More varied reasons apply for not conceding more space to discussing Celan's ekphrastic poems ('Einkanter', 'Unter ein Bild', 'Bei Brancusi, zu zweit', 'Blitzgeschreckt'; 'Hüttenfenster' may have been inspired by Chagall).[70] Many of these poems ('Bei Brancusi, zu zweit', 'Blitzgeschreckt', 'Hüttenfenster', 'Unter ein Bild') did not lend themselves as readily to demonstrating Celan's conception of the image and his notions of *archetypos* and *typos* as the poems under consideration in this study.[71]

Celan's preoccupation with a poetic image that is not merely *typos* but tends towards an *archetypos* is, I believe, incommensurable with post-structuralist approaches to Celan. Thus, on many occasions in this study, my arguments about Celan's image here take positions against post-structuralism even when I do not explicitly state so. Celan's preoccupation with notions such as 'Wahrheit', the prominence of 'Atem' in his poetry, his notions of poetry as a dialogue and of the poem as a handshake suggest the presence of a breathing, living speaker who testifies to the truthfulness of his poetry, rather than inviting post-structuralist interpretive aporia. Furthermore, Celan's privileging of the handwritten as opposed to the printed written word[72] (we will encounter Celan's association between 'sie schrieben' and 'sie logen' in chapter 4), and his untiring, fervent insistence that his poetry is decipherable despite its difficulties pose significant obstacles to enlisting Celan in a grammatological programme of endlessly deferring signifiers.[73]

Furthermore, the very core of my argument, namely that Celan seeks out an archetypal image, goes against such approaches as will become more apparent throughout this study. On the other hand, as we will see below, du Bouchet's image can more persuasively be read through a post-structural lens.

Given the prominence of the image in du Bouchet, it is not surprising that various aspects of the image in his poetry have received critical attention. There are studies on du Bouchet's image as visual image with regard to his *blancs*[74] and on his *livres d'artistes*,[75] on his early thought about the image in its Reverdian context,[76] and the image as a more general abstract concept.[77] However, none of them fully consider the genesis of du Bouchet's early thought about the image which has recently become widely accessible thanks to the publication of selections from his *Carnets* and particularly the publication in *Aveuglante ou banale* of du Bouchet's collected early essays written at the CNRS. We gain completely new insights into the development of the poet's early notion of the image and its impact on his later thought, which remains largely unstudied.[78] Du Bouchet's early conception of the image, still framed in a discourse on *archetypos* and *typos*, can be traced through his discussions of Maurice Scève, Friedrich Hölderlin, Victor Hugo, and Charles Baudelaire. Du Bouchet ultimately develops his own conception of the image as divested from an *archetypos*, straddling the visible and the invisible (see chapter 2). His abandoning of notions of the *archetypos* should also compel us to keep a respectful distance from some of the ontologizing or more Heideggerian readings of du Bouchet.[79] I do not believe that du Bouchet pursues a 'théologie négative' when his poetry tends towards absence or disappearance, as Champeau holds.[80] Even though du Bouchet is regularly read through various types of dialectical terminology, e.g. 'figure' and 'fond',[81] 'Grund' and 'Abgrund',[82] 'figure' and 'défigure',[83] as well as 'je' and 'dehors',[84] the dialectical terms are often not in equipoise and one term is given preference over the other or even a form of Hegelian synthesis is suggested. For instance, Martinez emphasizes that we are to read du Bouchet's white space not as 'substantialisation[s] de l'absence' but as 'une indication du rapport'.[85] However, these assertions fly in the face of Martinez's later reinstating, through the back door, of an ontology of absence, 'au-delà de tout phénomène visible',[86] that is metaphysically described as 'constitu[ant] la *réalité ultime* de ce que nous nommons le réel'.[87] Similarly Bishop interprets du Bouchet's paradoxes to be 'moins oppositionelle qu'unificatrice',[88] asserting an 'ontologie [...] de l'attente'.[89] In this ontology enshrouded in Platonic terms, he sees 'la manifestation aléthique d'une opacité'[90] from which du Bouchet's poetic reality springs, but that is also somehow 'sans transcendance'.[91] To then implicate all ontology as being entangled in paradoxes and difficulties, as Bishop does,[92] merely relegates the problem to a discourse outside of poetry.

Layet seems to me to frame du Bouchet's poetics in much more apposite terms by leaving aside questions of ontology and focusing on the logical and semantic nature of the contradictions inherent in du Bouchet's image, which he poses as irresolvable.[93] In du Bouchet, there is not only tension within the semantics but also between the different visual aspects of his poetry. I will share ground with other researchers who believe that du Bouchet's white space is a bearer of signification in that it makes signification possible, while it at the same time disrupts signification by the nature of the white gaps' interrupting his writing.[94] We will see that du Bouchet's image is constituted by relations negotiated intra-semantically between notions of absence and presence, but also visually between the white page and the ink inscribed upon it. While an interpretation of the white gaps in du Bouchet's poetry from a semantic and visual perspective is not without precedent,[95] no clear framework has been developed for how these different tensions within the semantics and between the semantics and the visuality of the text should be approached.

Although I do not explicitly embrace a post-structuralist approach to du Bouchet, my readings of his image as one that encompasses *absence* and *presence* is open to the possibility of understanding his poetry in this way. Du Bouchet's embracing of non-finality and the continuous deferral of meaning in the repetitions of his poetry, his constant reworkings, revisions, and republication of his poetry in different forms,[96] his fragmented notion of self (see chapters 2 and 8),[97] his privileging of the written over the spoken word,[98] and the fact that he is the only one of the *L'Éphémère* poets who also contributed to the post-structuralist *Tel Quel*[99] all speak to the possibility of interpreting du Bouchet in a post-structuralist manner.

I will not be looking at the *livres d'artistes* to which du Bouchet contributed. This is for similar reasons as with Celan. On the one hand, at least in his collaborations with Tal-Coat, du Bouchet had already written the text to which the painter then would add his illustrations,[100] and thus if our interest lies with du Bouchet's conception of the image, his particular poems seem to have been conceived prior to and without the artistic contribution. On the other hand, leaving out of close consideration those works that sprang from true collaboration between du Bouchet and other artists strengthens possibilities of comparison between du Bouchet and Celan. While the aesthetic appeal of each of the *livres d'artistes* is unique and they seem to be more central to the poetics of du Bouchet than Celan's collaborations with his wife are to his respective poetics, the fundamental points about the conception of du Bouchet's image will remain unchanged by this omission (as should become clear from our discussion in chapter 5).

Overview of Chapters

We will follow an overall chronological structure with respect to the development of Celan's and du Bouchet's thinking. We will begin by looking at Celan's conception of the image in his early text 'Edgar Jené: Der Traum vom Traume' as inflected by Breton's surrealism, and his image as a surprising, chance conjunction of disparate elements. Yet, we will see that despite the influence of surrealism, *archetypos* and *typos* and their philosophical and theological contexts constitute the fundamental tenets of Celan's thinking (chapter 1). In the subsequent chapter, we observe that du Bouchet, in his early critical and philosophical discussions written while researching at the CNRS, pursues a similar line of thinking about the image in terms of *archetypos* and *typos* and retraces it in the poetics of Maurice Scève, Friedrich Hölderlin, Victor Hugo, and Charles Baudelaire. As we approach du Bouchet's discussion of the notion of the image in Hugo and Baudelaire, however, we will see that particularly (du Bouchet's) Baudelaire and, indeed, du Bouchet himself increasingly move away from conceiving of the image in terms of *typos* and *archetypos*. In du Bouchet's interpretation of Baudelaire this seems to be a consequence of the fact that the poet is perennially confined to the limits of his own subjectivity, having been uprooted from subjectivity's connection to the objectivity of divine vision (chapter 2). Returning to Celan, we discover a similar scepticism towards a divine *archetypos* and the poetic subject's rootedness in the divine as *imago Dei* as well as a distrust in a divine paragon as such, which Celan associates with the Holocaust in his poem 'Tenebrae' (chapter 3). Ultimately and unlike du Bouchet, Celan does not give up thinking about the image in terms of *archetypos* and *typos*. Thus in Celan's poem 'Bei Wein und Verlorenheit', poetic speech is closely linked to the *archetypos* as opposed to its translation into written language that is a mere *typos*-image (chapter 4). Celan's notion of writing as *typos*-image contrasts quite starkly with the conception of the image of the mature du Bouchet, who embraces the visual and material character of his poetry. The mature du Bouchet develops a polychotomous image in which the semantics and the visual aspects of his poetry contrast and interact (chapter 5). Du Bouchet's paradoxical and visual image is contrasted with Celan's archetypal image in his 'Halbzerfressener' where the poetic act of creation becomes an act of continually shaping oneself into an image (chapter 6). In the last two chapters (7 and 8) we can compare most clearly the different conceptions of the image in the poetics of Celan and du Bouchet as we examine their reciprocal translations. After outlining the notion of translation and its relation to the image in each poet's respective poetics (chapter 7), we will scrutinize how their respective conceptions of the image informed their translations (chapter 8).

A note on terminology: as pointed out briefly towards the beginning of this introduction, whenever I speak of an image as an originary model or paradigm in the sense of the German *Urbild*, I will use the word *archetypos*. On the other hand, when I speak of the image in the common sense as a representation of something else, that is in the German sense of *Abbild*, I will call it *typos* or — if the relations have to be made especially clear — *typos*-image. I opted for these Greek terms over simply importing the German ones, because the terms 'archetype' and 'type' are already present in the English language, even if they usually carry slightly different meanings. To avoid confusions with the ordinary English usage of, for instance, archetype, I have left the original Greek ending '-os' unaltered when I use these terms with respect to the image. The term 'image' will generally be used as an umbrella term which can, depending on the context, encompass visual, semantic, and conceptual aspects of poetry and will also generally denote both the *archetypos* and *typos*. The terms *archetypos* and *typos* introduce into English designators for the two aspects of the image that reflect the German *Urbild* and *Abbild*. Both *Urbild* and *Abbild* contain the word *Bild*, and thus when Celan uses the word *Bild* he can mean either of the two, depending on the context, whereas in English the word image commonly excludes the former and only denotes the latter sense. Consequently, my using *archetypos* and *typos* makes it clearer that both *archetypos* and *typos* pertain to the image. Finally, when I occasionally speak of Celan's image or du Bouchet's image this is shorthand for Celan's or du Bouchet's *conception of the image*. I will *not* be using the word 'image' to denote a specific or extended metaphor, as in the common English usage of the word 'imagery'.

Notes to the Introduction

1. Philip Nicholas Furbank, *Reflections on the Word 'Image'* (London: Secker & Warburg, 1970), p. 4.
2. Ibid.
3. Bernhard Asmuth, 'Seit wann gilt die Metapher als Bild? Zur Geschichte der Begriffe "Bild" und "Bildlichkeit" und ihrer gattungspoetischen Verwendung', in *Rhetorik zwischen den Wissenschaften: Geschichte, System, Praxis als Probleme des 'Historischen Wörterbuchs der Rhetorik'*, ed. by Gert Ueding, Walter Jens, and Joachim Dyck (Tübingen: Niemeyer, 1991), pp. 299–311;

Furbank, pp. 25–34; Ray Frazer, 'The Origin of the Term "Image"', *English Literary History*, 27.2 (1960), 149–61.
4. Particularly notable in this respect is Loginus' treatment of visualization and imagination, cf. *Plato, Aristotle, Horace, Longinus: Classical Literary Criticism*, trans. by Penelope Murray and T. S. Dorsch, new edn. (London: Penguin Books, 2000; repr. 2004), pp. 133–66. Cf. also Furbank, p. 26.
5. Some of the most exhaustive studies on this are: James Engell, *The Creative Imagination: Enlightenment to Romanticism* (Cambridge, MA: Harvard University Press, 1981); Jochen Schmidt, *Die Geschichte des Genie-Gedankens in der deutschen Literatur, Philosophie und Politik, 1750–1945*, 2 vols (Heidelberg: Winter, 2004), I.
6. Furbank, p. 20.
7. Hans G. Gadamer, *Gesammelte Werke*, 6th edn, 10 vols (Tübingen: Mohr Siebeck, 1985–1995), IX: *Ästhetik und Poetik II: Hermeneutik im Vollzug* (1993), pp. 403, 406.
8. Celan writes for example: 'Sinnbild und das Bild ist nicht Metapher' (*M*, 69).
9. For instance, du Bouchet attributes the following conception of the image to his admired fellow poet Pierre Reverdy: 'les images de la poésie la plus imagée qui soit passent *inaperçues*; la syntaxe, portée par des images, reste entièrement soumise à leur avènement, et cependant ces images sont *invisibles*' (*AB*, 55; my emphases).
10. To name only a few important titles: Erwin Panofsky, *Idea: Ein Beitrag zur Begriffsgeschichte der älteren Kunsttheorie* (Leipzig: Hessling, 1924); Werner Beierwaltes, *Denken des Einen* (Frankfurt a. M.: Klostermann, 1985), pp. 73–114; E. H. Gombrich, 'Icones Symbolicae: The Visual Image in Neo-Platonic Thought', *Journal of the Warburg and Courtauld Institutes*, 11 (1948), 163–92.
11. Michael Syrotinski, 'Image', in *Dictionary of Untranslatables: A Philosophical Lexicon*, ed. by Barbara Cassin, Steven Rendall, and Emily S. Apter (Princeton: Princeton University Press, 2014), p. 478.
12. Kreuzer also discusses Johannes Scotus Eriugena and Eckhart von Hochheim: Johann Kreuzer, 'Was heißt es, sich als Bild zu verstehen? Von Augustinus zu Eckhart', in *Denken mit dem Bild: Philosophische Einsätze des Bildbegriffs von Platon bis Hegel*, ed. by Arno Schubbach and Johannes Grave (Munich: Fink, 2010), pp. 75–99. Of fundamental importance is also Cusanus: see Thomas Leinkauf, 'Der Bild-Begriff bei Cusanus', in *Denken mit dem Bild*, ed. by Schubbach and Grave, pp. 99–129.
13. All quotations from the Bible are from the *King James Version* (Glasgow: Collins, 1991).
14. Emmanuel Alloa, 'Bildwissenschaft in Byzanz: Ein iconic turn avant la lettre?', in *Philosophie des Bildes. Philosophie de l'image*, ed. by Anton Hügli (Basle: Schwabe, 2010), pp. 11–35 (pp. 23–31); cf. also Gerhart B. Ladner, 'The Concept of the Image in the Greek Fathers and the Byzantine Iconoclastic Controversy', *Dumbarton Oaks Papers*, 7 (1953), 1–34; Kurt Bauch, 'Imago', in *Was ist ein Bild?*, ed. by Gottfried Boehm (Munich: Fink, 1994), pp. 11–39; Georg Ostrogorsky, *Studien zur Geschichte des Byzantinischen Bilderstreites* (Wrocław: Marcus, 1929).
15. Alloa, p. 31.
16. Ibid., pp. 30–31.
17. Panofsky traces this conception to antiquity, where 'forma' or 'species' was a 'Zwitterbildung aus dem aristotelischen ενδον εἶδος, mit dem sie die Eigenschaft teilt, eine bewußtseinsimmanente Vorstellung zu sein, und der platonischen Idee, mit der sie die Eigenschaft der absoluten Vollendung, des "perfectum et excellens" gemeinsam hat' (Panofsky, p. 10).
18. E.g. in Albrecht Dürer, cf. Dieter Mersch, 'Materialität und Formalität: Zur duplizitären Ordnung des Bildlichen', in *Materialität und Bildlichkeit: Visuelle Artefakte zwischen Aisthesis und Semiosis*, ed. by Marcel Finke and Mark A. Halawa (Berlin: Kadmos, 2012), pp. 21–49.
19. Cf. e.g. Giorgio Vasari, *The Lives of the Artists*, ed. by Julia Conaway Bondanella (Oxford: Oxford University Press, 2008), p. 501.
20. Kreuzer, 'Von Augustinus zu Eckhart', p. 89. Cf. also Wolfgang Wackernagel, 'Subimaginale Versenkung: Meister Eckharts Ethik der Bild-ergründenden Entbildung', in *Was ist ein Bild?*, ed. by Boehm, pp. 184–207.
21. Anthony Ashley Cooper Shaftesbury, *Characteristics of Men, Manners, Opinions, Times*, ed. by Lawrence Eliot Klein (Cambridge: Cambridge University Press, 1999), p. 93; Schmidt, I, p. 258.
22. F. W. J. Schelling, *Sämmtliche Werke*, ed. by K. F. A. Schelling, 14 vols in 2 parts: I [1–x] & II [1–

IV] (Stuttgart: Cotta, 1856–61), I, III (1858), 626–27. For a more extensive history of philosophical notions of the imagination, focusing on the 'Urbild' and 'Abbild' distinction in eighteenth-century German philosophy (especially Immanuel Kant and Schelling) as opposed to notions of the imagination in English and French philosophy, see my forthcoming article 'The "Urbild" of "Einbildung": The Archetype in the Imagination in German Eighteenth-Century Aesthetics, *Journal of the History of Ideas*, 82.4 (2021).

23. Cf. among others: Wendy Steiner, *The Colours of Rhetoric: Problems in the Relation between Modern Literature and Painting* (Chicago: University of Chicago Press, 1982), pp. 6–11; Yvonne Al-Taie, *Tropus und Erkenntnis: Sprach- und Bildtheorie der deutschen Frühromantik* (Göttingen: Vandenhoeck & Ruprecht, 2015), pp. 99–134.
24. Linking word and image also has a long tradition, from Plato's conception of names as images in *Cratylus* to Horace's *ut pictura poesis*. Cf. Plato, *Cratylus. Parmenides. Greater Hippias. Lesser Hippias*, trans. by H. N. Fowler (Cambridge, MA: Harvard University Press, 1939), 430 E, 439; Horace, *Satires, Epistles, and Ars Poetica*, trans. by Henry Rushton Fairclough (London: Harvard University Press, 1936), p. 480, l. 361.
25. Cf. Johann Jakob Breitinger, *Critische Dichtkunst worinnen die poetische Mahlerey in Absicht auf die Erfindung im Grunde untersuchet und mit Beyspielen aus den berühmtesten Alten und Neuern erläutert wird* (Zurich: Orell und Comp., 1740), esp. p. 9.
26. Emile Mâle, *The Gothic Image: Religious Art in France, 13th Century*, trans. by Dora Nussey (New York: Harper, 1958), p. 2.
27. Gotthold Ephraim Lessing, *Laokoon; oder, Über die Grenzen der Malerei und Poesie: Studienausgabe*, ed. by Friedrich Vollhardt (Stuttgart: Reclam, 2012), chapters 11 and 6, respectively.
28. Wendy Steiner, p. 197.
29. Probably the most illuminating study on Celan's notion of language without arbitrary signifiers is that of Winfried Menninghaus, *Paul Celan: Magie der Form* (Frankfurt a. M.: Suhrkamp, 1980).
30. As Celan stated in a conversation with Hugo Huppert, he despised 'konkrete Poeten'. Cf. Hugo Huppert, '"Spirituell": Ein Gespräch mit Paul Celan', in *Paul Celan*, ed. by Werner Hamacher and Winfried Menninghaus (Frankfurt a. M.: Suhrkamp, 1988), pp. 319–25 (p. 320). On the often ambivalent and perhaps predominantly negative relationship between Celan and the concrete poets, see the excellent study by Bronac Ferran, '"A Language that No-One Speaks": Celan and the Concrete Poets', in *Celan-Perspektiven 2019*, ed. by Bernd Auerochs, Friederike Felicitas Günther, and Markus May (Heidelberg: Winter, 2019), pp. 107–25.
31. See, for instance, the compilation of documents and discussions of the image in Symbolism by Guy Michaud, *La Doctrine symboliste: Documents* (Paris: Nizet, 1947).
32. Willard Bohn, *The Aesthetics of Visual Poetry, 1914–1928* (Cambridge: Cambridge University Press, 1986), pp. 1–3.
33. Even half a century after Mallarmé's death, du Bouchet was to say that 'to be a poet in France is to already write "sous le harnais post-mallarméen."' Cited in Michael Sohn, 'In Mallarmé's Harness? André du Bouchet and Stéphane Mallarmé', *French Forum*, 32.1/2 (2007), 117–35 (p. 117).
34. Bohn, *The Aesthetics of Visual Poetry, 1914–1928*, p. 49. Sohn likewise emphasizes that Mallarmé saw the paper's visuality not 'beyond [its] immediate "operational" quality in the text' (Sohn, p. 19).
35. Cited in David Scott, *Pictorialist Poetics: Poetry and the Visual Arts in Nineteenth-Century France* (Cambridge: Cambridge University Press, 2009), p. 16.
36. Bohn, *The Aesthetics of Visual Poetry, 1914–1928*, p. 49. Cf. also the very comprehensive anthology and commentary: *Text als Figur: Visuelle Poesie von der Antike bis zur Moderne*, ed. by Jeremy D. Adler and Ulrich Ernst (Konstanz: VCH, 1988).
37. Sohn, p. 118; Serge Linares, 'Quant au blanc', *Poétique*, 160.4 (2009), 471–84 (pp. 471–75). On the influence of Mallarmé on du Bouchet and for du Bouchet's allusion to 'Un coup de dés', see François Rannou, 'André du Bouchet, lecteur de Mallarmé', in *Présence d'André du Bouchet*, ed. by Michel Collot and Jean-Pascal Léger (Paris: Hermann, 2012), pp. 28–39; cf. also Victor Martinez' remarks on du Bouchet's syntax in his *André du Bouchet: Poésie, langue, événement* (Amsterdam: Rodopi, 2013), pp. 66–68.

38. Cf. particularly Yves Peyré, *Peinture et poésie: Le Dialogue par le livre, 1874–2000* (Paris: Gallimard, 2001), esp. pp. 32–34.
39. Gordon Norton Ray, *The Art of the French Illustrated Book, 1700–1914*, 2 vols (New York: Pierpont Morgan Library, 1982), II, 487–88.
40. Cf. Marc Eigeldinger and Arthur Rimbaud, *Lettres du voyant (13 et 15 mai 1871). Précédées de: La Voyance avant Rimbaud* (Geneva: Droz, 1975).
41. Scott, p. 12: 'It was not until the 1840s and 1850s, with the formulations made by Baudelaire in his *Salons* (especially those of 1846 and 1859) that the implications of the romantic theory of the Imagination for the arts of poetry and painting were, in France, fully to be worked out.'
42. Furbank, pp. 34–38.
43. Remy de Gourmont, *Le Problème du style* (Paris: Société du Mercure de France, 1902), p. 69.
44. Ibid., p. 68.
45. Ibid., p. 67.
46. Gourmont does not simply equate the visual and written arts. Drawing on Lessing's argument from the eighteenth chapter of his *Laocoon*, Gourmont holds that 'le tableau donne une impression synthétique et le poème une impression analytique ou successive' (ibid., p. 150). Yet, the shared roots in sense impressions bind these arts together.
47. Ibid., p. 81.
48. Remy de Gourmont, *La Culture des idées* (Paris: Société du Mercure de France, 1900), p. 74.
49. For a more elaborate discussion of the image, see Etienne-Alain Hubert's 'Autour de la théorie de l'image de Pierre Reverdy', in *Bousquet, Jouve, Reverdy: Colloques poésie-Cerisy*, ed. by Charles Bachat, Daniel Leuwers, and Etienne-Alain Hubert (Marseille: Sud, 1981), pp. 289–317.
50. Ibid., p. 304. See also Klaus Dirscherl, 'Wirklichkeit und Kunstwirklichkeit: Reverdys Kubismustheorie als Programm für eine a-mimetische Lyrik', in *Lyrik und Malerei der Avantgarde*, ed. by Rainer Warning and Winfried Wehle (Munich: Fink, 1982), pp. 445–80. Jacques Derrida regards Mallarmé as the prime exponent of a non-mimetic poetry that becomes its own reality rather than merely representing one, see Jacques Derrida, 'The Double Session', in *Dissemination*, trans. by Barbara Johnson (London: The Athlone, 1981), pp. 173–287. For non-mimetic literature and poetry, see also Gottfried Willems, *Anschaulichkeit: Zu Theorie und Geschichte der Wort-Bild-Beziehungen und des literarischen Darstellungsstils* (Tübingen: Niemeyer, 1989), esp. pp. 159–63.
51. Pierre Reverdy, 'L'Image', *Nord–Sud*, 13 (March 1918), n.p.
52. Willard Bohn, *The Rise of Surrealism: Cubism, Dada, and the Pursuit of the Marvelous* (Albany, NY: SUNY, 2012), p. 138.
53. Philippe Geinoz, *Relations au travail: Dialogue entre poésie et peinture à l'époque du cubisme. Apollinaire — Picasso — Braque — Gris — Reverdy* (Geneva: Droz, 2014), pp. 426–28; Bohn, *Rise of Surrealism*, p. 136–37; cf. also Hugo Azérad, 'Parisian Literary Fields: James Joyce and Pierre Reverdy's Theory of the Image', *The Modern Language Review*, 103.3 (2008), 666–81 (pp. 674–75).
54. Peter Goßens, Markus May, and Jürgen Lehmann, 'Leben und Werk — eine kurze Chronik', in *Celan-Handbuch: Leben, Werk, Wirkung*, ed. by Peter Goßens, Markus May, and Jürgen Lehmann, 2nd rev. and ext. edn (Stuttgart: Metzler, 2012), pp. 7–15 (p. 11).
55. Ibid., p. 12.
56. Bertrand Badiou, '"...vivant et redevable à la poésie": Le Dialogue entre Paul Celan et André du Bouchet à travers sept lettres écrites au tournant de l'année 1968', *Europe: Revue Littéraire Mensuelle*, 89.986/87, special issue: *André du Bouchet*, ed. by Nikolaï Zabolotski (2011), 208–31 (pp. 208–09).
57. Michela Lo Feudo, 'Paul Celan and Jacques Dupin in the Journal "L'Éphémère"', trans. by Alexander Booth and Peter Douglas, *Studi Germanici*, 3/4 (2013), 129–54 (pp. 137–37).
58. See the extensive chronology by his wife Anne de Staël: 'Chronologie d'André du Bouchet', *L'Étrangère*, 14/15, special issue: *André du Bouchet 1* (2007), 355–88. Du Bouchet also continues a different tradition of poetic engagement with the image in his ekphrastic theoretical and poetic writing on Giacometti's drawings: André du Bouchet, *Qui n'est pas tourné vers nous* (Paris: Mercure de France, 1974).
59. Most of du Bouchet's early essays revolve around this question, as we will see in chapter 2.

60. For this difference between the two poets, see Bernhard Böschenstein, 'André du Bouchet im Gespräch mit Paul Celan', in *Celan-Jahrbuch*, 8, ed. by Hans-Michael Speier (2001/02), 225–35 (p. 235). On the imperative of Celan's poetry to remain engaged with and rooted in reality despite its often enigmatic character, see: Marlies Janz, *Vom Engagement absoluter Poesie: Zur Lyrik und Ästhetik Paul Celans* (Frankfurt a. M.: Syndikat, 1976).
61. This is the case, for instance, in Gerhard Neumann, 'Die "absolute" Metapher: Ein Abgrenzungsversuch am Beispiel Stéphane Mallarmés und Paul Celans', *Poetica*, 3 (1970), 188–225; Menninghaus, *Paul Celan*, pp. 80–166; Christine Ivanović, 'Eine Sprache der Bilder: Notizen zur immanenten Poetik der Lyrik Paul Celans', *Études Germaniques*, 55.3 (2000), 541–59. See also Gadamer, discussed earlier.
62. Frank Brüder, 'Kunst', in *Celan-Handbuch*, ed. by May, Goßens, and Lehmann, pp. 278–85; Sabine Könneker, *'Sichtbares, Hörbares': Die Beziehung zwischen Sprachkunst und bildender Kunst am Beispiel Paul Celans* (Bielefeld: Aisthesis, 1995); Otto Pöggeler, ' "Schwarzmaut": Bildende Kunst in der Lyrik Paul Celans', in *Die Frage nach der Kunst: Von Hegel zu Heidegger*, ed. by Otto Pöggeler (Freiburg i. Br.: Alber, 1984), pp. 281–375.
63. Christine Ivanović, ' "des menschen farbe ist freiheit": Paul Celans Umweg über den Wiener Surrealismus', in *'Displaced': Paul Celan in Wien 1947–1948*, ed. by Peter Goßens and Marcus Patka (Frankfurt a. M.: Suhrkamp, 2001), pp. 62–70.
64. Christine Ivanović, 'Kunst — der von der Dichtung zurückzulegende Weg: Pablo Picasso und Paul Celan', in *Stationen: Kontinuität und Entwicklung in Paul Celans Übersetzungswerk*, ed. by Jürgen Lehmann and Christine Ivanović (Heidelberg: Winter, 1997), pp. 27–53.
65. Otto Pöggeler, 'Schwerpunkt: Wort und Bild. Paul Celan und Gisèle Celan-Lestrange', *Sprache und Literatur*, 33.89 (2002), 3–42; Barbara Wiedemann, ' "Und sie auf meine Art entziffern" ', *Jahrbuch des freien Deutschen Hochstifts* (2001), 263–92. Celan created two *livres d'artistes* with his wife Lestrange: Paul Celan, *Atemkristall. Radierungen von Gisèle Celan-Lestrange* (Frankfurt a. M.: Suhrkamp, 1990); Paul Celan, *Schwarzmaut. Radierungen von Gisèle Celan-Lestrange* (Frankfurt a. M.: Suhrkamp, 1990).
66. Catherine Fournanty-Fabre, 'Images et réalité dans l'œuvre de Paul Celan' (unpublished doctoral thesis, Paris 4, 1999).
67. Cf. Wiedemann, ' "Und sie auf meine Art entziffern" ', pp. 267–69, 278; Pöggeler, 'Schwerpunkt: Wort und Bild. Paul Celan und Gisèle Celan-Lestrange', pp. 21, 33. Likewise, Celan's interest in Théodore Guéricault and Vincent Van Gogh seems to have been sparked by his personal interest in the artist (see Brüder, 'Kunst', p. 278).
68. Huppert, pp. 320–21.
69. For Celan, the collaborative projects with his wife appear to have been driven mostly by private concerns, and it seems that at least for *Schwarzmaut* Celan had written the poems independently of Celan-Lestrange's illustrations. See Wiedemann, ' "Und sie auf meine Art entziffern" ', pp. 267–69, 278; Pöggeler, 'Schwerpunkt: Wort und Bild. Paul Celan und Gisèle Celan-Lestrange' (pp. 21, 33); Könneker, p. 123, on Celan and the *livre d'artiste*, p. 144.
70. Klaus Mönig, *Malerei und Graphik in deutscher Lyrik des 20. Jahrhunderts* (Freiburg i. Br.: Rombach, 2002), pp. 231–58; Könneker, pp. 42–47, 57–77.
71. Furthermore, some of these poems have already found eloquent interpreters, e.g. 'Unter ein Bild': Timothy Bahti, 'A Minor Form and its Inversions: The Image, the Poem, the Book in Celan's "Unter ein Bild" ', *Modern Language Notes*, 110.3 (1995), 565–78.
72. See Julian Johannes Immanuel Koch, 'The Allegorical Image and Presence in Celan's "Wortaufschüttung" ', *Seminar — A Journal of Germanic Studies*, 56.1 (2020), 22–36 (esp. p. 25).
73. Aris Fioretos, for example, focuses with much ingenuity on the materiality of language in Celan (e.g. dashes, quotation marks and guillemets, asterisks, etc.) 'which cannot be translated into the spoken language of voice without an unaccountable remainder', ultimately posing a 'singular resistance to hermeneutic unraveling'; see Aris Fioretos, 'Nothing: History and Materiality in Celan', in *Word Traces: Readings of Paul Celan*, ed. by Aris Fioretos (Baltimore: Johns Hopkins University Press, 1994), pp. 295–341 (pp. 295 and 332, respectively). No doubt, one of the hallmarks of post-structuralism is that anyone, no matter how recalcitrant, can be deconstructed, even when it goes against their own views, and the ultimate deconstructionist

trick is to show how the deconstruction somehow inheres in the unwitting author's own views. See, e.g., Derrida's deconstructionist exercises with Edmund Husserl and John Searle: Jacques Derrida, *La Voix et le phénomène: Introduction au problème du signe dans la phénoménologie de Husserl*, 2nd edn (Paris: Presses universitaires de France, 1998); Jacques Derrida, *Limited Inc* (Evanston, IL: Northwestern University Press, 1988). Of course, against this premise of deconstruction as all-engulfing I can only set the premise that this is not so, and any adjudicating between these two premises in favour of one or the other would itself have to presuppose one or the other. Thus, ultimately, my approach can only rely on matters of plausibility which I believe I have sufficiently made clear above.

74. E.g. Sohn; Martinez, *Poésie, langue, événement*, pp. 63–98; Henri Maldiney, *Art et existence* (Paris: Klincksieck, 2003), pp. 213–28.
75. Emma Wagstaff, 'André du Bouchet and Pierre Tal Coat: "Sous le linteau en forme de joug"', in *The Dialogue Between Painting and Poetry: Livres d'artistes, 1874–1999*, ed. by Jean Khalfa (Cambridge: Black Apollo, 2001), pp. 105–27; Emma Wagstaff, 'Francis Ponge and André du Bouchet on Giacometti: Art Criticism as Testimony', *The Modern Language Review*, 101.1 (2006), 75–89; Emma Wagstaff, *Provisionality and the Poem: Transition in the Work of du Bouchet, Jaccottet and Noël* (Amsterdam: Rodopi, 2006), pp. 154–55.
76. Clément Layet, '"Annuler les images, les casser": L'Image dans la poésie d'André du Bouchet', *French Forum*, 37.1 (2012), 137–47; Michael Bishop, *Altérités d'André du Bouchet: De Hugo, Shakespeare et Poussin à Celan, Mandelstam et Giacometti* (Amsterdam: Rodopi, 2003), pp. 63–68; Serge Linares, 'Reverdy et du Bouchet: Deux poètes en regard', in *Présence d'André du Bouchet*, ed. by Collot and Léger, pp. 41–57.
77. Michel Collot, *L'Horizon fabuleux* (Paris: Corti, 1988), pp. 179–211; Victor Martinez, 'La "Phénoménologie de l'inapparent" dans les œuvres de Heidegger et du Bouchet', in *Figuren der Absenz*, ed. by Anke Grutschus (Berlin: Frank & Timme, 2010), pp. 59–71; Martinez, *Poésie, langue, événement*, pp. 58–63; Glenn Fetzer, 'Du Bouchet et la dynamique de l'image', *Dalhousie French Studies*, 111 (2018), 35–41.
78. Layet's and Fetzer's work are an exception. Clément Layet, 'Temps apparent', in *Présence d'André du Bouchet*, ed. by Collot and Léger, pp. 227–43; Layet, 'Annuler les images, les casser'; Fetzer, 'Du Bouchet et la dynamique de l'image'.
79. For instance: Martinez, 'La "phénoménologie de l'inapparent"'; Maldiney, pp. 213–28; Serge Champeau, *Ontologie et poésie: Trois études sur les limites du langage* (Paris: Vrin, 1995), pp. 101–69.
80. Champeau, p. 139; Stéphane Bacquey seems to share a belief very similar to that of Champeau, cf.: Stéphane Baquey, 'Le Sens du dehors', *Europe: Revue Littéraire Mensuelle*, 89.986/87, special issue: *André du Bouchet*, ed. by Zabolotski (2011), 84–93 (p. 85).
81. Pierre Schneider, 'La Figure et le fond', in *Autour d'André du Bouchet: Rencontres sur la poésie moderne. Actes du colloque des 8, 9, 10 décembre 1983*, ed. by Michel Collot (Paris: Presses de l'École Normale Supérieure, 1986), pp. 101–09.
82. Collot, *L'Horizon fabuleux*, pp. 179–211.
83. Michel Collot, '"D'un trait qui figure et défigure": Du Bouchet et Giacometti', in *André du Bouchet et ses autres*, ed. by Michel Minard and Philippe Met (Paris-Caen: Lettres modernes Minard, 2003), pp. 95–107. These terms are in fact du Bouchet's own.
84. Champeau, p. 106.
85. Martinez, 'La "Phénoménologie de l'inapparent"', p. 64. I believe more justice to du Bouchet's preoccupation with perception would have been done had Martinez not only considered du Bouchet's volume on Giacometti (*Qui n'est pas tourné vers nous*), but Giacometti's writings themselves, particularly his lifelong quest to reproduce the act of seeing: 'la vision de l'objet et non simplement l'objet vu', as Christian Berner puts it in his '"Se rendre compte de ce qu'on voit": À propos de *La Jampe* de Giacometti', in *Puissances de l'image*, ed. by Jean-Claude Gens and Pierre Rodrigo (Dijon: Éditions universitaires de Dijon, 2007), pp. 187–99 (p. 192); cf. also Alberto Giacometti, *Écrits* (Paris: Hermann, 2007), p. 284.
86. Martinez, 'La "Phénoménologie de l'inapparent"', p. 59.
87. Ibid., p. 70 (my emphasis).
88. Bishop, *Altérités d'André du Bouchet*, p. 25.

89. Ibid., p. 24.
90. Ibid., p. 93.
91. Ibid. For more discussion of du Bouchet's presumed ontology: Michael Bishop, 'Longer, sans attache: Neuf remarques pour une ontologie dubouchettienne', in *Présence d'André du Bouchet*, ed. by Collot and Léger, pp. 213–25.
92. 'Mais toute ontologie tourne autour de telles difficultés' (Bishop, *Altérités d'André du Bouchet*, p. 216).
93. Clément Layet, 'Demain diamant', *Europe: Revue Littéraire Mensuelle*, 89.986/87, ed. by Zabolotski (2011), 27–39 (p. 33). Wagstaff similarly rejects ontologizing approaches, even if she takes a somewhat different route from mine by focusing on du Bouchet's notion of attention. Emma Wagstaff, *André du Bouchet: Poetic Forms of Attention* (Leiden: Brill Rodopi, 2020), p. 31.
94. Cf. e.g. Collot: '[c]ette coupure qui permet à l'insignifiance du fond de transparaître, est paradoxalement nécessaire à la constitution de toute signification' (Collot, *L'Horizon fabuleux*, p. 197). Cf. also Wagstaff, *Provisionality and the Poem*, pp. 31–32.
95. Cf. Martinez, *Poésie, langue, événement*, pp. 63–94; Collot, *L'Horizon fabuleux*, pp. 179–211.
96. Wagstaff minutely traces some of du Bouchet's constant reworkings of his poetry (see chapter 6 of her book) and judges that such a 'reject[ing of] the notion of an origin' makes him 'postmodern' (Wagstaff, *André du Bouchet*, p. 192).
97. Wagstaff similarly notes that du Bouchet's rejection of an 'impassioned, expressive self' and his embrace of a self 'as the outcome of writing' puts him in close contact with the 'textualist poets' of *Tel Quel*, rather than the poets of presence of *L'Éphémère*; it should also be noted that this textual self in du Bouchet is, like his texts themselves, fragmented and not unified (ibid., p. 164). On the self in du Bouchet in the post-structuralist context of his time, see Julian Johannes Immanuel Koch, 'Translation as Poetics in the Works of André du Bouchet', *The Modern Language Review*, 114.1 (2019), 35–51 (pp. 36–37).
98. Wagstaff, *André du Bouchet*, p. 51.
99. Ibid, p. 29.
100. Wagstaff, 'André du Bouchet and Pierre Tal Coat', p. 195.

CHAPTER 1

Paul Celan's Early Conception of the Image

Our examination of the image in Celan commences with his text 'Edgar Jené: Der Traum vom Traume'. The text marks the beginning of Celan's poetological preoccupation with the image. As we have seen in the introduction, since about the late seventeenth and early eighteenth centuries, the image has come to be a metaphor for metaphor in a literary context.[1] However, the image — even in the literary context — is still very strongly associated with a specific form of visual representation of reality. Thus, the image also linked to much older discourses on representation than the conception of image as metaphor.[2] Both of these meanings of the term 'image' played a role when, in the early twentieth century, poets in France actively debated it. An avid reader of French poetry, having studied languages between 1940 and 1941 in Romania, Celan will certainly not have missed these discourses, not least since Breton's first *Manifeste du surréalisme* (1924) had borrowed significant passages from Pierre Reverdy's conception of the image[3] and made the image a centrepiece of his definition of surrealism.[4] In his brief surrealist phase after the war in Vienna (1947 and 1948), Celan was confronted by these questions surrounding the image, and his collaborations with the surrealist painter Jené, in particular his poetological text 'Edgar Jené: Der Traum vom Traume', are testimony to this.

The text is the earliest major poetological work by Celan,[5] and it clearly still bears traces of the poetic uncertainties of a young writer who had to find a foothold in poetry and the world. The text was written in 1948 during a time of reorientation in Celan's life. After the death of his parents in the Transnistria concentration camp, and having himself been intellectually and physically displaced during his time in a forced labour camp, Celan briefly lived in Vienna between 1947 and 1948 and then left for Paris. In Vienna, Celan made the acquaintance of the surrealist painter Edgar Jené who was to become a kind of leader to the surrealist movement in Austria that so far hadn't been put on the map of the artistic world after the Second World War.[6] At this time, Celan published his first volume of poetry, *Der Sand aus den Urnen* (1948), with the help of Jené (cf. KG, 582). The many printing errors in the final copy of the volume led to a cooling-off of his friendly relations with Jené. But there seems to have been more at stake as the friendship unravelled. Celan's remark, in 1957, that he retracted the publication not only because of the publication errors but also over a disagreement about the two lithographs by Jené which accompanied the text seems to indicate a difference in poetological and aesthetic outlook between Celan and Jené.[7] This difference may be particularly to do with Jené's rather uninspired visualization of the motifs of the fugue and serpents in Celan's Holocaust poem 'Todesfuge', which Jené had illustrated as organ pipes that turn into snakes in his eponymous lithograph. In fact, Jené's illustration, which entirely lacks a historical dimension and neglects the clear allusions to the Holocaust in Celan's poem, represents a kind of historical amnesia that seems to have already troubled Celan at the time of writing 'Der Traum vom Traume', a text in which the narrator already explicitly takes a position against ignoring or forgetting the past.

The rift with the surrealist Jené also seems to presage Celan's later turning away from not only surrealist doctrine — to which he never seems to have wholeheartedly and uncritically subscribed in the first place[8] — but also from surrealist metaphors and motifs. For instance, the frequency of oneiric tropes and mentions of the word 'Traum' almost abruptly declines in his 1955 cycle *Von Schwelle zu Schwelle* and is virtually non-existent by the time of his cycle *Sprachgitter* in 1959.[9] Celan's struggle and critical discourse with surrealism, as Johannes von Schlebrügge has particularly convincingly argued, is not only apparent from the immediate context and aftermath of 'Traum vom Traume', but can also be found in the text itself.[10] Schlebrügge argues that Celan seems to have taken a critical stance akin to that of Tristan Tzara, who in his lecture 'La Dialectique de la poésie' had provoked a rift with Breton by calling a surrealist poetry that is only preoccupied with itself and purged of history and mythology 'une nouvelle poésie parnassienne'.[11] Thus, while some formulations in Celan's text are reminiscent of Breton's conception of surrealism,[12] such as 'da Fremdes Fremdesten vermählt wird' (*CW* III, 158),[13] in crucial passages asserting the importance of history, Celan's text already turns away from surrealism.

What does Celan's reception of surrealism in 'Traum vom Traume' mean for his early conception of the image? Christine Ivanović believes that Celan's text develops 'ganz bewußt das bildliche Sprechen als Gegenmodell zum rein begrifflichen Sprechen', in which the 'bildliche[s] Sprechen' is conceived as a 'Sprechen als einmalige[r], kreatürliche[r] Akt' that is opposed to the 'abstrakte Formen oder erstarrte Topoi' of a 'begriffliche[s] Sprechen'.[14] The implication thus seems to be that Celan follows Breton's first *Manifeste* regarding the exposed position the latter gives the image in his surrealist poetics. Indeed, Celan's first and only collaboration with a visual artist other than his wife was with Jené; furthermore the importance of the visual arts and, more abstractly, of the image can be gleaned from the last line of Celan's text which explicitly confirms the exclusive and exposed position of the image in his poetological thinking: 'Edgar Jenés Bilder wissen mehr' (*CW* III, 161).

Yet how is the assertion that 'Bilder wissen mehr' compatible with Celan's claim at the beginning of 'Traum vom Traume' that images are left behind at the surface of the water, below which the narrator travels in his search for truth and meaning ('unter seine [Jenés] Bilder'; *CW* III, 155)?[15] How can these seemingly contradictory tendencies of the text be reconciled? Furthermore, we must ask again: what is the nature of Celan's supposed 'bildliche[s] Sprechen'? Ivanović's notion of 'bildliche[s] Sprechen' may be understood as 'figurative language'. But the original publication by Celan was accompanied by visual images, so is Celan's 'poetic imagery' perhaps also 'visual' in a stricter sense of the word?[16] If so, his cooling relations with Jené shortly thereafter would indicate a quite sudden reversal and perhaps even inaugurate the demise of the image in Celan's poetics.

I would like to suggest that this is not so. The image remained a persistent part of Celan's poetics. When Celan says about twelve years after 'Traum vom Traume' that 'Bildhaftigkeit = nichts Visuelles, sondern etwas Geistiges' (*M*, 107), this should be seen less as a departure and rather as a continuation of his earlier assertion that 'Edgar Jenés Bilder wissen mehr'. In fact, Celan's formulation is reminiscent of Breton's citation of Reverdy's image in his *Manifeste*: '[l]'image est une création pure de l'esprit.'[17] Celan's 'Traum vom Traume' gives us the first traces of his conception of the image that we will encounter, successively developed further, in the poems we discuss in the following chapters of this book. In particular, the nature of Celan's image as something that is not visual but spiritual and mental (i.e. 'geistig') is already prefigured in his text 'Traum vom Traume', when Celan confidently proclaims at the end that 'Edgar Jenés Bilder wissen mehr' and thereby associates the image with cognition. But in the same text we also find Celan's lingering suspicions about the image when he intimates at the beginning that our cognition goes further and deeper than any visual images can by going 'unter [die] Bilder'. These seeming inconsistencies in the conception of the image in Celan's 'Traum vom Traume' cannot be simply shrugged off as surrealist paradoxes. What the author implies here is that in these two instances he has in mind two different types of images and of seeing. The 'alten eigenwilligen Augen' that are still only habituated to an obsolete form of perceiving are simply not the same eyes that later look into the almost spiritually conceived, visionary 'Helligkeit' (*CW* III, 158). The spiritual dimension attributed to seeing the brightness and the divinatory form of cognition which Jené's images seem to give us ('wissen mehr') are reminiscent of Celan's later remarks about the image as 'etwas Geistiges' in the notes to his 'Meridian' speech. There, Celan more clearly than before distinguishes metaphorical and, as he implies, untruthful poetic speech from 'Wissen und Sehen von nacktester Evidenz' (*M*, 128). He also repeatedly emphasizes that seeing that is not merely visual perception is connected to truth, as the German word for perceiving or cognizing, '*wahr*nehmen' (my emphasis), already seems to insinuate: 'Sehen als <u>Gewahren</u>, Wahrnehmen, Wahrhaben, Wahr<u>sein</u>' (*M*, 134; underlined in original).

The Notion of the Image in Celan's 'Traum vom Traume'

The text is narrated from the first-person perspective and is roughly split into two parts. The first constitutes a more abstract poetics which arises out of a fictional conversation with a friend. The dialogical structure mirrors that in Heinrich von Kleist's essay 'Über das Marionettentheater' which Celan explicitly cites in his text.[18] The second part of 'Traum vom Traume' is a quite liberal ekphrastic description of Jené's paintings which then concludes in words that abdicate their own power of expression and endow the realm of images with true cognition and expression: 'Edgar Jenés Bilder wissen mehr.' From our analysis of the more abstract and poetological first part of Celan's text it should, however, become clear that this form of further, truer cognition is not exclusive to Jené's visual images or to visual images as such. It is also shared by poetic words which Celan conceives as images, making extensive use of visual, perceptual vocabulary and metaphors.[19] In my analysis of 'Traum vom Traume', I will focus on the first part of the text, which is of greater poetological importance, rather than the ekphrastic second part. Only the first part clearly transcends the particular context of Jené's drawings and lets us extrapolate a fundamental conception of the image that will inform Celan's later poetics.[20]

The first-person narrator describes a journey into the depths of the sea beyond the reality of the 'Meeresspiegel' that is presumed to be superficial: '[i]ch schlug eine Bresche in die Wände und Einwände der Wirklichkeit und stand vor dem Meeresspiegel' (*CW* III, 155). The mirror, the '-spiegel' of the 'Meeresspiegel', takes on a new significance beyond the literal meaning of sea level, because as we supposedly leave behind reality, we also leave behind a realm of art and of perception and cognition through art in which art merely creates mimetic *typos-images* of reality. Such a turn away from a pre-established notion of reality is not only implied in the passage cited above but also reinforced later when the narrator's mouth, in a disembodied monologue (i.e. acting independently of body and self) accuses his eye of being an 'Identitätskrämer', merely seeking to compare its current perceptions to already known objects and concepts: '[k]ein Wunder, daß ich in diesem Augenblick [in dem der Erzähler unter die See und Bilder geht], da ich noch meine alten eigenwilligen Augen hatte, um zu schauen, Vergleiche anstellte, um wählen zu können' (*CW* III, 155). Rather, the eye should turn inward and only then will it truly see. The mouth says to the eye: '[h]ol dir lieber ein paar Augen aus dem Grund deiner Seele [...]: dann erfährst du, was sich hier ereignet!' (*CW* III, 155). Only in leaving behind the idea of a pre-established reality and the desire to mirror that reality in art, only in breaking the mirror of the 'Meerespiegel', do we turn inward and inquire into the truths 'auf der anderen, tieferen Seite des Seins' (*CW* III, 155).

What is the role of the image in this inward turn? The narrator seems to imply that as we leave behind pre-established reality and break its mirror image in the sea, we also leave behind the realm of images: '[ich folgte] Edgar Jené unter seine Bilder' (*CW* III, 155). Insofar as the images by Jené open up the passage into the depths in which the narrator makes discoveries that break with the habits of reality, they, and perhaps images more generally, are the catalyst of the experience of an inner reality or truth described by the narrator. Yet, as we seem to leave the images behind in our going below them ('unter die Bilder'), they also fail to embody this new inner realm. In this interpretation, images are a mere instrument through which an aesthetic experience is rendered. The research seems to agree on this understanding of the failure of the images to realize this realm fully themselves.[21]

However, the role of images is patently more complex in Celan's essay, not least because we arrive at the conclusion that 'Jené's Bilder wissen mehr' after we have supposedly left Jené's images behind in going below them. The status of the image is already ambivalent in the motion of going 'unter die Bilder'. The dominant reading is that we go below the images, but we may also understand the going 'unter die Bilder' as a going amongst the images — 'unter die Bilder' supports both interpretations. Indeed, our turning inward and looking into our soul, as is implied later (*CW* III, 157–58), may coincide with the motion of not merely going below the images but going amongst them — becoming images. In this interpretation, images are not simple purveyors of the aesthetic experience. They are not just an intermediary that is to be left behind by going below and beyond them. Rather, if we are to go amongst the images in order to experience a deeper kind of seeing and speaking, images are essential to the new aesthetics the narrator envisions. This may seem too strong an interpretation; and yet only in taking this second reading of 'unter' into account can we explain why visionary forms of cognition later in 'Traum vom Traume' are described in visual terms ('blicke ich der neuen Helligkeit ins Auge'), and only in this reading do we eventually arrive at the conclusion that 'Jené's Bilder wissen mehr'.

What, then, does it mean to go amongst the images or even to become image in going 'unter die Bilder'? It should be quite clear that this 'becoming image' is not to be understood literally as the narrator's being visualized in, for instance, one of Jené's drawings. Rather, the image seems to encompass and embody a form of perception that enables a new form of cognition and artistic expression ('die Dinge bei ihrem richtigen Namen nannte'; *CW* III, 156), be it in poetry or painting. This new type of perception is anticipated and hinted at very early in the essay, namely as soon as the narrator goes below and amongst the images when he enters into the realm in which he faces new paths, each implying a different form of seeing ('ein anderes Augenpaar'; *CW* III, 155). In becoming image in the broader sense, the narrator hence partakes in a new form of perception. What this exactly entails is not very clear. To examine in more detail what constitutes this new form of perception we must outline what it is not: rational reflection in the mind's eye.[22]

Rational reflection is regarded as precisely the form of perception that involves comparison between newly perceived objects and already known ones. Thus, reflection is rejected as 'Identitätskrämer[ei]' in the interior monologue of the narrator. Only when reason is, as it were, asleep, as the narrator implies, is the new perceived as truly new and without prejudice (*CW* III, 157). The antirational discourse is elaborated further as the narrator depicts a discussion with an unnamed friend about how to truly leave behind the false reality in which we found ourselves at the beginning of the essay before we went 'unter die Bilder', and about how the new form of perception is to be attained. The friend holds that only through a 'vernunftmäßige[-] Läuterung unseres unbewußten Seelenlebens' is it possible to see in an unprejudiced, new manner (*CW* III, 156). We learn that the new form of seeing is conflated with the originary state before the Fall of Man and is situated outside of time, in eternity. The new form of seeing, according to the friend, would purge words of their historically accrued meanings: '[e]in Baum sollte wieder ein Baum werden, sein Zweig, an den man in hundert Kriegen die Empörer geknüpft, ein Blütenzweig, wenn es Frühling würde' (*CW* III, 156).²³ Only in getting rid of the historical 'Asche ausgebrannter Sinngebung' could a tree be seen for what it truly is: a tree.

While the narrator wishes to regain the state of prelapsarian purity before this linguistic Fall of Man, he does not agree that it can be realized or regained by obliterating history and by means of rational purification — it is here that we most clearly see Celan as Holocaust survivor in the figure of the narrator who cannot tolerate a *Geschichtsvergessenheit*.²⁴ The past has not merely left a mark on the present that could be whitewashed. The past has transformed the very essence of the present. For the narrator, the new form of seeing is thus not to be understood as having been cleansed of any history by means of reason. Rather, the vision of 'das Neue also auch das Reine' is achieved in a state 'jenseits der Vorstellungen meines wachen Denkens' (*CW* III, 157). In a manner similar to that of the first-person narrator in Kleist's essay 'Über das Marionettentheater',²⁵ the narrator in Celan's essay comes to his ultimate conclusions during a momentary pause for thought. When Celan's narrator says '[n]un habe ich mir selber gelauscht, während einer letzten Gedankenpause' (*CW* III, 158), the implication is that this pause is as much a temporal pause *for* thought indicated by the temporal preposition ('während') as it is a pause *of* thought. So, if the new and pure are not obtained by rational reflection, how are they obtained? The narrator asks the same question, but outlines how the new and pure come about only in highly metaphorical terms:²⁶

> Aus den entferntesten Bezirken des Geistes mögen Worte und Gestalten kommen, Bilder und Gebärden, traumhaft verschleiert und traumhaft entschleiert, und wenn sie einander begegnen in ihrem rasenden Lauf und der Funken des Wunderbaren geboren wird, da Fremdes Fremdesten vermählt wird, blicke ich der neuen Helligkeit ins Auge. (*CW* III, 157–58)

The new, visionary brightness appears to be constituted by irrational paradoxes in the narrator's 'entfernteste[-] Bezirke[-] des Geistes' which are reminiscent of Reverdy's image as seen through the antirationalist lens of the surrealist, according to which two realities 'plus ou moins eloignées' are merged in the 'esprit'.²⁷ It is perhaps in this paradoxical spirit that the visionary brightness, although seemingly 'heraufbeschworen' by the narrator's gaze, takes on a life of its own as though it were an independent agent. As soon as the narrator gazes into the brightness, it reciprocates the gaze: '[ich] blicke [...] der neuen Heiligkeit ins Auge. Sie sieht mich seltsam an [...]' (*CW* III, 158). The brightness is not mere mimetic display, a *typos*-image of something known that could be recognized by the narrator: 'sie ist von Gestalten bewohnt, die ich nicht *wiedererkenne* sondern *erkenne* in einer erstmaligen Schau' (*CW* III, 158; emphases in original). The customary relation between the onlooking subject, the narrator, and the displaying entity — the brightness — is reversed when the latter reciprocates the narrator's gaze and transforms, indeed, entirely renews the narrator's vision.

How is the narrator's gaze turned around? Let us try to outline what happens to the narrator's vision here as a line of inferences (although not in the strict logical sense). If the onlooking subject looks into the brightness and the brightness is constituted by this gaze ('heraufbeschworen'), gaze and brightness seem to coincide and to be coextensive. If the brightness is 'jenseits der Vorstellungen meines wachen Denkens' and comes from the 'entfernteste[-] Bezirke[-] des Geistes', it is new to the narrator's thinking, so that seeing it implies an altogether novel form of seeing ('erstmalig[e] Schau', 'neue[s] Augenpaar'; *CW* III, 158). His looking into the brightness opens up such a new form of seeing to him that he does not seem to *re*-cognize the gaze as his own ('nicht *wiedererkenne* sondern *erkenne*'). The brightness and the mode of seeing it are so new to the narrator as to seem disembodied and independent, but they actually originate in him, and it is perhaps in this sense that the brightness returns the narrator's gaze.

We need to remind ourselves that this cognition by and in the narrator is not rational reflection, even if it appears to be a form of introspection since the narrator's eyes are closed (*CW* III, 158). Rather, this vision is ascribed transcendent and spiritual qualities surpassing all rational grasp, leading to a form of synaesthetic ecstasy.[28] A 'neue Welt des Geistes' now lies before the narrator's eyes (*CW* III, 158), but we should remember that, new as this world may be, it has not obliterated history. Although this is not explicitly said and it is unclear how exactly it comes about, the previously described desire to regain paradise (which was to be achieved without obliterating history by means of reason) appears to have been fulfilled in the originary form of vision. The spiritual connotations of this 'neue Welt des Geistes', its mythological link to the Fall of Man, and the ever-significant trope of brightness seem to suggest that the image ultimately attained in 'Traum vom Traume' is the *archetypos* in which seer, the act of seeing, and what is seen coincide.

Celan's early text 'Traum vom Traume' provides us with the clearest and most unrestrained conception of the image as *archetypos* that we will find in his poetry and poetics. In his later works, Celan will tone down the patent optimism and spiritual enthusiasm that is captured in the archetypal image of his early poetics of 'Traum vom Traume'. His notion of the image will also lose its particularly surrealist hue — that is its paradoxical nature in which 'Fremdes Fremdesten vermählt wird'. Yet even the later Celan will ultimately strive for an archetypal image. This archetypal image is not quite equivalent to a Platonic or Neoplatonic notion of the *archetypos* as absolute and transcendent.[29] Celan will place an emphasis on the secular 'terrestrialness' of his poetry in his 'Meridian' speech and deny the possibility of absolute poetry.[30] Nonetheless, the question of absoluteness or purity in poetry — often associated specifically with the poetic programme of Stéphane Mallarmé whom Celan mentions in his speech — is not simply negated:[31] 'Aber es gibt wohl [...] diesen unerhörten Anspruch [auf Absolutheit, bzw. das absolute Gedicht zu sein]' (*M*, 10). Thus, poetic absoluteness is affirmed as constituting every poem's tentative goal ('Anspruch'), which it seeks to approximate and yet is too audacious to be fulfilled. In the adjective 'unerhört' resonate both the meanings of 'audacious' and of 'unattainable' (as in *nicht erhört*). Celan's preoccupation with the image in his notes to the 'Meridian' speech similarly betrays a striving for an *archetypos* in that he conceives of the image as something not visual or material but mental or spiritual (i.e. *geistig*; cf. e.g. *M*, 101). It is not a coincidence that the adjective *geistig* can designate something spiritual as well as mental in German. When we analyse Celan's poem 'Halbzerfressener' in chapter 6, we will see a similar ambiguity of the spiritual and the secular — that we also found in *geistig* — in the connection between the image and 'Himmel', since 'Himmel' can mean both sky and heaven (cf. *KG*, 195). The recurrence of polysemic words taking both secular and spiritual meanings, in turn, would indicate that these ambiguities between the secular and the spiritual are deliberate and consistent in Celan's poetry and poetics. Such Platonic or Neoplatonic vestiges in his poetics can also be seen in Celan's notion of an archetypal, pre-Babel state from which we and our language have fallen; this idea informs his work, starting with 'Traum vom Traume' and continuing until his later poetry (see especially chapter 4 on 'Bei Wein und Verlorenheit').

The prominent role of the image and of visuality more generally in the surrealist movement had a lasting impact on Celan's poetics. Celan's early poetological essay 'Traum vom Traume' thus marks the starting point in his conception of the image. His collaboration with Jené in bringing out the bibliophile volume containing the essay 'Traum vom Traume' will remain Celan's only such engagement, given that Celan's artistic collaborations with his wife Gisèle Celan-Lestrange on *Atemkristall* and *Schwarzmaut*, as pointed out in the introduction to this study, seem to have been predominantly motivated by private and amorous concerns rather than poetological or art-theoretical ones.[32] We should not infer that the later Celan developed a disdain for the visual arts and the visual image altogether. Nonetheless, Celan distanced himself from surrealism after moving to Paris in 1948. His use of colour words drops sharply from his publication of *Von Schwelle zu Schwelle* onward,[33] and in the late fifties we find exclamations that the image is 'nichts Visuelles' in his notes to the 'Meridian' speech (*M*, 101). Thus we can trace an increasing tendency in Celan not to understand the image as visually representing something to the eye — which would characterize it as *typos* — but as transcending its outer appearance.

We already analysed this tendency in his 'Traum vom Traume', in which Celan splits the world along a quite distinct line separating an outward reality above the sea level from a truer, inner reality below ('Tiefsee', 'Innenwelt'). To truly see means to abolish our sense of vision as we know it and develop a new one: '[h]ol dir lieber ein paar Augen aus dem Grund deiner Seele' (*CW* III, 155). These notions of depth and introspection remain at the heart of Celan's poetics as we will see in 'Halbzerfressener' and as is clear from Celan's notes: 'ich versuche mir das Gedicht vor Augen zu führen und es (denkend) anzuschauen' (*Mikro*, 147); 'Der Prozeß der Perzeption → Apperzeption im Gedicht' (*Mikro*, 149).[34] While introspection hence remains at the heart of his conception of the image, in his later poetics from about the late fifties onward Celan tones down or even abolishes the dualist worldview in 'Traum vom Traume', separating a false outer reality from an inner, truthful one. When Celan says in his 'Meridian' speech that poetry — and, implicitly, the image — is something 'Immaterielles, aber Irdisches, Terrestrisches' (*M*, 12), the implication is that poetry and the image do not pertain to an ontologically different sphere but can be seen or divined in this world if only one is willing to look beyond outward visuality (see also chapters 7 and 8). It is in this sense we should understand

Celan's remark that the image is 'nichts Visuelles': it is not a downright rejection of visuality (and by extension the visual arts) but asks us to look for more and more deeply.[35]

This development in the mature Celan's poetics is influenced by the phenomenology of Edmund Husserl with which Celan engaged closely in this period, as we will see in more detail in chapter 6. Husserl's concept of 'Wesensschau' — *eidos*, essence, or also eidetic insight — proposes a form of seeing in which the onlooker abstracts from the individuating properties of the particular object that is perceived and arrives at a universal essence, a process Husserl called 'eidetic reduction'.[36] For instance, by looking at a concrete cube, a dice perhaps, the eidetic reduction can be achieved by stripping away all the particularities of this dice to arrive at its abstract, geometric form, its universal essence — the cube shape — according to Husserl.[37] Although the image we see through eidetic insight is not sensory,[38] it can be the result of abstraction from a sensory intuition. In seeing the essence of something through eidetic insight, we hence do not see something that is fundamentally separate from the outer world. Celan's image as something that is mentally or spiritually divined but nonetheless terrestrial is therefore very reminiscent of Husserl's 'Wesensschau'. The later Celan can thus conceive of an image that is archetypal yet is not in opposition to, but based on reality, towards which Celan always felt a historical responsibility.

Another source for the later Celan's image that is archetypal but still terrestrial, is the painter Jean Bazaine, whose *Notes sur la peinture d'aujourd'hui* Celan translated in 1959.[39] Although Bazaine rejects 'jed[e] Art von Nachahmung' of reality, as did Celan in 'Traum vom Traume',[40] Bazaine's desired artistic creation does not divest itself of this world but rather embraces it to make us see more:

> die Verinnerlichung des Visuellen, dieses Mehr-als-Sehen, wie es jeder wahre Schöpfungsakt impliziert, hängt nicht von der größeren oder geringeren Ähnlichkeit von Werk und äußerer Wirklichkeit ab; sie hängt vielmehr von dem Grad der Ähnlichkeit mit einer inneren, die äußere einbegreifenden Welt ab.[41]

Such introspective 'Mehr-als-Sehen' seems to be echoed in Celan's 'Sehen als Gewahren, Wahrnehmen, Wahrhaben, Wahrsein' (*M*, 134), where the eye does not perceive an outer representation but a supposed inner truth. Significantly, this inner truth is not in juxtaposition or contradiction with outer reality, rather it encompasses outer reality and more ('einer inneren, die äußere einbegreifenden Welt').

Like Celan in 'Traum vom Traume' and later writings, Bazaine mourns the loss of a paradisiacal state, which is implied in the 'nicht mehr' when he writes that 'Sie [die Malerei] ist eine Seinsweise, sie ist das Atmenwollen inmitten einer Welt, deren Luft nicht mehr atembar ist',[42] or more explicitly when he declares the more originary, primitive art to already be merely 'Abglanz eines verlorenen Paradieses'.[43] Akin to Celan, Bazaine's hope to achieve a 'Mehr-als-Sehen' through which we prospectively perceive a truer, inner reality is thus also a retrospectively sought reattainment of an archetypal state now believed to be lost.

The Conception of the Image in the Early Celan and Du Bouchet

Although an unspecific notion of a lost archetypal state in which there was a truer connection between words and things seems to be shared by du Bouchet,[44] his poetry and poetics do not appear to be invested in it. Quite to the contrary, as we shall see in the next chapter, du Bouchet's poetics does not know a mythico-historical origin but emphasizes the present moment, that is a perennially continuous present, passing as soon it arrives. Du Bouchet first discovers this 'présent réel' (*AB*, 106) that cannot hold on to anything for longer than an instant in his early essays on Baudelaire: 'la perte de l'{*image*} crée' (*AB*, 298; parentheses and italics in original). These insights would inform his own poetics; for instance, when he writes in an early version of 'Image à terme': '[p]oésie.   Déjà, ce n'est plus d'elle qu'il s'agit. [...] Et dans cet instant où, la parole en place, de nouveau elle se révèle en défaut.'[45] Du Bouchet's extreme interpretation of the present eschews any notions of a quasi-mythological sense of history with an archetypal origin as well as any sense of an *archetypos*. In the following chapter, we will trace du Bouchet's discussion of the different conceptions of the image as *archetypos* in Maurice Scève, Friedrich Hölderlin, and Victor Hugo, arriving at a notion of the image in Baudelaire that abrogates the *typos–archetypos* distinction together with its spiritual dimension and its implied hierarchy.

Du Bouchet, who had returned from the United States to France in 1948, thus seems to have taken root in a very similar poetic soil as Celan did in 1948 Vienna, but the poetics that came to grow out of these similar circumstances were different. Celan engaged with the conception of the image in Breton's surrealism and, through Breton's *Manifeste*, with 'L'Image' in Reverdy. Du Bouchet, on the other hand, would have encountered Reverdy's image at its source, due to his great appreciation for and close engagement with the elder poet. The reception of Reverdy's image by Celan and du Bouchet seems to have been substantially inflected by the surrealist context in which the two poets engaged with it. We should recall that Reverdy had published his 'L'Image' in 1918, which Breton took up in his *Manifeste* in 1924. The surrealist interpretation of Reverdy's image focused on a presumed clash between two distant realities that are brought together in the image ('rapprochement de deux réalités'). In so doing it ignored that, even though these realities can be remote or distant in Reverdy, Reverdy had still noted that 'l'association des idées [doit être] lointaine et juste' and that this rapport is established and the image is created in a conscious mind ('l'esprit').[46]

As we move 'unter die Bilder' with Celan's narrator in 'Traum vom Traume', we recognize this surrealist understanding of Reverdy's image in Celan's negotiation of the image as irrationally clashing 'Fremdes [mit] Fremdesten'. As Celan later moves away from surrealism, this irrational clash of alien and different entities turns into a sought-out and mutually respectful encounter between two strangers: 'zweierlei Fremde — dicht beieinander' (*M*, 7).[47] A rapprochement of distinct entities inspired by the 'deux réalités' brought together without a pre-existing comparison or *tertium comparationis* — in contrast with Reverdy's image and more akin to the image of surrealism — will also underlie du Bouchet's poetic endeavour, but with fundamental alterations.[48] Rather than suggesting a conjoining of two realities similar to Reverdy's image, du Bouchet's image juxtaposes ink and paper visually and the notions of *absence* and *présence* semantically. These tensions in du Bouchet's image remain unresolved and his image is perennially 'inquiet' (see chapter 5).[49] The almost complete lack of a resolution is quite possibly the most marked characteristic of du Bouchet's poetry and poetics. It is in this retention of a 'tension qui ne fléchit pas' and the perennial 'circulation du sens', which is a 'continuité de tension de texte',[50] that du Bouchet departs from Reverdy's image and its 'rapports [...] justes' as well as from Celan's envisioned *archetypos* that is a 'Mehr-als-Sehen'.

Hence, for both Celan and du Bouchet discussions of the image in the late 1940s and early 1950s provided a crucial impetus for a continued engagement with this notion even as both would follow quite different poetological paths. As Celan later distanced himself from surrealism, what most conspicuously remained from his early conception of the image in 'Traum vom Traume' was the notion of an *archetypos*, placing him in an altogether different tradition of thinking and writing than surrealism or even Reverdy (see introduction).

Notes to Chapter 1

1. See Frazer; Asmuth.
2. See Syrotinski.
3. Reverdy.
4. André Breton, *Manifestes du Surréalisme: Premier Manifeste, Second Manifeste, Prolégomènes à un Troisième Manifeste du Surréalisme ou non, Position politique du Surréalisme, Poisson Soluble, Lettres aux voyantes, Du Surréalisme en ses œuvres vives*, ed. by Jean-Jacques Pauvert (Montreuil: Pauvert, 1962), pp. 13–65.
5. He had previously collaborated with Jené and published a pamphlet-like text called *Eine Lanze* in 1948 (*HKA* xv/1, 87–89).
6. Pöggeler, 'Bildende Kunst in der Lyrik Paul Celans', pp. 292–93.
7. Celan called these lithographs 'Beweis[e] äußerster Geschmacklosigkeit'. Cited in *Fremde Nähe: Celan als Übersetzer. Eine Ausstellung des Deutschen Literaturarchivs*, ed. by Axel Gellhaus (Marbach am Neckar: Deutsche Schillergesellschaft, 1997), p. 70; cf. also Pöggeler, 'Bildende Kunst in der Lyrik Paul Celans', p. 300–01.
8. Johannes von Schlebrügge, *Geschichtssprünge: Zur Rezeption des französischen Surrealismus in der österreichischen Literatur, Kunst und Kulturpublizistik nach 1945* (Frankfurt a. M.: Lang, 1985), pp. 91–95. For further context, see also Ivanović, '"des menschen farbe ist freiheit"'.
9. Fournanty-Fabre's research corroborates this finding. She has charted colour terms in Celan's works and their frequency of usage drops by more than half after *Mohn und Gedächtnis* (Fournanty-Fabre, p. 370).
10. Schlebrügge, pp. 95–122.
11. Cited in Schlebrügge, pp. 94–95. Heinrich Stiehler confirms that Celan was among the audience when Tzara gave the lecture in 1946 (cf. Heinrich Stiehler, 'Vom Bistilismus zum Zweitsprachengebrauch: Tristan Tzara', in *Horizont-Verschiebungen: Interkulturelles Verstehen und Heterogenität in der Romania. Festschrift für Karsten Garscha zum 60. Geburtstag*, ed. by Karsten Garscha, Claudius Armbruster, and Karin Hopfe (Tübingen: Narr, 1998), p. 97).
12. Michael Jakob, *Das 'Andere' Paul Celans; oder, von den Paradoxien relationalen Dichtens* (Munich: Fink, 1993), p. 157.
13. This phrase is also reminiscent of the 'deux réalités plus ou moins éloignées' in Pierre Reverdy, 'L'Image'.
14. Ivanović, 'Eine Sprache der Bilder', p. 553.

15. The notion that somehow the narrator has to go beyond images and eyesight to achieve 'true' seeing or speaking is also echoed by many scholars, e.g.: Dorothee Kohler-Luginbühl, *Poetik im Lichte der Utopie: Paul Celans poetologische Texte* (Berne: Lang, 1986), p. 17; Schlebrügge, p. 98.
16. It seems to be due to this muddled terminology, conflating the visual image with the metaphorical image, that it is rarely recognized by Celan researchers that Celan in fact went to great lengths to juxtapose the positively conceived non-visual image with the image that is mere metaphor and plays only a negative role (cf., e.g. *M*, 128).
17. Breton, *Manifestes du Surréalisme*, p. 34. Certainly, the nature of this 'esprit' already differs crassly between Breton and Reverdy, and by the time Celan wrote his notes for the 'Meridian' speech, his understanding of 'geistig' with respect to 'Bild' in turn differed from the ideas of the former two (although it is perhaps more sympathetic to Reverdy's 'esprit'). Nonetheless, given Celan's poetic starting point, Reverdy's conception of the image as received via Breton seems to be a likely source of inspiration for his later utterance.
18. The dialogical structure and the topos of the puppet may in fact go back to Plato's *Nomoi*, cf. Wilhelm Blum, 'Kleists Marionettentheater und das Drahtpuppengleichnis bei Platon', *Zeitschrift für Religions- und Geistesgeschichte*, 23.1 (1971), 40–49. Schlebrügge believes that Celan's mention of Kleist is an allusion to Johann Muschik's text 'Vom Adel des Verstandes' which had argued, citing Kleist's 'Marionettentheater', not for an abolition but a heightened use of reason to regain the state of innocence. Schlebrügge believes that to Celan this notion of progress and restauration in the post-World War II German-speaking world was 'leichtfertig' and 'geschichtsblind'. Schlebrügge, pp. 100–01.
19. It should be noted that I use the term 'metaphor' from the perspective of a critic, which contrasts with Celan's own negative conception of 'metaphor' (see above and chapter 7). There is no doubt that Celan was using metaphors despite his assertions to the contrary (perhaps most forcefully here: *M*, 158). Thus, the term should not be purged from our critical vocabulary when we engage with Celan's poetry. We are hence inquiring into the specific metaphorical qualities of Celan's conception of the image and of 'wahrnehmen'.
20. Ryland states as much: 'Celan's analyses of these [Jené's] works take a secondary position in the treatise, which is conceived as a reflection on the experience of viewing Jené's art and is dominated by a theoretical discussion of the nature of perception and expression.' Charlotte Ryland, *Paul Celan's Encounters with Surrealism: Trauma, Translation and Shared Poetic Space* (London: Legenda, 2010), p. 49. Kohler-Luginbühl seems to agree when she emphasizes, '[d]ass es sich nicht um einen eigentlichen Kommentar zu Jenés Bildern handelt, wird dem Leser bald klar. Bilder scheinen eher Anlass zu sein' (Kohler-Luginbühl, p. 16).
21. E.g. Kohler-Luginbühl, p. 28; Schlebrügge, p. 98.
22. Kohler-Luginbühl also notes that 'auch die Reflexion überwunden werden [muss], bis der Zugang zur "Tiefsee" frei wird' (Kohler-Luginbühl, p. 17).
23. Cf. also Kohler-Luginbühl, who investigates the millenarian and mythological notions of history in the essay and links it to Jewish and Christian mysticism (Kohler-Luginbühl, pp. 20–26).
24. The 'tausendjährige Last falscher und entstellter Aufrichtigkeit' could perhaps be seen as an allusion to the *tausendjähriges Reich* of Nazi Germany (*CW* III, 157).
25. Kleist's narrator reaches a conclusive moment of full insight in a state of absent-mindedness ('sagte ich ein wenig zerstreut'): Heinrich von Kleist, *Werke und Briefe in vier Bänden*, ed. by Siegfried Streller, 4 vols (Weimar: Aufbau, 1978), III: *Erzählungen, Anekdoten, Gedichte, Schriften* (1978), p. 480.
26. As already indicated in note 19, I use 'metaphorical' here from the perspective of a critic, not following Celan's usage of the word. Thus, while Celan in this essay suggests that metaphorical language is merely typified speech, his description of a more archetypal form of speech heavily draws on — in the critical use of the term — metaphors.
27. The merging of paradoxes was already envisioned by the narrator's friend, who spoke of a unification of tomorrow and yesterday yielding 'das Zeitlose, das Ewige, das Morgen-Gestern' (*CW* III, 156).
28. '[M]ein Gehör ist hinübergewandert in mein Getast, wo es sehen lernt' (*CW* III, 158).

29. Cf. e.g. Beierwaltes, *Denken des Einen*, pp. 73–114.
30. 'Das absolute Gedicht — nein, das gibt es gewiß nicht, das kann es nicht geben!' (*M*, 10); 'Ich finde etwas — wie die Sprache — Immaterielles, aber Irdisches, Terrestrisches' (*M*, 12).
31. Ute Harbusch provides an excellent overview and discussion of the frequently debated issue of absolute poetry in Celan; see her *Gegenübersetzungen: Paul Celans Übertragungen französischer Symbolisten* (Göttingen: Wallstein, 2005), pp. 84–92.
32. Cf. Wiedemann, ' "Und sie auf meine Art entziffern" ', pp. 267–69, 278; Pöggeler, 'Schwerpunkt: Wort und Bild. Paul Celan und Gisèle Celan-Lestrange', pp. 21, 33.
33. Cf. Fournanty-Fabre, p. 370.
34. The notion of apperception so prominent in Gottfried Wilhelm Leibniz's and Kant's philosophy denotes an inner and conscious self-perception. Celan, who had read Leibniz (c.f., e.g., *Mikro*, 120), clearly uses the word in this sense. For Leibniz's notion of apperception, see Manfred Frank, *Ansichten der Subjektivität* (Frankfurt a. M.: Suhrkamp, 2012), p. 39. It should be noted that Celan's use of 'apperception' here also marks a departure from the antirationalist, anticonsciousness rhetoric we witnessed in 'Traum vom Traume'.
35. 'Es gibt Augen, die den Dingen auf den Grund gehen. Die erblicken einen Grund. Und es gibt solche, die in die Tiefe der Dinge gehen. Die erblicken keinen Grund. Aber sie sehen tiefer. Frankfurt, 13.5.60' (*Mikro*, 25).
36. Dagfinn Føllesdal, 'Husserl's Reductions and the Role They Play in his Phenomenology', in *A Companion to Phenomenology and Existentialism*, ed. by Hubert L. Dreyfus and Mark A. Wrathall (Malden, MA: Blackwell, 2006), pp. 105–15 (pp. 109–10).
37. Føllesdal, p. 110.
38. Edmund Husserl, *Husserliana*, ed. Stephan Strasser and others (Den Haag: Nijhoff, 1950–), II: *Die Idee der Phänomenologie: Fünf Vorlesungen*, ed. by Walter Biemel (Den Haag: Nijhoff, 1950), §§4–6. Cf. also Dermot Moran and Joseph Cohen, ' "Eidetic Insight" ', in *The Husserl Dictionary* (London: Continuum, 2012), pp. 91–92 (p. 91).
39. Jean Bazaine, *Notizen zur Malerei der Gegenwart*, trans. by Paul Celan (Frankfurt a.M.: Fischer, 1959). According to Wiedemann and Badiou it was Celan's expressed wish to translate Bazaine's work (cf.: *Mikro*, 226).
40. Bazaine, p. 29.
41. Ibid., pp. 35–36.
42. Ibid., p. 52.
43. Ibid., p. 22.
44. Elke De Rijcke, 'Entretiens avec André du Bouchet', *L'Étrangère*, 16/17/18, special issue: *André du Bouchet 2* (2007), 277–300 (p. 295).
45. André du Bouchet, 'Image à terme', in *L'Incohérence* (Fontfroide-le-Haut: Fata Morgana, 1979), n.p. Cf. also the present book's introductory chapter to the reciprocal translations for a more elaborate discussion of time in Celan and du Bouchet (chapter 7).
46. Reverdy; Azérad, 'Parisian Literary Fields', pp. 673–74.
47. We may also think of the stanza in Celan's famous poem 'Sprachgitter': '(Wär ich wie du. Wärst du wie ich. | Standen wir nicht | unter einem Passat? | Wir sind Fremde.)' (*KG*, 99). Perhaps more significantly, we may also already think of Celan's 'Brücken über Abgründe' in his conception of translation (see chapter 7).
48. '[L'Image] ne peut naître d'une comparaison' (cf. Reverdy).
49. Du Bouchet, 'Image à terme'; cf. Layet's very illuminating essay 'Demain diamant', p. 34.
50. De Rijcke, 'Entretiens avec André du Bouchet', p. 288.

CHAPTER 2

Du Bouchet's Early Essays on the Conception of the Image in his Poetic Predecessors

We saw in the previous chapter that Celan's early image drew inspiration from surrealism but was also informed by a Judaeo-Christian and Greek tradition of thinking about the image that would ultimately become much more influential in his poetics. This tradition conceives of the image as split between *archetypos* and *typos*. In this chapter we will see that du Bouchet also drew inspiration from this tradition. He engaged with it in his early *carnets*, in his own readings, and particularly in his essays written as a young researcher at the Centre National de la Recherche Scientifique (CNRS).

After having fled to the United States with his family in 1940,[1] du Bouchet returned to France in 1948[2] and in 1951 took up a research position at the CNRS under the supervision of Jean Wahl,[3] known for reigniting the study of Georg Wilhelm Friedrich Hegel in France.[4] Du Bouchet undertook his research at the CNRS under the title 'Poésie et représentation dialectique de l'élément visuel dans l'image poétique'.[5] This title already indicates the fundamental importance of his early research and his early essays — only relatively recently edited and published by Clément Layet and François Tison under the title *Aveuglante ou banale* — for gaining an understanding of du Bouchet's poetics of the image. Even before beginning his work at the CNRS, du Bouchet's private notes in his early *carnets* had already increasingly begun revolving around the image, visibility, and perception.[6] For our close examination of du Bouchet's early poetic image we will draw on some of these notes. However, our main concern will be his essays and research summaries as well as proposals written for the CNRS, because they provide the most concise and focused account of his early conception of the image. In these essays, du Bouchet engages with the notion of the image in his poetic predecessors, particularly Maurice Scève, Friedrich Hölderlin, Victor Hugo, and Charles Baudelaire. From these texts we can also glean some of his readings of Neoplatonic philosophies of the image, such as Plotinus (*AB*, 344), Dionysius the Areopagite (*AB*, 290), and Giordano Bruno (*AB*, 18, 344). From such readings we would guess that du Bouchet's early thinking about the image was framed within the terms of the *archetypos*–*typos* dichotomy. While this assumption is certainly true, we will trace how du Bouchet increasingly departed from formulating his thought on the image in terms of *archetypos* and *typos*. The early du Bouchet seems to believe in a form of ulterior, transcendent reality to which we gain access through poetry and particularly through what du Bouchet believes to be the 'image'. However, through his analyses of Hugo and particularly Baudelaire du Bouchet comes to believe that the image is not objectively given. Since we can perceive reality only in images given by our vision, we have to realize that any 'vision réelle' is subjective and any attainment of an archetypal reality is thus altogether impossible (cf. e.g. *AB*, 75).

Celan would agree with du Bouchet's early analyses of Hugo and Baudelaire insofar as for Celan the *archetypos* is unachievable. Yet du Bouchet goes further in his analyses of Baudelaire: this supposed ulterior reality, which du Bouchet also calls 'fond', is paradoxically seen as 'vide' (*AB*, 106). At this point, du Bouchet's thought already touches on ways of conceiving of the image which we encounter in his later works. The more mature du Bouchet will move away from any such archetypal conception of reality: he posits reality or the image as a paradoxical relation between the visible and the invisible, between 'fond' and 'vide', a unification that is also a difference, as we will discuss more elaborately in chapter 5. In light of du Bouchet's rejection of any evocation of the absolute or the *archetypos*, whether negatively or positively, we will scrutinize du Bouchet's later image in terms of a mutually contingent *présence* and *absence*. This change from an image constituted by *archetypos* and *typos* to an image being constituted by *absence* and *présence* can already be traced in du Bouchet's early essays.

Du Bouchet's Discussion of Hölderlin's Image *Découpée*

In July 1950, du Bouchet writes in his notebook on the image in Hölderlin:

> [l]a vision nette de Hölderlin. L'encadrement de la fenêtre
> qui découpe le ciel etc. sans sourciller. Cette vision parfaite,
> qui élimine l'impureté et le vague de l'espace — mouches,
> phosphènes, bouillons, bavures, — lucidité de Dieu. Le
> médium: *nommément* (nämlich) il se conforme soigneusement
> avec l'objet pur. Tel quel. Miracle.[7]

We may be startled by the many incommensurable elements which du Bouchet ascribes to Hölderlin's image here. It seems clear that the 'vision nette' of the first line is a vision or a look through the 'fenêtre'. Yet how can the supposed 'vision nette', which seems so unimpeded in its being 'nette', be reconciled with '[l]'encadrement de la fenêtre', which in turn appears to narrow, perhaps even obstruct the field of this vision? Furthermore, the metaphorical, prophetic, and transcendent connotations of 'vision' are diminished in the second line, in which this 'vision' turns into a more mundane and literal instance of 'vision', understood as perceiving the sky through a window.

Indeed, it seems it is not the limitless expanse of the sky or heaven which constitutes what we originally presumed to be a transcendent 'vision parfaite'. The supposed purity of this vision is not constituted in 'le vague de l'espace', in the unformed infinitude and vastness of space. Rather the *découpage* of vision by the frame of the window — a liminal entity between outside and inside — appears to be that which constitutes the perfection of this 'vision'. We may even say that the purity and eventual 'lucidité de Dieu' is made possible by the vision's being framed by the window. The pure, transcendent vision is enabled precisely by the delimited field of vision which eliminates the 'impureté et le vague de l'espace'. Hence, the piece of sky cut out by the window frame is the 'vision parfaite'.

Reframing du Bouchet's note in our terms of *archetypos* and *typos*, we realize the unusualness of du Bouchet's assertion about Hölderlin. The 'vision parfaite' or the 'vision pure' would ordinarily be understood as the *archetypos*. In the *archetypos*, the act of seeing and that which is seen coincide, because any contingent and non-immediate relation between the act of seeing and that which is seen would render the *archetypos* relative rather than absolute and archetypal. If the *archetypos* somehow depended on the prophet's or onlooker's way of perceiving things, the *archetypos* would be relative to the latter's perception and would by definition not be archetypal. The *archetypos*, then, is independent of the onlooker's perception. Consequently, if we were to truly see the *archetypos*, then we could do so only in an act of vision in which perception and that which is perceived coincide as *archetypos*. Du Bouchet's 'vision parfaite' initially seems to intimate precisely this coincidence.[8] However, du Bouchet's 'vision parfaite', framed by the window, subsequently does not turn out to be this unconditioned and immediate perception. As du Bouchet writes, the limitless expanse of the sky is cut and framed by the window through which we look at the sky, rendering the image we see more *typos* than *archetypos*. Instead of seeing the sky in itself and as such — as an *archetypos* (it is surely no coincidence that 'ciel' can mean sky and heaven) — we see it through an intermediary — a windowpane — whose framed dimensions moreover limit our view and thereby remind us of the incompleteness of the image before our eyes. In the western philosophical tradition such an image would typically be considered a mere *typos*, not least since the onlooker's position behind a window suggests a fundamentally mortal (as opposed to divine) point of view. And yet, du Bouchet declares this very image to be the 'vision parfaite'. Hence, if we are to believe du Bouchet (at least up until line four of his note), what makes this vision an archetypal 'vision parfaite' is that the sky or heaven we see is *découpé*, that is — a *typos*.

This conception of Hölderlin's image finds some justification in Hölderlin's poetry and thought. Insofar as the divine or the 'Spirit must go out of itself and become manifest in matter' to reveal itself to humans,[9] the divine reveals itself by becoming *typos*. The poet is accorded a special role as mediator between the divine and the human, conveying the *archetypos* through the poetic word.[10] Accordingly, Hölderlin as a poet himself is foremost concerned with the *archetypos* in mediated form, in which 'der Mensch, der heißet ein Bild der Gottheit' 'misset nicht unglüklich [...] sich mit der Gottheit' (*SA* II/1, 372). And yet, the *archetypos* is not reducible to and fully comprehensible in this mediated form as *typos*. God can avert his 'Angesicht von den Menschen', leading to a questioning of the poetic vocation: 'wozu Dichter in dürftiger Zeit?' (*SA* II/1, 94; see also the following chapter). Ultimately, the *archetypos* in Hölderlin therefore cannot be captured in a *vision découpée*.

Perhaps it is partially for this reason that in the last two lines of his note, du Bouchet cuts back the radicalness and paradox of Hölderlin's 'vision parfaite', somehow typal and archetypal. Here, the 'encadrement de la fenêtre', which had delimited our view of the sky or heaven, 'se conforme soigneusement | avec l'objet pur', that is the sky or heaven. This conforming of the *typos* with the *archetypos* thus falls back into the traditional template of thinking about the *archetypos* and *typos* distinction, according to which the *typos* is modelled after the *archetypos* (e.g. in the well-known example of man as *imago Dei*). Therefore, the unilateral forming of the *typos* after the *archetypos* in the last lines of the note breaks with the previously established notion of the 'vision parfaite' which was perfect and pure precisely because the 'encadrement de la fenêtre' did not conform to the *archetypos* but rather gave us a *vision découpée*. Ultimately in this note, du Bouchet's rendition of Hölderlin's image reverts to the classic model of *archetypos* and *typos*.

Why does du Bouchet backtrack here? Why does he not conceive of *typos* and *archetypos* as relative and relational? In 1950, du Bouchet was still experimenting with his conception of the image in working through ideas of the image in other poets. Yet, what we can already glean from du Bouchet's note is his interest in the interstice, in the space or gap between *typos* and *archetypos*. Thus six years later, in 1956, in his application for an extension of his research stay at the CNRS, he revises his ideas in the earlier note on Hölderlin and much more clearly emphasizes the interstice: 'Hölderlin semble situer l'essentiel dans un intervalle qui séparerait, sans les infirmer, l'objet de son image' (*AB*, 288). Here the *typos* does not ultimately approximate the *archetypos*. Instead of the *typos*' conforming to the archetypal 'objet pur', as it did in the 1950 note, the 'objet' and its 'image' are separate in 1956. Furthermore, in 1956 there is no archetypal 'objet pur' to which the image or vision conforms. If there is anything archetypal at all, it is 'l'essentiel' which in turn is precisely that which separates image and object. The *archetypos* would then be the difference between object and image.

With this designation of the *archetypos* as essential difference, du Bouchet is halfway between his later, more radical conception of the image and more traditional thinking about it. It is not uncommon, especially in Neoplatonic philosophies, to think of the *archetypos* as absolutely different from the *typos* and the world of objects.[11] Hence in characterizing the *archetypos* as essential interstice, du Bouchet still follows to some extent this traditional strand of thinking about the image — at least when he is characterizing the image of Hölderlin. Nonetheless, du Bouchet's focus on the *archetypos* as interstice between entities paves the way for his later conception of the image. Rather than striving toward an *archetypos* that is an absolute or essential difference, his late image is constituted by the relative and relational difference between the visible and invisible, the 'figure' and 'fond', or what we will call in general terms *présence* in relation to *absence*.

There are two reasons why du Bouchet does not yet arrive at his own, more radical conception of the image in the note on Hölderlin. First, du Bouchet's own poetics of the image have not yet matured, and second, Hölderlin is only at the beginning of what du Bouchet perceives to be a historical, intellectual trajectory of the image which slowly moves away from the classic *archetypos–typos* dichotomy.[12]

Thus the more radical departure from the traditional notion of the image is not to be found in Hölderlin, but in Baudelaire. Du Bouchet does not draw the possible, radical conclusion of refraining from thinking of the image in terms of *archetypos* and *typos* altogether, because Hölderlin is still part of this heritage. He still holds onto the *archetypos–typos* dichotomy in relatively traditional terms, since he is only part of a larger historical development in thought about the image at whose limits this distinction becomes unstable.

Du Bouchet attests a notion of the image similar to that of Hölderlin to the French Baroque poet Maurice Scève (*c.* 1501 to *c.* 1564), which may help us shed further light on thinking about the image in more traditional terms of *archetypos* and *typos*. In Scève, the traditional conception of the image — between *archetypos* and *typos* — shows itself in his attempt to resolve the tension between the visible and invisible. For Scève, it is 'dans l'image d'une transparence que les termes du visible et de l'invisible s'équilibrent et assument une valeur égale' (*AB*, 285). The tension between the invisible and visible propels forward Scève's poetry, according to du Bouchet, but is ultimately resolved by arriving at what Scève terms transparency (*AB*, 285). As Layet notes on du Bouchet's discussion of transparency in Scève: '[a]ussi bien dans la tradition classique que dans les œuvres qui la transgressent, la transparence est le moment d'effacement de l'image.'[13] Transparency combines qualities of the invisible with the visible, since transparency denotes an entity that enables our seeing by letting us see through it, while at the same time this transparent entity itself is invisible. But in Scève this transparency is not just a mediator *between* the visible and the invisible but is spiritually charged. The 'trans' in transparency is to be understood as leading us beyond the duality of the visible and the invisible into an eternity, and consequently becomes archetypal.[14]

Following du Bouchet's discussion of how this contradiction in the notion of transparency in Scève is resolved, we realize that du Bouchet envisions a similar form of dissolving contradiction in the 'heilignüchterne[s] Wasser' of Hölderlin (from the poem 'Hälfte des Lebens') that 'résout la contradiction de l'absence et de la présence' (*AB*, 286). In both Hölderlin and Scève, this resolution occurs as 'dénuement' or a process of privation, which divested from all materiality presents us with the 'sacré' (*AB*, 289) and plenitude: 'le "dénuement" nous donne en même temps accès aux vertus positives de la vue, à des qualités substantielles telles que la *limpidité* ou la *transparence*' (*AB*, 288; emphases in original).[15]

Even though du Bouchet's Hölderlin, like Scève, seeks to resolve the contradictory and mutually exclusive dualities, Hölderlin seems to differ from Scève in one particular respect: that which conjoins and thus avoids being caught in the dichotomies of the visible and invisible manifests itself not as a form of transparency and transcendence, as in Scève, but as the discrepancy itself. In Hölderlin's image 'c'est l'écart même, l'étendue qui la [l'image de Hölderlin] sépare de l'objet envisagé qui lui fournit l'indice de sa propre essence' (*AB*, 287).[16] Whereas in Scève the dichotomies are overcome by an archetypal transcendence, in Hölderlin the difference — the image *découpée* — itself between (*typos*-)image and object is archetypal and transcends them insofar as it is beyond either. According to du Bouchet, Hölderlin situates 'l'essentiel dans un intervalle' and thus conceives of the *archetypos* as interstice (*AB*, 288).

The Subject and the Image in Du Bouchet's Early Essays on Hugo

Du Bouchet's declaring the difference — the gap — to be the seeming essential quality of the *archetypos* in Hölderlin prepares a fundamental shift which, for du Bouchet, occurs in Hugo and then, fully, in Baudelaire. In Hugo and especially Baudelaire, as du Bouchet holds, the *archetypos* ceases to be an absolute and essential difference to the *typoi*, effectively reducing the *archetypos* to another *typos*. In Hugo, the notion of transparency in the spirit of Scève is already declared to be an illusion (cf. *AB*, 71). Baudelaire in turn abolishes the idea of the *archetypos* by destabilizing its relation to the *typos*. It is at this point of divesting the *archetypos* of any absolute or transcendent characteristics that we will begin using the terms *présence* and *absence*. They denote an image which is conceived as constituted by the two equal poles of *présence* and *absence* without privileging one over the other.[17]

Before we can fully fathom du Bouchet's interpretation of Baudelaire's image, we will take a closer look at du Bouchet's ideas on Victor Hugo. He is the hinge to what du Bouchet — utilizing Rimbaud's term — calls the era of the *poètes voyants*.[18] Hugo is only very briefly mentioned in du Bouchet's essay on the conceptual evolution of the image which he outlines in his application for researching at the CNRS in 1956 (*AB*, 290). As his other essays show, however, Hugo's importance to du Bouchet's thought and to his implied intellectual and poetic history of the image is significant. The era of the *poètes voyants*, which Hugo initiates, is announced by a change of perspective in works of literature, but also on man and his place in science and nature:

> De la description du XVIII siècle, rendant compte de la topographie du paysage, de sa disposition matérielle, même teintée d'affectivité, à l'appréhension visionnaire du monde [syntax *sic*]. Le naturaliste devient voyant. Nodier entre Buffon et Hugo. La toile de fond envahit la scène pour occuper le premier plan. (*AB*, 148)

Du Bouchet attests to the era of naturalists that in their works the narrator becomes a spectator who does not and cannot train an omniscient and impartial eye on the scene. Rather, the narrator has become a part of the scene and as such does not convey absolute knowledge of what happens. The omniscient narrative perspective of the '*Dieu-Œil*' has lost its absolute vision (*AB*, 148–49). Such a relativity of the position of the spectator or narrator also entails that his perspective is unstable. The spectator is not an external, impartial onlooker. Since we only gain access to the 'toile de fond' of the narrated scene by means of the spectator, and since furthermore the narrator is a part of the scene, all accounts of the narrated scene are subjective. The increasing awareness of the subjectiveness of our point of access to the scene,[19] however, renders the spectator and what is seen through him unreliable: '[l]es rapports autrefois fixes deviennent fluctuants: vacillement incessant de ce qui est vu à ce qui voit, fusion occasionnelle de l'objet et du sujet' (*AB*, 148).

From the eighteenth century onward, according to du Bouchet, perception or narrative perspective is no longer removed from what takes place, like an omniscient narrator would be.[20] The narrator integrates himself into his own account of what is perceived and is aware of his (subjective) role in shaping the object of their perception. On the one hand, as part of the scene, the narrator is an object of his perception. As onlooker and narrator, however, he is also the perceiving subject. In the act of perceiving a landscape, the subject always also perceives itself as part of the landscape, resulting in a 'fusion occasionelle de l'objet et du sujet'.[21]

Yet, this fusion does not return the spectator to some form of originary or harmonious unity with the perceived world, in which the act of perception does not influence what is perceived. The hope for such an originary act of seeing does inhere in the act of looking, as du Bouchet believes to be the case in Hugo: '[v]oir cristallise le rêve d'agir sur ce que l'on décrit, de faire corps avec la réalité extérieure' (*AB*, 148). Nonetheless this desire cannot be fulfilled, because this act of looking entails a fundamental paradox. The spectator or narrator is partial to what he describes and perceives. He has integrated himself into the scene ('faire corps'; cf. *AB*, 148), making his awareness of his subjective viewpoint part of the narration. At the same time, however, this consciousness of his subjective viewpoint also always implies the impossibility of both, an entirely objective gaze onto what is narrated as well as the narrator's full integration into the scene. The narrating subject is split between being an object of its own perception (insofar as it is part of the scene) and being the subjective onlooker whose privileged position as an observer is precisely what sets it apart from the object of its perception. Therefore, his looking onto the 'réalité extérieure' and his perception of his spectatorship condemns the act of 'faire corps' to being a dream, an illusory vision. The new form of viewing or looking which du Bouchet claims begins in the eighteenth century hence implies a double thrust: the integration of the spectator into the scene as received by sensory perception, and his intrinsic distance from this scene, as his introspective gaze on his sensory perception reveals. Thus, as we pursue the dream to 'faire corps avec la réalité extérieure' through the act of viewing, we are confronted by the realization of 'la vue en tant qu'*effraction*' (*AB*, 148). The spectator's perception of the subjectiveness of his viewpoint also prevents his becoming part of the reality he describes, and this is the split inherent to the act of viewing. Clément Layet summarizes appositely:

> [l]es objets ne sont plus observés et exposés comme si le sujet lui-même n'en faisait pas partie. Le spectateur *sait* qu'il voit et que son regard conditionne la forme de la réalité. Puisqu'il la modifie en la percevant, la chose elle-même ne lui est jamais donnée, et le rapport avec le réel lui apparaît comme un 'défaut'.[22]

Du Bouchet's discussion of this subjective narrator remains abstract and most of his arguments are fragments. Yet, looking at a few excerpts in Hugo's *Les Misérables* might concretize what du Bouchet had in mind. As becomes clear in selected passages of the novel, the narrator is conscious of the act of narration ('celui qui écrit ce livre').[23] It is exactly because this third-person narrator himself takes part in the narration and, to a certain extent, narrates himself, that he becomes aware of the limitations of his own perception. As he is part of the narration, he has no access to an objective vantage point and needs to rely on hearsay from others — often other characters — and common knowledge in order to tell the tale of his characters. These limitations become particularly apparent at the start of the novel, where we frequently stumble upon gaps in the story. Turns of phrases recur that attest to this uncertainty, for instance: '[n]ul n'aurait pu le dire'; '[q]u'y avait-il de vrai, du reste, dans les récits qu'on faisait sur la première partie de la vie de M. Myriel ? Personne ne le savait.'²⁴ Although this narrator is not altogether unreliable, we notice the limitations owing to the narrator's subjective viewpoint and his integration of himself into the scene. The narrator thus draws into question the truthfulness of his own 'récits' and the question marks demarcate the boundaries of the narrator's own knowledge.

The more the reliability of the narration itself becomes a concern, the more the 'réalité extérieure' is distanced and an objective access to this reality increasingly impossible. We notice the narrator's integration into the narration as well as the persisting separation between the narrator and characters and the narrated reality. This should help us understand why du Bouchet speaks of the '[t]hème de la vue en tant qu'*effraction*' in Hugo (*AB*, 148). According to du Bouchet, we must ultimately draw the act of vision itself into question, since there is no transcendent eye independent of perceiver and perceived. As du Bouchet says in his 1953 essay 'Vision et connaissance' (which is, in part, a revision of his 'Vue et vision chez Victor Hugo'): '[l]e voyant ne peut plus voir que par truchement' (*AB*, 167).²⁵

Let us turn back to the short notebook entry from 1950 on Hölderlin's image, cited above. When we look more closely at it, we also find terminology from du Bouchet's discussion of Hugo, which allows us to compare the two conceptions of the image by Hölderlin and Hugo as seen by du Bouchet. Although the note antedates du Bouchet's essays on Hugo, it already contains some core terms of du Bouchet's later analyses of Hugo. The seemingly random occurrences of the 'mouches, phosphènes, bouillons, bavures' are nowhere to be found in Hölderlin's work. They stem in fact from du Bouchet's thinking on Hugo. They are recurring motifs particularly in his early essay (1951) on 'l'infini et l'inachevé' in Hugo's posthumously published fragments (*AB*, 65–81).

In the notebook entry on Hölderlin, the 'mouches, phosphènes, bouillons, bavures' to be eliminated by Hölderlin's 'lucidité de Dieu' for their 'impureté[s]' are precisely what for Hugo are the necessary 'truchement[s]' to render the onlooker seeing. They are what sets Hugo's poetry apart from that of his predecessor, Hölderlin. For Hölderlin, according to du Bouchet, the archetypal and unifying 'vision pure' is achieved by the *typos*'s eventual forming into the *archetypos*: '[l]e médium [...] se conforme soigneusement | avec l'objet pur.' In his proposal for the CNRS in 1956, du Bouchet would also phrase Hölderlin's *archetypos* as 'l'identité de ce [que l'image] parvient à enclore et de ce qui lui échappe' (*AB*, 287). This folding of the *typos* into the *archetypos* in du Bouchet's Hölderlin still clings to traditional notions of the *archetypos*, as we have already shown. Hölderlin's *archetypos* is reached in recognizing the difference ('la connaissance déchirante') between the archetypal 'objet pur' and its limited representation in the *typos*. Du Bouchet also calls Hölderlin's *archetypos* 'lucidité' in his various essays on the German poet (cf. *AB*, 287 and the note already quoted), co-opting traditional representations of the *archetypos* as 'light' or 'clarity'. The notion of the *archetypos* as 'lucidité' conjoins the notion of light as a metaphorically abstract, mystical entity which is seen and the fact that light enables seeing and visibility in the first place. The notion of 'lucidité' thus unites the act and possibility of seeing with that which is seen — a classic conception of the *archetypos*.²⁶

For Hugo, as opposed to Hölderlin, this type of originary 'vision' or 'lucidité' is not possible. This is because in du Bouchet's interpretation of Hugo everything is contingent on an act of seeing which is not anchored in an omniscient vantage point anymore. The act of seeing itself has become differential, at least in the interpretation by du Bouchet. It is split between the gaze (by the subject) onto the object and the subject's gaze on itself (and its gaze on the object). We saw that perception in Hugo was an act of seeing by 'truchement', as interpreted from an onlooking subject who itself is part of the scene upon which it looks. Such an act of seeing by proxy cannot achieve Hölderlin's visionary 'lucidité', joining the perceiver, perceiving, and the perceived in the *archetypos*. Even if in Hugo we find that, similar to Hölderlin, the 'désir immense de l'éternel, du continu, ne peut se satisfaire qu'en englobant son contraire', this thirst for unification and tendency toward an archetypal 'lucidité' is never quenched in Hugo. Du Bouchet does not shy away from phrasing it in contradictory terms. The desire for '[l]'infini, devenant l'inachevé, se disloque brutalement en éclats' (*AB*, 66). Paradoxically, in the same breath 'l'éternel' or 'l'infini' is unifying ('englobant') *and* breaks apart ('se disloque'). In other words, condensing this paradox into one sentence: '[l]'infini interrompu se contracte et se ferme sur une réalité d'une précision hallucinatoire...' (*AB*, 67).

The contradictory nature of that which is envisioned (i.e. '[l]'infini, devenant l'inachevé') and the radical questioning of an ulterior, archetypal reality ('une réalité d'une précision hallucinatoire') is immanent to the mode of seeing. This effectively amounts to perceptual solipsism. There is no reality independent of sight.²⁷ The act of perception, ever more subjective from the eighteenth century onward, according to du Bouchet, is in Hugo entirely contingent on and relative to the perceiving subject: '[t]out, n'existant qu'en vertu de la vision, ne peut que mutuellement s'entrevoir: l'existence devient une sorte de solipsisme visuel' (*AB*, 166). Even God and his powers are subject to and relative to being seen by an other: 'le dieu aveugle de Hugo qui ne crée des soleils qu'en devenant lui-même l'objet d'une autre vue' (*AB*, 166). Seeing is thus dependent on being seen by a subject which is other to that which is seen.²⁸ Seeing in Hugo is so utterly dependent on the 'truchement', on the proxy of the other through which reality is seen, that the existence of an independent external reality cannot even be postulated.

Hugo, for du Bouchet, goes even further than just drawing the possibility of accessing reality into question. Hugo's spectator is so radically dependent on being seen himself that he questions his own act of seeing when seeing someone who does not see: 'l'étonnement de ce qui voit face à ce qui ne voit pas, de voir, dans la logique d'une vision "intégrale", qu'on ne voit pas' (*AB*, 166–67). If our act of seeing is contingent on our being seen, then our seeing somebody who does not see, and therefore does not see *us*, is not possible in the first place. Hence, 'face à ce qui ne voit pas', we gain the insight ('une vision "intégrale"') that we do not see. This insight, in turn, becomes impossible, because if we do not see, we cannot have any in*sight*. We hence have to postulate with du Bouchet that we arrive at '[i]mages qui ne font qu'"autentifier" l'impossibilité de voir' (*AB*, 167).²⁹

These problems are hinted at in the note on Hölderlin by the inserted 'mouches, phosphènes, bouillons, bavures', which Hölderlin's 'vision nette' could transcend, but Hugo's 'voyant [...] par truchement' could not. In the vocabulary of du Bouchet's interpretation of Hugo's words, flies and phosphenes are treated as synonyms: '[l]a terre est sous les mots comme un champ sous les mouches' (cf. *AB*, 72, 153, 162). It is unclear whether the field upon which the black flies descend, similar to the black ink of the words on the page, is actually ever reached or is even reachable; this entirely depends on how 'sous' is understood. If the flies (and consequently words) are nothing but 'simples prête-noms d'une réalité innommable' (*AB*, 151), does this mean the existence of a reality (or a 'champ'), albeit nameless, is presumed? Or are the 'mouches' empty signifiers for a reality that does not exist? Du Bouchet does not seem to give a consistent answer to these questions.

A negatively evoked, unnameable reality could be considered a metaphysical cognate of the apophatic, nameless God (i.e. the *archetypos*) in negative theology.[30] Du Bouchet does seem to point to such a nameless reality, which words and images fail to describe: '[c]e n'est plus [...] un univers postiche à qui l'on prête un langage humain, mais le langage même que nous arrache cette insupportable présence dans un univers lucide et muet' (*AB*, 73, cf. also 151). In the 'univers lucide et muet', from which we have been torn according to Hugo, we recognize similarities to Hölderlin's 'lucidité'. However, we may go a step further and not only doubt our ability to express this universe in language, but even doubt the existence of that very reality in the first place. Given the epistemologically constricted account we get of that reality through the subjective perspective of the narrator, we have no certainty about the nature of this reality. Du Bouchet frequently cites Hugo's phrase 'mot-phosphène', which would imply that the unnameable reality, akin to the *archetypos*, is not evoked *ex negativo* by our fallible language, but rather that reality itself is an illusion. Phosphenes denote a sensation of perceiving light when no actual light enters the eye.[31] Thus, if words are phosphenes and are flies in du Bouchet's metaphor, then the 'champ' above which the flies fly does not exist. The reality evoked by words would be a visual sensation that is not rooted in anything visible.

If we took du Bouchet's thought on Hugo to its radical conclusion, we would find that the radical doubt of seeing and perception leads to a radical doubt of reality itself. Words such as 'prête-noms' and 'phosphènes' feign a visibility and nameability of a reality that this reality itself does not warrant, and there is therefore nothing to be actually said about the 'univers lucide et muet'. We are confined to speaking in images, without any presumption of an *archetypos*. However, as with Hölderlin, du Bouchet does not go so far with Hugo as to radically doubt an *archetypos* or an archetypal reality. Hugo, for du Bouchet, is 'à mi-chemin entre la fragmentation et la recherche de l'unité: une unité visuelle' (*AB*, 149).[32]

We thus discover vestiges of notions of the *archetypos* in Hugo's *Post-scriptum de ma vie*, which du Bouchet cites: '"[j]e me rappelle qu'en 1828, tout jeune, j'avais des taches obscures dans les yeux... elles semblaient envahir lentement la rétine... et voilà que je me mis à espérer que je serais peut-être un jour aveugle comme Homère et comme Milton"' (*AB*, 149). Like Milton and Homer, Hugo had hoped to reach a higher form of poetic vision through (sensory, perceptual) blindness. Accordingly, the heading of this chapter in du Bouchet's essay is called 'Victor Hugo: de la vue à la vision' (*AB*, 148), insinuating a progression from visual sight to spiritual vision.[33] In this light, Hugo's seeing what one does not see ('voir [...] ce qu'on ne voit pas') and his '[i]mages qui ne font qu'"autentifier" l'impossibilité de voir' could also imply a progression from sensory to visionary perception.

However, du Bouchet ultimately regards Hugo as being sceptical about the possibility of an archetypal 'vision'. As du Bouchet states in 'Vision et connaissance', that is, the last revision of his essays on Hugo:

> [l]e point de convergence des termes contradictoires de l'image localise effectivement le champ d'une intuition 'aveuglante', mais il n'y a là rien à 'saisir': le point précis où nous aiguille la convergence de leur action n'est qu'un lieu de disparition, un point de fuite. (*AB*, 167)

The unification of opposites, of subject and object, of representation of reality and reality in an archetypal image and vision ultimately yields an 'intuition "aveuglante"'. Given Hugo's desire to reach a higher vision through blindness, we could now assume that this blind intuition also entails an archetypal cognition. But this is not the case. The blind intuition only shows that 'il n'y a là rien à "saisir"'. This 'rien', clearly, is not an apophatic evocation of an archetypal nothing.[34] Rather, it perennially defies our grasp. It is fitting that the term 'point de fuite' in the art of painting does not denote a transcendent *locus*, but the vanishing point which lies just beyond the means of what can be visually represented to the onlooker by the painter. If there is an *archetypos* at all in du Bouchet's Hugo, this *archetypos* is such a 'point de fuite' that is not absolute but relative to the subjective onlooker.[35]

Baudelaire's Image *Présente* and *Absente* in Du Bouchet's Early Essays

In the brief history of the poetic image which du Bouchet submits to the CNRS in 1956, it is Baudelaire who completes the conceptual trajectory (*AB*, 289). As du Bouchet states in his essay 'Théâtre de la répétition' written around the same time: 'Baudelaire: le premier totalement engagé dans l'antinomie de l'apparence et du fond qui s'échangent' (*AB*, 296). According to du Bouchet in his 1956 essay 'Baudelaire irrémédiable', Baudelaire's poetry begins with the realization that 'l'infaillibilité dans la production poétique' cannot be achieved and thus we inescapably (*irrémédiablement*) face the limitations of our perception:

> Au point où l'infaillible se révèle comme étant l'irrémédiable, nous touchons à l'essence de la poésie de Baudelaire, puisqu'elle ne fait qu'énoncer l'impossibilité de retrouver sa vie *ailleurs*: ailleurs que dans sa durée réelle. Baudelaire s'attend à autre chose, mais cet 'autre', Baudelaire découvre qu'il n'est autre que Baudelaire. Baudelaire non pas infaillible, mais un Baudelaire atteint et susceptible de mourir. (*AB*, 96)

The 'essence' of Baudelaire's poetics, according to du Bouchet, is consequently the very lack of an essence, the impossibility to reach beyond the prison bars of his 'durée réelle' into an 'ailleurs'. This limitation is most evident when Baudelaire probes the boundaries of his 'durée réelle' by evoking his own death and thereby attempting to witness it as an independent spectator — as du Bouchet discusses with respect to Baudelaire's 'Le Rêve d'un curieux'. Let us look at the poem and try to outline what du Bouchet means by 'l'impossibilité de retrouver sa vie *ailleurs*':

> Connais-tu, comme moi, la douleur savoureuse
> Et de toi fais-tu dire: 'Oh! l'homme singulier!'
> — J'allais mourir. C'était dans mon âme amoureuse
> Désir mêlé d'horreur, un mal particulier;
>
> Angoisse et vif espoir, sans humeur factieuse.
> Plus allait se vidant le fatal sablier,
> Plus ma torture était âpre et délicieuse;
> Tout mon coeur s'arrachait au monde familier.
>
> J'étais comme l'enfant avide du spectacle,
> Haïssant le rideau comme on hait un obstacle...
> Enfin la vérité froide se révéla:
>
> J'étais mort sans surprise, et la terrible aurore
> M'enveloppait. — Eh quoi! n'est-ce donc que cela?
> La toile était levée et j'attendais encore.[36]

The double perspective, the split gaze, is apparent from the very first line of the poem. The poetic voice of the poem addresses a second person, a 'tu', which we suspect is the poetic voice itself. Indeed, as soon as the poetic voice has finished putting words into the mouth of the second person and the singularity of the second person is pronounced ('Oh! l'homme singulier'), we as readers are cast into the first-person poetic voice which we do not leave before the poem concludes. It is already clear after the second line of the poem that the attempt by the poetic voice to witness itself from the standpoint as an independent spectator fails. The voice experiences nothing but its own 'durée réelle'. This confinement to the ineluctable subjectivity of its personal experience crystallizes particularly in the two tercets.

Here again the spectator's perspective is split. The first-person poetic voice envisages another person — 'l'enfant avide du spectacle' — and it is in this refraction of its own gaze in the gaze of another that the gaze of the poetic voice is bent back on itself, reflected. The taking of another's perspective to return the gaze on the poetic voice itself is already implied in the comparative particle 'comme', which from the start makes the fictionality of the infant's gaze apparent. It is, in fact, the (split) gaze (on itself) of the poetic voice itself. In the second, final tercet, the illusion of this out-of-body experience by the poetic voice is once and for all evident. It is impossible for the voice to transcend its own perspectival confines and experience an 'ailleurs'. The enunciation of the event of its own death ('[j]'étais mort'), which the poetic voice seems to witness as if in the body of an infant, is a fiction. The enunciation of the voice's death turns out to be rather the pronunciation of the death of the possibility of an objective perspective on one's own subjectivity. As the curtain is lifted and the 'vérité froide se révéla', the poetic voice awakens to the terrible realization that the lifted curtain is its eyelid and the dawn enveloping it like a sheet constitutes the confines of its experience. It is due to its opening its eyes to the dawn that the voice wakes up and comprehends — as indicated by the exclamation '[e]h quoi! n'est-ce donc que cela?' — that everything it witnessed was a dream. Confronting the unimaginable image of witnessing our own death, we admit the inevitability of the confines of our 'durée réelle'.

This is precisely the conclusion du Bouchet draws as he makes Baudelaire's poem 'Le Rêve d'un curieux' the site of his philosophical inquiries about the image:

> Baudelaire manifeste son désir de transformer sa mort en représentation pure, — d'être le spectateur de sa mort, d'assister à sa mort, donc de ne pas mourir. [...] Le spectateur demeure toujours indemne, le spectateur ne meurt pas de la mort qu'il considère. Or la scène est vide. Il n'y a pas de spectacle, la vie n'est pas un spectacle, et ce vide nous donne la mesure réelle de Baudelaire. [...] La mort, en effet, *n'est que cela*: elle n'est pas ce spectacle prévisible auquel, lorsqu'il a lieu, un spectateur survit. (*AB*, 102–03)[37]

This 'cela' of death becomes the expression of that which resolutely lacks expression: Baudelaire's own death. One's own death cannot be expressed, cannot be imagined. The 'image' of one's own death has no representation,[38] because there is no looking beyond the existential confines of the subject:[39] '[c]ar nous ne pouvons pas imaginer autre chose que la vie, et, à la limite de la vie nous touchons à la limite de l'expression' (*AB*, 106). Thus, death surpasses the capacity of the imagination and can only be conceived 'sous les traits de la vie'[40] as that which escapes life: 'sa mort inimaginable, il ne peut l'imaginer autrement que comme l'expression la plus nue de sa vie' (*AB*, 105). As long as we live, death cannot be conceived: it is a void. Consequently, speaking about death and trying to grasp it in any way — even as a void — suggests an inadvertent conceptualization or imagination of that which is unimaginable. Facing the limitations and incapacity of our vision and imagination we are continuously forced to confront our own, very real existence:

> [m]ais l'inclusion de ce vide [de la mort] entre deux images, de cet intervalle et de ce vide par où l'inimaginable se fait jour, nous impose un moment la vérité que nous croyons connaître, la vérité familière, avec une violence et une intensité inconnues [*sic*]. Elle suffit à transformer ce désir incessant d'un infini qui se trouverait *ailleurs*, en une présence dont Baudelaire peut éprouver la force, puisqu'elle se confond avec la sienne — un peu à la manière de ce ciel dont l'évidence s'impose à notre attention d'une façon plus décisive dans le vide qui sépare deux rochers. (*AB*, 107–08)

The 'vide' risks conceptualizing and representing that which cannot be represented — the infinitude of an unspecified beyond ('*ailleurs*') — and eventually turns the unrepresentable and absent into a non-metaphysical presence. This *présence* is not a metaphysical antonym of an equally metaphysical *absence*, but a mundane, perhaps even banal *présence* of a here and now. The impossibility of imagining an '*ailleurs*' transforms our desire for the infinite *archetypos* ('transformer ce désir [...] d'un infini') into a ground upon which we tread ('[c]ette limite, ce sol que Baudelaire atteint au cœur de son œuvre'; *AB*, 107).

We will elaborate on this notion of a 'sol' or 'fond' in a final comparison of Hölderlin's 'encadrement de la fenêtre' with a seemingly similar metaphor by

Baudelaire, which radicalizes Hölderlin's image and concludes the intellectual trajectory in du Bouchet's 1956 CNRS proposal. In his discussion of the image in both Hölderlin and Baudelaire, du Bouchet focuses on the interstitial, or the intermediary, character of the image. However, whereas in Hölderlin the interstice or the intermediary is transformed into the *archetypos* ('Le médium [...] se conforme soigneusement avec | l'objet pur'), in Baudelaire it is through confrontation with the other, the unimaginable, or the absent that we realize the ultimate impossibility of reaching the *archetypos*. Instead of making the window frame conform perfectly with the sky, as in the note on Hölderlin, du Bouchet's Baudelaire stresses that the evidence of the 'ciel [...] s'impose à notre attention d'une façon plus décisive dans le vide qui sépare deux rochers'. Paradoxically we see the sky as 'vide' between two rocks better than in an unimpeded field of vision.

An archetypal vision independent of the onlooker's perspective is hence rejected. Furthermore, as we face the void or interstice, that is the absence of an unmediated perspective on the sky, we become aware of our own presence: '[t]el est, en effet, le ciel de Baudelaire. [...] Ce morceau de ciel qui est la seule forme concevable de la durée réelle hors de laquelle Baudelaire ne songe pas à inscrire son œuvre' (*AB*, 93). Therefore, we become conscious of our 'durée réelle'[41] through the confrontation with the other or with that which is absent and unimaginable. *Présence* presumes *absence* and vice versa.[42] This co-contingency of *présence* and *absence* is, for instance, suggested in 'l'antinomie de l'apparence et du fond qui s'échangent' in Baudelaire (*AB*, 296). Only in being confronted with the unimaginable, facing that which is absent and cannot be presented, can we form an idea of our 'durée réelle', our own presence.

The Subject in the Early Celan and Du Bouchet

Let us conclude our discussion of du Bouchet's early essays here and turn briefly to a comparison with Celan's early conception of the image. We see that both authors drew their initial poetic inspirations from quite different sources after the war. For a brief but informative period, Celan's poetics was influenced by the surrealist notion of the image but also clearly the idea of the image as spanned by the two opposing terms *typos* and *archetypos*. Most of du Bouchet's early essays on the image in his poetic predecessors similarly seek to grapple with traditional thought of the image as situated between *typos* and *archetypos*. But we can already see that the direction du Bouchet's thinking takes seems to move away altogether from the notion of the *archetypos*. Unlike Celan's 'Traum vom Traume', du Bouchet's early essays do not betray a strong bearing of surrealism on his thought (see also chapter 5). Thus, at an initial glance both authors' starting point after the war seems to reveal diverging sources of inspiration.

However, du Bouchet and Celan share some fundamental assumptions about the image and the notion of subjectivity, assumptions which they also have in common with surrealism.[43] We saw in du Bouchet's discussion of Hugo and Baudelaire that we cannot divest ourselves from our subjective standpoint. Furthermore, especially in Baudelaire our awareness of our subjectivity (and its limitations) and our *présence* in the 'durée réelle' is brought about by the experience of the 'ailleurs' or other. Although Rimbaud's *Lettres du voyant* are only alluded to in passing in du Bouchet's early essays (cf. *AB*, 149), the conception of subjectivity du Bouchet discovers in Baudelaire prefigures the experience of subjectivity through or as other articulated in Rimbaud's expression 'je est un autre'.[44] The confrontation with the other of the subject, in the form of the subject's unconscious as harbinger of a new cognition, is also apparent in Celan's 'Traum vom Traume': 'ich [blicke] der neuen Helligkeit ins Auge. [...] [O]bwohl ich sie heraufbeschworen habe, lebt sie doch jenseits der Vorstellungen meines wachen Denkens' (*CW* III, 158). At least in Celan's early surrealist phase, the narrator in 'Traum vom Traume' gains his archetypal vision from experiences that originate in himself, insofar as they are his 'Vorstellungen', and yet are other to himself, since they are not conscious (see chapter 1).[45] The importance of the other in 'Traum vom Traume' is also already evidenced by the fact that the text is written in the form of a dialogue.[46]

The later Celan would attenuate this notion of the subject that in 'Traum vom Traume' was split between conscious and unconscious. Yet, we will see in the discussion of Celan's mature poem 'Halbzerfressener' that the idea of the other or the 'Du' continues to be crucial for the conception of subjectivity in Celan's poetics (see chapter 6). Only in the experience of its other does the subject achieve, tentatively, an archetypal vision. Even though Celan's mature subject is primary to and precedes the other, the subject's engaging and communicating with the other is pivotal to Celan's poetics insofar as the purpose of the poetic subject is determined by its quest to speak truthfully and to be understood. In du Bouchet's more mature position on subjectivity and its relation to the image, comprising *présence* and *absence*, we will see that his subject, the 'je', does not precede and is not primary to the 'tu' (see chapters 6 and 7). The 'tu' and 'je' are 'l'écart que l'on prend sur soi'.[47] Unlike in Celan, the split between 'tu' and 'je' is primary to the subject in du Bouchet's mature writings. In this more radical position on the subject, we are reminded of the subject in Baudelaire, which realized the 'fond' of its own present existence only in facing the 'vide' image of its own absence (i.e. death). The subject became conscious of its subjectivity in the interaction of *présence* and *absence*.[48]

Du Bouchet had to leave his research post at the CNRS after 1956.[49] But we see that the cornerstones for the image in his own poetry had been laid in his early essays and interpretations of his predecessors. These analyses culminate in the reading of the poet who, in du Bouchet's eyes, has driven the image to its extremes: Baudelaire. In du Bouchet's own early writings, we find echoes of what in his essays he ascribes to Baudelaire. Baudelaire's image reveals 'l'essentiel [...] comme un échec', which resonates in du Bouchet's own conception of the 'image parvenue à son terme inquiet' (*AB*, 88; see also chapter 5) or in the paradoxical formulation that '[l]a vie accrue de la poésie à l'instant où elle constate sa mort' (*AB*, 87). In 1956 du Bouchet had already emphasized the 'dialectique du dénuement' in Baudelaire — a conception of the image which lacks an *archetypos* and is constituted by the two contrasting poles of *absence* and *présence* interacting with each other. This engagement with the image in Baudelaire foreshadows the direction of du Bouchet's own conception of the image in his poetry. Daniel Leuwers fittingly describes du Bouchet's poetry as an 'entrevoir': 'c'est-à-dire de voir entre — entre les choses, entre les mots, et même "*entre les lignes*"', as opposed to a divining Christian 'vision' or the Mallarméan 'vue' in his 'Prose pour des Esseintes', which are 'toujours prompte à venir résoudre les contradictions'.[50] In 1979 du Bouchet would discuss again the importance of Baudelaire for his own poetry in an interview with Alain Veinstein, in which he re-emphasizes his reading of Baudelaire's poetry as a contradictory oscillation between *présence* and *absence*: 'une contradiction sans borne et sans aboutissement'.[51]

Notes to Chapter 2

1. See the indispensable chronology published by his wife Anne de Staël, which also contains letters and crucial information about the earlier parts of du Bouchet's life (de Staël, p. 361).
2. Ibid., p. 370.
3. Layet, 'Demain diamant', p. 30.
4. Jean André Wahl, *Le Malheur de la conscience dans la philosophie de Hegel* (Paris: Presses Universitaires de France, 1951); cf. Bernhard Waldenfels, *Phänomenologie in Frankreich* (Frankfurt a. M.: Suhrkamp, 1986), p. 28; cf. also Henriikka Tavi, 'Rezeptionen des deutschen Idealismus in Europa', in *Handbuch Deutscher Idealismus*, ed. by Hans Jörg Sandkühler (Stuttgart: Metzler, 2005), pp. 355–89 (p. 368).
5. Layet, 'Demain diamant', p. 30.
6. André du Bouchet, *Une lampe dans la lumière aride: Carnets 1949–1955*, ed. by Clément Layet (Paris: Le Bruit du temps, 2011).
7. Du Bouchet, *Carnets 1949–1955*, p. 65.
8. We should note that the etymology and meaning of the word 'vision' already suggests both, the act of vision and that which is seen. Cf. 'Vision, N.', *OED Online* (Oxford University Press, 2016) <http://www.oed.com/view/Entry/223943> [accessed 31 March 2016].
9. Ian Cooper, *The Near and Distant God: Poetry, Idealism and Religious Thought from Hölderlin to Eliot* (London: Legenda, 2008), p. 25. Kreuzer makes the same point: Johann Kreuzer, 'Philosophische Hintergründe der Gesänge "Der Einzige" und "Patmos" von Friedrich Hölderlin', in *Geist und Literatur: Modelle in der Weltliteratur von Shakespeare bis Celan*, ed. by Edith Düsing and Hans-Dieter Klein (Würzburg: Königshausen & Neumann, 2008), p. 107–37 (p. 108).
10. 'Wir verfügen — als endliche Wesen — nicht über den Standpunkt eines unendlichen Geistes. Gäbe es einen, der Gott allein faßt, er wäre wie Gott. [...] Wir bedürfen — der Geist bedarf — der Zeichen und der Sprache. Deshalb müssen die "Dichter [...] auch | Die geistigen weltlich seyn"' (Kreuzer, 'Philosophische Hintergründe', p. 133).
11. Most notable in this respect is Plotinus, but also Meister Eckhart and Nicolaus Cusanus, who carry on Plotinus' legacy. Cf. Werner Beierwaltes, *Identität und Differenz* (Frankfurt a. M.: Klostermann, 2011), p. 26 (on Plotinus), p. 97 (on Eckhart), pp. 116–17 (on Cusanus).
12. In his proposals to the CNRS, du Bouchet's trajectory is often only implicitly a historical one, in that du Bouchet follows a historical chronology in discussing the authors he researches, starting with Scève and Hölderlin and ending up at Baudelaire. Yet, in his essay on 'Vue et vision chez Victor Hugo' (*AB*, 148–59), du Bouchet explicitly frames Hugo's poetics of vision in historical terms. Hence, I disagree with Layet here that 'le fil historique dégagé dans le projet de l'automne 1953 semble définitivement rompu' in du Bouchet's discussion of Scève (cf. Layet, 'Temps apparent', p. 234).
13. Layet, 'Temps apparent', p. 234.
14. Cf. du Bouchet's citation of Scève's verse: '[s]i transparent m'était son chaste cloître... | Je verrais l'âme ensemble et le corps croître | Avant le temps, en leur *éternité*' (*AB*, p. 285; my emphasis).

I thus partially disagree with Layet who believes that the image of du Bouchet's Scève, as for instance that of Baudelaire, 'aboutit à aucun terme final' (Layet, 'Temps apparent', p. 234). Layet is more apposite when he speaks of 'transparence' as 'le signe de l'invisible absolu' (ibid., p. 235), in which 'les opposés sont vus à partir du point où ils s'identifient' (ibid., p. 236). Scève's notion of growing and transcendence in connection to vision and the image resonates in the 'Bild' of Celan's poem 'Halbzerfressener' which 'sich entwächst, entwächst' (*KG*, 195; see chapter 6).

15. The notion of privation as giving access to an *archetypos* is reminiscent of negative theology. With regard to du Bouchet's Hölderlin, I believe, the association with negative theology is justified. To anticipate our discussion of du Bouchet's Baudelaire, we should note that du Bouchet declares Baudelaire's image, on the other hand, to be 'loin' of any apophatic evocation of a 'présence efficace du sacré' (*AB*, 289).
16. This conception of the *archetypos* as an essential and absolute difference to the world of *typos* images (worldly objects as well as actual images) is, at heart, Neoplatonic.
17. Du Bouchet calls this 'dialectique du dénuement' (*AB*, 289). We need to emphasize here that this dialectic is not to be understood in Hegelian terms. In Hegel's dialectics, thesis and antithesis are overcome by their synthesis, whereas in du Bouchet's perception of a dialectic in Baudelaire there is no synthesis which follows upon and dissolves the contradiction. Layet has argued that du Bouchet himself also does not subscribe to a Hegelian dialectics (cf.: Layet, 'Demain diamant').
18. 'Hugo ouvre définitivement l'ère des poètes "voyants"' (*AB*, 149). This notion of Hugo as *voyant* and in this role precursor to Rimbaud seems to be shared by some scholars. For instance, Eigeldinger states: '[l]e véritable initiateur de Rimbaud à la voyance doit être à coup sûr Victor Hugo, tant par son génie apocalyptique et visionnaire que par son expérience spécifique de la création poétique.' Eigeldinger also touches upon many of the same works of Hugo as du Bouchet does, especially *Océan* and *Les Travailleurs de la mer* (cf. Eigeldinger and Rimbaud, pp. 60, 76).
19. With respect to Hugo and particularly Baudelaire, du Bouchet, significantly, speaks not only of the image as an abstract entity situated outside the narrator or poetic voice, but considers the image as springing from the imagination ('imaginaire'), underlining the subjective origin of the image (cf. *AB*, 106).
20. Cf. also Layet, 'Temps apparent', p. 228.
21. Martinez remarks with respect to the image in du Bouchet more generally: '[u]ne "phénoménologie de l'inapparent" débouche sur une "aphanologie" qui est un redoublement de la question perceptive, "voir ce que l'on voit"' (Martinez, 'La "Phénoménologie de l'inapparent"', p. 68).
22. Layet, 'Temps apparent', p. 231.
23. Victor Hugo, *Les Misérables*, 10 vols (Brussels: Lacroix, Verboeckhoven, et Cie, 1862), I, 17. (I found some of the passages on Hugo's narrator in *Les Misérables* discussed here on the following website which uses the English version of the text: 'Les Misérables Narrator Point of View', *shmoop* <https://www.shmoop.com/les-miserables/narrator-point-of-view.html> [accessed 18 September 2017]. For a more general discussion of Hugo's narrators which 'swin[g] back and forth between moments of overomniscience and lapses in this omniscience that undermine the narrative voice', see Isabel Roche, *Character and Meaning in the Novels of Victor Hugo* (West Lafayette, IN: Purdue University Press, 2007), p. 47.
24. Hugo, *Les Misérables*, I, 5.
25. This conclusion by du Bouchet is certainly more radical than at least the example from *Les Misérables* can warrant.
26. This is not an uncommon idea in Neoplatonism, as Beierwaltes shows with respect to Cusanus's *visio absoluta*, in which 'Subjekt des Sehens, Akt des Sehens und Sehbares' coincide: Beierwaltes, *Identität und Differenz*, esp. p. 151.
27. This is reminiscent of George Berkeley's 'esse est percipi': cf. George Berkeley, *Principles of Human Knowledge and Three Dialogues*, ed. by Howard Robinson (Oxford: Oxford University Press, 1999), p. 25.
28. Du Bouchet does not consistently follow through on his thoughts here. For this subject itself to

be and be seen, another subject would have to see the subject, and this act of seeing the subject seen would only be realized by yet another subject's gaze on the subject's gaze on the subject's gaze, *ad infinitum*. The only escape from this infinite regress is an assumption contradictory to the visual solipsism du Bouchet ascribes to Hugo: the mutual act of seeing that is the premise of such solipsism can only be posited by implicitly acknowledging a vantage point from which this *mutual* act of seeing can be observed, but whose very existence negates the premise of this solipsism.

29. Of course, seeing that one does not see is still a form of seeing. We run into fundamental epistemological problems and the possibility of an ultimate solution is doubtful. Even though du Bouchet's critical examinations of other authors engage with philosophical problems, it should be borne in mind that they are poetological considerations which, in the end, do not require philosophical rigour.
30. E.g. Dionysos the Aeropagite in his work on *Mystical Theology* and *On the Divine Names*, who is also briefly mentioned by du Bouchet in his 1956 application to the CNRS (*AB*, 290). Cf. Kevin Corrigan and L. Michael Harrington, 'Pseudo-Dionysius the Aeropagite', *The Stanford Encyclopedia of Philosophy* (2015) <http://plato.stanford.edu/archives/spr2015/entries/pseudo-dionysius-areopagite/> [accessed 18 April 2016].
31. 'Phosphène, subst. masc.', *Le Trésor de la Langue Française informatisé* <http://atilf.atilf.fr/> [accessed 25 February 2021].
32. The context of this citation from 1953 suggests that Hugo is halfway on a trajectory from fragmentation to unity, which would imply that the further we go in time, the more unity is sought out and achieved. However, in du Bouchet's 1956 proposal for the CNRS, Hugo's successor Baudelaire is placed at the opposite end of unity, realizing the impossibility of unifying contradictions ('[l]a révélation de l'essentiel est ressentie par lui comme un échec'; *AB*, 289). Such contradictions and implicit revisions demonstrate the immense challenge of pursuing a linear argument through du Bouchet's early works.
33. This is a theme in Hugo's poem 'À un Poète aveugle': Victor Hugo, *Les Contemplations* (Paris: Nelson, 1856), p. 64
34. See also chapter 8, where we look at how du Bouchet translates Celan's 'Nichts' — which is a nominalized nothing with spiritual, archetypal connotations — into a *rien*, which lacks such connotations.
35. Du Bouchet's conclusion on Hugo (and its implications for Rimbaud's notions of 'voyance') differ markedly here from that of Eigeldinger: '[c]onformément à la tradition et au goût obstiné de Hugo pour l'antithèse, le poète aveugle "voit dans l'ombre un monde de clarté", il est le véritable voyant, en ce sens que la cécité physique lui ouvre les yeux de l'esprit, qu'elle accroît par un phénomène de concentration l'intensité de la vision intérieure et spirituelle' (Eigeldinger and Rimbaud, p. 64).
36. Charles Baudelaire, *Œuvres complètes*, ed. by Alphonse Lemerre, 7 vols (Paris: Lemerre, 1888), I, 321.
37. Du Bouchet treats the poetic voice in Baudelaire's writings as identical with the poet himself.
38. 'L'essentiel se précise dans l'incompatibilité de l'être et de la représentation: il se définit en tant que lieu d'une représentation annulée' (*AB*, 288).
39. 'Baudelaire se trouve donc uniquement réduit à sa vie — sa vie irrémédiable (*AB*, 105).
40. An expression purloined from du Bouchet who makes this remark elsewhere about the notion of 'uniqueness' with regards to another Baudelaire poem (*AB*, 255).
41. Du Bouchet also calls this 'durée réelle' 'le fond que Baudelaire découvre en un présent réel' (*AB*, 106), which is reminiscent of Hugo's 'toile du fond' into whose background the narrator retreats.
42. At least in the case of 'absence' this dependence on 'présence' is already suggested by the prefix 'ab-'. Cf. Wolfgang Ernst, 'Absenz', in *Ästhetische Grundbegriffe: Historisches Wörterbuch*, ed. by Karlheinz Barck and others, 7 vols (Stuttgart: Metzler, 2010), I, 1–15 (p. 1).
43. It is worthwhile noting that both Celan and du Bouchet experienced an intellectual environment in post-war Paris in which the primary position of the subject (with respect to an other) and the idea of a self-transparent subject with unmitigated access to itself came increasingly under attack.

For an extensive contextualization see: Manfred Frank, *Was ist Neostrukturalismus?* (Frankfurt a. M.: Suhrkamp, 1984): on the subject in Derrida, pp. 336–39; in Jacques Lacan, pp. 376–99; in Gilles Deleuze and Félix Guattari, pp. 400–21. While both poets remained at a distance from deconstruction, Lacanian psychoanalysis, and the philosophical circle around the magazine *Tel Quel*, the elevated importance of the other in their poetics perhaps indicates the influence of this environment on the writing of both poets. Particularly du Bouchet's more radical notion of the subject might have been inspired by this intellectual context (see below).

44. Arthur Rimbaud, *Œuvres complètes*, ed. by André Guyaux and Aurélia Cervoni (Paris: Gallimard, 2009), p. 340.
45. That this position is paradoxical is apparent: if these experiences are from 'jenseits der Vorstellungen meines wachen Denkens' and remain there, as Celan states, it is not possible that the narrator becomes aware of them.
46. Effectively all of Celan's poetological texts are dialogues either due to their textual form ('Traum vom Traume'), their being an interview (his radio talk on Osip Mandelstam), or their being addressed to an attending audience (his speech for the Bremer Literaturpreis and his 'Meridian' speech for the Büchner prize).
47. *Entretiens d'André du Bouchet avec Alain Veinstein*, ed. by Alain Veinstein (Strasbourg: Institut National de l'Audiovisuel & L'Atelier Contemporain, 2016), p. 42.
48. Du Bouchet shares this notion of the alterity of the poetic subject with his French poetic contemporaries, such as Yves Bonnefoy and Bernard Noël. For more context, see my article 'Translation as Poetics in the Works of André du Bouchet', pp. 36–37.
49. His application for another year of funding in 1957 was unsuccessful, as Layet notes (*AB*, 356).
50. Daniel Leuwers, 'Le Carnet et ses autres', in *André du Bouchet et ses Autres*, ed. by Michel Minard and Philippe Met (Paris-Caen: Lettres modernes Minard, 2003), pp. 43–53 (p. 46).
51. Veinstein, p. 23.

CHAPTER 3

The Typified Image in 'Tenebrae'

In the last two chapters, we discussed the inspiration Celan and du Bouchet drew in their thinking about the image from poetic predecessors and contemporaneous discourses. Whereas Celan's early discourse of the image was informed by the renascent post-war surrealist movement, du Bouchet's discourse of the image drew inspiration from sources predating the surrealist movements, with which he never sympathized but whose importance at the time, together with the encounter with the poetry of Reverdy, possibly foregrounded the question of the image for du Bouchet as well. In any case, it is quite clear from the preceding discussion that both young authors sought to articulate their first poetic attempts around and in conceptions of the image.

As we have seen in chapter 2, du Bouchet's philosophical and poetological engagement with the poetic image of his predecessors had successively led him to increasingly doubt the existence of an *archetypos*. The early du Bouchet believed that he had discovered in Baudelaire's image a liminal quality which confronted us with what lies just beyond the reach of our imagination, making visible to us, as it were, our own inability to see further. The confrontation with the invisible, unimaginable makes us realize our subjectivity. Yet, this invisible and unimaginable *absence* is not an *archetypos* independent of our engaging with it. Rather the unimaginable is contingent on our ability to see and imagine and vice versa. Hence, du Bouchet abandoned the concept of *archetypos*. The lack of an *archetypos* in du Bouchet's poetry also explains why a first-person poetic voice plays a much less prominent role in his verse than in Celan's. In du Bouchet, our subjectivity seems grounded not only in what we can imagine but also determined by what lies outside of what we can represent to ourselves, splitting the subject into a 'je' and an other, a 'tu'. Du Bouchet would later say that the 'tu' is 'l'écart que l'on prend sur soi'.[1] Furthermore, he would claim that 'il s'agit d'abord de me traduire moi-même' (see chapters 7 and 9),[2] making our understanding of the poetic subject relative to its being translated. Thus, in du Bouchet, we find much more rarely than in Celan that poetry is expressed by and centred around a poetic voice.

In this chapter, we will see that Celan shares some of du Bouchet's doubts regarding the *archetypos* but does not quite go as far as his younger French contemporary and soon-to-be friend in undermining or abolishing notions of an *archetypos*. Some doubts about regaining an archetypal meaningfulness of poetic language lost in the wake of historical atrocities (among them, most prominently, the Holocaust) had already announced themselves in his early essay 'Traum vom Traume', in which words were claimed to have accumulated 'Asche ausgebrannter Sinngebung' (*CW* III, 157) in the past. Yet these doubts were swept away later in the essay in a mesh of metaphors through which Celan emphatically proclaimed the possibility of a new poetic writing that bore many characteristics ascribed to the *archetypos*. Yet, Celan's growing distance from the surrealist movement, his emigration to Paris in 1948, and his increasingly finding his poetic voice in the publication of his poetry volumes (*Mohn und Gedächtnis* in 1952, followed by *Von Schwelle zu Schwelle* in 1955), reveal a more toned-down poetic voice compared to his initial, youthful poetic enthusiasm. The question of engaging with the past and especially with the Holocaust through poetry, although ever-present even in Celan's earliest poetry after the war, would continuously lead him to challenge notions of the *archetypos*. As we will discover in the following analysis, Celan's questioning of the *archetypos* also affects his conception of the poetic subject, even if both *archetypos* and poetic subject are not as radically probed as in the later poetry of du Bouchet.

The poem 'Tenebrae', which we scrutinize in this chapter, is perhaps Celan's most explicit critical engagement with the traditional conception of the *archetypos* in his volume *Sprachgitter*, published in 1959. The title of the poem alludes to a Christian Easter mass, which takes place in church after dark in the last three days of Holy Week. During the ceremony candles are extinguished, symbolizing the dying of Christ at the cross, while religious hymns are sung. As anticipated by the title, we encounter allusions to the Eucharist and the crucifixion of Christ in the poem. Formally, it most closely resembles a religious song or plaint to God, although as we will see the traditional direction of address, from man to God, is inverted.[3] On a slightly less apparent level, 'Tenebrae' is also an engagement with Friedrich Hölderlin's poem 'Patmos' whose opening lines 'Nah ist | Und schwer zu fassen der Gott' (*SA* II/1, 165) are echoed in reverse in the first lines of Celan's poem: '[n]ah sind wir, Herr' (*KG*, 97). Furthermore, the Eucharist as communion between man, particularly the poet, and divinity is a typical motif in Hölderlin's poetry (cf. especially 'Brod und Wein'; *SA* II/1, 90–95). Therefore, through his inversion of Christian tropes of salvation in 'Tenebrae', Celan also voices the difficulty in sharing his celebrated predecessor's belief in poetic expression, not least in German, and its ability to mediate between man and God (or the gods) after the Holocaust.[4] To some degree Celan thus shares du Bouchet's reading of Hölderlin's image — which du Bouchet had characterized as 'lucidité de Dieu' (see chapter 2) — and, like du Bouchet, rejects the notion that poetry and the poet have unique access to the divine *archetypos*.

The loss of absolute anchorage in the *archetypos* and of any perceived purity or absoluteness of poetic expression leads Celan to problematize the position of the subject or speaker in the poem. Insofar as the poem is a plaint to God or even against God, Celan's poetic voice in 'Tenebrae' seems to be constituted in its speaking against the divine *archetypos* and in realizing the absence of an *imago Dei*. Celan thus shares with du Bouchet some doubt of a fully self-present or self-sufficient poetic subject: as we saw in the previous chapter, the poetic voice in du Bouchet's interpretation of Baudelaire realizes its subjectivity only in confrontation with the image of its own non-existence, that is the image of its own death. The subject in Celan's 'Tenebrae' is equally threatened, but unlike du Bouchet's Baudelaire it persists through poetic speech despite, not because of, its confronting the image of its death. In Celan's 'Tenebrae', as in du Bouchet, the continuation of the poetic voice's speaking comes at the loss of the Archimedean point constituted by the conception of the *archetypos*. However, we will see in 'Tenebrae', and more expressly in the following chapter on Celan's 'Wein und Verlorenheit', that this loss of the *archetypos* is not absolute or final, even if any notion of pure poetic speech from an absolute vantage point remains problematic in Celan. In this respect du Bouchet and Celan will turn out to increasingly differ the more du Bouchet radicalizes his polychotomous conception of the image.

Unlike for du Bouchet, the loss of the *archetypos* in Celan constitutes an existential problem and, in 'Tenebrae', threatens to condemn the poem's voice to silence and death. As we have seen in previous chapters and particularly in the introduction, the *typos*-image is traditionally conceived as an entity whose existence is derived from the *archetypos*.[5] Thus, if humankind as *imago Dei* experiences the loss of the divine *archetypos*, our entire constitution as human beings seems to be undermined. The source of this existential threat to the *archetypos* and, concomitantly, the *typos* is the historical trauma of the Holocaust.[6]

The Lack of an *Imago Dei* in Celan's 'Tenebrae'

TENEBRAE

Nah sind wir, Herr,
nahe und greifbar.

Gegriffen schon, Herr,
ineinander verkrallt, als wär
der Leib eines jeden von uns
dein Leib, Herr.

Bete, Herr,
bete zu uns,
wir sind nah.

Windschief gingen wir hin,
gingen wir hin, uns zu bücken
nach Mulde und Maar.

Zur Tränke gingen wir, Herr.

Es war Blut, es war,
was du vergossen, Herr.

Es glänzte.

Es warf uns dein Bild in die Augen, Herr,
Augen und Mund stehn so offen und leer, Herr.
Wir haben getrunken, Herr.

> Das Blut und das Bild, das im Blut war, Herr.
>
> Bete, Herr.
> Wir sind nah. (*KG*, p. 97)

The poem begins somewhat innocuously with an address to God, invoking a proximity of the poetic voice, speaking for a collective, to God in the first line. Subsequently the intimacy of this address seems to be emphasized and confirmed in the acknowledgment of closeness through the 'Greifbarkeit' of the speaker. Up to this point, the adjective 'greifbar' would presumably be translated as 'being within reach'. But in line three, this last word of the first stanza very suddenly ('schon') transmutes into the past participle 'gegriffen', a state of being seized or gripped that transforms the experience of closeness into an uncomfortable sensation. As soon as 'gegriffen' morphs into 'verkrallt' it becomes clear that this intimacy is painful and coarse. In short succession, we have seen the transformation of a close physical encounter into an embodiment of menace which evokes Holocaust reports of gassed victims who clasp each other in their struggle with death. We now realize that through death we achieve our proclaimed proximity to God. To the vivid corporality of this state of inescapable violence a further, darkly ironic twist is added: our bodies claw into each other as if these bodies we are clasping were not our own, existentially limited mortal husks, but the body of God himself ('dein Leib, Herr').

The biblical allusion running through these lines, from the body of Christ in the Last Supper (from Matthew 26. 26) to Genesis 1. 26, in which God says '[l]et us make mankind in our image, in our likeness', are obviously enunciated with a forked tongue. It is the confluence of these distinct passages of the New and Old Testament in Celan's poem which makes these lines blasphemous even while they superficially follow the ecclesiastical tradition of lamentation.[7] Man may well be created in the *likeness* of God, but this likeness does not extend to physical verisimilitude. In the context of the second commandment even the intimation ('als wär') of divine corporality and its likeness to that of man is heretical. On the other hand, the evocation of a divine 'Leib' alludes to the ritual tradition of the Eucharist to break bread and distribute wine in the belief that these transubstantiate into the true body and blood of Christ. Celan brings these two traditions — and their respective trajectories of visual apophasis as opposed to physical embodiment — to a clash in the purposeful ambivalence of his lines. The juxtaposition of these traditions marks a turning point in the poem that announces itself by the poetic voice's demand to invert the position of addresser and addressee ('bete zu uns') in the subsequent lines and ultimately results in a spectacle that undermines the traditions pervading Christian metaphors and (Neoplatonic) metaphysics of vision. The double violation of the traditions of transubstantiation and the prohibition of images in the second commandment is presaged by Celan's transformation of divine proximity from 'greifbar' into 'verkrallt' and turns on the poetic voice's reversal of addresser and addressee, culminating in the abolition of the *archetypos* in the conception of the divine image.

Thus, in the third stanza, the plaintive prayer characterized by the frequent invocations of 'Herr' changes from being a prayer to God to being a prayer of God: 'Herr, | bete zu uns'. Just like his believers had prayed for the tortured figure of Christ nailed to the cross, God, as the imperative appeal in the poem seems to imply, should now pray for these dying bodies. But this divine prayer is not merely a praying *for* those who suffer from the violent proximity, but a prayer *to* them, as if they themselves were to be worshipped. The victims of the Holocaust seem to take the position of the body of Christ, but it should be noted that this is only in the conditional tense ('als wär').[8] Celan opts for the conditional mood and only establishes a likeness between the 'wir' of the poem and the Body of Christ rather than an identity that could do away with Celan's 'als wär'. This decision is not to be misunderstood as self-restraint on the part of Celan — e.g. for fear of appearing too blasphemous — for otherwise the previous and succeeding lines would not have been written in the first place. Rather Celan intimates that in contradistinction to Christ's sacrifice on the cross, the death of the 'wir' (or the Jews in the Holocaust) does not lead to the absolution of sins and does not promise eternal salvation.[9] Indeed, Beate Sowa-Bettecken even believes that in the 'Irrealis [des "als wär"] auch die Erlösung durch den Tod des Einen in Frage gestellt [wird]'.[10]

The subversion of God in the plaint of the poetic voice in the poem does seem to run deeper than just being a momentary expression of doubt akin to Christ's 'My God, My God, why hast thou forsaken me?' (Psalms 22. 2; Matthew 27. 46), because there can be no hope of resurrection from death for the victims of the Holocaust. A certain ambivalence in the poem toward Christ could be regarded as being motivated by the fact that, on the one hand, he was Jewish but, on the other, the 'Bild des Gekreuzigten' was 'das Sinnbild des rasendsten Hasses, ihrer [der Juden] Vernichtung selbst',[11] as Jews, in the Christian tradition since the second century, had been accused of having killed Christ.[12] Yet the subversion of God runs deeper than just ambivalence. It is obvious that Christ's suffering has not cleared mankind of sin and given us salvation, and Celan reminds us that it is precisely the mass murder of millions of Jews which must undercut any such unshaken belief.[13] As we will see in the following analysis, the reversal of the emblematic meaning of Christ on the cross through the suffering of the poetic voice culminates in the evocation of the divine image in the penultimate stanza.

In a superficial reading, the following stanza seems to revert back to the traditional hierarchy between God and man by evoking Psalm 23 — 'The Lord is my shepherd [...]. [...] [H]e leadeth me beside the still waters. He restoreth my soul.'[14] In the poem, the poetic voice goes to a maar and bows to drink. The poetic voice seems to suit the role as obedient sheep given by Psalm 23 not only because of its act of bowing, but also because the infinitive form 'zu trinken' suggests that it follows an order, as does the later 'Wir haben getrunken, Herr'.[15] However, on a closer reading we realize that any such idea of following God conveyed in these constructions is hollowed out by Celan, since they betray the senselessness of the violence suffered by the poetic voice. The grammatical elision of the conjunction 'um', the apparent lack of any explanation for our motivation to pilgrimage to the trough, and the passivity apparent in the construction 'uns zu bücken' make it sound as if these acts just happen gratuitously. The crimes alluded to in the poem are violent not only because of their vivid evocation of states of pain ('verkrallt'), but because there is absolutely no reason that what happens should take place at all.

Celan has deprived the acts that come to pass in the poem of all intention. While in the Psalms, the motivation to go 'beside the still waters' is grounded in an ultimate faith in God, this is not the case in 'Tenebrae'. It is not grammatically the case, as we have seen, but also not semantically. 'Tenebrae' shows that we have no grounds for such ultimate faith. The extent to which Celan expresses his doubt in and undermines traditional representations of God becomes clear in the following analysis, as we discuss the conceptions of perception and image in 'Tenebrae'. As the image of God materializes in the trough, we realize that the suggestively obeisant gesture of bowing to the frequently invoked divine Lordship is controverted (even further), since we do not gaze up to look for signs of God but bend over to behold the image of God. The act of bending over implies an inversion of above and below in and through the formation of the divine image in the trough at our feet.[16] The spatial deposition of God entails an entire complex of value changes that occur within the traditional Christian framework of meanings which governs perceptions of the below. An all too speculative interpretation could elaborate on connotations of hell and underworld here; such an endeavour, however, would rely on thin evidence in the text itself. That which is below the poetic voice is not an otherworldly realm, an absolute below. Rather, what lies below the poetic voice is relative to its position as beholder — to its position as plaintiff, reader, and victim. The fact that the poetic voice sees God below itself nonetheless carries connotations of God's abjectness and inferiority of power. God's image in the trough beneath the poetic voice is a display on the surface of the blood and therefore lacks profundity and depth. The surface of blood with God's image in 'Tenebrae' is not the sea surface in Celan's 'Traum vom Traume' (see chapter 1), below which the narrator goes to gain a new sense of vision in the hidden depths. Such epiphanic vision or even hopeful revelation of a meaningful ground (in the extended sense of the word) is lacking in 'Tenebrae'. Rather, the lack of a ground reinforces the figurative lack of a ground due to the elision of an explicatory conjunction indicating reasons ('um') and the passivity intimated by perfective constructions such as 'wir haben getrunken', as discussed above.

The words of Psalm 23 echoed in the poem, according to which God leads the psalmist to the water and restores his soul, now get a cynical twist as we find out that the trough is filled with 'Blut, [...] was du vergossen, Herr'. Depending on whether we read the verb 'vergossen' as transitive or ditransitive, the shed blood can be interpreted as either coming from God, evoking Christ's blood on the cross, or as that of the poetic voice (and, by implication, the victims of the Holocaust), accusing God of the crimes of the Holocaust. Many critics follow both readings and believe that Celan underlines the similarity between Christ's sacrifice and the massacred Jews.[17] Werner Wögerbauer is appreciably careful in asserting that '[l]e poème dit qu'il y a une relation entre les deux sangs', rather than prematurely affirming, like Joachim Seng, that this relation consists of an 'Annäherung an Christus'.[18] Given our reading up to this point, this caution is well justified, because what would this 'Annäherung' consist of? In light of Christ's divine provenance and the resurrection after his crucifixion, as well as the theological and teleological purposiveness of his sacrifice — none of which applies to the senseless murder of the Jews during the Holocaust — such attestations seem imprudent.[19] The sarcastic tone of the opening lines, that had evoked a proximity to God due to the impending death of the poetic voice, has not changed by the time the poetic voice gazes into the trough filled with blood. We should take a closer look at the nature of the relation between the two bloods and between poetic voice and God which culminates in the image that forms in the trough.

In this image, Celan not only contradicts the traditional hierarchy of vision in the Judaeo-Christian tradition by inverting the direction of the gaze (below, into the trough, instead of above, into the heavens), but also through a perverted form of transubstantiation of God in the image in the trough. The senselessness of the crimes is embodied and symbolized by the image that forms in the trough. The violence, of course, is already signified by the image's material constitution: it is an image reflected in blood. But the senselessness is also more subtly intimated by the structure of the image. Images in bodies of water are mirror-images,[20] they are copies of an original, that is, *typoi* of an *archetypos*. However, the mirror-image to which we bend down does not seem to have an *archetypos*; in fact, God's substance seems to transform into a mere, substanceless image which is (re)producing itself in what is either the fluid resulting from God's own disembodiment or the blood of his victims. In either case, the theological underpinning of the Christian conception of the image is dissolved from within in Celan's evocation of the divine image here; and with it, all corollaries of the divine *archetypos* — its theological, teleological transcendency, and, since God is implied to be complicit in the crimes, its ultimate status as moral paragon — are abandoned. The collapsing of the *archetypos* into the *typos* not only renders God visible in explicit contradiction to the second commandment, but such a complete trespass of the divine into the visual realm inscribes upon His image the discrepancy that adheres to the conception of the *typos*. The copy that is the mirror-image in the trough is a copy at variance with itself, a reproduction without an original.[21] Such a copy's copy is, of course, entirely vacant[22] and, indeed, the divine image cast into our eyes — an almost violent act of intrusion into our retina[23] — elicits their emptiness of expression:

> Es warf uns dein Bild in die Augen, Herr,
> Augen und Mund stehn so offen und leer, Herr.

The *typos*-image displayed on the blood is reminiscent, as Wögerbauer points out, of the *typos*-image in Celan's poem 'Bei Wein und Verlorenheit', which we will examine in the next chapter.[24] The mirror-image in 'Tenebrae' expresses a further aspect which can be read in quite explicit contrast to Celan's later poem 'Halbzerfressener' (see chapter 6). The image is fundamental to the poetic subject's ability to reflect on itself and perhaps even to its constitution as poetic voice, which is also the role of the image in 'Halbzerfressener'. In contradistinction to such an image enabling self-reflection, the *typos*-nature of the image in 'Tenebrae' undermines the voice's ability to assert itself. The seeming diminution of God's power as *typos*-image does not concomitantly augment our own powers of self-determination as is the case, for instance, with Goethe's Prometheus who formed 'Menschen | Nach [s]einem Bilde'.[25] It is not only the conception of the divine image which Celan controverts in 'Tenebrae'. In making a (liquid) mirror the mediator between God and our (self-)perception, Celan also picks up on another foundational metaphor of Christian philosophy in the tradition of Augustine. The poet undermines the traditional role of this reflecting interface in the conception of the *imago Dei*, and, in turn, undermines how humankind can comprehend God as well as, through the contemplation of God, itself as *mens humana*.[26]

In his *De trinitate*, Augustine had used the metaphor of the mirror as a core element in his exposition of how humankind comes to reach an understanding of God and recognize itself as an image of God. According to Augustine, as man is looking at his image in the (metaphorical, intellectual) mirror, he recognizes himself as an image of and as bearing a likeness to God.[27] Since this form of mirror-reflection is an intellectual act, looking and recognition are not a mere passive display on a mirror (as on a projection screen), but an activity of constituting that which elevates humankind above other beings and distinguishes it from other creatures: its *mens*.[28] Looking or contemplating and recognition are part of the same activity in which the mind becomes a mirror *through* which (*per speculum*)[29] man realizes his being a finite image of God.[30] From Augustine onward, this conception of the intellectual act of mirroring and image formation becomes immensely productive in Christian philosophical thought, and is foundational to, for instance, Meister Eckhart's conception of 'Bildung'[31] and to the mirror motif as perpetuated by Cusanus in his conception of the *imago Dei*.[32] Such self-acting image production on the intellectual mirror has a strong tendency towards the iconoclastic in that the (*typos*-)image deposes of its visual tabernacle and is entirely elevated into the spiritual realm in approximating the *archetypos*.[33]

Yet, the bloody mirror of Celan's poem, which casts the divine image into our eyes, is not an active production of our contemplating intellect, as in the Augustinian tradition. We have already discussed how the mirror reflects the divine image without an original, collapsing the *archetypos* into the *typos*, whereby the *typos*' difference from itself is totalized, effectively uncreating the entire image. But the mirror metaphor in Celan goes further. Instead of situating the mirror in our *mens humana* as the patristic tradition had done, the mirror is located in and constituted by the blood. In this line of reading, the '*archetypos* become *typos*' implies the physical disembodiment of the poetic voice by exsanguination as well as the lack of an *archetypos* through which the voice could recognize itself as subject, as *imago Dei*. The image in the blood is therefore doubly outside of its proper domain. The reflected image exists outside of our mental faculties — for which, according to the Augustinian tradition, our body serves as tabernacle — depriving us of the possibility to recognize ourselves as human subjects (in recognizing ourselves as *imago Dei*). Further, even this tabernacle itself is deprived of its life-giving essence by its bleeding out. Hence, in a crassly sarcastic contortion of Augustine's metaphor, in 'Tenebrae' the mirror does form *in* us, or rather in a *part* of us: our blood that has been shed. Consequently, the emptiness of expression of the divine image cast into our eyes is not just a nonentity in and of our perception but affects our very self-perception and constitution.

Indeed, Celan undermines the conception of God through the image and concomitantly the conception of ourselves so completely — death already having loomed in the subtext of the second stanza — that the entire fabric of the poem is threatened. And this fabric is, of course, poetic speech. Accordingly, the empty expression is not only in our eyes, once the image strikes our retina, but the mouth, too, is 'offen und leer'. Similar to the divine de-substantiation in and as *typos* which is constituted in perpetual difference to itself, diminishing the *archetypos*, verbal expression seems consumed by the emptiness and senselessness of the deeds committed against us as victims and readers of violence. This emptiness resonates phonetically in the echo of 'Herr' in 'leer' which represents sonically what is inherent in the structure of the divine image in the trough. The echo of 'Herr' in 'leer' has expressly nothing as its origin: *Leere*.[34] The negative, empty visuality of the image now seems to have encroached upon our possibility to speak.

The poem could end here. But it does not. The eyes seem to be permanently blinded, incapable of further perception — indeed, this is already programmatically projected by the title 'Tenebrae', which means obscurity. The mouth, however, almost silently returns in the subsequent stanza:

> Wir haben getrunken, Herr.
> Das Blut und das Bild, das im Blut war, Herr.

Poetic speech seems to somehow persist through the act of drinking, which Wögerbauer believes 'devient constitutif d'un nouveau langage' that is, however, a 'contre-langue' to the language of Christianity and belief.[35] The act of swallowing, especially in the perfective tense of '[w]ir haben getrunken', suggests the passivity and powerlessness of victims of violence. In his commentary on the poem Fred Lönker even goes so far as to suggest that the swallowing and the last lines of the poem confirm the death of the poetic voice.[36] Once again Celan inverts the supposed spiritual replenishment of the Eucharist. Unlike what Matthew 26. 28 suggests, the act of drinking the blood does not imply a 'remission of sins', and unlike in John 6. 58 the blood does not appear to be a source of life. Indeed, the consumption of the blood by the poetic voice seems to be the climax of Celan's inversion of Christian tropes and motifs. The poetic voice consumes itself by consuming the blood — possibly its own — and the image, insofar as it consumes God as image and therefore consumes itself as *imago Dei*.[37]

At the same time, despite the implications of self-consumption and self-abnegation in the act of drinking, the poetic voice seems to defiantly persevere by having drunk the blood and in the last lines of the poem calls on God to pray. The poetic voice is still not entirely the arbiter of its own fate. It does not assertively tell God to pray *to* it anymore, as it did in the third stanza. It is also still not an agentive subject of verbs in the present tense, which would indicate that it is in control of its acts. However, the imperative appeal to God to pray attests to the continuation of poetic speech beyond the presumed death of the speaker and beyond the *typification* of God. Poetic speech survives as plaint.

Even though the violence committed against the poetic voice and the subversion of God pose extreme threats to the poetic subject as well as the notion of the *archetypos* in 'Tenebrae', neither poetic subject nor *archetypos* are fully extinguished. But they are also not positively affirmed or reinstated. Celan did not write a poem in which God or faith would not be problematically addressed and ambivalently expressed. His interest in mysticism, religion, and religious philosophy is widely attested,[38] even though he never fully subscribed to any specific school of thought or dogmatic belief. Yet thinking about the *archetypos* remains at the heart of Celan's poetry. In his 'Meridian' speech of 1960, given three years after writing 'Tenebrae', Celan would reaffirm his striving toward a higher, more unified, and more truthfully expressed word, even if it cannot exist in absolute form (cf. *M*, 10; see chapters 1 and 7). In his speech, Celan makes use of a common denomination of God when he evokes 'dieses "ganz Andere"' (*M*, 8).[39] The demonstrative adjective and abstract singular by which God is designated as other contrast with Celan's use of scare quotes, betraying a certain distance and scepticism to this other. And yet, this tension between his intimations of the *archetypos* and its being cast into doubt at once is sustained throughout much of Celan's poetry.

The *Archetypos* and *Typos* in Celan as Opposed to in Du Bouchet

The groundlessness and gratuitousness of what happens to the poetic voice in the poem clearly relies on the traditional framework of *archetypos* and *typos*, whose inversion in the poem constitutes the violence and is the subject of the poetic plaint. In this reliance on such a traditional framework, even in the moments of most radical doubt, Celan differs quite markedly from du Bouchet's later thinking, which is outside the *archetypos–typos* dichotomy (as we will see in chapter 5). His 'fond', in the many senses of the word, is only one side of a binary and reciprocal relation. In Michel Collot's words it is a '*Grund* qui fonde toute manifestation, mais échappe lui-même, puisqu'il est aussi *Abgrund*'.[40] Thus, as we will see, the paper's underpinning and quite literally underlying the written poetic word in du Bouchet only becomes conceivable as the 'fond' of writing in its being displaced by the written word, whose purpose is, in turn, to bring out the foundational quality of the paper. Celan, on the other hand, remains committed to a framework of meaning hinged on an *archetypos*, even when doubting and making accusations against it. His commitment to the traditional framework is probably explained by the fact that an equipoise between ground and abyss as well as a poetic reality that relativizes the notions of *archetypos* and *typos* would also seem, for Celan, to relativize the suffering of Holocaust victims and the grounds of accusing those responsible. Only by means of the plaint to God in 'Tenebrae' can the poetic voice express the violence suffered. Implicating the highest power in being complicit in the crimes ('Blut, [...] | was du vergossen') and showing the Almighty's powerlessness by calling upon him to pray ('Bete, Herr') indicates how fundamentally the divine has fallen short of its archetypal standards in the Holocaust. If Celan had relativized these standards rather than affirmed them *ex negativo* by lamenting that they have not been kept, he also would have relativized the absoluteness of the crime.

Thus instead, as we have seen in 'Tenebrae', the poetic address is still directed at the divine *archetypos* even after its typification, and the poetic voice speaks even after its physical and spiritual disembodiment. The suffering in the poem and the existential threat to the poetic subject manifest themselves as the typification of an *archetypos*, and it is the very lamentation of this absence which reinstates the *archetypos* (the 'ganz Ander[e]') at least as a notional reference point (as 'bekanntes Hilfswort'; *M*, 10).[41] Thus, neither the position of the *archetypos* nor that of the poetic subject are fully undercut in Celan, because they constitute the foundation that enables poetic speech. This relation between poetic subject and the *archetypos* also underlies Celan's poem 'Bei Wein und Verlorenheit', which we examine in the following chapter, where our focus will shift to the relation between the image and the conception of language in Celan.

Notes to Chapter 3

1. Veinstein, p. 43.
2. De Rijcke, 'Entretiens avec André du Bouchet', p. 277.
3. It is a 'Kirchenlied contrefait', according to Werner Wögerbauer: cf. *Sur quatre poèmes de Paul Celan: Une lecture à plusieurs. Analyses et présentation des débats*, ed. by Jean Bollack, Jean-Marie Winkler, and Werner Wögerbauer (Villeneuve d'Ascq: Université de Lille 3, 1991), p. 129.
4. Cf. Götz Wienold, 'Paul Celans Hölderlin-Widerruf', *Poetica*, 2 (1968), 216–28, esp. p. 222.
5. This is, for instance, the case in Meister Eckhart, whom Celan read. Cf. Mauritius Wilde, *Das neue Bild vom Gottesbild: Bild und Theologie bei Meister Eckhart* (Freiburg, Switzerland: Freiburg Universitätsverlag, 2000), p. 84.
6. Fred Lönker notes that three different texts documenting the Holocaust seem to underlie Celan's poem: the motif of the trough may have been inspired by a report by the Hungarian doctor Miklos Nyiszli; dead bodies clawing into each other resembles a passage in Gerald Reitlinger's *Endlösung: Hitlers Versuch der Ausrottung der Juden Europas 1939–1945*; finally, the open eyes and mouth in the poem probably stem from Jean Cayrol's documentary *Nuit et brouillard*, whose French script Celan translated: cf. Fred Lönker, 'Tenebrae', in *Kommentar zu Paul Celans 'Die Niemandsrose'*, ed. by Jürgen Lehmann and Christine Ivanović (Heidelberg: Winter, 1997), pp. 187–96.
7. While most critics of the poem note these divergent biblical passages (including the 'Ecce Homo' motif later in the poem), it escapes most that the blasphemous character of the poem is not only sparked by the inversion of address demanded by the poetic voice, i.e. God's praying to man, but by Celan's conjunction of these incongruent biblical passages. See Ruth Lorbe, 'Paul Celan, "Tenebrae"', in *Über Paul Celan*, ed. by Dietlind Meinecke (Frankfurt a. M.: Suhrkamp, 1970), pp. 248–49; Irène Elisabeth Kummer, *Unlesbarkeit dieser Welt: Spannungsfelder moderner Lyrik und ihr Ausdruck im Werk von Paul Celan* (Frankfurt a. M.: Athenäum, 1987), p. 129; Beate Sowa-Bettecken, *Sprache der Hinterlassenschaft: Jüdisch-christliche Überlieferung in der Lyrik von Nelly Sachs und Paul Celan* (Frankfurt a. M.: Lang, 1992), p. 191.
8. Cf. also Sowa-Bettecken, p. 182.
9. For similar points, cf. ibid. pp. 182–83. We should note here that the commonly used term 'Holocaust', at least etymologically, suggests a sacrifice to the gods: 'holokauston' means 'whole burnt' in Greek and was used e.g. in the Septuagint to describe sacrifice by fire. See James E. Young, *Writing and Rewriting the Holocaust: Narrative and the Consequences of Interpretation* (Bloomington: Indiana University Press, 1988), p. 87. When I use the term 'Holocaust', I do

not also adopt its etymological meaning, which is inappropriate here (for reasons made obvious above), but to refer to the Nazi's attempt to kill all Jews. Many thanks to an anonymous reviewer for pointing this out.
10. Ibid, p. 183.
11. Margarete Susman cited in Joachim Seng, *Auf den Kreis-Wegen der Dichtung: Zyklische Komposition bei Paul Celan am Beispiel der Gedichtbände bis 'Sprachgitter'* (Heidelberg: Winter, 1998), p. 212.
12. Matthias Blum, 'Gottesmord', in *Handbuch des Antisemitismus: Judenfeindschaft in Geschichte und Gegenwart. Begriffe, Theorien, Ideologien*, ed. by Wolfgang Benz and others, 8 vols (New York: De Gruyter, 2009–15), III, compiled by Brigitte Mihok (2011), 113–14.
13. I thus emphatically reject Gadamer's reading that 'das so furchtbar vereinzelnde Sterben nicht nur jeden mit jedem anderen, sondern gerade auch mit dem sterbenden Jesus in eine eigene Verbundenheit versetzt' (Gadamer, p. 456).
14. Cf. Wögerbauer, in *Sur quatre poèmes de Paul Celan*, ed. by Bollack, Winkler, and Wögerbauer, p. 129; Lönker, p. 191.
15. Cf. also Kummer, p. 130.
16. Cf. also Wögerbauer on these lines: '[u]ne fois de plus, le poème inverse ce que dit le psaume: Yahvé retient tous ceux qui tombent, redresse tous ceux qui sont courbés (Ps. 145, 14). Dans le poème de Celan, ceux qui ploient sous le joug ne sont pas redressés, bien au contraire: ils se courbent et se baissent davantage encore (uns zu bücken | nach Mulde und Maar)' (*Sur quatre poèmes de Paul Celan*, ed. by Bollack, Winkler, and Wögerbauer, p. 129).
17. Cf. Sowa-Bettecken, pp. 187–88; Kummer, p. 130; Seng, *Auf den Kreis-Wegen der Dichtung*, p. 211.
18. Seng, *Auf den Kreis-Wegen der Dichtung*, p. 211.
19. We should also remember that Celan had criticized Nelly Sachs for her attempts at a 'deutsch-jüdische Symbiose' as 'Versöhnungsversuche im Geiste christlicher Liebe und eines ungebrochenen Gottesglaubens'. See Tobias Tunkel, *Das verlorene Selbe* (Freiburg i. Br.: Rombach, 2001), p. 37.
20. Sowa-Bettecken also interprets the image as a mirror-image, and she believes the fact that it is not the poetic voice whose image is reflected but the image of God is a further sign of their closeness. She also points out the possibility that 'im Spiegelbild der Sprechenden das Bild des Herrn aufsteigt'. These readings of unification or approximation between Christ and the poetic voice, however, gloss over the violence with which this image enters the eyes of the poetic voice. She rephrases the violent intrusion of 'warf uns dein Bild in die Augen' in religious terms as an entering or merging into (*eintreten*) (Sowa-Bettecken, p. 189).
21. The notion of a reproduction without an original may echo Benjamin's conception of *Das Kunstwerk im Zeitalter seiner technischen Reproduzierbarkeit*, but the implications here are quite different as the following above shows (*GS*, 1/1, 431–508).
22. The vacancy of God's image here is not related to the use of 'Nichts' in the poem 'Mandorla', by which Celan evokes mystical connotations of God as a substance that can only be described apophatically (from our human perspective) as nothing (cf. *KG*, 142). This positively connotated, substantial nothing is discussed in chapter 9, where we discover a discrepancy between Celan's use of the word 'Nichts' in the poem 'Erblinde' (similar to his evocation of the word in 'Mandorla') and du Bouchet's translation thereof by 'rien'.
23. That violence occurs in the image's being cast into the eyes of the poetic voice is very clear from the great similarities this passage bears to Jean Cayrol's description of dead Jews in *Nuit et brouillard* (cf. Lönker, p. 192).
24. 'Le sang, et l'emblème qu'il contient, trouvent leur adéquation dans le vide. Cet accueil engloutit également l'image, dénonçant ainsi les langues imagines, inauthentiques et mensongères. La vacuité et l'ouverture renvoient à l'absence de langage, au silence' (Wögerbauer in *Sur quatre poèmes de Paul Celan*, ed. by Bollack, Winkler, and Wögerbauer, p. 131).
25. Johann Wolfgang von Goethe, 'Prometheus', in *Berliner Ausgabe*, ed. by Siegfried Seidel u.a., 23 vols (incl. 1 supplementary vol.) (Berlin: Aufbau, 1960–78), I: *Poetische Werke* (1960), 327–29 (p. 328).
26. Kreuzer, 'Von Augustinus zu Eckhart', p. 82.
27. 'Indem sie sich als Bild erkennt, realisiert die *mens humana*, wovon sie sich als Bild denkt — zumindest wird diese Erkenntnis zu ihrem Anspruch' (ibid.).

28. Aspects of this thought can already be found in Philo of Alexandria and from then on in the entire Eastern Christian theology, e.g. Pseudo-Dionysius the Areopagite (cf. Ladner, pp. 11, 13).
29. Kreuzer, 'Von Augustinus zu Eckhart', p. 84.
30. Ibid.
31. Ibid., p. 89.
32. 'Indem der Mensch — als selbstaktiver Spiegel der Bildhaftigkeit der Wirklichkeit — eben diese Bildhaftigkeit auch tatsächlich einsieht und denkt, realisiert er erst sein Bild-Sein' (Leinkauf, p. 106).
33. Kreuzer points to John Scotus Eriugena for his 'ikonophobe[] Aufhebung der Bilder in einer rein geistigen Schöpfung zu der die "sinnliche Kreatur verwandelt wird"' (Kreuzer, 'Von Augustinus zu Eckhart', p. 84). Likewise, Meister Eckhart speaks of 'entbilden' in much the same spirit (see ibid., p. 85).
34. Sowa-Bettecken and Felstiner, among others, have commented on this imperfect rhyme: cf. Sowa-Bettecken, p. 190; John Felstiner, *Paul Celan: Poet, Survivor, Jew* (New Haven: Yale University Press, 2001), p. 145.
35. In *Sur quatre poèmes de Paul Celan*, ed. by Bollack, Winkler, and Wögerbauer, p. 131. Sowa-Bettecken and Kummer, in broad terms, seem to share this belief that the suffering of Jews has now replaced that of Christ (cf. Sowa-Bettecken, p. 191; Kummer, p. 131). Gadamer is mostly alone in proclaiming that the closing lines of the poem reaffirm the Christian doctrine of incarnation and the position of God as 'Herr' (cf. Gadamer, p. 458).
36. Lönker, p. 192. Eminently, the swallowing in 'Tenebrae' reminds us of the prominence of swallowing in Celan's 'Todesfuge', which also evokes the Holocaust and where swallowing is likewise associated with death.
37. Schulz very appositely reads the act of swallowing as 'auto-consommation': 'il s'agirait donc (car je pense, à l'évocation de l'image, à l'homme fait à l'image de Dieu, qui — sous la forme de l'image de Dieu — se reflète dans le sang) d'une sorte d'auto-consommation' (in *Sur quatre poèmes de Paul Celan*, ed. by Bollack, Winkler, and Wögerbauer, p. 140).
38. One of the first to study this interest with respect to Celan's poetry was Joachim Schulze: *Celan und die Mystiker: Motivtypologische und quellenkundliche Kommentare* (Bonn: Bouvier, 1976).
39. For a more complete discussion of this passage of Celan's speech, see Florence Pennone, *Paul Celans Übersetzungspoetik: Entwicklungslinien in seinen Übertragungen französischer Lyrik* (Tübingen: Niemeyer, 2007), pp. 53–57. It is also worth pointing out the astonishing similarities between Celan's work and Martin Buber's philosophy of dialogue, in which 'das ganz Andere' very clearly denotes God: James K. Lyon, 'Paul Celan and Martin Buber: Poetry as Dialogue', *PMLA*, 86.1 (1971), 110–20 (p. 112).
40. Collot, *L'Horizon fabuleux*, p. 180.
41. See also Celan's utterance: '[d]er Gott des Gedichts ist unstreitig ein *deus absconditus*' (*Mikro*, 136). For a brief discussion, see Julian Johannes Immanuel Koch, 'The Image in Celan's Poetics', *German Life and Letters*, 71.4 (2018), 434–51 (p. 446).

CHAPTER 4

Writing as *Typos* in Celan's 'Bei Wein und Verlorenheit'

In our analysis of 'Tenebrae' in the previous chapter, we have seen how the first-person poetic voice, as presumed *imago Dei*, was almost extinguished along with the divine *archetypos* and yet was somehow able to carry on speaking, despite the typification of the *archetypos*. The near silence of the poetic voice in conjunction with the typification of the *archetypos* already indicated that there is a negative relation between (*typos*-)image and language, and we will scrutinize this relation more closely now by analysing Celan's 'Bei Wein und Verlorenheit' in this chapter. As we are going to discover, Celan makes a distinction between written, that is, visual language, which he characterizes as *typified*, and spoken language, which bears the marks of the *archetypos*.

> Bei Wein und Verlorenheit, bei
> beider Neige:
>
> ich ritt durch den Schnee, hörst du,
> ich ritt Gott in die Ferne — die Nähe, er sang,
> es war
> unser letzter Ritt über
> die Menschen-Hürden.
>
> Sie duckten sich, wenn
> sie uns über sich hörten, sie
> schrieben, sie
> logen unser Gewieher
> um in eine
> ihrer bebilderten Sprachen. (*KG*, 126)

In 'Bei Wein und Verlorenheit', Celan seems to hint at a purer poetic language which is evoked in proximity to archetypal divinity. This language is in contraposition to the languages of man in the poem, whose plurality ('Sprachen') and mistranslation ('umlügen') seem to point to an underlying conception of language in which the Fall of Man and the loss of the original language after Babel are reimagined as one and the same event (see also chapter 7).[1] Celan's poetry is written in a language which comes *After Babel*, to speak with George Steiner.[2] Yet in contrast to the scripture, for Celan the event that brings about the confusion of tongues is devoid of Judaeo-

Christian mythology and historiography and is reimagined as the historical trauma that is the Holocaust.[3] Hints of this thinking were already evident in Celan's earliest poetological text 'Traum vom Traume', where he attested that our languages carry the 'Asche ausgebrannter Sinngebung' after the 'Sündenfall' and longed for 'jene Ursprünglichkeit' in language in which 'Anfang und Ende zusammen[fielen]' (*CW* III, 156). This thinking resurfaces when in 1960 he re-emphasizes that he wants to build 'Brücken von Sprache zu Sprache, aber — Brücken über Abgründe'.[4]

Since we cannot simply reconstruct the archetypal linguistic state, translation becomes the medium of interlingual relations and for bridging the abyss between languages. Only in a translation that fully respects the other, without effacing traces of the other (i.e. the source text), can we at least partially overcome not only inter- but also intralinguistic gaps.[5] This conception of language and translation manifestly underlies Celan's 'Bei Wein und Verlorenheit' and is further inflected by particular circumstances at the time of writing the poem. The poem is in part a reaction to Celan's critics who saw in his poetry absolute poetry and abstractions that were removed from all reality, including or especially the reality of the Holocaust. Thus former Nazi Hans Egon Holthusen detaches Celan's poetry from the Holocaust and claims that it flies away from 'der blutigen Schreckenskammer der Geschichte [...], um aufzusteigen in den Äther der reinen Poesie'.[6]

Such misunderstandings shaping the German discourse on his poetry, intentional or not, and even if said in praise, would pose a doubly existential threat to Celan. It was the Germans who had killed his parents and whose misinterpretations further undercut his poetry's quest to communicate the historical atrocities and commemorate the victims of the Holocaust. Even more menacing to Celan's poetic and personal identity than the tide of misreadings[7] were the (deliberately) false accusations of plagiarism by Claire Goll, the widow of the surrealist poet Yvan Goll. Celan had agreed on Yvan Goll's deathbed to translate his French poetry into German. Subsequently, Celan's early and unpublished translations were used and manipulated by Claire Goll to support her accusations of plagiarism. In a vicious public campaign Claire Goll rallied supporters for her accusations, staining Celan's public image and leaving Celan in need of psychiatric help.[8]

Claire Goll's campaign and the viciousness of the public discourse in Germany on Celan's purported plagiarism grew worse throughout the late 1950s and reached their peak in the early 1960s, that is around the time of writing 'Bei Wein und Verlorenheit'. Thus, 'Bei Wein und Verlorenheit' is at least in part a reaction to how his poetry was received, given that it was written on the same day as the publication of yet another piece of fraught interpretation of Celan as the 'Meister der im Schwange befindlichen Technik, der assoziativen Reihung von Traumbildern' (cf. Wiedemann's notes in *KG*, 126).[9] Consequently, the excoriating characterization of mankind's mistranslation and of false images in the poem clearly speaks out against readings of his poetry as merely metaphorical.[10] Furthermore, the poetic voice in the first person, which self-assertively steers the poet's horse,[11] suggests Celan's drive to affirm his poetic stance and his poetry's ability to still communicate to the keen and attentive ear ('hörst du') in the face of such a reception.

To construe the poem as a momentary affective response to the Goll affair or to his reception, however, means overlooking how fundamentally the poem addresses and integrates itself into Celan's poetics. Celan's mytho-poetological desire to overcome or at least bridge the abyss between languages as well as his striving to regain an originary and more truthful language that does not speak in false images or *typoi* is informed by continuous confrontations with his critics and reviewers. If poetry could transcend the existential linguistic predicament of language after Babel, if it could regain an archetypal way of communicating without a separation between signifier and signified, misunderstandings of his poetry such as that of Holthusen and others would be impossible.

To be sure, as we have seen in 'Tenebrae', Celan is highly sceptical of a naive affirmation of the *archetypos* or even of an assumed rapprochement with it. He eschews any unambiguously positive declaration of a reunification of language with the *archetypos*. Indeed, given that the poetic voice in 'Tenebrae' just barely survived through the act of speaking, and given that the mode of speech in the poem is a plaint, we could not claim that archetypal speech has been attained or expressed in the poem. As we will see, Celan's hesitancy to positively proclaim the *archetypos* in his writing is also evident in his poem 'Bei Wein und Verlorenheit'. Here, even the most assertive expressions of the poetic voice are undermined by the loss projected by the title-giving first lines of the poem ('Verlorenheit') and the impossibility of translating and expressing the supposed song of the God-horse *as such* in the poem.

Before we start our close reading, we should consider another context of the poem. Celan shares the notion of the loss of the *archetypos* with Hölderlin's 'Brod und Wein', to which the first lines of Celan's poem allude, as well as to parts of Hölderlin's 'Patmos'. In our analysis of 'Tenebrae' we noted briefly that the poem was inspired by Hölderlin's 'Patmos' in which the author was also struggling to express the relationship between man and God through poetry. In 'Tenebrae', Celan rejected Hölderlin's eventual resolution at the end of 'Patmos', that through the poetic cultivation of the 'feste Buchstab, und Bestehendes gut Gedeutet' divine benevolence is assured (SA II/1, 172).[12] After the Holocaust such a belief in poetically mediated approximation of the divine *archetypos* must have seemed problematic to Celan, especially if Hölderlin envisaged 'deutscher Gesang' to play an exceptional role in this mediation (SA II/1, 172).

Man's mistranslation of divine song in Celan's 'Bei Wein und Verlorenheit' seems to re-emphasize Celan's rejection of Hölderlin's stout belief that man-made 'deutscher Gesang' could bring us closer to God. Hölderlin's elegy 'Brod und Wein' is less optimistic than his hymn 'Patmos' (cf. SA II/1, 90–95). In his famous elegy, Hölderlin develops a syncretistic, poetic theology in which Greek gods are merged with the Christian God through the Eucharistic sacraments of bread and wine. Yet, this sacramental and symbolic evocation of the God(s) is only necessary, because the divine has withdrawn into its heavenly abode.

This withdrawal in Hölderlin's 'Brod und Wein' is rendered in visual terms as God divests himself of his typified countenance ('[a]ls der Vater gewandt sein Angesicht von den Menschen'; SA II/1, 94) and retreats as *archetypos*. The poet's capability to inaugurate the proximity of man to the gods through worldly festivities and by means of song, bread, and wine is eventually cast into doubt. The impediment to accessing the divine has linguistic ramifications which eventually query poetry itself, leading to the question: 'wozu Dichter in dürftiger Zeit' (*SA* II/1, 94). In Hölderlin's view, the poet who writes after Christ's ascension, 'bears witness to what is absent through the power of his poem to evoke and recollect, to celebrate and to commemorate, but not to embody or to reveal directly that which can no longer be experienced as present and immediate'.[13]

In the absence of God, God can only be represented by signifiers like bread and, particularly, wine, which, as Eucharistic sacraments and as celebratory elements in the Dionysia, conjoin the two different traditions of Greek antiquity and Christianity. Bread and wine 'provide a consolation and a reassurance concerning divinity in its absence'; yet, they, as Cyrus Hamlin writes,

> do not actually become the body and blood of Christ during the service of Communion; they merely signify as signs that which is absent, so that they may communicate to the mind the memory or the thought of what they signify.[14]

In Celan's 'Bei Wein und Verlorenheit', the human experience of divine absence is, similar to its conception in Hölderlin's elegy, suffered on the level of language and becomes absolute. The first lines already programmatically project this loss and intensify the withdrawal of the divine even compared to Hölderlin's elegy.[15] The symbolic representatives of the divine, bread and wine, are broken up and we are left with wine only, which furthermore is running out. Ironically, the *locum tenens* for the absence of the bread is absence itself — 'Verlorenheit' — augmenting the sense of loss. Compared to Hölderlin's bread and wine which would at least 'signify as signs that which is absent' (Hamlin), Celan's poem begins at a point where these symbolical proxies for the divine are already in decline. Furthermore, not only is the wine drying up but also 'Verlorenheit' ('bei beider Neige'). If in Hölderlin's elegy, in keeping with the dithyrambic tradition, inebriation and wine are instrumental to honouring and approaching God, and if in Celan's poem 'Verlorenheit' suggests drunken self-oblivion, then the decline (or loss) of both wine and abandon as elements of ritual adoration of divinity inevitably pronounces the insurmountable distance of man from God. Further, whereas in Hölderlin's poem 'die Sänger' sing 'den Weingott' (*SA* II/1, 94), in Celan's 'Bei Wein und Verlorenheit' singing is of divine provenance ('Gott [...] sang') and mankind does not partake in divine song.[16] By developing its radicalized diagnosis of the difficulties of poetic communication through communicating with Hölderlin's elegy, Celan's poem at once expresses and embodies the exacerbation of the problem to communicate poetically since Hölderlin. Indeed, as we will see, Celan's problematization of the possibilities of theological signification is so fundamental that it extends not only to mankind, but even to the self-assertive first-person poetic voice.

That the poetic voice and God are not entirely unified is already clear at the beginning. The poetic voice steers the God-horse.[17] The control of the poetic voice over the divine mount seems to imply the voice's confident affirmation of its power to write poetry, in what could be considered an ironic take on the notion of *poeta alter deus*. On the other hand, God's raising his voice alone in his act of singing ('er sang') seems to identify God as the author of that which is the traditional metaphor for poetry: song. Nonetheless, the degrees of separation between God and poetic voice as well as the blasphemous impetus of the rider-horse metaphor should also not be overstated: this God is not the same as the one accused of complicity in the Holocaust in 'Tenebrae'. Moreover, the apostrophic appeal to the 'du' to listen to the poetic voice relating God's song ('hörst du') underlines, even if indirectly, the importance of the divine word in 'Bei Wein und Verlorenheit'. Furthermore, in the second stanza, the poetic voice and God are unified in their spatio-temporal movement and direction ('unser letzter Ritt'), and in the third they are also unified in utterance ('unser Gewieher'). Celan renders the reciprocity of communicative interaction in a positive light, whether in the expression and reception of sounds ('er sang', 'hörst du') or in the complementary character of horse and rider.

This communication between horse and rider, and first and second person, eludes discrete and linguistically classifiable criteria. This form of communication is immediate and non-discursive. The communicative act between horse and rider, singer and listener, is expressed and understood.[18] The divine song has no content that can be expressed in the discursive languages of humankind, since the joint utterance of God and the poetic voice is unintelligible 'Gewieher' to the ears of man in stanza three. Similarly, the direction into which poetic voice and God are riding is indescribable in non-paradoxical terms: 'die Ferne — die Nähe'. But we should already indicate at this point that these inconcrete or even paradoxical poetic circumscriptions, that is direction as indirection and divine expression as song, not only problematize the languages of man in stanza three but will eventually also call into question poetic expression itself. We should keep in mind that poetry after Babel always remains problematic in enunciating the divine *archetypos*, and Celan is mindful of this.

Nonetheless, however large the degree of separation between the archetypal song of the divine mount and the poetic rider is, they are united in their superior form of communication — superior, that is, if one compares it to mankind's efforts of understanding. This superiority of communication is a quite literal one. It is expressed semantically ('unser letzter Ritt über Menschen-Hürden') as well as spatially by the fact that the second stanza is positioned above the third stanza. The semantic juxtaposition of the stanzas is amplified by the spatial barrier of the white line that renders visual the spatial opposition expressed in the poetry itself. The poem could have ended after the second stanza, which would have given it an outlook somewhat similar to the last lines of the famous poem 'Fadensonnen' Celan wrote four years later: 'es sind | noch Lieder zu singen jenseits | der Menschen' (*KG*, 179).[19] The eschatological prospect of the last ride over and beyond mankind in 'Bei Wein und Verlorenheit' would then have been comparable to the songs to be sung 'beyond mankind' in 'Fadensonnen', both spelling the possibility of a superhuman realm. Yet, 'Bei Wein und Verlorenheit' does not end on this prospect. The white space after the second stanza marks a turning point in the poem similar to the blank line that divides 'Halbzerfressener' into two parts (see chapter 6).[20]

Language struggled to express the direction of the ride and evoked the divine song heard by the 'du' and the poetic voice in stanza two. In the blank line, then, language cedes. When words return in the third stanza, they speak to us as typified languages. After the blank line's empty *typos*-image, meaningful expression has become impossible. Unlike the appeal to the 'du' to attentively listen in the second stanza, the reaction of man elicited by the riding above is that of an obsequious and fearful ducking. Thus, inherent to man's act of veneration is the failure to (re)gain a linguistic bond with God. Man dodges away from any engagement with divine song and neighing and speaks in *typos*-images. This failure was already foreshadowed by the loss of the traditional sacraments of the Eucharist ceremony (bread and wine) to which, as to Hölderlin's 'Brod und Wein', the first lines of Celan's poem had alluded. Yet the extent of the failure to create a communicative bond with God through the sacraments as well as through speech only becomes clear in the blank line and the following stanza. So utterly deprived of meaning and expression in its emptiness, the visual vacuity of the white line separating the stanzas prefigures the languages of writing, filled with images, mentioned in the final line: 'sie | schrieben [...] | um in eine | ihrer bebilderten Sprachen.' What coincides with the visual, written character of these languages is that they are a false, typified misrepresentation ('sie logen [...] um') of what is supposed to remain an untranslated auditory expression, that is 'Gewieher' and song.

Inherent to this typification of language is also the fact that it is mute and written rather than articulated like the 'Gewieher' or divine song. Celan's privileging of verbal speech over written speech in this poem is also apparent throughout most of his poetry. It is fitting for a poet who stresses the importance of dialogical exchange in the form of a 'Gespräch' that his most important poetological work was a speech delivered in front of an audience. Similarly, Celan's emphasis on the pneumatic presence of the poetic voice is apparent in the title of his poetry volume *Atemwende* as well as throughout his notes, for instance: '[d]as Gedicht ist [...] der Atem dessen, der — sterblich — durch das Gedicht geht' (*Mikro*, 142; underlined in original). Celan's preference for the spoken word bespeaks his partiality to the living individuality of a speaker as opposed to signification *in absentia* particular to the written word.[21] Thus, Celan only speaks positively of the written word if it bears testimony to the individuality of the writer. It is for this reason that Celan says '[n]ur wahre Hände schreiben wahre Gedichte' (*CW* III, 177), as the hands attest to the provenance of the written poem. Roland Reuß reports that Celan wrote his poem 'Einkanter, Rembrandt' 'mit der Feder ins reine [*sic*]', because only a person's handwriting could reveal the individual behind the symbolic abstraction of the written word and therefore express the personal importance of this poem to Celan.[22]

Writing in Celan as Benjamin's Allegorical Image

Celan's emphasis on the living, breathing, audible word as opposed to the written one echoes Walter Benjamin's conception of the latter as allegorical image in his *Ursprung des deutschen Trauerspiels*: '[d]ie Lautsprache ist [...] der Bereich der freien, ursprünglichen Äußerung der Kreatur, wogegen das allegorische Schriftbild die Dinge in den exzentrischen Verschränkungen der Bedeutung versklavt' (*GS* I/1, 378–79). Thus, according to this interpretation spoken language breathes the free and creative spirit of the speaker, whereas the written word is removed from the personal intentions and the voice of the writer. The written word, or the allegorical image, thus betrays the arbitrariness of meaning. Allegory is removed from the object or person it expresses, because as written word it stands in for the absent object it denotes. If the relation to the object is supposed to give allegory its meaning, then the latter's meaning becomes arbitrary, since it is, as a written image, removed from this very object. In his edition of Benjamin's *Ursprung des deutschen Trauerspiels*, Celan had underlined the following sentence in which Benjamin ascribes arbitrariness to allegory: '[j]ede Person, jedwedes Ding, jedes Verhältnis kann ein beliebiges anderes bedeuten.'[23] Hence, in the arbitrariness of allegory, as Benjamin holds, the relation between (allegorical) sign and signified object is untethered, and allegory precisely expresses anything but the presence of the object: 'Allegorie bedeutet etwas anderes als es ist. Und zwar bedeutet es genau das Nichtsein dessen, was es vorstellt' (*GS* I/1, 406). The allegorical image thus creates an 'Abgrund zwischen bildlichem Sein und Bedeuten' (*GS* I/1, 342). Benjamin's theory of allegory is embedded in the larger context of his conception of linguistic signification, according to which the arbitrariness of the allegorical image is a consequence of the Fall of Man and the events at Babel. Benjamin believes that the Fall of Man had already created a disorder between objects themselves and mankind's relation to these objects and thus holds that 'Zeichen müssen sich verwirren, wo sich die Dinge verwickeln. [...] In dieser Abkehr von den Dingen, die die Verknechtung war, entstand der Plan des Turmbaus und die Sprachverwirrung mit ihm' (cf. *GS* II/1, 155).[24] The diagnosed arbitrariness of meaning of the allegorical image is thus twice removed from the archetypal state and thereby embodies the very arbitrariness of meaning after Babel and the Fall of Man.[25]

With Benjamin's notion of the allegorical image in mind we can now turn back to Celan's 'Bei Wein und Verlorenheit'. In his poem, the falsity of man's expressions as 'umlügen' is asserted immediately after man attempts to capture God's and the poetic voice's expression in writing, which reminds us of Benjamin's 'allegorische[s] Schriftbild':

> [...] sie
> schrieben, sie
> logen unser Gewieher
> um in eine
> ihrer bebilderten Sprachen.

The notion of writing as an image that is removed from the true (and nondiscursive) meaning of the archetypal song in the poem reminds us of the abyss allegory creates between 'bildlichem Sein und Bedeuten' in Benjamin. The written image does not breathe the divine pneuma. It is a transformation into mute and dead letters of what already sounds like mere neighing to mankind's ears. Man's transformation of the neighing in the form of 'umlügen' betrays the arbitrary character of these written images which are anything but what they feign to be: divine song. The derivative and deviating character of these *typos*-images that are man's languages inheres in the very nature of these languages after Babel. Benjamin and Celan are thus significantly informed by the Judaeo-Christian discourse of the image as split between *typos* and *archetypos* which underpins their conception of language after Babel. As we saw in the introduction, in the philosophical tradition the image's difference to the *archetypos* is embodied in its being *typos*. In representing or seeking to represent the *archetypos*, the *typos* necessarily differs from the *archetypos*. Benjamin's allegorical image is a radicalization of this understanding of the *typos*, when he says that it 'bedeutet [...] genau das Nichtsein dessen, was es vorstellt'. Similarly, in Celan's poem, the plurality of man's typified languages embodies the difference to archetypal song.[26] They express anything but divine language. They only signify the absence of the divine in their deviance from it through mistranslation.

This differential character to archetypal song governs man's languages internally, even down to their typographically broken-up grammatical structure. Hence in another, further sense, the Divine Word is betrayed by man in 'Bei Wein und Verlorenheit'. By means of the syntactical symmetry between '[s]ie duckten sich', 'sie schrieben', and 'sie logen' Celan uses parallelism to turn the Bible's most important poetic device against the Divine Word.[27] The typification of man's writing is conveyed visually by the jagged syntax which fragments the third stanza of the poem. The typifying character of man's language in the third stanza leaves no line unscarred; no line forms a grammatically complete phrase or clause. Significantly, the first time a verb phrase is split up by the white space at the end of a line is when writing is mentioned — 'sie | schrieben' — reinforcing our conjecture that Celan thinks of writing along the lines of Benjamin's allegorical image.[28] Once again we discover in Benjamin's *Ursprung des deutschen Trauerspiels* a similar association of fragmentation with writing, which Celan underlined in his own edition:

> [d]ie Heiligkeit der Schrift ist vom Gedanken ihrer strengen Kodifikation untrennbar. Denn alle sakrale Schrift fixiert sich in Komplexen, die zuletzt einen einzigen und unveränderlichen ausmachen oder doch zu bilden trachten. Daher entfernt sich die Buchstabenschrift als eine Kombination von Schriftatomen am weitesten von der Schrift sakraler Komplexe.[29]

The strict codification of sacred writing thus cannot be divested from the latter's content. Ultimately, form and content of scripture express one unchangeable complex, as Benjamin terms it, that bears strong similarity to how the Judaeo-Christian tradition conceived the *archetypos*. This strict codification of sacred writing is in stark contrast with the fragmented 'Buchstabenschrift' and its arbitrary combination of letters. The Divine Word pronounced in the scripture is furthest removed from the allegorical, written image. Man's act of writing and translating into a written lie in Celan's 'Bei Wein und Verlorenheit' therefore appears to be a perpetuation of the linguistic confusion after Babel, strongly resembling what Benjamin believes Baroque allegory embodies.[30]

The Poetic Voice Speaks after Babel

The impossibility of truthful expression in language after Babel is most densely encapsulated in the polyglot pun of 'Neige'. 'Neige' is not only the German word for decline — which in the context of the poem's title seems to have connotations of loss — but also the French word for snow, echoed in its German equivalent 'Schnee' here, and additionally bears resemblance to the 'Nähe' in the poem and the English word 'neigh'.[31] We realize that the heterology of languages even encroaches upon the speaker position of the first-person voice. Celan, too, writes after Babel. The sense of loss conveyed by 'Neige' is also enacted by its relation to *Nähe/neige/*neigh, evoking the confusion of tongues and a distance to archetypal speaking. The 'Nähe' towards which the poetic voice rides the God-horse, passing through 'Schnee' or *neige*, becomes linked to the sensation of loss and linguistic confusion via the polyglot 'Neige'.

Moreover, we realize that the poetic voice, which so seemingly confidently steers the divine horse, does not itself actually communicate divine song to us. Rather, the poetic voice has to evoke a 'du' as witness to divine song — 'hörst du' — and only through this address to the testifying 'du' do we know of the divine song. Hence, we only know, along with and through the 'du', *that* there is singing but not *what* is sung — indeed, testimony of divine singing is only borne by the written words of the poem. The text *as* (visual) text (rather than spoken word) draws itself into question via *Neige/Nähe/neige/*neigh, since as Yoko Tawada perspicaciously discerns: '[d]as englische Wort "neigh" (Gewieher) weicht zwar von dem deutschen Wort "Neige" orthografisch etwas ab, aber dennoch geht es hier eher um eine grafische Ähnlichkeit als um eine phonetische.'[32]

Thus, unlike Arno Schmidt, who envisions a form of *unio mystica* between poetic voice and God,[33] and Jean Bollack, for whom the 'Schnee', somewhat inexplicably, is 'etwas Abbildloses, Unbebildertes' and thus archetypal,[34] my interpretation sees the heteroglossia of 'Schnee' as 'neige' and its similarity to 'neigh' precisely as a mark of linguistic separation between the poetic voice and God. The plurality of tongues suggests an unbridgeable gap between the (absent) archetypal song and its indirect, textual representation in the poem. Indeed, the only time when the poetic voice and God-horse are described as speaking in unison, they are ironically characterized — from the perspective of mankind — as neighing ('Gewieher'). This neighing in turn embodies the confusion of languages in its similarity to *Neige/ Nähe/neige*. Thus, the seeming unity between poetic voice and God-horse already suggests an inherent gap between the poetic voice and the divine *archetypos*.

Certainly, even if the poetic voice cannot join the God-horse in its song, the use of the first-person plural pronoun ('unser') in opposition to the third person plural used for man also implies their fundamental difference. Whereas mankind ducks down, the poetic voice and 'du' listen to divine song. Nonetheless the confusion of languages which speak in images is already enacted in *Neige/Nähe/neige/*neigh and problematizes the position of the poetic voice, which then culminates in man's lying languages of *typoi,* as suggested by the false sonic and visual effigies of *Neige/ Nähe/neige/*neigh.

The fact that the poetic voice, too, speaks after Babel in 'Bei Wein und Verlorenheit' casts a new light on the claims Celan makes for his own poetry. Celan's poetic position in 'Bei Wein und Verlorenheit' became apparent when he severely restricted any unauthorized alterations and distribution of his work, including its translation.[35] He also frequently insisted on the untranslatability of his poetry:

> [e]s gibt kein Wort, das, einmal ausgesprochen, nicht auch seinen übertragenen Sinn mitbrächte; und doch meinen die Worte im Gedicht, unübertragbar zu sein; das Gedicht erscheint als der Ort, wo alle Metaphorik ad absurdum geführt wird. (*M*, 75)

The German 'übertragen' takes both senses here: 'metaphorical' and 'translated'. Celan does not deny that words have their 'übertragenen Sinn' which they carry with themselves ('mitbrächte'). His poetry is, of course, metaphorical and translatable, having been written after the Holocaust and thus after linguistic confusion. But his insistence on *Unübertragbarkeit* and truthfulness places the priority on what is not metaphorical or translatable in his poetry. Thus, rather than reading his poetry for its metaphorical abstraction and concluding that it flies away from 'der blutigen Schreckenskammer der Geschichte',[36] we should look for those instances in his poetry which are not metaphorical expressions: '[w]er im Gedicht nur die Metapher findet, der hat auch nichts anderes gesucht; er nimmt nichts wahr' (*M*, 138). And if the instances of 'truth' are not immediately apparent to us due to the tortured and confused language then this is a consequence of the Holocaust. Only at a closer look may we find that what initially seemed to be metaphorical is not:

> Schwarze Milch der Frühe:[37] Das ist keine jener Genitivmetaphern, wie sie uns [sic] von unseren sogenannten Kritikern vorgesetzt bekommen, damit wir nicht mehr zum Gedicht gehen; das ist keine Redefigur und kein Oxymoron <u>mehr</u>, das ist <u>Wirklichkeit.</u> (*M*, 158)[38]

What makes Celan's words 'unübertragbar' is thus a desire to overcome or even undo Babel and the Holocaust and communicate through song sung in the archetypal language now lost. Yet, untranslatability does not merely apply to his poetic words, but rather to what they seek to express: the untranslatable and pre-metaphorical archetypal speaking which antedates the split into signifier and signified. Celan experiences the Holocaust as a corruption and confusion of language that drove a wedge between the signifying words and that which they signify.[39] Thus, when critics consider his poetry to be merely metaphorical, *übertragen*, they perpetuate this very split in language. And while we are aware that Celan certainly did use metaphors, his own derogatory remarks about metaphor notwithstanding, Celan is nonetheless right to emphasize that the experience of injury and trauma expressed in his language and, not least, the 'schwarze Milch' of the crematoria is very real.

However, there is added complexity to Celan's conundrum of speaking after the Holocaust. His poetry is caught in two fundamental and interconnected paradoxes. The Holocaust as that which undid archetypal speech, poses the radical problem of how to speak truthfully and commemorate the victims. Furthermore, Celan's desire to return to an archetypal form of speaking, his commitment to poetic 'Sehen als <u>Gewahren</u>, Wahrnehmen, Wahrhaben, Wahr<u>sein</u>' (*M*, 134), at heart also express a desire to return to a language from before the Holocaust, that is, free of the Holocaust — but this is impossible because we cannot simply resign the Holocaust to oblivion. Celan is writing from within a language — in German no less — that cannot but bear the traces of the Holocaust and thus of the split between the signifier and signified, and to this extent metaphor persists. Thus, when Celan states that metaphor is reduced to absurdity, he does not simply mean that it is abolished. Instead, writing from within this state of language, Celan seeks to reduce metaphor ad absurdum and to insist on the *Unübertragbarkeit* of his poetry. Truthful commemoration of the victims of the Holocaust in words that are not to be shrugged off as merely metaphorical and the desire to regain the ability to sing archetypal song are Celan's twin motivations. In a sense, both are incommensurable, because archetypal speaking is immediate and in this sense absolute, whereas writing after the Holocaust — even in commemoration — is not and cannot be. Hence, what is reduced to absurdity is absolute, archetypal poetry after the Holocaust which always has an 'übertragenen Sinn'. However, for poetry to survive and commemorate it must also maintain its truthfulness, its *Unübertragbarkeit*, and not be done in by the absurdity and arbitrariness of Nazi crimes. Consequently, what remains possible[40] is to testify to the *archetypos* through poetic speech and through attentive listening and engagement on the part of the translator, poet, or listener and reader, and to repudiate those who simply perpetuate the confusion of tongues and speak in *typos*-images.

The Notion of Writing in Du Bouchet and Celan

We saw that poetic truth was in part warranted by the personal, breathing presence of witnesses, and even the *archetypos* characterized by oral, pneumatic expression as song. Celan's conception of an *archetypos* as speaking or singing as opposed to the written word in 'Bei Wein und Verlorenheit' stands in marked distinction to du Bouchet's poetic image which he conceives of as painting, as we will see in the next chapter. In other words, the visual, written character is constitutive to du Bouchet's image. It would be an overstatement to say that du Bouchet does not accord any place to the spoken word in his poetry. However, when he does, it often takes on characteristics of writing. This can already be gleaned from some of his titles, such as 'L'Écrit à haute voix'[41], or 'Ce balbutiement blanc' whose 'blanc' refers to the white space of the page.[42] According to Michaël Bishop we should understand even the spoken word as insufficiency: 'écrire, c'est [...] éprouver "l'insuffisance" de la parole, insuffisance due à la non-répétabilité de la parole.'[43] Similarly, Emma Wagstaff states that the 'poetry of du Bouchet [...] is written to be read rather than heard'.[44] She further emphasizes that '[d]u Bouchet [...] rarely read [his] work in public, and when [he] did so, [he] read written texts; [he] did not give performances'.[45]

As we will see in the following chapter, du Bouchet's image, 'présente | et absente',⁴⁶ requires the tension between the written word in black ink and the white page as well as the paradoxes that present themselves in du Bouchet's semantics.⁴⁷ This tension is conspicuous for its lack of an espousal of the written word or white page, or *présence* or *absence* over the other. The resolution of the polychotomous tension inhering in du Bouchet's poetry, enunciated through a range of contrasts, is projected into an infinity. However, this infinity is not a target or even eschatological telos or *archetypos*, but an expression of a continuous future, a not-yet which continually eludes being captured in the present or as *presence*: '[l]e sens d'un mot est toujours au futur, mobile, mouvant à l'infini.'⁴⁸ The biggest difference between Celan's and du Bouchet's poetic image lies in the former's pneumatic and teleological *archetypos* as opposed to the irresolvable polychotomy of the latter's image which is also, firmly, a written one. Du Bouchet's 'souffle' is not the privileged presence or voice of the poet but may also be a whiff of the wind whistling through du Bouchet's poetic landscape devoid of a personal presence.⁴⁹

Notes to Chapter 4

1. The Fall of Man and the confusion of tongues are also thought of in the same breath by Celan's intellectual kin Walter Benjamin (*GS*, II/1, 155). Benjamin seems to have greatly inspired Celan's thinking about language, and these similarities in the interpretation of Babel are not a coincidence. For more on the relation of Benjamin and Celan, see: Menninghaus, *Paul Celan*. For more on Benjamin's theory of language, see especially: Winfried Menninghaus, *Walter Benjamins Theorie der Sprachmagie* (Frankfurt a. M.: Suhrkamp, 1980); Werner Hamacher, 'Intensive Languages', trans. by Ira Allen and Steven Tester, *Modern Language Notes*, 127.3 (2012), 485–541.
2. George Steiner, *After Babel: Aspects of Language and Translation*, 3rd edn (Oxford: Oxford University Press, 1998).
3. Cf. Menninghaus, *Paul Celan*, p. 55.
4. Letter by Celan to Karl Dedecius of 31 January 1960], in Angela Sanmann, *Poetische Interaktion: Französisch-deutsche Lyrikübersetzung bei Friedhelm Kemp, Paul Celan, Ludwig Harig, Volker Braun* (Berlin: De Gruyter, 2013), p. 388.
5. In the language of Benjamin, the translator should seek an 'anbilden' instead of 'abbilden' of the original (cf. *GS*, IV/1, 18).
6. Cited in Wolfgang Emmerich, *Paul Celan*, 6th edn (Reinbek: Rowohlt, 2014), pp. 94–95.
7. Emmerich quotes a substantial but by no means complete list (ibid.).
8. Wiedemann has documented the affair with meticulous detail: cf. *Paul Celan, die Goll-Affäre: Dokumente zu einer 'Infamie'*, ed. by Barbara Wiedemann (Frankfurt a. M.: Suhrkamp, 2000). Perhaps the most prominent academic voices supporting Celan were Peter Szondi in the *Neue Zürcher Zeitung* (p. 272) and Walter Jens in *Die Zeit* (p. 365).
9. Cf. also Jürgen Lehmann, 'Bei Wein und Verlorenheit', in *Kommentar zu Paul Celans 'Die Niemandsrose'*, ed. by Christine Ivanović and Jürgen Lehmann (Heidelberg: Winter, 1997), pp. 61–64 (p. 62).
10. In the notes to his 'Meridian' speech, Celan would repeatedly speak out against interpreting his poetry as metaphoric: '[a]ls das Unübertragbare, selbst nicht leicht zu Tragende und oft Unerträgliche — unerträglich Schwere — haßt man das Gedicht. Wer das Gedicht nicht [...] mit-tragen will, überträgt und spricht gern von Metaphern' (*M*, 159).
11. The suggestions of a divine flying horse in conjunction with poetry quite plausibly alludes to Pegasus (see Lehmann, 'Bei Wein und Verlorenheit', p. 61).
12. For Celan's rejection of Hölderlin, see Wienold, 'Paul Celans Hölderlin-Widerruf'.

13. Cyrus Hamlin, 'German Classical Poetry', in *The Literature of Weimar Classicism*, ed. by Simon Richter (Rochester, NY: Camden House, 2005), pp. 169–210 (pp. 190–91).
14. Ibid., p. 190.
15. It should be noted that some echoes of Jeremiah 25. 15 can also be heard in Celan's poem. But Jeremiah's vengeful, commanding God of the Old Testament, who effectively commits mass murder by poisoned wine, could hardly be the God whom the first-person poetic voice of Celan's poem would ride and whom neither the author nor his poetic voice would describe as singing. Theo Buck and Jean Bollack both note that the parallels to Jeremiah hinder rather than facilitate the interpretation of Celan's poem; see Theo Buck, *Celan schreibt an Jünger*, Celan-Studien, 7 (Aachen: Rimbaud, 2005), p. 15. Bollack appositely writes that if the eschatological scenario of Jeremiah was applicable to Celan, then 'diese Endzeit [wäre] unmittelbar nach den Vernichtungslagern schon Geschichte' (Jean Bollack, 'Chanson à boire: Über das Gedicht "Bei Wein und Verlorenheit"', *Celan-Jahrbuch*, 3, ed. by Hans-Michael Speier (1989), 23–37 (p. 24)).
16. I therefore disagree with Jean Bollack here, who cryptically reads the decline or loss of 'Verlorenheit' as the state of self-oblivion in which the first-person poetic voice finds the most truthful expression of itself: '[a]uch die Verlorenheit geht zur "Neige"; in diesem Zustand findet das Subjekt des Gedichts am besten zu sich' (Bollack, 'Chanson à boire', p. 30).
17. Lehmann, 'Bei Wein und Verlorenheit', p. 61.
18. Celan seems to pursue similar ideas here as Walter Benjamin in his early theory of language. Benjamin attributed to pre-Babel language that it communicates in an immediate fashion, believing that a signifier denotes its signified 'unmittelbar' (see *GS* II/1, pp. 142–57).
19. Bollack also connects 'Bei Wein und Verlorenheit' with 'Fadensonnen' (Bollack, 'Chanson à boire', p. 34).
20. A similarly important blank line in Celan can be found in his poem 'Wortaufschüttung' (see Koch, 'The Allegorical Image and Presence in Celan's "Wortaufschüttung"').
21. On the importance of verbal utterance as opposed to the written, visual word, see also ibid.
22. Cited in Roland Reuß, *Im Zeithof: Celan-Provokationen* (Frankfurt a. M.: Stroemfeld, 2001), p. 18. I am thus qualifying Monika Schmitz-Emans's position according to which Celan accords fundamental importance to the written word, interpreting the world as a book. For Celan the written word is equal to the spoken one if it acquires the same qualities as the spoken word, is considered to have 'eine "sterblich-unsterbliche Seele"', and is a 'lebendige Wesenhei[t]'; Monika Schmitz-Emans, 'Paul Celan und die schriftmetaphorische Tradition', in *Der Glühende Leertext: Annäherungen an Paul Celans Dichtung*, ed. by Christoph Jamme and Otto Pöggeler (Munich: Fink, 1993), pp. 87–113 (p. 95).
23. Cf. Paul Celan, *La Bibliothèque philosophique. Die philosophische Bibliothek: Catalogue raisonné des annotations*, ed. by Alexandra Richter, Patrik Alac, and Bertrand Badiou (Paris: Presses de l'École Normale Supérieure, 2004), p. 280. One may add, in light of Benjamin's essay on *Das Kunstwerk im Zeitalter seiner technischen Reproduzierbarkeit* (as Burkhardt Lindner intimates), that the reproducibility of the allegorical sign is deprived of the 'aura' of the object that gives the allegory its meaning; cf. Burkhardt Lindner, 'Allegorie', in *Benjamins Begriffe*, ed. by Michael Opitz and Erdmut Wizisla, 2 vols (Frankfurt a. M.: Suhrkamp, 2000), I, 50–94 (p. 63).
24. Cf. also: '[u]m aber als rebushaftes Bild-Schriftzeichen dienen zu können, muß das Bedeutende immer schon zerstückelt, fragmentiert, anamorphisiert, entseelt und aus dem Kontext herausgerissen sein. Dies betrifft noch die Schrift selbst. Auch sie wird zum Stückwerk, dem der lebendige Sprachlaut ausgegangen ist [...]' (Lindner, p. 67).
25. For a further discussion of Benjamin's notion of the allegorical image in relation to Franz Kafka's *Trial* and Orson Welles's film thereof, see Julian Johannes Immanuel Koch, '"The False Appearance of Totality Is Extinguished": Orson Welles's *The Trial* and Benjamin's Allegorical Image', *Film-Philosophy*, 23.1 (2019), 17–34.
26. Celan seems to have Benjamin's allegorical image in mind when he specifically delineates a positively connoted conception of the image from Benjamin's conception of the allegorical image: 'diese Dichtung ist keine Emblematik [;] keine Stimmungspoesie [;] das Bild hat phänomenalen Charakter — <u>es erscheint</u>. [/] die Vision –' (*M*, 87; insertions in curly brackets by the editors of the *Tübinger Ausgabe*).{/;}{/;}

27. Stephen A. Geller, 'Hebrew Prosody and Poetics: Biblical', in *The New Princeton Encyclopedia of Poetry and Poetics*, ed. by Alex Preminger and T. V. F. Brogan (Princeton: Princeton University Press, 1993), pp. 509–11. See also the pioneering study of parallel syntax in Hebrew poetry by Robert Lowth, *Lectures on the Sacred Poetry of the Hebrews*, trans. by G. Gregory (Boston, MA: Buckingham, 1815).
28. Henriette Beese, who also analyses Celan's poetry in relation to Benjamin's thought, similarly discovers in Celan's poetry an association between linguistic fragmentation and what is perceived to be lifelessness in writing: '[w]ie thematisch in Celans Lyrik immer mehr das Abgespaltene und das Anorganische hervortraten [...], so ist in seiner Lyrik das, was in der Schrift als tot gilt, die Wörter, die Silben, die Buchstaben, bevorzugt vor dem von lebendigem Sinn durchatmeten Ganzen der Sprache' (*Nachdichtung als Erinnerung: Allegorische Lektüre einiger Gedichte von Paul Celan* (Darmstadt: Agora, 1976), p. 209, cf. also p. 214). Pöggeler also observes allegorical elements in Celan's poetry. However, he understands allegory not in the Benjaminian sense but rather in contrast to the symbol as stipulated by Johann Wolfgang Goethe (Otto Pöggeler, 'Symbol und Allegorie', in *Paul Celan, 'Atemwende': Materialien*, ed. by Gerhard Buhr and Roland Reuß (Würzburg: Königshausen & Neumann, 1991), pp. 345–61 (p. 350).
29. Celan, *La Bibliothèque philosophique*, p. 280; cf. Benjamin, GS I/1, 351.
30. In anticipation of our analysis of the poem 'Halbzerfressener', we may say that the 'umlügen' in 'Bei Wein und Verlorenheit' is quite the opposite of the 'umbrechen' in 'Halbzerfressener'.
31. Lehmann, 'Bei Wein und Verlorenheit', p. 62; Elizabeth Petuchowski, 'Bilingual and Multilingual "Wortspiele" in the Poetry of Paul Celan', *Deutsche Vierteljahrsschrift für Literaturwissenschaft und Geistesgeschichte*, 52.4 (1978), 635–51 (p. 641); 'Hyphen, n.', OED Online (Oxford University Press, 2017) <https://www.oed.com/view/Entry/90403?rskey=uXraDT&result=1&isAdvanced=false#eid> [accessed 25 March 2021].
32. Cited in Wiebke Amthor, *Schneegespräche an gastlichen Tischen: Wechselseitiges Übersetzen bei Paul Celan und André du Bouchet* (Heidelberg: Winter, 2006), p. 311.
33. Arno Schmidt, '"Bei Wein und Verlorenheit...": Bemerkungen zu einem Dithyrambos von Paul Celan aus der Sammlung *Die Niemandsrose*', *Archiv für Papyrusforschung und verwandte Gebiete*, 57.2 (2011), 345–55 (p. 350).
34. Jean Bollack, 'Chanson à boire', p. 35.
35. Dirk Weissmann, 'Poésie, judaïsme, philosophie: Une histoire de la réception de Paul Celan en France, des débuts jusqu'à 199' (unpublished doctoral thesis, Paris 3, 2003), pp. 277–78. <http://www.theses.fr/2003PA030084> [accessed 24 April 2017].
36. Holthusen cited in Emmerich, p. 94.
37. This expression stems from Celan's Holocaust poem 'Todesfuge', in which it describes the smoke of burning bodies in the concentration camps.
38. In a poem composed five years after the remarks in the context of his 'Meridian' speech, 'Ein Dröhnen' (KG, 206), Celan speaks of a 'Metapherngestöber' into whose midst, as he tells us in a sarcastic tone, truth has stepped. Of course, the mocking tone and the metaphoricity undermine the reader's belief that there is much truthfulness in this 'truth' or about the people who are said to be in the 'Metapherngestöber'.
39. See Menninghaus, *Paul Celan*, p. 55.
40. It is no coincidence that Celan's poetics revolves around the possible: 'die Sprache als Möglichkeit und Fragwürdigkeit' (*Mikro*, 102).
41. Text printed in *André du Bouchet*, ed. by Pierre Chappuis (Paris: Seghers, 1979), pp. 90–91.
42. André du Bouchet, *Openwork: Poetry and Prose*, trans. by Paul Auster (New Haven: Yale University Press, 2014), p. 56. Parts of this poem were later worked into the third section, 'Rudiments', of the volume *Dans la chaleur vacante* (CW IV, 178–79).
43. Bishop, *Altérités d'André du Bouchet*, p. 30.
44. In an insightful passage on the orality of du Bouchet's poetry, Wagstaff reminds us that the sonic features of poems served to facilitate the oral citation of the poems from memory. Insofar as du Bouchet's poetry 'incites forgetting' and lives in the immediate present tense (see also chapter 7), his eschewal of traditional oratory and sonic elements in poetry becomes understandable (Wagstaff, *Provisionality and the Poem*, p. 37). On du Bouchet's notion of forgetting, which is

inspired by Reverdy's, see Lucy-Jean Lloyd, 'Writing and Forgetting: Reading Reverdy through André du Bouchet', *Nottingham French Studies*, 28.2 (1989), 66–74.
45. Wagstaff, *Provisionality and the Poem*, p. 44.
46. André du Bouchet, *Openwork*, p. 56.
47. Even though most du Bouchet scholarship seems to confirm the importance of the visual over the sonic qualities of du Bouchet's texts, Chappuis emphasizes the 'concurrence [...] du parlé et de l'écrit' and their 'introuvable unité' (in *André du Bouchet*, ed. by Chappuis, p. 64).
48. Veinstein, p. 27.
49. Cf. Pennone, pp. 444–49.

CHAPTER 5

Du Bouchet's Polychotomous Image

I noted in the last chapter that du Bouchet conceived of the poetic image explicitly as a written and, thus, as a visual image. This set his image apart from that of Celan (see end of previous chapter). We also already indicated that du Bouchet's image appears to be constituted in an inherent tension which motivates his poetic writing. Du Bouchet's penchant for paradox and contradiction was already evident in his critical engagement with his poetic and intellectual forebears Hölderlin, Hugo, and Baudelaire (see chapter 2), where he was fascinated particularly by the moments in which these poets' image disappeared, surpassed the capabilities of the imagination, or even destroyed itself. In du Bouchet's own poetry, almost from the very beginning, the disappearance of the image is not only semantically thematized but is also visually apparent in the disappearance of text and the appearance of gaps on the page. In this chapter, we will continue to analyse du Bouchet's image as constituted by the interaction between *absence* and *présence*, and we will focus on the interaction between the semantics of the text and its visual character, which we had not considered in our previous discussion of du Bouchet.

Du Bouchet's attention to the visuality of the page as well as his interest in contradiction and paradox — which also pervades his early discussions of Scève, Hölderlin, Hugo, and Baudelaire — is informed by a more contemporaneous predecessor: Pierre Reverdy. Indeed, the sympathy for the elder poet and the prominence of his conception of the image in France, along with du Bouchet's fascination with the visual arts,[1] are likely among the main reasons why du Bouchet is preoccupied with the poetic and visual image throughout his life. We have already become aware of Reverdy's importance in the chapter on Celan's 'Traum vom Traume', where we saw Reverdy's considerable influence on Breton's surrealist image, which in turn had provoked the young Celan to respond with his own conception of the image with surrealist elements. Whereas Celan most likely came in touch with Reverdy's poetics only indirectly through surrealism, for du Bouchet the inverse applies. Du Bouchet's interest in surrealism seems to have been marginal at best, but his knowledge of Reverdy's poetry and poetics is first-hand. To gain a more complete understanding of the importance of Reverdy for du Bouchet's conception of the image, we shall cite Reverdy's influential formulation of the image at some length:

> [l]'Image est une création pure de l'esprit.
> Elle ne peut naître d'une comparaison mais du rapprochement de deux réalités plus ou moins éloignées.
> Plus les rapports des deux réalités rapprochées seront lointains et justes, plus l'image sera forte — plus elle aura de puissance émotive et de réalité poétique.
> Deux réalités qui n'ont aucun rapport ne peuvent se rapprocher utilement. Il n'y a pas création d'image.
> Deux réalités contraires ne se rapprochent pas. Elles s'opposent.
> [...]
> Une image n'est pas forte parce qu'elle est **brutale** ou **fantastique** — mais parce que l'association des idées est lointaine et juste.
> [...]
> On crée [...] une forte image, neuve pour l'esprit, en rapprochant sans comparaison deux réalités distantes dont **l'esprit seul** a saisi les rapports.[2]

The two realities Reverdy's image encompasses are, on the one hand, the exterior reality given by the senses and, on the other, the creative, secondary, artistic reality.[3] Both are unified in and by the artistic mind in its striving for an ulterior, absolute reality that is approximated in the process.[4] Under Breton's pen in his *Manifeste du surréalisme*, Reverdy's image was refocused on a presumed clash between the two 'réalités' that were now rather considered 'plus' than 'moins' 'éloignées'.[5] In the image of his 'Traum vom Traume', Celan had reiterated Breton's emphasis on contrast when he stated that 'Fremdes [wird] Fremdesten vermählt' (*CW* III, 158) in achieving a unified poetic *archetypos*.

Although du Bouchet felt much closer to Reverdy than to surrealism, his conception of the image seems not entirely untouched by Breton's reformulation of Reverdy. Particularly in two respects Breton's change of emphasis regarding Reverdy's image seems to have had some impact on du Bouchet. Firstly, Breton shifted his attention in the *Manifeste* to an image constituted by 'deux réalités *distantes*' (my emphasis), rather than 'plus *ou* moins eloignées' (my emphasis).[6] Secondly, Breton dispensed with Reverdy's notion that '"l'esprit a saisi les rapports" des deux réalités en présence'.[7] By denying us or the mind knowledge of a pre-existing relation between the realities, Breton thus doubly emphasizes the image as a juxtaposition of contrasting realities, because even if the approximated realities are not crassly distinct, their conjunction will come as a surprise to us. The tension in du Bouchet's image seems to consider Reverdy's early text particularly under its aspect of creating a contrast. In Breton's discarding with Reverdy's 'esprit', we can find the influence of his reading of Reverdy on du Bouchet. By disregarding Reverdy's (conscious) 'esprit', Breton, of course, implies that the image is created by the unconscious and goes on to say that '[i]l n'a [...] rien saisi consciemment'.[8] Although neither a conscious nor an unconscious 'esprit' of a poetic subject particularly centres du Bouchet's poetry,[9] the diminishing role accorded to the 'je' in his poetics and even in his interpretations of Reverdy is likely informed by Breton's shifted focus, away from an 'esprit' apprehending the world.[10]

Du Bouchet particularly focuses on those moments in Reverdy's poetry in which the '*je* disparaît dans les grands paysages, dans les marines', as he observes in his 1951 essay 'Envergure de Reverdy' (*AB*, 61, cf. also 50). The perceived disappearance of the 'je' into the scenery in Reverdy also betrays du Bouchet's more general fascination with the alternation of *absence* and *présence* and their interlacement governing the image. In his 1949 essay 'Le Chant des morts' on Reverdy's eponymous *livre d'artiste* with Picasso, parts of which du Bouchet later worked into his 'Envergure de Reverdy', he notes: 'Reverdy poussait à leur limite extrême les points de dilatation et de contradiction' (*AB*, 31). This interest in juxtaposition as appearance and disappearance in the image is quite possibly at least in part motivated by a reading of Reverdy's image as a clash of two juxtaposed realities.[11] However, we should not emphasize too much the importance of contradiction in du Bouchet's readings of Reverdy. On the whole du Bouchet, in 1951, still saw in Reverdy a resolution for stability in the struggle between stability and instability,[12] forming a unifying image in the 'aspiration towards some absolute reality', as Bishop says with regard to Reverdy's image.[13]

Even though du Bouchet, at least with respect to his discussions of Baudelaire and his own poetry, would refrain from such a explicit espousal of stability and uniformity, we see clear continuities between du Bouchet's early interpretive essays on Reverdy and his research output at the *CNRS* (examined in chapter two) about three years later. It is likely that du Bouchet's interpretations of the image in Scève, Hölderlin, Hugo, and Baudelaire are to some degree informed by his previous readings of Reverdy's poetry and the latter's conception of the image in particular. These authors' moving away from a Cartesian subject[14] or a 'point de vue de Dieu',[15] whose self-conscious self grounds perceptions and experiences, shows parallels to du Bouchet's focus on the disappearance of the 'je' in Reverdy. We see traces of du Bouchet's engagement with Reverdy when, in his reading of Baudelaire's 'Le Rêve d'un curieux' four years later, he focuses on the decentred subject trying to see the image of its own death that it itself cannot imagine. Consequently, it is possible that du Bouchet's engagement with Reverdy's clash of two realities in the image — which du Bouchet divested of a Cartesian 'je' — already predisposed him to read Baudelaire's conception of the image as comprising paradoxes without resolution.[16]

In anticipating the coming chapter on Celan, let us take a brief look at the poetic subject in Celan and its interrelation with his image, and compare this with the subject in du Bouchet. As we saw in 'Tenebrae' and 'Bei Wein und Verlorenheit', without the *archetypos* the poetic subject loses its ability to realize its own constitution as subject and to speak truthfully. Insofar as the poetic subject speaks after Babel, the *archetypos* is already lost. However, as we previously indicated with regard to 'Bei Wein und Verlorenheit' and will further discuss in our examination of 'Halbzerfressener', Celan's poetic subject can testify to the *archetypos* by communicating with an other, a 'du'. Insofar as the poetic subject needs the other to tend toward the *archetypos*, the poetic subject in Celan does not occupy an absolute position. Thus, Celan's subject speaks in times of existential threat and shares with the subject in du Bouchet (or the subject du Bouchet attests to Baudelaire) that it is not an absolute anchorage point. The reasons for the subject's loss of an absolute anchorage point in Celan's poetry certainly differ from those in du Bouchet. The Holocaust underlies Celan's poetry as a form of historical eventuation of the Fall of Man and Babel. Celan's (Jewish) poetic subject[17] therefore is fundamentally and continuously threatened — not least due to the resurfacing anti-Semitism in the Goll affair (see previous chapter). Clément Layet points out that du Bouchet was not raised Jewish and escaped the atrocities of Nazism by going into American exile during the war: '[i]l ne se représente pas lui-même comme un Juif survivant. La vie en général lui paraît une "survie insensée", à la fois exposée à l'absurdité, tendue vers le sens, incapable d'échapper absolument au non-sens.'[18] For du Bouchet the loss of an absolute anchorage point in the subject is thus of a poetological nature, an idea he had developed already in his early essays which predate most of his published poetry (cf. chapter 2). The consequences du Bouchet draws for the poetic subject are also more radical than with Celan. Hence, when he writes 'j'écris aussi loin que possible de moi' (*CW* IV, 220),[19] the poetic subject constituted through the written text we read also writes to erase itself from writing. We will return at more length to Celan's and du Bouchet's subject in chapters 7 and 8, where we will more closely examine the connection between du Bouchet's conception of writing and poetic voice.

White Space and Paradox in Reverdy and André du Bouchet

Reverdy's importance for du Bouchet is apparent not only in the latter's inclusion of contradiction or juxtaposition in the image, as evinced in the formulation above, but also for his use of the visuality of the page. While a comparison to Mallarmé and specifically his 'Un coup de dés' seems to naturally suggest itself,[20] du Bouchet's use of paginal space with only one invariant font is actually much closer to Reverdy's poetry.[21] We have already pointed out that this consideration for visuality in du Bouchet's poetry differs from the often very negative role of textual visuality in Celan — if Celan draws attention to it at all. Yet the visual aspect of du Bouchet's poetry is important for more than just the positive role it plays in his poetry. It fundamentally constitutes his poetry, and in this the influence of Reverdy's poetry makes itself felt once again. Like du Bouchet in his poetry, Reverdy often uses the paginal white space to fragment the continuity of the written discourse and to problematize any notion of a meaningful, coherent whole.[22] Underlying this attention to the irruption of the white space upon the written word is a specific understanding of reality for Reverdy:

> [r]*éel* peut désigner le monde concret, les apparences qui sont saisies par les sens; mais par *réel* on peut aussi entendre ce que Bonnefoy appelle la *présence* et qui précisément échappe à la perception. [...] La langage, s'il donne l'existence aux mots, fait s'évanouir la chose; mais les mots eux-mêmes disparaissent et créent l'absence.[23]

According to this view, Reverdy conceives of language as inherently incapable of grasping a form of truer reality hiding away from the word and perception. Du Bouchet's poetry has likewise been read 'as the movement across the heterogeneous towards "le réel"', which is similarly understood as the ulterior or even absolute reality of Reverdy.[24] If their notion of reality were interpreted this way, the irruption of the spaces of the page into the semantic space of the text (in both poets) would hence signify the reality which words have absented. Yet in this interpretation, just like language that had failed to grasp reality, the empty paginal space would only seem to be yet another signifier for the reality that eventually still escapes signification even by the empty space itself: 'un signe, le plus primitif et essentiel de tous, un signe en négatif'.[25] Such a conception of the space of the page as a negative sign — presumably for an absolute reality — is what Riley criticizes in du Bouchet: 'blank space cannot in itself bear semantic substance.'[26]

This merely negative characterization of blank space in Reverdy or in du Bouchet does not do justice to its complex role in their poetry. Serge Linares rightly criticizes such views[27] and Maldiney, likewise, emphasizes that the *blancs* are not to be understood as the 'résultat d'une négation'.[28] The white space should not be seen as mere negative displacement of words that in turn, just like the written word faltering to meaningfully describe reality, only fails to signify reality. It is not simply an absence (or signifier thereof) or silence. Linares emphasizes that it is the interaction, the 'communauté d'appartenance' and the 'réciprocité d'influences' of ink and page on a visual and semantic level, which constitutes poetry for both authors.[29]

In a positive embrace of visuality and white spaces in Reverdy and du Bouchet, some du Bouchet scholars call the blanks 'les *ressources* de son dire'[30] or 'support'.[31] Conceiving of the white space as the source of the poetic text would suggest that the spaces are primary to writing, which in turn would therefore be secondary. The white space as *L'Emportement de muet*, according to one of du Bouchet's poetry volume titles, or as 'fond'[32] would then be the foundation of everything sayable. It is consequently only a small step from this silent source of all meaning to the opinion of Serge Champeau that du Bouchet pursues a 'théologie négative': according to Champeau, the 'fond' is an apophatic evocation of an *archetypos*, which is only 'porté au paraître [...] par le silence'.[33] While other du Bouchet scholars do not seem to share this view of du Bouchet's poetry as a negative theology,[34] some fundamental problems remain with the conception of the white space as 'support' or 'fond'. The issues are apparent enough when du Bouchet's poetry is interpreted along the lines of Martinez, whose oracular description of du Bouchet's poetry in Heideggerian terms as '"l'être sans abri retourné dans l'entier de l'étant"'[35] or as 'réalité ultime de ce que nous nommons le réel' strongly resembles Champeau's theological interpretation, even if Martinez's theology is one in self-denial.[36]

But even if du Bouchet's spaces are interpreted as a surfacing of the source of language in entirely untheological and non-metaphysical terms, I contend that we still misjudge the white space in his poetry. When we think of the space as 'support' or as 'fond', we forget that these very notions of the blanks are enunciated not by the white space itself but by that which it is precisely supposed to provide a ground for: words. In other words, in the very act of ascribing to the white space the notion that it is 'fond' or 'support', it is displaced. On the other hand, any act of ascribing such notions to the blanks can only be meaningful in the presence of white space, in the white space's foregrounding its place in the poetry.

Therefore, in a paradoxical entanglement, the visuality of du Bouchet's texts is only apparent firstly in the interaction of black ink and white space, and secondly in the semantic discourse about this very interaction. The semantic discourse, in turn, is premised upon the visuality of the text. Since every text is visual, but since most texts' visuality is transparent insofar as we are not concerned with their visuality in and of itself but with the meaning the visual symbols of letters carry, I shall call a text 'pictorial' when it draws attention to its visuality for its own sake.[37] A text is pictorial if its visuality is more than just the bearer of linguistic semantic meaning.[38]

In their pictorial qualities, du Bouchet's texts function fundamentally like pictures. The pictorialness of a picture is apparent only by a complex interconnected network of conventions, such as institutional conventions (museums), perceptual conventions (verisimilitude between what is depicted and that which depicts it), and art theoretical and historical conventions (which tell us that, despite their seeming identity, Andy Warhol's Brillo boxes are art whereas those manufactured by Brillo are not; or in the case of abstract art, they tell us that abstract art is art despite the absence of verisimilitude).[39] The pictorialness of du Bouchet's texts is similarly only apparent against a complex framework of textual conventions. While the reader would readily recognize du Bouchet's texts as verse (and thus as poetry), their difference to traditional conventions of verse layout and the way they create (semantic) meaning through words, using visuality only as a means, draws the pictorial aspects of du Bouchet's verse to our attention. The latter create meaning in a way that differs from linguistic, semantic meaning (see footnote 38). Thus, because the white spaces in du Bouchet are pictorial, we should be wary of conflating verbal enunciations of the absence of words as well as semantically expressed instances of space, such as 'écart', 'vide', or 'passage', with the pictorial white space itself.

Du Bouchet is well aware of the *blancs*' dual nature as informing verbal *présences* and *absences* in the texts, while also being different to them:

> [l]es blancs peuvent être considérés comme de séparations, comme des différences qui sont marquées. Mais ces séparations sont des passages, le passage par lequel un mot *se transforme* dans le mot suivant. Le mot suivant d'ailleurs ne peut pas être entendu *dans une seule direction*, mais se retourne souvent sur le mot qui précède et lui donne une coloration tout à fait différente. La métamorphose du mot s'accomplit à l'instigation du mot qui le suit. C'est dans ce rapport, dans cette relation de réciprocité d'un mot à un autre que s'établit le courant poétique.[40]

Du Bouchet points out that the *blancs* both merge and separate the textual parts between which they emerge. External to the semantic discourse of his poems, the *blancs* enter into a differential relation with the text of the poem, their white space giving it quite literally 'une coloration tout à fait différente'. They raise an awareness of the pictorial aspect of his texts, which also lets us read the texts in a non-linear fashion, in ways we would ordinarily look at pictures. It is important to note the twofold and paradoxical manner in which he describes the *blancs* as 'passages' *and* 'séparations'. This is a very typical, contradictory characterization of his poetry, to which we will return in chapter 7, where we touch upon du Bouchet's conception of time as fractions that are also instances of fusion[41] and his understanding of translation as perpetuating but also reaching across a gap between languages. In this chapter we shall concern ourselves foremost with the differential, polychotomous relations between semantic characterizations of visuality (or space) and the pictorial aspect of his poetry. Together, the interactions between these poles constitute his conception of the poetic image.

Du Bouchet's Poetological Text 'Image à terme'

We find further support for our interpretation of du Bouchet's notion of the image as not striving toward an *archetypos* but rather as perennially oscillating between differing poles in his short text 'Image à terme'. Du Bouchet published it in 1954, at about the same time in which he was working on Hölderlin, Hugo, and perhaps already on drafts of his essay 'Baudelaire irrémédiable' (*AB*, 86–88). Layet's assertion that this text 'rassemble sa [de du Bouchet] conception définitive de la poésie'[42] has to be taken with a grain of salt, since this poetological essay was republished several times in different versions. Of the four versions published during his lifetime, three differ from each other in major ways. The first was entitled 'Image à terme' (1954; cf. *AB*, 86–89).[43] The second went by the title 'Résolution de la poésie' (1960). Almost twenty years later, in 1979, du Bouchet published it again under the previous title 'Image à terme' but subjected it to the most significant changes compared to the two earlier versions.[44]

It is already clear from chapter 2 that du Bouchet's interest lies not in any conventional understanding of the image as a visual entity, but in the moment of its destruction or disappearance. The image is both *présente* and *absente* for du Bouchet. This paradoxical understanding of the image grew out of our analysis of du Bouchet's discussion of Baudelaire, where we saw that imagining the moment in which our imagination quite literally ceases to exist, namely in death, grounds us all the more in the here and now, our 'présent réel' as du Bouchet calls it (*AB*, 106): 'sa mort inimaginable, il [Baudelaire] ne peut l'imaginer autrement que comme l'expression la plus nue de sa vie' (*AB*, 105). This expression of life is 'nue' in the two senses of the French word: it is life in its most deprived and naked stage,[45] but it is also life at its most truthful and pure.[46] This is why du Bouchet calls Baudelaire's unimaginable image not only 'vide', as that which evades representation, but also alternatively 'fond' or 'sol'. As such, the confrontation with the absent underlies that which is present and vice versa. It is in a similar light that the title of 'Image à terme' should be understood.

The title already emphasizes that the concept of the image oscillates between certainty and uncertainty; it also underlines how closely image and poetry are associated for du Bouchet.[47] The titular 'Image à terme' is the image at its most accomplished and most terminal, so to speak, in the moment of unrest. As du Bouchet writes in the earliest version (*AB*, 88) and the one published in 1979: '[i]mage parvenue à son terme inquiet.'[48] The poetic image is thus determined by and arrived at ('parvenue à son terme') in its being not final and determined ('inquiet').[49] Furthermore, even the expression 'parvenue à son terme' can be read in two contrasting ways. On the one hand we can understand it as the reaching of an end in the sense of having achieved a goal. However, on the other hand we could also see the image 'parvenue à son terme' as its having come to its end, i.e. as ceasing to exist or dying.[50] The image achieves its end, in the many senses of this phrase, but also continues its existence in its uncertainty.

What could be an example of such an image? Most of du Bouchet's passages that explain his conception of the image also already put this poetics into practice. Even if it is not explicitly introduced as such, we can read the following passage as an example:

> [v]ers le froid auquel ce feu a donné son sens qu'il préfigure, et qui, en récompense, fait mine de le prolonger. Ce feu qui ne tient pas en place. Cette image qui nous accompagne, une fois éteinte, jusqu'au froid, en conservant son pouvoir irradiant, au cœur de notre inattention. (*AB*, 86)

As is common for du Bouchet, he starts *in medias res*, the definite articles and demonstratives ('le', 'ce', 'cette') insinuate a familiarity with 'froid' and 'feu' which is not given by their actual context. Importantly, the beginning of the first main clause is also its end, semantically speaking. The first main clause is opened by '[v]ers le froid'. However, the meaning of 'froid' is prefigured by 'ce feu', as the phrase states. Yet, the 'feu' in turn is postpositioned to the 'froid' with regards to the sequence of words forming the sentence. Consequently, the two opposing terms mutually presuppose each other by virtue of the order of the words and the succession that is semantically implied. Such a reciprocal interaction between dichotomous elements is an integral part of du Bouchet's poetic image, and we have already pointed out that the relation between writing and the *blancs* is an equally reciprocal interaction as 'séparatio[n]' and 'passag[e]'.[51]

The interrelation between 'feu' and 'froid' is further emphasized in the second main clause of the cited passage. Fire prefigures the cold; the cold in turn appears to prolong the fire ('fait mine de le prolonguer'). And yet, fire 'ne tient pas en place', which in turn seems to undermine the entire previous phrase, given that 'feu' and 'froid' seem to be mutually contingent.

As should be clear by now, thinking of fire and cold in mutually exclusive terms is not apposite. Fire and cold both constitute '[c]ette image'. It is an image extinguished to the point of coldness and still retaining the power to radiate — presumably heat and light — like fire. If one initially conceives of 'éteinte' in opposition to 'image' and 'irradiant' in du Bouchet's poetry, it soon becomes clear that they are clearly to be seen as mutually presupposing. Du Bouchet's paradoxes become even stronger in his altered version of 'Image à terme', published twenty-three years later, allowing us to see the maturation and radicalization of his poetics. The above-cited passage, which is one of the few preserved at heart, even if slightly altered, from the first version, reads in the 1979 edition:

> [c]e feu qui, sans même adhérer au terme qui le désigne, ne tient pas en place (qu'on le nomme froid, aussi bien...)   Cette image déroutée qui, une fois éteinte, nous accompagne au cœur de notre inattention.   Cet élargissement
> de son premier éclat jusqu'à la banalité.[52]

The opposition of 'feu' and 'froid' is even more clearly dissolved in this passage. Du Bouchet straightforwardly says that fire may just as well be called cold. This paradoxical equivalence between 'feu' and 'froid' is underlined by a previously described reluctance of the fire to simply adhere to its own name ('sans même adhérer au terme qui le désigne'). Fire untethered from its linguistic designation also implies its uncoupling from any specific place, being spatially as well as temporally not locatable ('qui [...] ne tient pas en place'; already in the first version of 'Image à terme').

We can also revisit the titles of du Bouchet's essays 'Image à terme'. We have already seen that 'Image à terme' can be both the image brought to fruition and the image destroyed. Yet, in light of the above-cited phrase, 'à terme' seems to also play on the act of denoting, fixing something by a term ('adhérer au terme') and thereby also ending it ('à terme'). The image, however, is 'inquiet' and thus does not necessarily adhere 'au terme qui le désigne'. Thus, if 'Image à terme' is the essay in which du Bouchet explains what he means by the term 'image', this definition is pronounced and problematized at once. If du Bouchet has laid down his definitive conception of the image and poetry in this essay, as Layet says, then his image and poetry seek to evade the confines of definition at the same time. Of course, such an *inquiétude* that persists through infinity can only be insinuated in the finite space of poetic writing. Nevertheless, we should remark that the phrase 'image parvenue à son terme inquiet' keeps its promise: it does not conclude the essay just as it does not conclude what the image is. In both the earliest version and that of 1979, the phrase is only the penultimate sentence, thereby refusing to be the last, defining word on the image.

Let us now return to du Bouchet's *blancs*, which are so often conceived as 'fond' or 'support', as if they were a fixed 'image à terme' rather than an 'image parvenue à son terme inquiet'. Such an interpretation seems to be supported when he says in his 'Image à terme' from 1979: 'la parole débordée, dans son emportement, aille droit à une destruction [followed by white space, J. K.]', or when he writes: '[p]oésie. Déjà, ce n'est plus d'elle qu'il s'agit. Sa force est dehors, dans la | plénitude qui l'entame.'[53] Speech and language reach their point of destruction, since they cease as soon as the phrase ends and is replaced by white space. If we take these words at face value, true poetry lies in the 'dehors' outside of the text. However, an obvious question imposes itself: if the white 'dehors' is what constitutes poetry, why are du Bouchet's pages inscribed at all? The contours of an answer should already have emerged from our discussion of his texts and of du Bouchet's own characterization of the *blancs* thus far. The page signifies its being 'dehors' or 'emportement' only in its being inscribed as such. Du Bouchet's poetry embodies and expresses the conscious negotiation of these reciprocal interactions between page and text. Hence in the phrase '[p]oésie. Déjà, ce n'est plus d'elle qu'il s'agit. Sa force est dehors, dans la | plénitude qui l'entame', the power of poetry resides as much in the written word 'dehors' as in the paginal dehors or *blancs*. Poetry not only ceases when words appear on the page ('déjà, ce n'est plus d'elle qu'il s'agit'), but poetic inscription ceases as well in the *blancs*. Only in the interaction of the two do we encounter, for an instant in which they fuse,[54] the force of poetry. Du Bouchet's poetic image is thus nourished not by the white gaps between parts of the text but by the gaps, as it were, between the white gaps and the text. It is the difference between text and page and their reciprocal interaction based on this difference from which poetry springs.

A Framework for Reading Du Bouchet's Pictorial Image

We should now consider the distinct types of interactions possible between the different aspects of du Bouchet's text. If the blank space were in a simple oppositional relation to the text, or if the blank space were simply to be equated with the semantically enunciated 'support' or 'fond' as 'face | du papier',[55] we would end up with a binary relation between semantic text and space in either case. But as we know by now, the relation is more complex. Neither is the semantically expressed 'face du papier' the surface of paper itself, nor is the mere surface of paper sufficient unto itself to constitute the poetic image. Since poetry arises from the contrast and interaction between *blancs* and text, we get a sense of why du Bouchet could say of the *blancs* that 'ces séparations sont des passages'.[56] The nature of the interaction between *blancs* and text in practice perhaps becomes clearer when we take a look at the following:

> face
> du papier

The irruption of the paper surface clearly disrupts the pictorial continuity of the black text. Yet, in a different sense the white space between the textual fragments also provides continuity, because the semantically described irruption of the 'face | du papier' into the text is also enacted by the pictorial irruption into the text, thereby aligning to an extent the semantic with non-semantic meaning. Hence we understand the dual relation enacted by the *blancs* which du Bouchet described so paradoxically as 'séparations' and 'passages'. Because of the difference between the words 'face | du papier' and that very surface itself, they reciprocally ('cette relation de réciprocité') invest each other with meanings they could not have by themselves. The paper would be meaningless without the text with which it interacts. The text, on the other hand, would not make us aware of its visual or material properties without these properties' making themselves apparent as such.

Having explained the fundamental principles of du Bouchet's poetic image, its paradoxes and pictorial dimension, and having explained some examples in detail, we should now try to schematize the different types of interaction and contrast between paper and text. These manifold distinctions and possibilities of interaction within du Bouchet's text I call the 'polychotomous image'. As we see in the model below, the two horizontal levels are divided by pictorial and semantic elements. The horizontal line comprising the semantic level of the text is (1) divided by what I have previously called *absence* and *présence* (see chapter 2). An interaction or tension between *absence* and *présence* is felt in those intra-semantic moments in which the text enunciates its own *absence*. For example, when du Bouchet writes: 'dans le mot

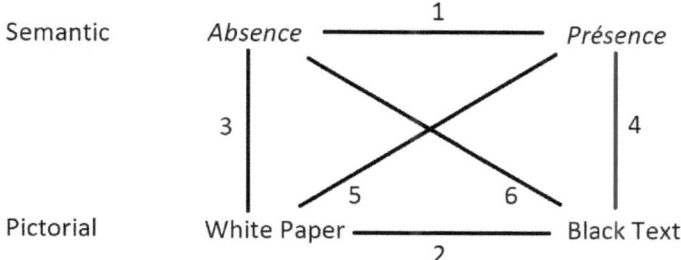

FIG. 5.1.: A framework for reading du Bouchet's pictorial image.

le silence,'[57] the words while speaking are claiming to be silent. These tensions between *absence* and *présence* can take on very different forms, and they have most explicitly preoccupied du Bouchet in his engagement with his poetic predecessors.

Number (2) is the basic visual difference between white paper and black text, as shown on the second horizontal line. Of course, any semantic and pictorial operation is contingent on the fact that there is a text and that there is therefore a distinction in colour between the text and that on which the text is written.[58] In this sense all the other distinctions, (1) to (6), hinge on (2).

The most striking interactions in du Bouchet's poetic image involve the four other categories. Number (3) denotes the interaction between white paginal space and verbal, semantic *absence* of text evoked by the text which is necessarily written and thus different to a pictorial absence of text. We already encountered an example of this above when we discussed the 'face | du papier' in du Bouchet's poem 'Essor'. Examples like this one are plentiful in du Bouchet, for instance when he writes:

> à l'écart de la parole
> le vif qui l'entretient[59]

We notice that 'parole' semantically absents itself by saying that it is 'à l'écart', to then be pictorially absented by the white space. Once again, we are reminded of du Bouchet's conception of his *blancs* as 'séparations [qui] sont des passages', when in the second line the 'écart' or the gap is described as the liveliness or the heart ('vif') which makes 'parole' possible. Thus, while the gap interrupts speech, it enables it at the same time. It does so on two levels: first, its pictorialness reminds us that the white space of the paper constitutes the foundation of the textual inscriptions in ink. Second, the poetic discourse on the *absence* of speech semantically points us to the significance of the paper as a foundation for our creating meaning (this significance is also pictorially embodied by the gaps).

We encounter number (4) when the text semantically affirms its *présence* while also raising our awareness of the pictorial, written dimension of the text, for instance when the inscription of words onto the page is affirmed by the meaning of these words themselves:

> mot en place[60]

To be sure, any semantic self-affirmation as word or text can necessarily only be realized as text, since the existence of semantic meaning is contingent on the existence of text (see also (2)). Nonetheless the effect of (4) is particularly strong when a discourse of semantic *présence* is further supported by a lack of pictorial gaps, ensuring textual continuity.

Number (5) points out the contrast between verbally expressed, semantic *présence* and the white paginal spaces which constitute an absence of black ink and thus also an absence of semantic *présence*. Numbers (5) and (3) are effectively the two opposing sides of the same coin. Hence in our example for (3), the 'parole' first semantically absented itself ('écart de la parole') to then be absented pictorially by white gaps in the text following upon the 'écart de la parole'. In (5), on the other hand, there is less of an agreement, so to speak, between the semantic and pictorial levels of meaning. The text semantically affirms its *présence* as text, yet its pictorial, textual presence is interrupted or immediately superseded by white space:

> un mot
> anime   comme à la route[61]

As we see in this example, the divergence between what is semantically expressed and pictorially realized does not have to appear as a conflict. The word 'un mot' clearly addresses its own constitution as (semantic) text, but what this *présence* of discourse animates is the white gap. Yet, this animation through the (semantic) word also appears to be nourished by the gap that is the line break between 'un mot' and 'anime'. Once again, while semantic *présence* and pictorial gaps here make us aware of their difference, in so doing they also remind us of their reciprocal dependence. We should also direct our attention back to (4) which, like (3), is in close relation with (5). Whereas in (4) semantic *présence* and pictorial presence of text are in agreement — just as semantic *absence* and pictorial absence of text were in agreement in (3) — (5) emphasizes the difference and mutual contingency between semantic *présence* and our awareness of the page's pictorial properties.

Number (6) indicates a difference between the black ink considered as pictorial phenomenon and a semantically professed *absence*. For example in the phrase 'papier sans un mot',[62] paper's *présence* is semantically affirmed. Thus, paper appears not as itself, as paginal space, but in the form of words. On the other hand, the words semantically announce their *absence* despite their obvious textual presence.

We should already have an inkling how much (1) to (6) interdepend, and we should be under no illusion that our model is more than a heuristic one. I have numbered the interactions and separated them to show the principal, combinatorial possibilities of relations between these four different main elements of du Bouchet's poetic image. Nonetheless, the boundaries between (1) and (6) are not to be seen as strict, since our judgment of which of the two cases applies depends upon how much text (and space) we take into consideration. Thus, if in the last example we consider the paginal layout surrounding the phrase, we discover that paper is not only semantically *présent* as 'papier', that is, as text *on* paper, but also *as* paper, of which we are *pictorially* made aware by the elaborate spacing:

> papier sans un mot

After having established this framework, it is now time to analyse more closely how these differences interact in full poems rather than excerpts. For this reason, we will be looking at du Bouchet's 'Peinture' from the volume *Ici en deux* first published in 1986.[63]

The Image in Du Bouchet's 'Peinture'

'Peinture' is one of several texts by du Bouchet bearing this title. In 1983 du Bouchet had published a volume of poetic meditations under this name,[64] and even within *Ici en deux* the title 'Peinture' for a poem occurs twice. Together, the two poems frame the text 'Notes sur la traduction', which are, in turn, framed by the two homonymous poems 'Fraîchir'. From the frequent occurrence of the title 'Peinture' we can infer that the relation between language and painting or visual arts more generally is at the heart of du Bouchet's poetic concern. Below, I will analyse the first of the two 'Peinture' poems from *Ici en deux*, which is representative for du Bouchet's conception of the image more generally.[65]

The poem's title, 'Peinture', alerts the reader to the fact that this poem seeks to be understood not only by verbal means. The *blancs* underline this impression by surfacing between the sections (the sections are separated according to the following scheme: 4+5+4+7), between lines, and even within lines. The discontinuous and incomplete syntax confronts us with considerable difficulties in understanding the poem. Nonetheless we can tentatively trace some continuities through the poem. In some parts, particularly in the second section, the poem seems to circumscribe a gaze out of a window or door with its mention of 'l'embrasure' and 'croisée'. Various mentions of flowering ('fleurit' and 'floraison') then appear to give us an impression of what is seen through the window or door. These motifs recur throughout the poem, forming a guiding thread.

On another level, however, the poem is clearly an examination or negotiation of seeing and displaying as such. We encounter classical tropes from poetic and artistic treatises, such as the 'ressemblance avérée',[66] and different forms of seeing and appearance or illusion suggest that this poem is concerned with fundamental poetological questions framed in the particular context of a gaze out of the window or door.[67] There seem to exist two worlds or realities in the poem. One is a form of received reality ('monde reçu') and the 'choses' with their 'air d'attente' also appear to be of this order of reality. A second reality seems to be the 'réalité [...] qui ne ressemble à rien', situated beyond appearance ('à travers toute apparence'). This reality is not received but pursued and seems to be associated with openings, interstices, and the motif of flowering. As soon as we have reached our object or reality of desire, however, it is lost ('elle se perde dans une différence infinie').

Much of this echoes du Bouchet's *Carnet* note on Hölderlin discussed in chapter 2. In the note du Bouchet discerned Hölderlin's 'vision nette' to be the opening and frame (the 'encadrement de la fenêtre') of vision, rather than being an ulterior, archetypal reality. The 'encadrement' as situated between the one who sees and that which is seen seemed almost to become the 'vision parfaite' itself. Thus, we saw that at a very early stage in du Bouchet's writing the interstice of vision became vision as interstice. Yet eventually this interstice was formed into an archetypal 'lucidité de Dieu' rather than forming the *archetypos* into the interstice and thereby abandoning this notion altogether. We will see in du Bouchet's 'Peinture' that he has abandoned the notion of the *archetypos*. The ulterior 'réalité' which seems to be desired and pursued in the poem may remind us of the notion of the *archetypos*. Yet as we will see, this 'réalité' is a relation rather than an absolute, as would be the case if it were archetypal. It lies somewhere between the poles of seeing and not seeing ('on [...] voit', 'on ne voit pas'), losing itself in a 'différence infinie'.

The first words of the poem suggest they had been awaiting the reader's gaze to traverse the indentation which had preceded them ('air d'attente'). The apparent tension of the first lines is not only owing to the poem's beginning with a gap rather than words, but also due to the two conflicting forms of temporality implied in these lines. The immediate present of 'aussitôt' stands in contrast to a sense of anteriority to this present insinuated by 'attente'. Since the 'choses' seem to await our gaze as soon as we see them, they must have been present before we had actually seen them. Thus, the notion that these 'choses' are waiting seems to retrospectively inject their presence into the gap which precedes their having become visible to us through the written mention of 'choses' (number 5 in our model). And yet, any such idea of anteriority is contingent on a temporal here and now expressed by 'aussitôt' and on the 'choses' being seen, as the apposition in the second line makes clear: we realize the 'air d'attente' of the 'choses' only 'aussitôt qu'on les voit'. It is not entirely certain that the 'choses' are to be equated with words (this interpretation would be supported by other passages in du Bouchet's poetry where the word or language is equated with things or matter).[68] The 'choses' could also include the opening gap, especially since the homophony of 'air d'attente' with 'aire d'attente' (waiting area) seems to put emphasis on the spatial aspect of the 'choses'.

While we are looking at the 'choses' we recognize them, as the second and third lines suggest. Yet, it is unclear what exactly they resemble. Do the 'choses' resemble each other? Do they, *in toto*, resemble an unknown other? We are confronted with a resemblance devoid of the binary relation it is supposed to establish. We can surmise that we verify this resemblance of the 'choses' at the same moment at which we perceive them and realize that they have been waiting for our gaze. Is it thus possible that the 'ressemblance avérée' of the 'choses' is their resembling the white space that preceded the phrase? Yet, this would imply that white space and 'choses' are not identical. Based on this assumption, we would presume that the poem begins in the white space before these words, so that these words are waiting for us until we read them. In the end, we are only able to determine that the 'choses' await our recognition, even if we do not know what the 'choses' are.

What obscures this passage's accessibility to a conventional reading is that the white spaces exert an unspoken influence not only on the pictorial qualities of the page, but also on how we understand the text. The blanks even appear to shape the text's grammar. Even though the sentence from lines two to five commences as a question ('est-ce'), it ends on a reaffirming 'ici' and a full stop. There is no location in the text in which we could pinpoint the question's turning into a normal sentence. The turn takes place outside the written text and we can only see the effect on the text, reinforcing the feeling of a semantic and grammatical absence already apparent the relations of 'ressemblance' whose relata remain unclear.

So far, we have focused on evidence of anteriority, whether expressed semantically in the text or, more subtly, attested by our inkling that changes in the text are caused by the gaps which are not part of the text. In turn, we only recognized these changes *ex post* as we read that the text had changed. However, as we read the deictic 'ici' it is clear that any sense of anteriority has vanished, and we also realize that the phrase is no longer a question. We seem to have arrived at the immediate present. Perhaps here we have reached the 'coïncidence de temps' in du Bouchet's poetry of which Yves Peyré speaks: the immediate present becoming the point of unification, into which past and future merge.[69] This arrival at a point of unity also seems to be suggested in the last lines of the first section. We apparently recognize the things ('nous les saurons') and concurrently recognize ourselves ('en même temps que nous'), a process which culminates in the 'ici'. The spacing which sets off 'ici' from the rest of the section seems to further emphasize the independence and self-containment of this recognition where recognizing subject and object coincide.[70]

Yet, this coincidence and union towards which du Bouchet's poetic image strives, these 'instant[s] [de] fusion' should also be considered as 'fraction'.[71] And, indeed, Michel Collot in his preface to du Bouchet's volume of poetry *Ici en deux*, from which this poem is taken, points out that 'ici' is not only a point of unity but also of doubling and deferment (number 1):

> Ce dédoublement s'inscrit dans la physionomie et l'étymologie du mot *ici*, avec ses deux *i* séparés par un *c*, qui nous rappellent que l'adverbe français ne vient pas du latin *hic*, mais de sa forme redoublée *ecce hic*, doublement déictique: 'voici ici'. Comme si la langue ne pouvait désigner le lieu où l'on est qu'au prix d'un redoublement qui, à la fois, le met en vue (*ecce*), et le met à l'écart, le scinde en deux, le dédouble (*ecce hic*). Le langage est ce pli par lequel le lieu, pour accéder à la conscience de soi, cesse de résider en lui-même.[72]

While these words by Collot are meant to introduce the reader to du Bouchet's volume of poetry *Ici en deux* in general, they are just as fitting for the 'ici' in this poem, because here, too, it 'cesse de résider en lui-même'. The 'ici' is not an absolute *locus*, nor is it a final point in time. The 'ici' breaks into two. This is not only true in the etymological sense Collot evokes, but also when the inherently dual nature of this painting-poem is called to mind again. Any form of seeing and knowing so central to the first section relies on the dual nature of the words and page as pictorial 'choses' and semantically meaningful entities.

It may be for this reason that the poem does not end on the climactic 'ici'. The 'ici' is merely a gateway to the second section, where the focus shifts. Instead of the 'choses' which we know and recognize, we encounter a 'réalité [...] qui ne ressemble à rien'. This other reality seems to escape our abilities to meaningfully and positively designate it. It is an 'autre' which we desire to bring into our compass of signification and knowledge, given the context of the first section where we recognized the 'choses'. After the first two lines in the second section which introduce this 'réalité' by negative description, we realize that 'déjà, dans l'embrasure, elle fleurit'. Reality flourishes in the gap or opening ('l'embrasure') and it has already been flourishing ('déjà') when we turn our attention to it, indicating its evasiveness to our grasp.

As we pointed out before, the motif of the opening ('embrasure') in 'Peinture' reminds us of the 'encadrement de la fenêtre' in du Bouchet's early note on Hölderlin.[73] Hölderlin's 'vision nette', despite initially being thought of as interstice and as that which demarcates the boundaries of sight ('encadrement'), eventually turned into a transcendent 'lucidité de Dieu'. In contrast, the 'réalité' in 'Peinture', thirty-six years later, remains an interval, in multiple senses of the word. The words 'l'embrasure' and 'le halo' insinuate that the 'réalité' is not something self-contained just as the various notions of flowering suggest that it is also not something stable and fixed. But this reality is not only semantically *présent* as opening and *absent* insofar as the centre of an opening is a void (number 1). This 'réalité' can also be considered as a pictorial interval. The 'embrasure' in which the reality already ('déjà') flowers — that is, before we read that it does — could be understood to be the gap preceding the 'déjà'. This gap is also (roughly) in the centre of the section, perhaps mirroring the opening of 'embrasure'. The reality thus enunciates its *présence* in words ('elle fleurit'), but its presence also somehow precedes its verbal expression. Thus, the flowering of this 'réalité' is realized in the interaction between the pictorial and semantic components of this poetic image (number 5). It is the oscillation or interaction between these two poles which constitutes the *poème-peinture*. Du Bouchet's poetry is nourished by these tensions and it is hence not a coincidence that this 'réalité' is paradoxically equivalent to something as intangible and immaterial as a 'halo', but also a static opening ('embrasure') through which we can look; and that it grows organically, while also being basically static ('presque sans émoi').[74]

In the first two sections we have encountered the 'choses' awaiting our recognizing gaze and a 'réalité' which we wished to apprehend, but which did not resemble anything and therefore could not be recognized. Reality was enigmatically both present and absent in a semantic and pictorial sense (numbers 1 and 5 of our model). In the third section we return to the reality or 'choses' we know from the first section, which here appears to us as 'monde reçu'. After traversing noun phrase fragments devoid of any movement induced by verbs (thereby fulfilling the promise of 'presque sans émoi' which had concluded the previous section), we see a sky broken up by branches. How did we arrive at this view? It is quite possible that what we see is enabled by the 'réalité' of the second section, which is an opening and light ('embrasure', 'halo') and thereby makes possible that we see something in the first place. The noun phrases, such as 'le carreau' and 'les pampres', in the third section would then be what offers itself to our gaze 'à travers' this door of the 'réalité'.

What is particularly noteworthy about this gaze in section three is that it seems devoid of depth. What we see is a two- rather than three-dimensional view. The description of the sky as being broken up, presumably by the 'branchages', especially lends itself to such a reading. Ordinarily we would assume that the branches are in front of the sky and thereby impede our view of it. In this perspective the sky would be whole and would only be perceived to be fragmented by branches. In the poem, however, the sky is broken. Pictorially speaking, our seeing the sky is also broken up by the line break between the preposition 'dans' and 'les branchages'. We examine the planarity of our gaze through the (metaphorical) door, because it reflects on the nature of this *poème-peinture* itself. Neither the semantic expression of the words nor the pictorialness of the poem are three-dimensional and hence visuality in the poem is reflected on and reflected as two-dimensional. The two-dimensional, dichromatic visuality is complemented by other sets of — often contrasting — dualities. Our 'monde reçu', viewed anew through the 'embrasure' of 'la réalité', appears fresh and tired, growing and broken before our eyes. All of these juxtaposing notions are joined into a paradoxical chain by the alliteration between 'se fêle', 'fleurit', 'fatigue', and 'fraîcheur'. More and more 'la réalité [...] qui ne ressemble à rien' seems not only to frame our vision but to underlie how we perceive the 'monde reçu'.

This seems to be what the following section expresses. As we saw the 'fraîcheur' of our 'monde reçu' in the last line of the previous section, presumably by means of 'la réalité', the last section of the poem indicates that we now are 'parvenus à cette chose même que nous avons désirée'. This 'chose même' seems to be nothing else than 'la réalité' itself from the second section, since we had desired but could not grasp it then and have arrived at it now. Our world, which we perceive, and the evasive 'réalité' seem to be moving closer together. The ostensibly increasing convergence of 'monde reçu' and 'réalité' seems to also be spatially indicated. The two sections can be considered as spatial complements, since they could be fitted together almost seamlessly ('il arrive' being preceded by 'reçu'), further reinforcing the semantic link between 'reçu' and 'il arrive'. We are reminded of du Bouchet's note on Hölderlin's 'vision nette' in 1950. In the note the 'vision parfaite' was initially conceived as lying in the interstice or the frame — the 'encadrement de la fenêtre' — rather than in an archetypal vision or envisioned *archetypos* itself. Yet ultimately, the frame and medium of vision became this very *archetypos*. Even though our 'monde reçu' and the 'réalité' seem to close in, and we seem to have arrived at the enigmatic 'chose même', there is no *archetypos*. The moment we arrive at our object of desire, 'elle [la chose même] se perde | dans une différence infinie.' Akin to the 'image parvenue à terme inquiet', we have reached ('parvenus') what we desired only to realize that it is inherently unreachable and cannot be transfixed ('inquiet', 'différence infinie').

Let us take a closer look at the nature of this 'différence infinie'. Hoyt Rodgers translates it as an 'infinite otherness'. The nominalization of 'other' by means of the suffix '-ness' places a substantial amount of stress on 'otherness' as an absolute state or even substance. As such, this otherness recalls Plotinus's absolute 'other'.[75] 'Otherness' here thus seems to point to an absolute beyond. However, the French 'différence infinie' appears to place its emphasis slightly differently on the act of differing. Du Bouchet's 'différence infinie' is more reminiscent of a differing *ad infinitum*. Rather than focusing on the 'other*ness*' of an absolute, du Bouchet seems to accentuate the *relation* between two terms, that is, their differing from one another *ad infinitum*.[76] We should keep du Bouchet's accentuation of a relational differing in mind when we look at his translation by 'rien' of the 'Nichts' in Celan's poem 'Erblinde' (chapter 8). Here, too, du Bouchet does not opt for the more absolute *néant*, which would have been reminiscent of apophatic mysticism, but rather uses the relative negation 'rien'. Whereas du Bouchet's poetic image is characterized by seeking to create a 'rapport' between the differing poles that constitute his poetic image 'à terme inquiet',[77] Celan desires to testify to an *archetypos* that proves to be similarly perennially elusive as du Bouchet's 'rapport' that is lost in infinite difference but is understood as an absolute Otherness.

To what does this infinitely differing relation in du Bouchet's 'Peinture' relate? As we have seen, there are two forms of realities or 'choses' which du Bouchet seeks to unite or at least join: 'la réalité [...] qui ne ressemble à rien' and the 'monde reçu'. This attempt at unification certainly recalls the 'rapprochement' of the 'deux réalités' in Reverdy's conception of the image. However, as should be clear from the many doublings and juxtapositions in 'Peinture', du Bouchet's 'rapprochement' of two realities does not mean that they become the same, nor do they seek to approach an absolute reality as did Reverdy (see above). Although there seems to be a semantic discourse of 'la réalité', taken to be *absente*, and a 'monde', understood as 'reçu' and *présente*, du Bouchet's interest is not in an ultimate 'réalité' as a form of *archetypos*, but rather in the relation of the two realities. Yet, this relation is perennially unstable as is not only suggested in the semantic discourse on the 'différence infinie', but also by the tension and interaction between black ink and *blancs*. It is these contrasting poles of du Bouchet's image between which the infinitely differing relations are established (as visually represented in our model). They are joined in an 'instant [de] fusion' that is also necessarily 'une fraction de temps'.[78] Given that what is sought to be unified in 'Peinture' are a 'réalité' inherently without resemblance to anything and a reality whose resemblance is affirmed, it is not surprising that their union bears the sign of their difference.

In the subsequent lines we do not escape du Bouchet's paradoxes. Initially, it seems we return to more concreteness and discover variations of certain motifs which we previously encountered. The 'bleu' reminds us of the colour of the 'ciel' of the 'monde reçu', whereas the 'croisée' can be linked to the 'embrasure' as a type of opening which had been associated with 'la réalité'. These two worlds now seem to merge. Yet du Bouchet's paradoxical description leaves open how and if this is achieved at all. Not only are we to have 'nulle illusion' in the moment of confusion over the two worlds, but furthermore that which is merged of the two worlds is a visibly coloured light ('lumière au bleu') which then somehow is not seen ('qu'on ne voit pas').

In this paradoxical tension 'qui ne fléchit pas',[79] we are confronted with the question: 'qui, alors, | dira le nom des choses reconnues ?' This question perhaps most explicitly exposes the problem of poetic expression in the poem. Since poetic expression is commonly thought of as being constituted by words, which often stand for objects, in this poem these 'choses' — at least the 'chose même' or 'la réalité' — have slipped away from our attempts to transfix them by denotation. We recall that from the beginning the 'choses' were awaiting our gaze and recognition and yet precisely that which we desired, the reality presumably underlying the 'monde reçu', would escape our recognizing gaze ('ne ressemble à rien'). The 'réalité' was already flowering in the interstice ('déjà, dans l'embrasure, elle fleurit') and would lose itself in an infinite difference when we thought to have grasped it ('se perde | dans une différence infinie'). We realized that this 'réalité' is characterized by the gaps, interactions, and differences in the poetic image. Indeed, the last question posed in the poem — 'qui, alors, | dira le nom des choses reconnues ?' — remains unanswered. Instead, we find out once again that the 'choses' 'ont fleuri' 'déjà, dans cette attente'. This flowering happens without the 'choses' being named. They bloom between the paradoxical poles of speaking and not speaking. The closing line makes this unmistakably clear. Here, in the *passé composé* of 'ont fleuri', we are confronted with a concluded action: once again, the final development has taken place elsewhere — presumably in the gap between the question and the assertion that the 'choses [...] ont fleuri'. The last line of the poem hence retains the polychotomous nature of du Bouchet's poetic image. It enunciates the final development but cannot embody it itself, as text. The '[choses] ont fleuri' only between the pictorial and semantic.

Let us take a step back from the close discussion of the poem and return to our comparative analysis of Celan and du Bouchet. In stark contrast to the previous chapter, in which we saw that Celan associated archetypal and truthful poetic speech with the spoken rather than the written word, we discovered in this chapter that du Bouchet's image conceives of itself and consciously displays itself as writing. Celan's desire for his poetry to communicate by tending toward an *archetypos*, unifying poetic discourse, and eliminating the possibility of misunderstanding, is in patent juxtaposition with du Bouchet's polychotomous image in which contradictions are not resolved. A seeming final resolution in du Bouchet, for instance in '[des choses] ont fleuri', is thus intimated only *between* the polychotomous poles of du Bouchet's image. Du Bouchet's emphasis on the interstice and continuous interactions between the different elements of his image evade the implied hierarchy in Celan's striving toward an *archetypos*. The difference in their notion of the image also has distinct implications for how Celan and du Bouchet conceptualize space. In our discussion of the poem 'Peinture' we saw that du Bouchet's space is often planar and horizontal. On the other hand, Celan's quest for archetypal speech implies a conception of space that is vertical, as we have already found out from the upward trajectory of the poetic voice in 'Bei Wein und Verlorenheit' and as will become clear in the poem 'Halbzerfressener' discussed in the following chapter. From our discussion in this chapter, we can also stipulate one further, last difference between Celan and du Bouchet: du Bouchet's 'other' is not an 'otherness' or a Neoplatonic absolutely 'Other'. Rather, the interactions between the differing elements of his image are 'other' to each other. That is, they perpetually express their reciprocal differing, their (relative) distinction from each other, and thus in du Bouchet's poetry there is no singular *archetypos*, a capital-O Other, but a perennial othering. While Celan does not unambiguously affirm that his poems speak for or are addressed to an absolutely Other, their seeking out a dialogical 'Du' that is other to the poetic voice also expresses the wish to speak for more, for a 'ganz Anderen' (*M*, 8), as we will see in the following chapter.

Notes to Chapter 5

1. Cf. also Michel Collot, 'Bouchet, André du', in *Dictionnaire de poésie de Baudelaire à nos jours*, ed. by Michel Jarrety (Paris: Presses Universitaires de France, 2001), pp. 85–89 (pp. 85–87).
2. Reverdy, n.p. (emphases in original).
3. Cf. esp. Michael Bishop, 'Pierre Reverdy's Conception of the Image', *Forum for Modern Language Studies*, 12.1 (1976), 25–36 (p. 27).
4. Ibid.
5. Cf. particularly Breton, *Manifestes du Surréalisme*, pp. 52–57.
6. Breton, *Manifestes du Surréalisme*, p. 52.
7. Ibid.
8. Ibid.
9. Layet, 'Temps apparent', pp. 239–40. We should also note du Bouchet's general disinclination to give in to biographical considerations with regards to his poetry. Layet has pointed out this tendency in contradistinction to Celan: Clément Layet, 'La Survie insensée', *Europe*, 94.1049/50 (2016), 176–87 (pp. 179–80).
10. Other influences on the shift away from a subject-centred perspective have been discussed in chapter 2.
11. Cf. also Bishop's remarks about movement and lack, or voidness ('vide'), in Reverdy and du Bouchet: Bishop, *Altérités d'André du Bouchet*, p. 68.
12. ' "L'œuvre d'art lutte contre le déséquilibre du mouvement", écrit-il [Reverdy] encore dans *Le Gant de crin*. Ce déséquilibre qui fait la nécessité du poème. Puis il ajoute: "Le mouvement n'est possible que dans l'ensemble universel où il retrouve toujours le sens de l'équilibre" ' (*AB*, 57).
13. Bishop, 'Pierre Reverdy's Conception of the Image', p. 29.
14. As Karin J. Dillman says of Rimbaud, who perceived himself to be the successor of Baudelaire (as the first of the *poètes voyants*); Karin J. Dillman, *The Subject in Rimbaud: From Self to 'Je'*. (New York: Lang, 1984), pp. 44–45.
15. Layet, 'Temps apparent', p. 232.
16. Cf. du Bouchet's remarks about contradiction in Baudelaire: 'une contradiction sans borne et sans aboutissement' (Veinstein, p. 23).
17. Cf. Marina Cvetaeva's dictum that '[a]lle Dichter sind Juden', which precedes his poem 'Und mit dem Buch aus Tarussa' (*KG*, 164). For a context of this quote, see Regina Grundmann, '*Rabbi Faibisch, Was auf Hochdeutsch heißt Apollo': Judentum, Dichtertum, Schlemihltum in Heinrich Heines Werk* (Stuttgart: Metzler, 2008), p. 426. See also Christine Ivanović, *Das Gedicht im Geheimnis der Begegnung: Dichtung und Poetik Celans im Kontext seiner russischen Lektüren* (Tübingen: Niemeyer, 1996), p. 288.
18. Layet refers to this passage as well. Layet, 'La Survie insensée', p. 179.
19. Also cited by Layet, 'La Survie insensée', p. 180.
20. Cf. e.g. Sohn.
21. For more on this idea, see particularly Linares, 'Quant au blanc'.
22. Cf. e.g. Michel Collot, 'La Syntaxe du visible: Reverdy et l'esthétique cubiste', in *Reverdy aujourd'hui: Actes du colloque des 22, 23, 24 juin 1989*, ed. by Michel Collot and Jean-Claude Mathieu (Paris: Presses de l'École Normale Supérieure, 1991), pp. 67–77 (p. 73).
23. Y.-A. Favre, 'Le "Réel absent" ', in *Le Centenaire de Pierre Reverdy: Actes du colloque d'Angers*, ed. by Yvan Leclerc and Georges Cesbron (Angers: Presses de l'Université d'Angers, 1990), pp. 25–34 (p. 27). Cf. also: 'la réalité est, pour Reverdy, insaisissable et mouvante; elle ne saurait

être captée dans sa totalité', in: Michel Collot, 'La Syntaxe du visible: Reverdy et l'esthétique cubiste', p. 74.
24. Glenn Fetzer, *Palimpsests of the Real in Recent French Poetry* (Amsterdam: Rodopi, 2004), p. 132.
25. Nina Catach cited inj Isabelle Chol, *Pierre Reverdy: Poésie plastique. Formes composées et dialogue des arts (1913–1960)* (Geneva: Droz, 2006), p. 208.
26. Peter Riley, 'The Apophatic Poetry of André du Bouchet', *The Fortnightly Review* (2015) <http://fortnightlyreview.co.uk/2015/04/andre-du-bouchet-riley/> [accessed 4 July 2015], n.p.. This is a rather premature point by Riley, because words, likewise, do not in themselves bear semantic substance either, unless one is to subscribe to pre-Saussurean traditions of thinking about language, assuming an inherent connection between 'ontos' and 'logos'. Rogers is right to correct Riley on this, see Hoyt Rogers, 'Translating André du Bouchet', *The Fortnightly Review* (2015) <http://fortnightlyreview.co.uk/2015/06/translating-andre-du-bouchet/> [accessed 31 May 2016].
27. Cf. Linares, 'Quant au blanc', p. 474.
28. Maldiney, pp. 215–16; cf. also Weissmann (p. 313), who agrees with Maldiney and Linares.
29. Linares, 'Quant au blanc', p. 474. Fetzer shares a similar view: '[c]e qui se dit, ce qui n'est pas dit: la matière de parole et le blanc typographique forme un tout organique' (Glenn Fetzer, 'Du Bouchet et la dynamique de l'image', *Dalhousie French Studies*, 111 (2018), 35–41 (p. 38)).
30. Maldiney, p. 219.
31. Linares, 'Quant au blanc, pp. 474–77.
32. André du Bouchet, *L'Emportement de muet* (Paris: Mercure de France, 2000), p. 63.
33. Champeau, p. 139. Riley seems to agree with this line of interpretation.
34. Some explicitly reject this view: '[u]ne forme de pensée issue de la dialectique, de l'hégélianisme, de la pensée négative ou théologique (juive ou chrétienne) reste étrangère à la sensibilité de du Bouchet' (Martinez, 'La "Phénoménologie de l'inapparent"', p. 65).
35. Ibid., p. 69.
36. Ibid., pp. 69–70.
37. I use the term 'pictorial' here in the sense of what Lars Ellestrӧm (drawing on Charles Sanders Peirce's semiotics) calls 'iconic', see Lars Ellestrӧm, 'Visual Iconicity in Poetry: Replacing the Notion of "Visual Poetry"', *Orbis Litterarum*, 71.6 (2016), 437–72. My notion of 'pictorial' here also shares much with Johanna Drucker's notion of 'diagrams' as 'literary works whose meaning depends on spatialized relations embodied in their texts', as opposed to 'ideograms' (images of abstract ideas, such as hieroglyphs or Chinese characters) or 'pictograms' (a pictorial representation of a word or thing, often found in concrete poetry): see Johanna Drucker, 'Stéphane Mallarmé's *Un Coup de Dés* and the Poem and/as Book as Diagram', *Journal of Philosophy: A Cross-Disciplinary Inquiry*, 7.16 (2011), 1–13 (pp. 2, 8). Several of Drucker's comments on the generation of meaning through spatial relations in Mallarmé's 'Un coup de dés' are also applicable to du Bouchet, although the loss of an originary state of language (as we will see) and the notion of chance ('hazard') do not play a fundamental role in du Bouchet.
38. For a more exacting analysis of how ordinary textual visuality differs from that of painting, see Nelson Goodman's seminal work *Languages of Art: An Approach to a Theory of Symbols* (Indianapolis: Hackett, 1976). In Goodman's theory of notation, the difference between what I have called pictorial here and the visual qualities of natural languages lies in the fact that the former are 'syntactically dense' whereas the latter are not (Goodman, pp. 130–41). W. J. T. Mitchell notes that '"speech acts" are not medium-specific' and that 'there is, *semantically* speaking [...] no *essential* difference between texts and images', because we can use images in the same way as language (and vice versa), i.e. images can 'tell stories, make arguments, and signify abstract ideas' (W. J. T. Mitchell, *Picture Theory: Essays on Verbal and Visual Representation* (Chicago, IL: University of Chicago Press, 1994), pp. 160–61). No doubt Mitchell is right, and he is effectively making the same point as Ellestrӧm here: all texts are visual and, to this (albeit limited) extent, images are already used in the same way as language. Nonetheless, Goodman's point still stands: the conventional usage of texts as (visual) language whose visuality is, so to speak, invisible implies that we are to treat the text as a categorically different signifying system compared to images, because linguistic writing systems use discrete signifying entities (letters,

diacritics, radicals, ideograms, etc.), whereas visual images are 'syntactically dense'. While it is dictated by convention (which is thus arbitrary and not essential) *when* our attention is directed towards the discrete entities of linguistic writing systems as opposed to the continuous and syntactically dense elements of images, *once our attention is so directed* the difference between images and language is a categorical one. It is precisely because du Bouchet's poetry does not abide by the conventions of typical textual layout that the nonconventional visual aspects of his poetry are foregrounded and their pictorial (or iconic, syntactically dense) nature comes to our attention. Du Bouchet's text is thus not only seen as or under the 'aspectual shape' of being a piece of language (to use Searle's terminology), but also under the aspectual shape of having pictorial qualities. While du Bouchet's texts have both the qualities of texts and pictures and while I maintain that, once identified as one or the other, pictures and texts signify differently, there is no contradiction in seeing the same thing under two different aspects with quite different implications for that which is seen. For a discussion of 'aspectual shape', see John R. Searle, *The Rediscovery of the Mind* (Cambridge, MA: MIT Press, 1992), pp. 156–59.
39. This is not the place to argue this point in more detail. For many of the points made here, see Arthur Danto's seminal essay: 'The Artworld', *The Journal of Philosophy*, 61.19 (1964), 571–84 (esp. pp. 580–01).
40. De Rijcke, 'Entretiens avec André du Bouchet', p. 282.
41. Ibid., p. 287.
42. As Layet says in the preface to his edition of du Bouchet's early essays (*AB*, 19).
43. Originally published in *Cahier G.L.M.* but reprinted in the volume *Aveuglante ou banale* edited by Layet. Further drafts and manuscripts, originally entitled 'Banalité' (cf. *AB*, 331), are in the Bibliothèque Littéraire Jacques Doucet in Paris (ADB Ms 2 Image à terme (GLM, 1954)).
44. Du Bouchet, 'Image à terme' (1979). The essay was published once more (unchanged apart from a slight alteration to the title) during du Bouchet's lifetime: André du Bouchet, 'Image parvenue à son terme inquiet', in *Dans la chaleur vacante. Suivi de Ou le soleil* (Paris: Gallimard, 1991), pp. 109–18.
45. Cf. the third sense listed: 'Nu, Nue, adj. et subst.', *Trésor de la Langue Française informatisé* <http://atilf.atilf.fr/> [accessed 9 March 2021].
46. This is exemplified in the expression 'la vérité toute nue' (ibid.).
47. Cf. Layet's discussion of the notion of contradiction in du Bouchet's work and his evocation of this phrase: 'Demain diamant', p. 34.
48. Du Bouchet, 'Image à terme' (1979), n.p. Unaltered in André du Bouchet, 'Image parvenue à son terme inquiet', p. 115. This passage does not exist in the 1960 version of the text, however (cf. André du Bouchet, 'Résolution de la poésie', *Arguments*, 4.19 (1960), 42–44).
49. See also du Bouchet's utterance: 'IL N'Y A PAS D'IMAGE FIXE' (*AB*, 170).
50. Cf. sense 1α in: 'Terme, subst. masc.', *Trésor de la Langue Française informatisé* <http://atilf.atilf.fr/> [accessed 9 March 2021].
51. I agree with Fetzer here, who similarly suggests that the 'binarité sous-entendue du dynamisme [de l'image] repose sur deux particularités opposées, deux forces contradictoires, dont la juxtaposition l'exprime, chez le poète, en termes de "l'aller et [du] retour", du "foyer et [du] remous", de "l'arrivée et [du] depart", et d'un "va-et-vient"' and emphasizes that 'les deux conditions ou particularités dépendent l'une de l'autre' (Fetzer, 'Du Bouchet et la dynamique de l'image', p. 39).
52. Du Bouchet, 'Image à terme' (1979), n.p. I have tried to preserve the spacing of the original.
53. Du Bouchet, 'Image à terme' (1979), n.p.
54. For a clearer explanation of du Bouchet's conception of 'instant', see chapter 7.
55. Du Bouchet, *L'Emportement de muet*, p. 58.
56. De Rijcke, 'Entretiens avec André du Bouchet', p. 282.
57. André du Bouchet, *Carnet 2* (Fontfroide-le-Haut: Fata Morgana, 1999), p. 177.
58. There are (theoretically) infinite different possibilities to arrange the gaps on the written page. While it remains questionable whether a line break of 2 cm compared to one of 2.1 cm gives a wholly different meaning to the pictorial aspect of a text (if we notice the difference at all), it would be difficult to argue that salient differences in the size of the gaps and where they occur are insignificant. As he reports in an interview, du Bouchet also hung up pages from his poems

58. [continued] on the wall in his room, suggesting that their pictorial impact was fundamentally important to how he wanted his poetry to be considered (Veinstein, p. 48).
59. I have tried to remain as faithful as possible to the original spacing in the *Carnets* (see Du Bouchet, *Carnet 2*, p. 75).
60. André du Bouchet, *Annotations sur l'espace non datées* (Fontfroide-le-Haut: Fata Morgana, 2000), p. 71.
61. Du Bouchet, *Carnet 2*, p. 137.
62. Du Bouchet, *Annotations sur l'espace non datées*, p. 73.
63. André du Bouchet, *Ici en deux* (Paris: Mercure de France, 1986).
64. André du Bouchet, *Peinture* (Fontfroide-le-Haut: Fata Morgana, 1983).
65. Du Bouchet, *Ici en deux* (1986), n.p.
66. Cf. e.g. Hans Blumenberg's instructive discussion of the terms 'Wahrscheinlichkeit' and 'vraisemblance' in his 'Paradigmen zu einer Metaphorologie', *Archiv für Begriffsgeschichte*, 6 (1960), 7–143 (pp. 88–105).
67. Du Bouchet's fundamental or even perennial poetic concerns arise only in specific and quite ordinary contexts, they are never engaged with merely on an abstract level. However, du Bouchet's vocabulary, though mostly mundane and ordinary, is so stripped of overt literary devices or even ornamentation that these ordinary 'choses' almost become abstract entities.
68. For instance, in several interviews with Veinstein du Bouchet treats 'langage' synonymously with 'matériau' or 'matière' (see Veinstein, pp. 25, 43). This conception of poetry and words as material is in stark contrast to that of Celan who speaks negatively about the 'Herumexperimentieren mit dem sogenannten Wortmaterial' (*CW* III, 177).
69. Yves Peyré, 'La Coïncidence de temps', in *Autour d'André du Bouchet: Rencontres sur la poésie moderne*, ed. by Collot, pp. 41–53. Cf. similar assertions by du Bouchet in his early 'Image à terme': '[l]e point où se confondent enfin l'évidence admise et l'évidence qu'on repousse' (*AB*, 87). And: '[e]lle [in the text, the pronoun can refer to any of the following: 'poésie', 'image', 'réalité arbitraire', 'montagne', 'lampe qui ingore le jour...', J. K.] part si loin qu'elle semble nette de passé, que nous la retrouvons sans cesse devant nous, comme non avenue, et comme si son point d'origine ne pouvait désormais se localiser que dans un ordre de progression indéfinie, où elle s'est affranchie de tous les sens restrictifs que nous lui avions imposés. Si loin qu'il semble qu'elle aille droit à sa destruction' (ibid.).
70. As many critics of du Bouchet have discerned, the notions of (semantic) time and (paginal or semantic) space in du Bouchet's poetry often seem to overlap. Peyré, for instance, believes that '[l]e temps, en s'appropriant l'espace, en se spatialisant donc, élève les rapports du moi et du monde à la tension dynamique du monde-moi qu'est le poème': Yves Peyré, *À hauteur d'oubli: André du Bouchet* (Paris: Galilée, 1999), p. 13. See also Wagstaff, 'André du Bouchet and Pierre Tal Coat', pp. 105–27 (particularly p. 117). Wagstaff, among others, notes about du Bouchet's frequent use of future perfect (a tense otherwise rarely used in French) that it incorporates 'the gap between the present and an anticipated moment of looking back' and destabilizes any sense of temporal permanence or stability — an instability which he also put into practice by revising his earlier poetry, not least by changing the tense to future perfect. See Wagstaff, *André du Bouchet*, pp. 51–53 and (on his later revisions and use of future perfect) 178.
71. De Rijcke, 'Entretiens avec André du Bouchet', p. 287.
72. André du Bouchet, *Ici en deux*, ed. by Michel Collot (Paris: Gallimard Education, 2011), p. 11.
73. Du Bouchet, *Carnets 1949–1955*, p. 65.
74. This proclivity for expressing both movement and stasis is one of the many characteristics du Bouchet shares with Alberto Giacometti, famous for his walking sculptures whose uneven surfaces insinuate an oscillation between 'figure' and 'fond'. As Wagstaff says: 'Giacometti himself frequently commented that he could conceive of an object or a person only in the context of his field of vision, which is why his figures so often appear to be moving towards us, but without ever seeming to arrive'; Emma Wagstaff, 'Francis Ponge and André du Bouchet on Giacometti: Art Criticism as Testimony', *The Modern Language Review*, 101.1 (2006), 75–89 (p. 82). Giacometti writes in his *Écrits*: '[e]t on continue, sachant que plus on s'approche de la chose, plus elle s'éloigne ... La distance entre moi et le modèle a tendance à augmenter sans cesse: plus

on s'approche, plus la chose s'éloigne, c'est une quête sans fin'; quoted in Collot, ' "D'un trait qui figure et défigure": Du Bouchet et Giacometti', p. 96. Jacques Depreux examines du Bouchet's notion of walking extensively; see his *André du Bouchet; ou, La Parole traversée* (Seyssel: Champ vallon, 1988).
75. Plotinus' reasoning is this: everything is relatively different with respect to everything else and relatively identical with respect to itself. The 'One' is absolutely other with respect to everything else and absolutely identical with respect to itself (this absolute identity here also implies an array of qualities, such as being self-constitutive without being or existing in the ontological sense). Beierwaltes, *Identität und Differenz*, pp. 26–28.
76. Cf. also Layet, 'Demain diamant', p. 33.
77. On the question by Veinstein: '[c]'est une tension, donc, qui est au départ, plutôt que la langue?', du Bouchet answers: '[l]e point de départ, c'est peut-être un rapport avec la langue. [...] C'est peut-être toujours dans la langue, ou en-dehors de la langue, mais en tout cas en rapport avec la langue' (Veinstein, p. 48).
78. De Rijcke, 'Entretiens avec André du Bouchet', p. 286.
79. Ibid., p. 285.

CHAPTER 6

The Self-Surpassing Image in Celan's 'Halbzerfressener'

In the previous chapters we analysed Celan's desire to overcome the perceived gap between languages and approximate a linguistic *archetypos*. The loss of this linguistic *archetypos* implied the confusion of tongues and therefore also entailed misunderstandings and untruthful speaking, according to Celan. Only the genuine engagement with the other and the other's language — be this a different natural language or just individual inflections of tone and diction — without neglecting or glossing over any differences would let us approach some form of truthful understanding.

In 'Traum vom Traume', 'Tenebrae', and 'Bei Wein und Verlorenheit', Celan had conceived of the *typos* as a merely imitative and false image which served as a negative contrast to the truthful dialogical conversation and engagement with the other on the way to the *archetypos*. We have also pointed out the Judaeo-Christian influences on Celan's conception of the image as split between *archetypos* and *typos*, dividing the image into good and bad, simply put. Furthermore, we saw that Celan's conception of the *archetypos–typos* dichotomy at the heart of the image differs from that of du Bouchet whose image is nurtured by the positive tension between polychotomous poles. These differences also manifest themselves in the relation of Celan's and du Bouchet's respective image to notions of depth, height, and visuality. Thus in 'Traum vom Traume' and 'Tenebrae', the visual *typos* had formed on a watery surface, being a falsifying copy of the *archetypos*.[1] Moreover in 'Traum vom Traume', we were impelled to go deeper and therefore beyond the *typos*-images. In a similar manner, 'Bei Wein und Verlorenheit' and, as we will see, 'Halbzerfressener' situate the *archetypos* in an unspecified above. This above is not quite transcendent, but also clearly goes beyond typified representation. Du Bouchet on the other hand does not formulate his image in such traditional terms of a positively connotated depth or (hierarchical) height. His image springs in equal part from the surficial visuality of black ink and white page and the non-visual semantics of the page, which conceives positively of visuality.

The tropes of depth or height in Celan will return in 'Halbzerfressener' as we examine his conception of introspection and subjectivity in the poem. We discovered in previous chapters that Celan's poetry is oriented toward an other which is of fundamental importance for the constitution of his poetic language and therefore also for the poetic voice or subject. In 'Bei Wein und Verlorenheit', testimony of the archetypal was only possible in communication with a 'du'. In our analysis of 'Tenebrae', on the other hand, we looked at the role of the image in our self-recognition as human subjects. Celan had inverted the traditional Augustinian understanding of ourselves as *imago Dei* through which we understand ourselves to be human beings and thus conscious subjects. The lack of an *imago Dei* had deprived the poetic voice of any positive sense of itself as human, which Celan also captured viscerally as physical destruction by describing the poetic voice as bleeding out. Hence in 'Tenebrae', Celan seems to negatively confirm Augustine's notion of the image. In 'Halbzerfressener' these two elements so essential for poetic subjectivity in Celan are combined: the Augustinian notion of our self-recognition by means of the image and Celan's conception of the other towards which all action and speech of the poetic voice seems to tend.

The Poetic Subject in Celan and Du Bouchet

Before we go into an in-depth analysis of 'Halbzerfressener', we need to make sure we understand the poetics of Celan's other more fundamentally. Celan's other is nearly omnipresent in his poetry. Apart from the many apostrophes to a 'du',[2] we can also read Celan's many translations — his translational oeuvre is about twice as large as his own — as an engagement with a poetic other. The presence of other authors also makes itself felt in Celan's frequent textual allusions to other poets.[3] Given the evident importance of these various aspects of the other for Celan, one may be swayed to declare, with Tobias Tunkel, that a radical notion of alterity pervades Celan's poetry:

> [d]as Paradigma lyrischer Subjektivität wird auf den Kopf gestellt: Alterität ist der Identität vorgängig; nicht mehr das Du verdankt seinen Ort und seine Gestalt einer ästhetischen Inkorporation durch das reflexiv sich die Welt aneignende Ich, sondern das Ich verdankt sich einer Anrede durch den Anderen und nimmt sich wahr als eine Spur und als Zeugnis des abwesenden Anderen.[4]

Certainly, the assessment that 'Alterität ist der Identität vorgängig' must be considered premature as it begs the question who or what identifies the 'du' in Celan's texts in the first place. The designation by 'du' cannot but originate in an explicitly or implicitly present first person, who precedes or at least coincides with the appearance of the second person. Only from the perspective of an I can the 'du' be addressed, described, or designated as 'du' in Celan. Indeed, given that we are reading a poetic text, the initial situation is quite the inverse of what Tunkel ascribes to Celan, as Michael Jakob correctly observes:

> Literatur ist zunächst alles andere denn der Ort eines *Dialogs*. Schriftlichkeit, Mittelbarkeit, einseitige (individuelle) Setzung, relative Intentionalitätslosigkeit und das Fehlen eigentlicher Zielgerichtetheit (Entpragmatisierung) — sie alle kennzeichnen das Literarische als einen einsamen, isolierten Akt.[5]

We have seen that the written language of the poem in Celan is always only a tentative testimony to the *archetypal Other*. Particularly in our analysis of 'Bei

Wein und Verlorenheit', we outlined this fundamental conundrum constituted by written language. Here, the written word only evinced the absence of originary speaking and proliferated the 'bebildert[e] Sprachen' perpetuating the falsification of archetypal song. Indeed, the multilingual pun of *Nähe/Neige/neige/*neigh seemed to suggest that Celan knew the poem itself could only be an indirect testimony to divine song, even if it was a genuine attempt at listening to and rendering archetypal song. Our doubts raised about language, including poetic language, thus extended even to the poetic voice, which could only linguistically mediate archetypal song (see chapter 4). In 'Tenebrae', these doubts even threatened the existence of the poetic subject. Poetic language is only an indirect signifier, a *locum tenens* for something that is absent, whether the second-person other or the *archetypal Other*. Hence, the 'du' does not precede the first-person poetic voice. The opposite is the case, as Celan stated in his 1960 'Meridian' speech:

> [d]as Gedicht will zu einem Anderen. [...] Erst im Raum dieses Gesprächs konstituiert sich das Angesprochene, versammelt es sich um das ansprechende und nennende Ich. (*M*, 9)

The first-person poetic voice is thus unambiguously at the centre of poetic speech and the 'du' is constituted in and as the apostrophe of the poetic voice. The 'du' doubly attests to the loss of an *archetypos*. On the one hand, always reminding us of the loss of non-mediated, archetypal speech, the 'du' only exists as an element of poetic speech created by the poetic voice without the 'du' itself being directly present. On the other hand, in Celan's view genuine poetic language is necessary in order to communicate even just traces of the *archetypos*. Only the presence of a witness could testify to the *archetypos* in 'Bei Wein und Verlorenheit'. In 'Tenebrae', the poetic voice only persisted through the linguistic, communicative endeavour by directing its speech toward the other. It is consequently undeniable that this engagement with the other in poetic speech forms a fundamental part of the poetic voice's subjectivity in Celan. Celan's tending toward a 'du' is an attempt within the poems' language to undo linguistic solipsism, as pointed out by Jakob, and overcome its own insufficiency as a medium. As we saw with regard to 'Bei Wein und Verlorenheit', only in communicating with an other can the poetic voice, together with this other, attest to non-mediated archetypal speech.

We can now go further. The poetic voice itself is present as poetic speech. Thus, as the poetic voice addresses a 'du' and seeks to bridge the abyss within or between languages and even approach archetypal speech, the poetic voice also approaches and restores itself. The other that is constituted through the speaking of the poetic voice embodies the linguistic alterity of the poetic voice itself. Anticipating our analysis of 'Halbzerfressener', we may even say that the 'du' bears the image of the poetic voice. In the act of communicating with the other, in this 'Begegnung', the poetic voice thus also restores and recognizes itself: 'Ich bin ... mir selbst begegnet' (*M*, 11).

We have already emphasized at several points (cf. chapters 2 and 5) that du Bouchet's poetry evinces the loss of a self-certain subject, which contrasts with the subject in Celan. Indeed, in an interview with his fellow poet Alain Veinstein du

Bouchet made remarks very similar to those cited of Celan above, but differing in some fundamental respects:

> '[t]u' peut être 'je', n'est-ce pas. Il n'y a pas de 'tu' qui ne commence par un 'je'. C'est d'abord l'écart que l'on prend sur soi et, ce faisant, on rencontre quelqu'un qui est tantôt soi-même, tantôt quelqu'un d'autre. Pour qu'il y ait rencontre, il faut commencer par prendre cet écart sur soi-même. Mais il ne peut se prendre qu'en s'appuyant sur soi-même. La relation avec la langue implique deux personnes qui n'en sont qu'une, 'un' qui se dédouble.[6]

As in Celan, the 'je' initially seems to take a primary position, since the existence of a 'tu' for du Bouchet also implies a 'je', and since there is no 'tu' without a 'je'. However, it becomes clear that the 'tu' is not a 'je' in the sense of being identical, but that the 'tu' inheres the 'je' as its other, as 'l'écart que l'on se prend sur soi', as '"un" qui se dédouble'. Particularly the last sentence of the citation presses a point more clearly and more radically than Celan does. As a linguistic entity, the written 'je' is already an other to the 'je' that is writing.[7] In this sense, as soon as the 'je' enters into a relation with language, the written 'je' becomes a linguistic expression of the writing 'je', which the written 'je' denotes but itself is not (see also my discussion of du Bouchet's notion of translation and his 'je' in the following chapter). As such it is inherently split as an 'écart sur soi-même'. Hence when du Bouchet uses the word 'rencontre', it's in a similar but also markedly different sense to Celan's notion of 'Begegnung'. Celan starts with the 'Ich' which in addressing the 'du' returns to itself to recognize itself in the other. Du Bouchet's 'rencontre' on the other hand acknowledges that it is contingent on the split that precedes any potential togetherness of 'je' and other: '[p]our qu'il y ait rencontre, il faut commencer par prendre cet écart sur soi-même.' In the manner of the polychotomous poles that create tensions and interact in du Bouchet's image, du Bouchet's 'je' paradoxically oscillates between constituting a unity that precedes any notion of otherness and being inherently other to itself (see also the next chapters).[8] Whereas Celan's 'Ich' recognizes itself in the other, du Bouchet's 'je' recognizes the other in itself.

The Subject and the Image in 'Halbzerfressener'

With these insights in mind, we can now approach the poem 'Halbzerfressener' (1964), where we find such a positive self-recognition of the poetic voice in the 'du'. In the poem, we move from the visual outside of the corbel to an inside that withdraws from the perceptual grasp of the onlooker. The partially eroded corbel that opens the poem is a representation whose representationality is patently visible: 'maskengesichtig'. The 'visual mask' is emphasized further by the mid-word enjambment after 'masken-'. This enjambment, which so ostentatiously foregrounds the pretence of the mask's display, calls to mind the prominent enjambments in 'Bei Wein und Verlorenheit' where 'sie | schrieben, sie | logen' had so emphatically condemned the typified visuality of mankind's 'bebildert[e] Sprachen'. We should not necessarily think of the mask as concealing the corbel's face, but rather we should think of the mask as the face of the corbel, since the word 'Maske' as a technical term in the arts is synonymous with 'Kragstein'.[9] Thus, the mask-character and the associations of deceitfulness which go along with this word pertain not to an assumed visual display or wilful deceit by the corbel but concern the very nature of the corbel as such, as artifice. That the very nature of the corbel is concerned is important because it entails that the opposition in the poem is not between a false (masked) and a true (unmasked) appearance, but rather between outward appearance and inner being or self. Thus, when we look under or beyond the corbel's mask, we do not arrive at the face of the corbel, but we are looking inside the 'Schädelinnre' of the corbel. We hence move from the outward appearance exposed to someone's gaze, to an inwardly oriented gaze that seems to be the corbel's own.[10] The word 'gesichtig', so critically separated from the visual pretence of the mask, can mean both: visible to an external onlooker and looking inward.[11] '[M]asken- | gesichtig' thus expresses the two poles that create the tension operating in the poem: a visibility, which, indiscernible to itself, services someone else's gaze, and a self-active introspection.

In the next few lines, our gaze shifts from the face of the corbel to the crypt in its eyes. The direction of the poem is inwards, into the depth of the 'Augenschlitz-Krypta'. Paradoxically this means, as the eye cannot see itself, we see ourselves focusing on that which lies beyond the perceptual reach of the very organ that enables vision.[12] This becomes most apparent when we consider that the word 'Krypta' comes from the old Greek *kruptós*, meaning 'to conceal'.[13] Perception, ultimately, has turned inward and on itself. Moving inward into the corbel's 'Schädelinnre', where the corbel 'pflanzt sein Bild', hence implies that the corbel as an object of perception now becomes a perceiving object. In this 'turn' or rather in the act of turning, as we will see, the corbel's perception and image become defined and, indeed, seem to coincide.

This move beyond mere appearance into the depths and heights ('[h]inein, hinauf') of the 'Schädelinnre' is not merely a move away from outward display, but it further seems to be a form of survival of the 'Schädelinnre' in contrast to the transience and moribundity of the decaying outside.[14] The '[h]albzerfressen[e]' corbel shows signs of the ravages of time, and the proximity of the words 'crypt', as a specific burial vault underneath churches, and 'masken-gesichtig' distinctly remind us of death masks.[15] This external moribundity predominant in the first stanza contrasts with the motifs of growing and organic life in the second stanza, whose spatial dimensions of height and depth are also juxtaposed with the emphasized superficiality of the corbel's surface being described as mask.

Inside the skull, into which we have entered through the eye slit, a dialogical 'du' becomes active, and we encounter motifs of fecundity. The image is pivotal for this productivity: the 'du' prepares the ground for the corbel's image, which in turn cultivates it and lets it grow. It is in the 'Schädelinnre' of the corbel, in this inward turn of the corbel's gaze, that it encounters the 'du', which in turn ('in Furche und Windung') forms its image. The 'du' is thus a part of the corbel's introspection. Hence in passing through this reflective other and its actions, the corbel can plant and nurture its own image, which is the image of the corbel's self-reflection. Thus, it seems that in the introspective encounter of the other in its 'Schädelinnre' and in the objectivation of itself as image, the corbel gains cognition of itself. What the poem thus seems to depict in the last stanza is the act of the corbel's recognizing the 'du' as the image of itself in its mental reflection.

The metaphor of mental self-reflection or self-consciousness is, of course, derived from the recognition of oneself in the mirror. We step before a mirror and realize that the person in front of us is really just an image of ourselves. But only in the mirror's forming an image of us, that is only in the self-objectivation of ourselves as image, can we recognize the mirror-image as image and, specifically, as an image of ourselves. Our idea of mental self-reflection, which was most prominently formulated in Augustine's and René Descartes's conceptions of self-consciousness, operates effectively in the same manner as perceptual self-reflection.[16] When we talk of mental self-reflection, we imagine that the mind watches itself in the act of thinking. In other words, a subject watches someone or something in the act of thinking and realizes that this someone or something is nothing other than the subject itself.

In a very similar manner, Celan's introspective corbel watches the 'du' act and reaps its own image as the fruit of this act of reflection. The perceiving subject that is the corbel seems to coincide with the perceived object in the image. Celan expresses an analogous and spelt-out notion of this self-reflection in engaging with a 'du' when he writes in his notes to his 'Meridian' speech that: 'Ich — Du: keine fixe Relation[.] Ich — Du (Unendlichkeitsrelation[)... .] Wesentlich: das Du des Gedichts gibt, auch da wo es "wörtlich" antwortet, niemals Antwort [...]. Ständiges Hin und Her des Ich' (*M*, 143). Celan describes a relation between 'Ich — Du' which self-reflexively leads back to the subject and continuously constitutes or partakes in the subject by means of this relation. The relation of 'Ich — Du' is consequently effectively nothing other than a 'Hin und Her des Ich'. This continuous oscillation between 'Ich — Du' constituting the 'Ich' seems to be echoed in 'Halbzerfressener', where the image in the reflecting 'Schädelinnre' of the corbel is continuously — 'wieder und wieder' — renewed by the 'du' and the corbel (or 'er'): 'sein Bild, | das sich entwächst, entwächst'.

This mental self-reflection through the image reminds us of the Augustinian *mens* contemplating its likeness to the divine *archetypos* in its own image as *imago Dei*, which we discussed in 'Tenebrae'. Whereas in 'Tenebrae', Augustine's notion of the *imago Dei* was only negatively present through its absence, as it were, in 'Halbzerfressener' we encounter what appears to almost be a positive counterpart to the missing *imago Dei* in 'Tenebrae'. Further corroborating our suspicion that the idea of the *imago Dei* informs this poem, the 'Schädelinnre' of the corbel in 'Halbzerfressener' is also the 'Himmel', that is the traditional *locus* of the divine *archetypos* as image of which the Augustinian *mens* would recognize itself. Yet, we should be more cautious in our interpretation. 'Himmel' can mean both a divine heaven and a terrestrial sky; furthermore, the rather sober and anatomical description of the *mens* as 'Schädelinnere' and possibly the brain as 'Windung'[17] secularizes Augustine's solemnly spiritual concept and quite literally grounds it, considering the agrarian vocabulary. The *archetypos* from which an image is formed hence is not divine but rather that of the corbel contemplating itself as (mental) image.[18]

Nonetheless, the *double entendre* of 'Himmel' as heaven and sky as well as the fact that this is a mental image call to mind the many notes to his 'Meridian' speech in which Celan had sought, time and again, to draft his conception of the image as something 'geistig', that is spiritual and mental: 'Bildhaftigkeit = nichts Visuelles, sondern etwas Geistiges' (*M*, 101). Celan further describes introspection in his notes to the 'Meridian' speech as 'Intensives Wahrnehmen: Inne<u>werden</u>' (*M*, 193) and says that 'Wahrnehmen' is also always a 'Wahr<u>sein</u>' (*M*, 134). Like the traditional introspective seeing of the *archetypos* by means of the mental mirror, Celan regards the gaze which turns inward as truthful and in a sense as self-constitutional ('Inne<u>werden</u>', my emphasis). In Celan's translation of Bazaine's *Notes sur la peinture*, published around the same time as Celan was writing down the cited notes, we discover very similar passages in which Celan associates introspection with a truer form of seeing and with archetypal creation: 'die Verinnerlichung des Visuellen, dieses Mehr-als-Sehen, wie es jeder wahre Schöpfungsakt impliziert.'[19]

These ideas developed between 1959 and 1960 had remained present in Celan's thought when he wrote 'Halbzerfressener' in 1967, in which, having left behind the visual outside, the corbel sees its mental or spiritual image sowed, reaped, and thus created in heaven or the sky. Thus, even if the corbel's image is not absolute and entirely archetypal in the traditional sense, it shares with the Augustinian contemplation of the *archetypos* many characteristics, including its tending inward and upward as well as its being not merely visual. The corbel's image, in other words, is more than just the visual and false *typos* of the previous poems by Celan we discussed. The image's continuously outgrowing its own perceptual or representational grasp in 'Halbzerfressener' ('sich entwächst, entwächst') hence stands in a long tradition of thinking about the divine *archetypos* after which mankind continually strives, but which ultimately escapes full comprehension.

However, there is potentially even more to this corbel, and the 'Windung' and 'umbrechen' in the poem provide a clue: they are German variants of the Latin 'versus'. The self-contemplating act takes place in and through verse. Consequently, the contemplator or corbel is none other than the voice of poetry which (re-)constitutes itself — continuously — in the act of writing. Celan had said in his 'Meridian' speech that '[d]as Gedicht will zu einem Anderen. [...] Erst im Raum dieses Gesprächs konstituiert sich das Angesprochene, versammelt es sich um das ansprechende und nennende Ich' (*M*, 9). The contemplating poet thus becomes a 'wahrnehmende[s] Du' in his self-reflection, which is nothing other than 'ein Sichvorausschicken zu sich selbst, auf der Suche nach sich selbst' (*M*, 11). This self-recreation of the 'Ich' via the contemplating and complementing 'du', perhaps, for the briefest of moments, turns and returns to recognize and meet itself as self-defining, secular *archetypos*: 'Ich bin ... mir selbst begegnet' (*M*, 11).

The poetic verse of 'Halbzerfressener' in its 'umbrechen', 'wieder und wieder', hence tentatively seems to bridge the abyss between different languages as well as between poetic voice and other, and in so doing poetry approaches the *archetypos*. Unlike the narrator's dialogical partner in 'Traum vom Traume' who wanted to rid language of its historical baggage in order to purify it (see chapter 1), in 'Halbzerfressener' the image's ever growing toward the *archetypos* is not created by forgetting the dead. We should remember that we entered the 'Schädelinnre' by passing from the eroded outside through the crypt of the eye. Even the action of 'brechen' and the prefix 'ent-' in the second stanza are not without connotations of loss and violence. Hence, while in a certain sense the poem survives the moribundity and decay of the first stanza, the moribundity of outer reality is not simply obliterated. We are not oblivious of the dead in 'Halbzerfressener'.

The dead are probably why the image never transcends reality as absolute *archetypos*, despite Celan's insistence that the image does more than just display outer reality. There are obvious reasons for Celan to persist in acknowledging the outer reality in which six million people, including his parents, were murdered, instead of simply seeking to transcend it. Hence while Celan's poetic striving toward an *archetypos* projects the desire to move beyond this outer reality and to somehow undo this loss, the irremediable reality of this loss and the will to commemorate it at the same time prevent a fulfilment of this archetypal desire in an absolute detachment from this outer reality.[20] In other words, the *archetypos* as absolute and transcendent cannot be reached. Rather, true introspection in poetic speech includes outside reality. Purloining an expression from Celan's translation of Bazaine, 'dieses Mehr-als-Sehen [...] hängt [...] von dem Grad der Ähnlichkeit mit einer inneren, die äußere einbegreifenden Welt ab.'[21]

We gain further insight into the possibilities of a 'Mehr-als-Sehen' as a looking inward that is not entirely separate from the outer world when we consider Celan's engagement with Husserl's phenomenology, which can be gleaned from his notes from a similar time period as his Bazaine translation. One of these notes states: '[l]es essences des choses, et non leur existence, présence | eidetische: Wesens- wissenschaften | äußere = innere Wahrnehmung' (*M*, 210). This remark was probably inspired by Celan's reading Husserl's *Ideen zu einer reinen Phänomenologie und phänomenologischen Philosophie*.[22] The turn towards the essences of things bears strong resemblance to what Husserl in his work from 1913 onward would call eidetic reduction or 'Wesensschau', which in the act of intuition abstracts from the concrete empirical object to reach its form, in the extended sense of the word, or, in Plato's term, its *eidos*.[23] Husserl's reformed notion of this Platonic *archetypos*, arrived at through eidetic reduction in the mind of a thinking subject, possibly contributed to Celan's conception of the image as 'nichts Visuelles, sondern etwas Geistiges' (*M*, 101), and informs Celan's poetics when he writes that he 'versuch[t] [sich] das Gedicht vor Augen zu führen und es (denkend) anzuschauen' (*Mikro*, 147). Husserl, like Bazaine, does not advocate Plato's dualist worldview and hence would regard the realm of inner and outer perception as ontologically commensurable.[24] The *eidos* as a form of *archetypos* does not belong to a metaphysical and transcendent realm. Perhaps most unequivocally we find the influence of (particularly Husserl's) phenomenology when Celan affirms that the 'Bild hat phänomenalen Charakter — es erscheint. | die Vision — ' (*M*, 87).[25]

Thus, Celan is interested in the phenomenal rather than the mere sensory-visual character of the image, that is, he is interested in the image as seen, thought, and in a sense constructed by the conscious mind.[26] Yet, in the climactic culmination of the above-cited note in 'Vision' — a term Husserl does not use — Celan's statement seems to point beyond Husserl's project of a strict phenomenological science and has undertones that are mystical.[27] It is perhaps no coincidence then that in his reading of Husserl's *Die Idee der Phänomenologie* Celan marks a moment — one of only a few — in which Husserl draws an analogy between his idea of a 'schauende Erkenntnis der Vernunft' and the 'intellektuelle Schauen' in the 'Rede der Mystiker'.[28] The idea of cognizing the essence of things or, as in the (Neoplatonic) mystics, of God,[29] by abstracting from particular experiences to arrive at an absolute vision[30] through introspection would have resonated with Celan's idea that 'Bild = Vision' (M, 109) and that '[d]as Bild ist die Erlösung des Geistes von dem Ding' (M, 160).[31]

Yet, we are reminded that even Celan's most assertive remarks about the *archetypos* are not without reservations, and this is where he differs most markedly from the traditional conception of the *archetypos* which otherwise fundamentally informs his image. Even if the poetic voice is riding the God-horse over 'Menschen-Hürden' 'in die Ferne — die Nähe' in 'Bei Wein und Verlorenheit' and though he proclaims 'es sind noch Lieder zu singen jenseits | der Menschen' in 'Fadensonnen', Celan insists that his poetry is 'Immaterielles, aber Irdisches, Terrestrisches' (M, 12). We may also think of the poet's tentative evocation of the traditional denomination of God as 'ganz Andere[r]' in his 'Meridian' speech as a typically reserved expression of the *archetypos*: '[v]ielleicht, so muß ich mir jetzt sagen, — vielleicht ist sogar ein Zusammentreffen dieses "ganz Anderen" [...] mit einem nicht allzu fernen, einem ganz nahen "anderen" denkbar — immer und wieder denkbar' (M, 8). The iteration of 'vielleicht' emphasizes the tentative character of this thought, which is even further accentuated by the interjective phrase and the dash as well as the scare quotes.[32]

To preliminarily conclude our discussion of 'Halbzerfressener', we recall that from outside perception we move to an introspective inside that is more than the former yet does not obliviate it. Poetic speaking is, to borrow the words of Celan's translation of Bazaine, directed toward the *archetypos* by means of 'die Verinnerlichung des Visuellen'.[33] The 'du' or other, as reflected in the corbel's 'Schädelinnren', is pivotal in the constitution of the corbel's image of itself. That is, even if the 'du' 'versammelt [...] sich um das ansprechende und nennende Ich' (M, 9) and in so doing leads to a *Selbstbegegnung* of the 'Ich' (cf. M, 11), the 'Ich' or the corbel recognizes itself in the other through the other.[34] The corbel thereby achieves a 'Mehr-als-Sehen' or a form of Husserlian *Wesensschau* of itself.[35] Yet, the *archetypos* cannot be fully reached, only approximated in the continuous turning of Celan's verse and the image constantly outgrowing itself.[36]

Writing, Image, and Earth in Celan and Du Bouchet

The continuous act of 'umbrechen' and cultivating the image also means that it is, as turning verse, linguistic and poetic rather than visual. This motif of cultivation in Celan's 'Halbzerfressener' provides an interesting point of comparison to du Bouchet's figure of the 'charrue' in 'Le Moteur blanc' from his volume *Dans la chaleur vacante* (*CW* IV, 254–305, esp. 264). As Wiebke Amthor has pointed out, the 'charrue' can be understood as encapsulating the act of writing more generally for du Bouchet: '[s]o zieht die Schrift, wenn sie sich auf das Papier legt, eine Spur, die der Furche des Pflugs auf dem Acker ähnelt, der den Boden wendet und lockert.'[37] The metaphorical parallels between written paper and ploughed field hinge on the visual similarity in the metaphor between the black line on the 'bouche blanche' of the paper and the 'membres | de terre écorchés par une charrue'. The emphasis on visuality as eventuated by the semantic discourse is further amplified by the layout of du Bouchet's page that foregrounds visuality. In the emphatically visual association of 'charrue' with poetic writing, du Bouchet's motif thus differs from the cultivation of the image in 'Halbzerfressener'. The image's outgrowing itself and, presumably, outgrowing its visuality is a result of the cultivation by and the turning ('umbrechen') of poetic verse.

Another point of comparison suggests itself. The image of du Bouchet's verse, like the image in Celan's 'Halbzerfressener', also never seems to cease turning, in its seeming disinclination to settle and take a final form (see chapter 5). Once again, however, the continuous cultivation of du Bouchet's verse by the 'charrue' is not directed into unspecified heights and does not move inward. Du Bouchet's verse is not impelled by an *archetypos* but by the internal tension between the polychotomous poles constituting his image.

Amthor's examination of agricultural motifs in Celan and du Bouchet points us to yet another difference between Celan and du Bouchet that also implies differences in their conception of the image. In an essay on the poetry of Mandelstam, Celan identified the notion of 'Pflug' with poetry, which 'reißt die untersten Zeitschichten auf, die "Schwarzerde der Zeit" tritt zutage' (*Mikro*, 203).[38] With respect to du Bouchet's 'charrue', on the other hand, Amthor notes that '[sich die] poetologische Arbeit des Pfluges vor allem auf der Oberfläche der Seite ansiedelt' and therefore also has no historical dimensions.[39] Although the historical dimensions in 'Halbzerfressener' are not clear by the act of 'umbrechen' as such, the decaying corbel and the crypt through which our gaze proceeds into the 'Schädelinnre' clearly bear the marks of time's passing. A historic element thus underpins the entire movement in the poem and anything that happens in time, including the act of 'umbrechen', necessarily places itself in a temporal relation to the past, whether implicitly or explicitly. Du Bouchet's 'charrue' on the other hand is constituted entirely in the present, and the whole poem moves from one present moment to the next (cf. *CW* IV, 264). Past and future, whether semantically indicated or as grammatical tense, are markers of a formerly present moment or a moment whose eventuation in the present is still to materialize. Past and present thus unite in the present tense as 'l'instant d'une fusion' that is also 'une fraction de temps'.⁴⁰ In the following chapter, we will take a closer look at Celan's and du Bouchet's conceptions of time and their respective implications for the poets' notions of translation and the image.

Notes to Chapter 6

1. The watery surface as the locus of *typoi* is a recurrent motif in Celan. See also my discussion of his poem 'Wortaufschüttung' (*KG*, 180) in Koch, 'The Allegorical Image and Presence in Celan's "Wortaufschüttung"'.
2. Lyon gives a numerical table for an overview: Lyon, 'Paul Celan and Martin Buber', p. 114.
3. Cf. e.g. Monika Schmitz-Emans, *Poesie als Dialog: Vergleichende Studien zu Paul Celan und seinem literarischen Umfeld* (Heidelberg: Winter, 1993).
4. Tunkel, p. 29.
5. Jakob, *Das 'Andere' Paul Celans*, p. 85.
6. Veinstein, p. 42–43; the original interview was carried out in 1989.
7. The paradoxes of framing the irreducibility of the first-person perspective in language has led to lively discussions in the philosophy of language (and mind). Cf. particularly Manfred Frank's discussion of Carlos Castañeda's groundbreaking work: *Selbstbewusstsein und Selbsterkenntnis: Essays zur analytischen Philosophie der Subjektivität* (Stuttgart: Reclam, 1991), pp. 280–304. Frank likes to quote Molière's Amphitryon on this occasion: 'Mercure: Qui va là? | Sosie: Moi! | Mercure: Qui, moi?' (ibid., p. 18).
8. Du Bouchet's reflections on the subject here closely resemble Friedrich Schlegel's and Novalis's thinking about subjectivity and self-consciousness. Cf. Manfred Frank, *Einführung in die frühromantische Ästhetik: Vorlesungen* (Frankfurt a. M.: Suhrkamp, 1989), pp. 309–10, 312–13. There is also some resemblance with Schelling's conception of subjectivity when subjectivity is already objectified in the subject's attempt to grasp the nature of its own subjectivity propositionally or through self-reflection. Thus, the subject 'ist nur da, inwiefern ich es nicht habe, und inwiefern ich es habe, ist es nicht mehr' (Schelling, *Sämmtliche Werke*, I, IV, p. 357).
9. Cf. entry 7 on: 'Maske, *f.*', *Wörterbuchnetz — Deutsches Wörterbuch von Jacob Grimm Und Wilhelm Grimm* <http://woerterbuchnetz.de/cgi-bin/WBNetz/wbgui_py?sigle=DWB&mode=Vernetzung&lemid=GM02008#XGM02008> [accessed 12 May 2017].
10. In the following discussion, I am assuming that 'er' refers to the 'Kragstein'. While there is the theoretical possibility that 'er' refers to a third party, different from 'du' and the 'Kragstein', it seems to me implausible that the vital action of *Bild pflanzen* (whose significance will become clearer soon) is carried out by an otherwise unspecified third party whose relation to 'du' and 'Kragstein' is unclear and that appears from nowhere. Typically, the only poetic personae in Celan that can remain at such a level of implicitness are the first- and second-person personae, because their relationship to each other is always already clear at the very least due to the fact that there is no poetic voice, no speaking in a poem without a speaker, and there is no apostrophic 'du' without a speaker addressing it. Third parties are usually introduced, and only then are pronouns used to refer to them (e.g. the 'sie' of the 'Menschen-Hürden' in 'Bei Wein und Verlorenheit' or the 'sie' of 'Bildern' in 'Erblinde', which we will encounter in chapter 8), and I am assuming the same to be the case here.
11. 'Gesichtig, *adj. und adv.*', *Wörterbuchnetz — Deutsches Wörterbuch von Jacob Grimm Und Wilhelm Grimm* <https://woerterbuchnetz.de/?sigle=DWB&mode=Vernetzung&lemid=GM02008#3> [accessed 16 March 2021]. Sieghild Bogumil says something very similar about the conception of the eye in general in Celan's poetry: '[k]onkret mit Celan gesprochen, besitzt das Auge die Doppelfunktion. Es ist sinnlich-geistig, halb ist es Wahrnehmungsorgan und halb Mittel der Erkenntnis, getragen durch die Sprache [...]. Wahrnehmen ist das Wahrnehmen der Außenwelt mittels der Erkenntnis der Innenwelt oder umgekehrt das Erkennen der Innenwelt mittels der Wahrnehmung der Außenwelt'; Sieghild Bogumil, 'Geschichte, Sprache und Erkenntnis in der Dichtung Paul Celans', in *Der Glühende Leertext: Annäherungen an Paul Celans Dichtung*, ed. by Christoph Jamme and Otto Pöggeler (Munich: Fink, 1993), pp. 127–42 (p. 133).

12. This movement into an eye, i.e. into that which the eye itself cannot see, is a frequent motif in Celan's poetry. See also the poems 'Zuversicht' and 'Ein Auge, offen' (*KG*, pp. 93, 109).
13. 'Κρυπτός' [Kruptós], *Etymological Dictionary of Greek*, ed. by Robert Beekes (Leiden: Brill, 2010), 786.
14. Cf. also Klaus Voswinkel, *Paul Celan: Verweigerte Poetisierung der Welt. Versuch einer Deutung* (Heidelberg: Stiehm, 1974), p. 44.
15. Hermann Burger and Voswinkel speak about the motifs of moribundity in the first stanza, see Hermann Burger, *Paul Celan: Auf der Suche nach der verlorenen Sprache* (Zurich: Fischer, 1974), pp. 20–21; Voswinkel. Klaus Weissenberger even claims that the connection in 'Halbzerfressener' between the motifs 'Stein' and 'Totenschädel', through which 'das "Geheimnis" der Erhöhung erwachsen kann', exemplifies a general tendency in Celan's poetry: Klaus Weissenberger, *Zwischen Stein und Stern: Mystische Formgebung in der Dichtung von Else Lasker-Schüler, Nelly Sachs und Paul Celan* (Berne: Francke, 1976), p. 82.
16. Cf. Gareth Matthews's introduction in: Saint Augustine, *On the Trinity: Books 8–15*, ed. by Gareth B. Matthews (Cambridge: Cambridge University Press, 2002), especially p. xi. For an influential reading of Descartes's conception of self-consciousness and Johann Gottlieb Fichte's attempt at a solution of its problems, see Dieter Henrich, 'Fichtes ursprüngliche Einsicht', *Wissenschaft und Gegenwart*, 34 (1967), 7–48.
17. Cf. Markus Taibon, '"Ein Wort nach dem Bild des Schweigens": Zur Sprachmetaphorik im Werk Paul Celans', *Sprachkunst*, 24 (1993), 233–53 (p. 242). I cannot subscribe to the main line of Taibon's interpretation who holds that 'Innenraum' and 'Außenraum' are united in the poem, whereas I perceive that the poem follows a clear movement from inside to outside.
18. Burger goes further and states that: '[d]er Dichter — das Du kann sich nur auf seine Person beziehen — bricht den "Himmel" um, damit das Bild Früchte tragen kann. [...] [D]as Bild [wird] durchtränkt [...] vom Göttlichen, das im Dichter waltet. Dieser Umbruch führt aber auch dazu, daß das Bild sich "entwächst"' (Burger, p. 20). The identification of 'du' with the poet and with the 'Bild', in turn, also implies that Burger identifies the 'du' with the corbel whose 'Bild' is planted. Why I do not fully agree that the image is imbued by the divine should become clearer in the explanations below, but the reasons can already be gleaned from my previous discussions of the *archetypos* in Celan.
19. Bazaine, p. 35. Celan's translation of Bazaine has the added importance that it was one of only a number of translations which Celan expressly wished to do (cf. *Mikro*, 226).
20. Hence his emphasis that the absolute poem does not exist in his 'Meridian' speech. Cf. also: Janz.
21. Bazaine, pp. 35–36.
22. Celan, *La Bibliothèque philosophique*, p. 423. Cf. also *M*, 249.
23. Føllesdal, pp. 109–10. Cf. also Moran and Cohen, p. 91.
24. Husserl, however, does differentiate quite strictly between inner and outer intuition, which is particularly the subject of his sixth chapter in: Edmund Husserl, *Logische Untersuchungen*, 4th edn, 2 vols in 3 (Tübingen: Niemeyer, 1968), II/2, 128–65. See also the appendix, pp. 222–44.
25. In several other notes Celan describes the 'Bild' as 'phänomenal' or with similar connotations (e.g. *M*, 69, 71, 74, 117). We should be aware, however, that he does not always seem to use the word 'Phänomen' and its cognates in a strictly phenomenological sense (cf. e.g. *M*, 87, 96, 230). For a further illumination of Husserl's impact on Celan, see Markus May, '"Bild-Poetik/-Politik: Anmerkungen zu Paul Celans Hinwendung zur Phänomenologie"', *treibhaus: Jahrbuch für die Literatur der fünfziger Jahre*, 13 (2017), 72–97 (pp. 87–88). For an attempt to read Celan in light of Maurice Merleau-Ponty's phenomenology, see Frank König, *Vertieftes Sein: Wahrnehmung und Körperlichkeit bei Paul Celan und Maurice Merleau-Ponty* (Heidelberg: Winter, 2014).
26. Cf. Celan's underlining of a passage in Husserl's *Phänomenologie des inneren Zeitbewusstseins* in which Husserl points out that '[m]it der Wirklichkeit haben wir es nur zu tun, insofern sie die gemeinte, vorgestellte, angeschaute, begrifflich gedachte ist' (Celan, *La Bibliothèque philosophique*, p. 420). May sees resonances of this passage in the notion of 'Wirklichkeit' in Celan's 'Bremer Rede' (cf. May, pp. 87–88).
27. Cf. 'Vision, f.', *Wörterbuchnetz — Deutsches Wörterbuch von Jacob Grimm und Wilhelm Grimm

<http://woerterbuchnetz.de/cgi-bin/WBNetz/wbgui_py?sigle=DWB&mode=Vernetzung&lemid=GV09255#XGV09255> [accessed 15 April 2019].

28. Celan, *La Bibliothèque philosophique*, p. 420; cf. Husserl, *Die Idee der Phänomenologie*, p. 62.
29. Cf. Augustine, *Confessions*, trans. by William Watts, 2 vols (London: Heinemann, 1912), II, 47 (book 9, chapter 10). I have also already discussed Meister Eckhart in the introduction. For illuminating discussions of this tradition, see Kreuzer, 'Von Augustinus zu Eckhart'; and see Leinkauf.
30. Husserl calls it 'reine Evidenz' or '[a]bsolute Gegebenheit' (Husserl, *Die Idee der Phänomenologie*, p. 61). Cf. also Christoph Grube, 'Phänomenologie', in *Celan-Handbuch: Leben, Werk, Wirkung*, ed. by Markus May, Peter Gossens, and Jürgen Lehmann, 2nd rev. and ext. edn (Stuttgart: Metzler, 2012), pp. 250–54 (pp. 251–52). Grube also briefly connects the notion of the 'Uneigentlichkeit des Gedichts' in Celan with Husserl's idea of the 'absolut Selbstgegebenen' (ibid.).
31. This is a quotation Celan may have falsely attributed to Friedrich Schlegel, where it is not to be found (cf. *M*, 241).
32. Once again we see in the 'immer und wieder' of Celan's utterance the constantly reconstituted 'Unendlichkeitsrelation' between poetic voice and other. The relation between poetic voice and other has to be established 'immer und wieder', echoing the many doublings of the second stanza of 'Halbzerfressener', into which we go 'Hinein, hinauf' and where the corbel cultivates the image 'wieder und wieder', 'das sich entwächst, entwächst'.
33. Bazaine, p. 35.
34. We have seen above that du Bouchet takes this thought a step further by stating that the 'je' is inherently *dédoublé*.
35. Bazaine, p. 35.
36. A notion reminiscent of Eckhart's 'entbilden' on the subject's path toward the divine *archetypos* (cf. Wackernagel, pp. 185–89).
37. Amthor, pp. 76–77.
38. Cf. Amthor, p. 79.
39. Ibid. Amthor goes on to state that time for du Bouchet is simply the 'Verstreichen der Zeit in der natürlichen Abfolge des Jahres' (ibid.). A treatment of du Bouchet's complex conception of time and a fully argued rejection of Amthor's interpretation of time in du Bouchet would require more space than suits our argument here. Nonetheless, from the discussion in the following chapter it should become clear why I do not fully agree with Amthor on du Bouchet's notion of time.
40. De Rijcke, 'Entretiens avec André du Bouchet', p. 287.

CHAPTER 7

The Conception of Translation in Celan and Du Bouchet

Celan and du Bouchet translated each other — a rare historical case. Translations are attempts at engaging with, forming, and perhaps reforming or even adopting the other in one's own voice. But the case of du Bouchet's and Celan's translations is even more than an engagement with each other's poetry. For both authors, translation is a cornerstone of their poetics and, as we will see, closely entwined with their notions of the image; and thus their practice of translation is also an encounter with their poetic selves. Celan's famous remarks in his 'Meridian' speech cannot only be read as referring to the poem's address to a reader but also as a poetological esquisse of translation: '[d]as Gedicht will zu einem Andern, es braucht dieses Andere, es braucht ein Gegenüber. Es sucht es auf, es spricht sich ihm zu. [...] Erst im Raum dieses Gesprächs konstituiert sich das Angesprochene' (*M*, 9). We already discussed this passage in chapter 6, when we examined the importance of the other in order to bear testimony, however tentatively, of the *archetypos*. But we can also look at Celan's utterance from the perspective of translation. Indeed, his remark can almost be taken at face value when bearing the act of translation in mind: the translated poem needs this other, that is the poem in its native tongue, because only through the engagement or dialogue with this other does the translation come into being. But there are other, more direct remarks by Celan which establish that he believed his translations to be part and parcel of his poetics. For Celan translations are 'Begegnungen' in which '[ich] mit meinem Dasein zur Sprache gegangen [bin]'.[1] It is thus not only the translation that turns back to the original, but it is also the original poem which seeks to engage with and meet a translational other.

Although du Bouchet was a less prolific translator in practice, for him the act of translation is similarly identified with the act of writing poetry as such.[2] The words he uses to describe translation bear some resemblance to those quoted above from Celan's 'Meridian' speech: '[e]n traduisant ce qui m'échappe, je me distingue de ce que je traduis. Il faut qu'en écrivant je rende compte de ce que je n'ai pas saisi.'[3] Here, too, an other is necessarily present in translation insofar as it determines translation's trajectory or direction in its attempt to grasp that which escapes translation ('ce qui m'échappe'). Similarly, he says in his *Notes sur la traduction*:

> mais traduire est une séparation aussi.   traduire
> la séparation.[4]

For du Bouchet translation is exemplary for poetic writing in general in its seeking out an other, from which it is perennially separate but which separation impels the act of writing and translating akin to the 'différence infinie', the perennially differing image we encountered in chapter 5.

There seems to exist further poetological kinship in Celan's and du Bouchet's use of tropes of circularity. Celan's circular passage along the metaphorical meridian to the other and back to himself is reminiscent of du Bouchet's 'circulation du sens'[5] in writing and translating which continually departs from and returns to the 'moi-même'.[6] In this light, du Bouchet's and Celan's reciprocal translations are more than mere coincidence or acts of sympathy that arose from their years of mutual and close friendship. They agree on the poetological importance of translation.

Despite these substantial similarities in their conception of language — and of poetry in particular — as inherently translational, there are notable differences that can already be gleaned by a closer look at the quotations above. Celan's, eventually, holistic figure of the meridian does not quite match du Bouchet's 'circulation du sens', however similarly circular the motions may be. Celan's 'Meridian' speaks of a poem in need of an other which is sought and to which the poem speaks, thereby emphasizing the complementariness between the poem and the other. This complementariness of poem and other is also clear from Celan's notion of a dialogue ('Gespräch'). Celan's 'Meridian' is conceived as a coming full circle.[7] Certainly, Celan does not wish to nullify the difference of the other to the speaker or to the speaking poem: '[a]ber in diese Gegenwart [des Gesprächs] bringt das Angesprochene und durch Nennung gleichsam zum Du Gewordene auch sein Anderssein mit' (*M*, 9). Nevertheless, Celan's diction of '*mit*sprechen' (my emphasis), of constitution ('Gewordene'), and of 'Gespräch' (*M*, 9–10) — even if it is, at times, a desperate one ('verzweifeltes Gespräch') — emphasize a shared point of contact between poem and other, and by extension between translation and original. The point of contact ('berühren'), conceived as a coming full circle — 'etwas Kreisförmiges, über die beiden Pole in sich selbst Zurückkehrendes' (*M*, 12) — is also what closes Celan's 'Meridian' speech. He addresses his audience before which he delivers his speech, thereby engaging them in a dialogue. There is another sense in which his turn toward the audience implies a coming full circle: Celan's speech had begun and closed with an address to the audience.[8]

While du Bouchet also conceives of translation as an overcoming of separation — 'traduire | la séparation' — or, in Celan's words as a shared point of contact, the separation that is constitutive to translation is much more pronounced: 'mais traduire est une séparation aussi.' Consequently, du Bouchet's 'circulation du sens' is as much driven by a tension — 'un niveau de tension qui ne fléchit pas'[9] — between translation and original as it is by bringing them together. Du Bouchet's 'traduire | la séparation' very appositely describes both the approximating and distancing acts inherent to his conception of translation, which even informs his notion of poetic subjectivity. We have already touched upon the otherness of the first person in du Bouchet in chapter 6. As we thus might surmise from du Bouchet's poetic subject that is conceived as both 'je' and 'tu', the otherness of translation is part and parcel of the act of writing and constitutive to the subject: '[j]e traduis parce que j'entretient un rapport de difficulté avec ma propre langue: il s'agit d'abord de me traduire moi-même en français.'[10]

Furthermore, the separation inherent in du Bouchet's idea of translation — 'traduire | la séparation' — is also highlighted by means of spacing. An aspect integral to du Bouchet's but not to Celan's poetry is the pictorialness of du Bouchet's text. The separation constitutive to translation which translation, seemingly self-effacing, seeks to overcome is not only the separation between the translated text and its original, but also that between the semantic and the pictorial (see also chapter 5). Du Bouchet had made this link between his conception of translation and the 'niveau visible du poème'[11] explicit in his interview with Elke de Rijcke: '[l]es blancs peuvent être considérés comme des séparations, comme des différences qui sont marquées. Mais ces séparations sont des passages.'[12] It is thus in multiple, paradoxical senses that the utterance 'traduire | la séparation' has to be read: the space between verb ('traduire') and its object ('la séparation') pictorially marks the separation that is verbally enunciated. The separation in the act of translation, between the translated text and its original, is transposed into the separation between the poem's semantics and its pictorialness (see chapter 5). Yet the spatial gap, in 'traduire | la séparation', does not constitute the separation as such. The gap is not an embodiment of the separation. Rather, the separation lies in the (metaphorical) space between the separating space and the verbally pronounced 'séparation' (number 3 in our model; see chapter 5). The separation is the *difference between* these different forms of signification.[13] An invisible interstice even seems to run through the semantic level of 'traduire | la séparation' itself, separating different readings, each of which cannot be determined as the conclusive one. It is unclear whether 'traduire | la séparation' implies reaching across the separation or ensuring that the separation is carried across when translating.

Du Bouchet's conception of translation, thus, is suspended between two irreconcilable poles: (1) on the one hand, there is a unifying trajectory that seeks to re-establish the 'rapport' between 'mot' and 'chose' (or what he also calls 'imprononcé' or 'le réel'), translate across that gap, and make them coincide,[14] impelled by the imperative that 'la chose [...] doit *être* le mot'.[15] But this begs the question: if thing and word are to coincide, what is to be made of the word 'séparation' in 'traduire | la séparation'? If the word 'séparation' *is* already the 'chose', it does not need the relating across the gap that is translation (or *traduction*).[16] Yet, if the word is not the 'chose', then the word 'séparation' already indissolubly inscribes a gap — a separation — into du Bouchet's call for translational conciliation of 'mot' and 'chose'. How are separation and unification reconcilable? Since for du Bouchet there is no such thing as a 'coïncidence absolue' between 'mot' and 'chose'[17] or a Platonic essence that transcends time and space,[18] we are thus inescapably caught in the flow of time ('le cours du temps').[19] Consequently, there are only momentary '*instant[s] [de] fusion*'.[20] Time is the differentiating element that makes impossible the 'coïncidence absolue' in an atemporal, Platonic realm.[21] Therefore in that very instant of fusion and unification, we are confronted with separation, as du Bouchet says: '[c]e que vous appelez *fraction* est *l'instant d'une fusion*.²² La fusion entre le mot et la chose est une *fraction de temps*. C'est un instant.'²³ (2) This designates the second pole of du Bouchet's conception of translation which maintains the separation. Both unification and separation are part and parcel of the impetus of 'traduire | la séparation'.²⁴ Translation tentatively achieves a reaching across the gap in the multiple separations introduced by the spacing between words and by the word 'séparation' itself. Yet, it does so only in the fraction of an 'instant' and not by positing an accomplishment, but by negating separation or in du Bouchet's words by 'détruire ce qui est détruit'.²⁵

Considering du Bouchet's paradoxes and dichotomies, Sieghild Bogumil's assertion that du Bouchet's poetry, like that of Celan, tends toward an ultimate end ('jenes Letzte')²⁶ is in much need of further qualification. Her assertion is problematic especially since she arrives at the perceived similarities between Celan's and du Bouchet's ultimate poetic end only by abstracting from seemingly merely cosmetic differences in their 'Schreibverfahren' 'auf der Textoberfläche'.²⁷ We have argued that a consideration of the 'Textoberfläche' in the case of du Bouchet's pictorial text is indispensable to the conception of his poetics. It is no coincidence that du Bouchet departed from his initial discussions of the image in the 1950s as tending toward a form of *archetypos*. Rather, from the sixties onward his image is a polychotomous one whose display on the page is akin to the 'peinture' which du Bouchet so often evokes in his texts (not to mention his frequent collaborations with artists on *livres d'artistes*).

The ultimate end, or what Bogumil terms 'jenes Letzte', of du Bouchet's poetry, although conceivable as the re-establishment of the 'rapport' between 'mot' and 'chose', is never engendered by his poetry: 'le réel' 'se per[d] dans une différence infinie' as soon as it is supposedly grasped by the poetic word (see the analysis of 'Peinture' in chapter 5). 'Poésie. Déjà, ce n'est plus d'elle qu'il s'agit.'²⁸ The ultimate end of du Bouchet's poetry is in fact the poetic expression of the impossibility to end. Insofar as the 'différence infinie' cannot be encompassed by the finite poetic page and text, it can be considered as a *locum tenens* for something — namely an infinite action — that surpasses the scope of the 'Textoberfläche'. But it does not lead 'konkret zu jenem Letzten, Unaussprechbaren', which goes 'über das Weiß der Seite [hinaus]',²⁹ because the ultimate end cannot be realized in du Bouchet's poetry. The white space of the page and the discourse of *absence* and *présence* are markers not of *an other*, but of a continuous *othering* (see chapter 5). Negatively stated, the inevitable end of a poem is merely an interruption ('l'interruption de la fin du poème'),³⁰ which in turn calls for an interruption of this very end. Positively stated, the end of the poem calls for a continuation of the 'circulation du sens'.³¹ The finiteness of the poem is therefore both: on the one hand, the poem's end is a point of contrast with the infinite circulation of meanings outside of the poem's scope. On the other hand, the poem's end in its self-negation and in its tension with itself, calling for an end to its end, is also that which lets the poem continue to circulate meanings. The interruption *by* the end of the poem is also the interruption *of* the end of the poem. Through du Bouchet's insistence that he should 'traduire

| la séparation', we can say with Layet that 'du Bouchet se consacre à traduire la persistance des contradictions'.³² Just as the unification of word and thing in a fraction of time stands under the sign of separation — as implied by the very word 'fraction' — the end of a poem stands under the sign of a poem's continuation. Consequently, du Bouchet's major poetic text on translation, *Notes sur la traduction*, ends aporetically, without coming full circle:

> le français.　　　　il me reste à traduire du français.
> [page break, J. K.]
> on ne s'aperçoit pas que cela n'a pas été traduit.³³

Even if we were to read 'traduire | la séparation' as implying that translation means bridging the separation, the separation nonetheless would still inhere in the untranslated French of *Notes sur la traduction*: 'il me reste à traduire du français.' However, if translating the separation is understood as continuing the separation *in* the act of translation rather than cancelling it out,³⁴ the separation between original and translation has not yet been introduced to the French text of the *Notes* due to its being untranslated — which is perhaps why it has not been noticed that it was not translated in the first place. These two different poles (*fusion* and separation), as we previously called them, thus remain operative in du Bouchet's conception of translation until its end — that is, until the poem is interrupted.³⁵

In contrast to du Bouchet, bridging the separation, or rather bridging 'Abgründe', is clearly what Celan intends to do when translating. It almost seems as if Celan is directly replying to du Bouchet when he writes the following in a letter to Karl Dedecius (31 January 1960) that predates du Bouchet's *Notes sur la traduction* by sixteen years:

> Brücken von Sprache zu Sprache, aber — Brücken über | Abgründe. Noch beim allerwörtlichsten Nachsprechen des Vorgegebenen — Ihnen, lieber | Herr Dedecius, will es als ein 'Aufgehen' im Sprachmedium des Anderen erscheinen — : | es bleibt, faktisch, immer ein Nachsprechen, ein zweites Sprechen; noch im (scheinbar) | restlosen 'Aufgehen' bleibt der 'Aufgehende' mit seiner — auch sprachlichen — | Einmaligkeit, mit seinem Anderssein.³⁶

Despite this irremediable existential difference ('Anderssein') between translation and original, for Celan the envisioned trajectory when translating is a unifying one. That which remains untranslated and which makes any full merging into one ('Aufgehen') impossible is the distinguishing imprint time and history leave on the different speakers of languages, on poet and translating poet.³⁷ The notion of each speaker's uniqueness ('Einmaligkeit'), which has temporal connotations in German, constituting their untranslatable, existential difference is more elaborately laid out in Celan's 'Meridian' speech:

> Noch im Hier und Jetzt des Gedichts — das Gedicht selbst hat ja immer nur diese eine, einmalige, punktuelle Gegenwart — , noch in dieser Unmittelbarkeit und Nähe läßt es das ihm, dem Anderen, Eigenste mitsprechen: dessen Zeit. (*M*, 9–10)

Thus, as for du Bouchet, time is the differentiating element which is constitutive of the separation between translation and original and between word and thing.[38] Yet, for Celan, time's bearing on individual speakers has historical and existential import. In his conception of time he has more in common with Osip Mandelstam than with du Bouchet.[39] As perhaps Bogumil noted first, du Bouchet's conception of time fundamentally differs from that of Celan: 'Celan spricht über das Vergessen mittels der Erinnerung', whereas du Bouchet's poetry operates in the present (and in the presence of what she calls the poetic landscape), forgetting the past.[40] Du Bouchet himself, in his interview with Michael Jakob, makes explicit this difference in his understanding of time compared to Celan:

> ich [bin] auch gleichsam ohne Gedächtnis; ich stehe dem Unerwarteten offen gegenüber, und dieses Unerwartete kann ja auch ausbleiben. [...] [D]as unterscheidet mich z.B. von Paul Celan, der ein totales historisches Gedächtnis besaß, der Erinnerungen des Verwurzelt- und Entwurzeltseins besaß. Mir war dies nicht gegeben; ich habe nicht dieses Bewußtsein einer Tradition, zu der ich gehören würde.[41]

Wiebke Amthor remarks that du Bouchet's forgetting, which she believes to be expressed by his *blancs*, seems to mark 'den unweigerlichen Verlust' of memory which is declared to be '[das] eigentlich[e] Ziel' of his poetic endeavour.[42] Amthor here somewhat overemphasizes the idea that loss ('Verlust') is at the heart of forgetting and du Bouchet's *blancs*. After all, the forgetting of the past in the immediate present of the 'instant de fusion' also implies that writing can go on in du Bouchet's polychotomous poetics, in which 'ces séparations [des blancs] sont des passages'.[43] Nevertheless, Amthor and Bogumil touch upon a point in which du Bouchet's poetry fundamentally differs from that of Celan, for whom forgetting was impossible in a psychological, ethical, and linguistic sense.[44] Bogumil even believes that Celan engaged with and translated du Bouchet's poetry precisely because it allowed him to forget about the cruel history which underpinned his own poetry: 'Celan hat hier, in den geschichtslosen Worten eines rudimentären unberührten Landschaftsentwurfs, die leicht gewordene Sprache gefunden, die ihm im Deutschen nicht mehr zugänglich ist.'[45] That this was, in fact, Celan's motivation, is doubtful. Celan's contemporaneous translations of Giuseppe Ungaretti (around 1968), who is very much concerned with history and memory, certainly attest that a search for 'geschichtslos[e] Wort[e]' was not a general tendency of Celan's translational endeavours at the time.[46]

Furthermore, in a more fundamental sense, history cannot be glossed over or simply ignored in the act of translation for Celan. Indeed, given that in his work the 'Einmaligkeit' of each poem, that is the unique sequence of historical circumstances leading to the poem being written, constitutes the latter's irremediable, and untranslatable otherness,[47] history must be, ethically and factually, ever present in the act of translation. It is precisely the untranslatability of the unique historical provenance of each act of speaking or writing which calls for a translation that does not extinguish the otherness of that which is translated. In this superficial sense, Celan's conception of translation, like that of du Bouchet, seems to perpetuate the gap the translation is tasked to reach across. Yet where du Bouchet's conception of translation ends in inconclusiveness, Celan's conceived preservation of the otherness or the separation through the act of translation is conciliatory or at the very least unambiguously conclusive in its trajectory. In Celan's view, a poem only communicates when its unique historical provenance — the historical context from which it arises and the history that the poem itself gives voice to — is considered by the reader. The poem speaks only when the historical gap between the present instance of reading or translating, itself embedded in history, is considered vis-à-vis the unique history of the poem, its *Einmaligkeit*. This may mean, on the one hand, that the translator, due to her own history — and certainly we must think of the Holocaust here — cannot translate a poem in such a way that its translation conveys a belief in the harmony of language. Celan found such a belief in the harmony of language in Sergei Yesenin, whose poems he translated (see footnote 37). It may also mean that the translator must translate a text with particular attention to the unique history of a poem and its writer, as surely every translator of Celan must do. Thus, translation as understood by Celan cannot gloss over and smoothly relate across the history in which the original utterance is embedded. Only in retaining history can the poem speak to us. In this sense, too, Celan's poems are already translated: in retracing the 'untrügliche Spur' of the Holocaust,[48] they retain and commemorate the historic circumstances which gave rise to them, communicating, indeed, translating them to us.

Yet on a different, more abstract level Celan does hope to overcome and translate language across the division between word and thing.[49] This perceived division is embedded in a quasi-historical mythology which underlies his notion of translation as such. Celan's intense focus on the presence and *Einmaligkeit* of each poem, which is always a consideration of its writer's history, is itself,[50] of course, historically conditioned — a history Celan would have preferred undone. Past atrocities provide the trajectory of Celan's quasi-historical mythology which underlies his conception of translation (see also chapter 4). Winfried Menninghaus most appositely describes the trajectory, origin, and teleological direction of this mythology in the following way:

> Die Sprachmystik selbst hat diese Frage [des Ursprungs und des Ziels mystischen Schreibens und Strebens] seit je auf das Schema vom Sündenfall und die Restitution des Paradieses bezogen. [...] Indem Celan nun auch dieses (heils)geschichtliche Schema der Mystik des 'Namens' aktualisierend reinterpretiert, wird die scheinbar unhistorische Sprachontologie [der Mystik] an sich selbst auf eine Gestalt der Geschichte hin durchsichtig, und zwar oft sogar direkt im tradierten mystisch-theologischen Gewand. Immer wieder wird nämlich die Intention auf den 'Namen' [...] auf die Elemente der biblischen Sündenfallgeschichte und ihre sprachverwirrenden Folgen (Baum des Lebens, Baum der Erkenntnis, Babel) bezogen, und immer wieder wird dabei die Erfahrung des Faschismus als der historische Grund der Aktualisierung der Sündenfallgeschichte transparent.[51]

The quasi-historical mythology in its conjunction of the mythological Fall of Man and the confusion of tongues with the history of Nazism and the Holocaust is rarely explicitly uttered but seems to underlie Celan's entire poetics and poetry.[52]

However, there are moments where this mythology clearly rises to the surface. This is the case in Celan's first major attempt at a poetics with 'Traum vom Traume', in which the Fall of Man is interpreted foremost as linguistic event merging with the more implicitly evoked past of the Holocaust (*CW* III, 156, see also chapter 1). According to the early poetics of this essay, for instance, the word 'tree' is divested from the tree as its signified object by the fact that the meaning of the word would include historical atrocities, such as people being hanged on trees (*CW* III, 156). Throughout Celan's poetry (human) language is characterized by an inherent need for translation to cross the historico-mythically marked gap between word and thing and return to the originary state, as has been discussed in our interpretation of Celan's poem 'Bei Wein und Verlorenheit' (where the act of translation, however, fails).[53]

This quasi-historical mythology at the heart of translation and language is entirely lacking in du Bouchet. In an interview he admits that 'à cette époque-ci, les rapports [entre mot et chose] ne sont plus donnés,'[54] implying the existence of a previous state in which these 'rapports' were given.[55] However, this anterior state remains almost completely unspecified and abstract, being only loosely associated with the destruction of World War II. More importantly perhaps, this anterior original state and the socio-political contours it takes in the interviews,[56] does not present itself in his poetry, nor is it mourned in his poetry as a state of loss, whether historical or mythical. Du Bouchet's poetry is not embedded in a historical trajectory with an origin and a teleological or even eschatological end. Quite the opposite is the case, as Alain Mascarou observes:

> Chez André du Bouchet en effet, le sentiment, premier, de la pluralité des langues, antérieur dirait-on à celui d'une langue natale [...], suscite une rêverie matérielle sur l'incidence concrète des mots. 'Habité par le désir humain [...] [le nom, A. M.] reflète le degré de réel.' Mais cette notion du nom comme indice de réalité, témoin de notre prise sur les choses [...], n'est marquée, et pour cause, ni par la quête d'une 'métaphysique de l'origine [où, A. M.] les mots sont supposés continus aux choses', ni par la nostalgie d'une adéquation parfaite du mot à ce qu'il désigne. [...] La valeur concrète des vocables est donc acquise, temporaire, tributaire des zones de contact, de frottement, de déperdition, des mots et des choses.[57]

The tentative unification of word and thing in du Bouchet hence is not motivated by an ultimate metaphysical goal, nor does it seek to turn back to a primordial linguistic state. Precisely because such unification is only tentatively conceivable under the sign of separation and in a present instant of time, such a metaphysical trajectory projected into the distant future or past is impossible for du Bouchet.

Translation and the Image in Du Bouchet and Celan

These in some respects similar but essentially different approaches to language and translation in the two authors are reflected in their conception of the image. For du Bouchet, the image is conceived as an '[i]mage parvenue à son terme inquiet'. This image thus arrives at a state of non-arrival, a contradictory inconclusiveness reflected in his entire poetry suspended between different poles. The radical polychotomous form, which du Bouchet's image takes, not only pronounces itself in the semantics of *absence* and *présence*, but also in the pictorial thrust of the white page as opposed to the black ink (see chapter 5). In Celan's poetry and poetics, the image also evinces a dialectical tension between *typos* and *archetypos*, but one which Celan hopes to dissolve in favour of the *archetypos*. We have seen this, on the one hand, in our analyses of 'Tenebrae' and 'Bei Wein und Verlorenheit', where the image as *typos* has negative connotations. On the other hand, we observed in 'Halbzerfressener' that the image, when positively conceived, continuously transcends itself and approaches a form of secularized — or in the words of Celan's 'Meridian' speech: 'Immaterielles, aber Irdisches, Terrestrisches' (*M*, 12) — *archetypos*. Hence, where the image in Celan can grow out of its being dependent on a superficial representation of an outer reality — whose surface might also hide the traces of past crimes — it can regain its status as 'Sprache als geistige Gestalt' (*M*, 75).[58] The image as *archetypos* is therefore 'nichts Visuelles, sondern etwas Geistiges' (*M*, 101, also 107) which is recognized in an introspective, divinatory 'Vision' (*M*, 109, also 121), true to Celan's 'Seelenrealismus'.[59] This divination, however, is never an entirely transcendent act of seeing. As 'Wahrnehmen', it still retains its colloquial sense of 'perception', but also points toward a philosophical or theological form of cognition which ultimately leads to the truth already etymologically contained in the word (*Wahrheit*). Celan puts this very poignantly in the following note in preparation for the 'Meridian' speech: 'Sehen als <u>Gewahren</u>, Wahrnehmen, Wahrhaben, Wahr<u>sein</u>' (*M*, 134). The archetypal image is perceived and taken for truth.[60]

In both authors the gaps, separations, and moments of speechlessness that are part and parcel of the translational endeavour are negotiated and renegotiated in the image. Du Bouchet's 'image parvenue à son terme inquiet' is just the other side of the coin of his 'traduire | la séparation', insofar as both imply either reaching an end that is not finite ('parvenue à son terme inquiet') or a relating across a separation ('traduire') whose disjunctive qualities are perpetuated as well as nullified by the act of translation. For Celan, on the other hand, within the image, comprising *archetypos* and *typos*, the demarcating line is drawn between what he believes to be the false pretences of metaphor — as figurative and translated in such a way that history is obliterated or glossed over[61] — and untranslatable truth (cf. e.g. *M*, 75, 134, 159). Therefore, the image (as *typos*) has negative connotations in 'Tenebrae' and 'Bei Wein und Verlorenheit'. But it is also why the image seems to provide a solution which turns and returns us to the 'Sprache als geistige Gestalt' in 'Halbzerfressener' and in many notes for his 'Meridian' speech (*M*, 101). Thus whereas Celan has nothing positive to say about metaphor (akin to the *typos*-image) in his 'Meridian' speech notes (*M*, 70, 138, 158) and even speaks of an anti-metaphorical character of the poem (*M*, 74, 145), it is frequently in these very same passages that the image is evoked in contradistinction to metaphor (*M*, 69, 74, 87, 109, cf. also 128, 134).[62] Even in the final 'Meridian' speech itself, metaphor and image are only seemingly used synonymously, according to the prevailing usage of 'image' in literary studies as a metaphor for metaphor, as a closer look reveals:

Und was wären dann die Bilder?
    Das einmal, das immer wieder einmal und nur jetzt und nur hier Wahrgenommene und Wahrzunehmende. Und das Gedicht wäre somit der Ort, wo alle Tropen und Metaphern ad absurdum geführt werden wollen. (*M*, 10)

We have already seen that Celan understands *wahrnehmen* as more than just perception but also as some form of cognition of truth — albeit not an absolute,[63] but a terrestrial, even if immaterial one (*M*, 12). This *wahrnehmen* is ascribed to the 'Bilder' that truthfully display what is perceived, whereas the figurativeness of metaphor is to be abolished or reduced to absurdity. Or in other words, to purloin a phrase from Celan's notes, images are not 'als Metapher abzutun, sondern als ein Wissen und Sehen zu verstehen' (*M*, 128).

The Reciprocal Translations in Context

We will see in the following chapter how Celan's and du Bouchet's conceptions of the image and translation inform their reciprocal translations. Before we analyse the latter, we should outline current research on the two authors' translations and the general place of their reciprocal translations in their respective oeuvre. Whereas Celan's translations have been widely received — the first book-length study having been published in 1985,[64] followed by many other studies of and commentaries on his translations[65] — and have become canonical,[66] the translations of his younger contemporary du Bouchet still await such treatment. This situation may be in part due to the fact that Celan was much more prolific as a translator, working across French, Russian, Italian, English, Hebrew, Romanian, and Portuguese. Another reason may be du Bouchet's insufficient command of the languages (German and Russian) from which he translated, excepting English. Especially in the case of Celan's poetry he relied on the advice of his friend.[67]

For this reason, it is much easier to contextualize Celan's translations of du Bouchet and his translational methods within his great range of translations than it is do the same for du Bouchet. Due to the pioneering work by Leonard Olschner and Bernhard Böschenstein, we know that Celan's approach to translation changed around 1964.[68] His translations of du Bouchet fall into this period. Although neither Böschenstein nor Olschner concern themselves with du Bouchet in their respective studies, the differences they unveil in Celan's approach to translating the poetry of Jules Supervielle before and after 1964 support the assumption that Celan became more 'faithful' or *wörtlich* in his later translational work.[69] Some of Bogumil's speculations about why Celan chose to translate du Bouchet so faithfully[70] can be cleared up by looking at Celan's translations within the greater purview of his translations in this period.[71]

Unfortunately, a similarly extensive overview of du Bouchet's translations is not available and, consequently, his translations of Celan cannot be synoptically integrated into a potential spectrum of translational methods. We can only unambiguously affirm that Celan's poetry proved to be the most persistently translated and retranslated — perhaps also the most resistant to translation — by du Bouchet. Du Bouchet published three different book editions of Celan's poetry: *Strette* (1971),[72] *Poèmes* (1978),[73] and *Poèmes* (1986).[74] Du Bouchet thus translated Celan at a time when he had already found his poetic vocation and voice in his *Dans la chaleur vacante* (1961) and after he had gained experience in translating William Faulkner (1951), Shakespeare (1961), James Joyce (1961), and Hölderlin (1963), amongst others. Apart from Mandelstam, Celan is the only author whom du Bouchet translates so far into his own poetic maturity and on such a scale.[75]

It certainly does not help that the status of du Bouchet's translations of Celan — at least in *Strette* — is controversially discussed in scholarly literature. Böschenstein's comparative study of du Bouchet's translations of Hölderlin and Celan concludes that du Bouchet's greater fidelity to the original text in translating Celan is due to Celan's own involvement in the process of translation[76] and due to a sense of responsibility owed to the violent history experienced by his friend.[77] On the other hand, Henri Meschonnic reproaches du Bouchet's translations of Celan in unusually evaluative language. He surmises that du Bouchet, standing all too much in the Mallarméan tradition,[78] translated Celan without being sensitized to the latter's 'langage [...] occulté' and his poetological 'transfert de kabbale'.[79] Bertrand Badiou even conjectures that Celan was reluctant to have his poems translated into French, due to the poet's believing they were downright untranslatable.[80]

Only part of the controversy can be resolved by asserting that Böschenstein makes a relative, comparative assessment of du Bouchet's translations whereas Meschonnic judges du Bouchet's translations of Celan according to a different, more abstract measure of translation. The present study does not seek to resolve this controversy and it can certainly not hope to level the imbalance of research on the translations of the two authors. However, such a balancing of scales should not be necessary since the elaborate analyses of their respective poetics as well as of the similarities and differences between them will sufficiently equip us to discern the motivations behind their particular translational divergences from the original.

The focus on the poetological and translational differences should not mask the role their friendship played in their poetic and translational engagement with each other. If translation was, for both authors, a way to bridge the gap or at least an attempt to do so, their letters are testimony to the fact that both saw in the other an intimate point of contact ('instant de fusion') or a 'Brück[e] über | Abgründe'. Celan's belief that a poem is like a 'Händedruck' between two people engaging in a dialogue was surely doubly enacted in the translational and actual shaking of hands with du Bouchet.[81] Du Bouchet was, tragically, a bridge in more than just a poetological sense: he seems to have been Celan's only close friend in Paris in the late 60s, and during Celan's times in psychiatric clinics du Bouchet was one of the few visitors keeping the friend in touch with poetic life and the outside world.[82] The bridge over abysses provided by Celan's personal exchange with du Bouchet, in turn, became poetically manifest in his poetry. As a letter by du Bouchet reached Celan in early December 1968, Celan had — 'juste au moment' — 'terminé de transcrire, dans un cahier, un poetit poème' and the poem tellingly begins: 'Ungespalten die Rede'.[83]

For du Bouchet, on the other hand, the endorsement of the senior poet he admired seemed to wipe away all doubts and uncertainties about his poetic efforts which 'se poursuit si aveuglément': 'tout ce qui provient de vous a pour moi valeur de certitude et de confirmation.'[84] Through Celan, du Bouchet experienced 'l'instant dont je suis à la poésie — et à la poésie par vous — redevable'.[85]

Notes to Chapter 7

1. *Briefe an Hans Bender*, ed. by Ute Heimbüchel and Volker Neuhaus (Munich: Hanser 1984), p. 54; cf. Pennone, p. 1.
2. '[L]e travail personnel n'est pas tellement différent de celui d'une traduction' (de Rijcke, 'Entretiens avec André du Bouchet', p. 278).
3. Ibid.
4. Du Bouchet, *Ici en deux*, n.p.
5. De Rijcke, 'Entretiens avec André du Bouchet', p. 288.
6. Cf. ibid., p. 277.
7. Celan's understanding of his poetry and poetics as being in dialogue with other poets is perhaps almost universally discussed among Celan scholars. Leonard Olschner was the first to discuss this at length with respect to Celan's translation: cf. Leonard Olschner, *Der feste Buchstab: Erläuterungen zu Paul Celans Gedichtübertragungen* (Göttingen: Vandenhoeck & Ruprecht, 1985), pp. 13–34, 54. See also Pennone, pp. 1–15.
8. On the importance of cyclical structures in Celan's poetry up to about the time of his 'Meridian' speech, see Seng, *Auf den Kreis-Wegen der Dichtung*.
9. De Rijcke, 'Entretiens avec André du Bouchet', p. 288.
10. Ibid., p. 277. Wagstaff even speaks of an 'individual self [that] is effaced' in du Bouchet's poetry (Wagstaff, *Provisionality and the Poem*, p. 167).
11. De Rijcke, 'Entretiens avec André du Bouchet', p. 289.
12. Ibid., p. 282.
13. 'Je suppose que le blanc *n'est pas* l'imprononcé, mais nous le *montre*.' Question formulated by de Rijcke addressed to du Bouchet, which he affirms (ibid., p. 289).
14. Cf. ibid., pp. 286–87.
15. Ibid., p. 285. All italics in the original, except where indicated otherwise. Cf. also: '[m]ais dans cet écart seul réside la possibilité d'un déplacement, qui est le mouvement même de l'écrire et du traduire, leur unique vérité, qui n'est pas d'adéquation, mais d'approximation perpétuelle' (Michel Collot, 'Ici en deux: André du Bouchet, poète et traducteur', in *Génétique & Traduction*, ed. by Serge Bourjea (Paris: L'Harmattan, 1995), pp. 147–67 (p. 149).
16. Cf. 'Traduire, verbe trans.', *Le Trésor de la Langue Française informatisé* <http://atilf.atilf.fr/> [accessed 18 March 2021].
17. De Rijcke, 'Entretiens avec André du Bouchet', p. 287.
18. Ibid., p. 294.
19. Ibid., p. 287.
20. Ibid., p. 287.
21. Layet makes a similar point: '[o]r, sans tenir pour faux le principe énoncé par Aristote [le principe de non-contradiction], on peut néanmoins remarquer qu'il n'est vrai qu'à condition que la chose décrite soit considérée pendant un seul instant en sous un seul point de vue. Et puisque le passage du temps rend nécessairement partielle une telle description, la vérité exige de reconnaître qu'en un instant donné les choses ne se contredisent pas, mais s'apprêtent à le faire, et qu'au lieu d'un ensemble discontinu de choses différentes, le réel est bien plutôt cette continuité de relations conflictuelles qu'Héraclite nommait déjà un combat' (Layet, 'Demain diamant', p. 30).
22. For a similar but more enigmatic conception of time which we cannot discuss more fully here see: du Bouchet, 'Image à terme', 1979, n.p.
23. De Rijcke, 'Entretiens avec André du Bouchet', p. 287; cf. also Wagstaff's interpretation that du

Bouchet's time 'is not the linear passing of historical time, but rather the freshness of repeated newness' (Wagstaff, *Provisionality and the Poem*, p. 184).
24. Cf. also: 'puisque jamais nous ne pouvons sortir de la langue, comme entre deux langues, comme entre deux mots, sur l'impossibilité de sur une telle passer de l'un a l'autre, exclus alors, n'en disposant d'aucune': André du Bouchet, 'Tübingen, le 22 Mai 1986', *Hölderlin Jahrbuch*, 26 (1988), 343–59 (p. 345).
25. De Rijcke, 'Entretiens avec André du Bouchet', p. 298. This mirrors what Layet says about G. W. F. Hegel's dialectics which he believes underlie du Bouchet's poetological paradoxes: '[l]e mouvement d'ensemble auquel celle-ci entent se conformer est bien plutôt de *dépassement* du négatif, c'est-à-dire la négativité s'appliquant à la négativité elle-même, qui est, plus fondamentalement encore que le négatif, *positivement* à l'œuvre dans le réel' (Layet, 'Demain diamant', p. 31). However, as Layet holds, du Bouchet's poetry does not reach a final resolve, only a 'terme inquiet' (ibid., p. 34). Du Bouchet also phrases it this way: '[d]ans ce que j'écris, j'essaie de rester à un niveau de tension qui ne fléchit pas' (de Rijcke, 'Entretiens avec André du Bouchet', p. 288). Although Layet already makes some crucial distinctions between du Bouchet and Hegel, it should be added that du Bouchet's thinking does not have a Hegelian *Geist* and a historic dimension. As such, du Bouchet's position resembles more Hegel's early Romantic predecessors Novalis and Friedrich Schlegel. Whereas Hegel enters the realm of the absolute, the early German Romantics could only resort to a longing for the absolute not reached by the mutual negation — similar to du Bouchet's 'détruire ce qui est détruit' — of finite parts. There is a strong resemblance between some of the formulations and ideas of Novalis and du Bouchet's 'détruire ce qui est détruit'. Cf. Frank, *Einführung in die frühromantische Ästhetik*, pp. 309–10, 312–13.
26. Sieghild Bogumil, '"Ortswechsel bei den Substanzen": Paul Celan als Übersetzer von André du Bouchet und Jacques Dupin', in *Stationen: Kontinuität und Entwicklung in Paul Celans Übersetzungswerk*, ed. by Jürgen Lehmann and Christine Ivanović (Heidelberg: Winter, 1997), pp. 163–93 (p. 168).
27. Bogumil, '"Ortswechsel bei den Substanzen"', p. 169.
28. Du Bouchet, 'Image à terme', 1979, n.p.
29. Bogumil, '"Ortswechsel bei den Substanzen"', p. 169.
30. De Rijcke, 'Entretiens avec André du Bouchet', p. 287.
31. Ibid., p. 288.
32. Layet, 'Demain diamant', p. 34.
33. Du Bouchet, *Ici en deux*, n.p.
34. Evelyn Dueck emphasizes this separation inherent in du Bouchet's notion of translation when she states: '[s]elon du Bouchet, le but d'une traduction n'est pas de réduire cet écart, mais de le rendre manifeste, puisque "nous sommes, pour le dire, sans langue natale"' (Evelyn Dueck, *L'Étranger intime: Les Traductions françaises de l'œuvre de Paul Celan* (Berlin: De Gruyter, 2014), p. 257. The French that du Bouchet thinks still remains to be translated is very reminiscent of Derrida's notion of 'une sorte d'"aliénation" originaire qui institue toute langue en langue de l'autre; l'impossible propriété d'une langue' — a point which Derrida later (I believe wrongly) associates with Celan, but is much more fittingly applied to du Bouchet: Jacques Derrida, *Le Monolinguisme de l'autre; ou, La Prothèse d'origine* (Paris: Galilée, 1996), pp. 121, (on Celan) 129. Clémence O'Connor makes this point about du Bouchet as well in 'Poetry as a Foreign Language in Heather Dohollau and André du Bouchet', *Nottingham French Studies*, 56.2 (2017), 188–200 (p. 195).
35. George Steiner notes that in a sense all of Celan's own poetry has already been translated into German. Celan's poetry has already passed through the difficulties of translation to find its expression in German, a language 'qui reste, douloureusement, mienne', whereas the French of du Bouchet's poetry remains in an aporetic 'reste à traduire'; cited in Olschner, *Der feste Buchstab*, p. 41.
36. Cited in Sanmann, pp. 388–89. Cf. also Celan's letter to Werner Weber of 26 March 1960 in which he likewise speaks of 'Abgründe' between languages and emphasizes that a translation has to remain conscious of and even retain this 'Anders- und Verschiedensei[n]' (Gellhaus, pp. 397–400).

37. Olschner gives Celan's translations of poems by Sergei Yesenin as an example of what we have called existential difference. Yesenin had not participated in the hermetic poetic development of his western contemporary colleagues (approximately 1895 to 1925) and his work still exhibited a 'Vertrauen in die Sprache und ihre potentielle Harmonie'; Olschner writes further: 'Es wäre, so paradox dies klingen mag, ein Akt der Untreue, ja der Sabotage am eigenen Werk gewesen, wenn Celan diese Entwicklung hätte leugnen wollen und beispielsweise für seine Esenin-Übertragungen eine frühere, angeblich "intakte", vertrautere und somit letztlich verfehlte Sprache verwendet hätte. Die historischen und sozialen Konfrontationen, denen Celan seine Sprache aussetzen mußte, waren bei Esenin nicht gegeben' (Olschner, *Der feste Buchstab*, p. 23).
38. The idea of time as an obstacle to the possibility of poetic expression — an obstacle which nevertheless should not simply be nullified but be considered — is already apparent in Celan's early text 'Der Traum vom Traume' (*CW* III, 156–62).
39. Cf. Amthor, p. 76.
40. Bogumil, ' "Ortswechsel bei den Substanzen" ', p. 172.
41. 'Gespräch mit André du Bouchet', in *Aussichten des Denkens*, ed. and trans. by Michael Jakob (Munich: Fink, 1997), pp. 57–85 (pp. 84–85).
42. Amthor, p. 139.
43. De Rijcke, 'Entretiens avec André du Bouchet', p. 282.
44. Theo Buck has formulated poignantly that, for Celan, German was 'Muttersprache, Mördersprache'; cf. his *Muttersprache, Mördersprache*, Celan-Studien, 1 (Aachen: Rimbaud, 1993).
45. Bogumil, ' "Ortswechsel bei den Substanzen" ', p. 182.
46. Cf. Olschner, *Der feste Buchstab*, pp. 309–18. Cf. also: Peter Goßens, 'Nachwort', in *'Angefügt, nahtlos, dem Heute'. 'Agglutinati all'oggi': Paul Celan übersetzt Giuseppe Ungaretti. Zweisprachige Ausgabe. Italienisch, deutsch. Handschriften. Erstdruck. Dokumente*, ed. by Peter Goßens (Frankfurt a. M.: Insel, 2006), pp. 185–222; Peter Goßens, *Paul Celans Ungaretti-Übersetzung: Edition und Kommentar* (Heidelberg: Winter, 2000). A clearing away of accrued historical senses in language was also already rejected by Celan in his essay 'Traum vom Traume' (see chapter 1).
47. 'Das Gedicht ist das Einmalige Unübertragbare Gegenwärtige' (*M*, 145).
48. Cf. the first lines of Celan's 'Engführung' (*KG*, 113).
49. That Celan had the desire to overcome the separation between word and thing seems to be implied when Klaus Reichert believes to discover in Celan's poetry 'die Restitution eines sehr alten Sprachdenkens: im Hebräischen bilden nämlich Wort und Ding, Wort und Sache eine Einheit, es gibt für sie nur das einzige Wort *dabar*.' Menninghaus dedicates his entire Celan study to this subject. Cf. Klaus Reichert, 'Hebräische Züge in der Sprache Paul Celans', in *Paul Celan*, ed. by Werner Hamacher and Winfried Menninghaus (Frankfurt a. M.: Suhrkamp, 1988), pp. 156–69 (p. 164); see also Menninghaus, *Paul Celan*, p. 31.
50. 'Wer es [das Gedicht] schreibt, bleibt ihm mitgegeben' (*M*, 9).
51. Menninghaus, *Paul Celan*, p. 55. Menninghaus uses the somewhat esoteric vocabulary of Walter Benjamin, e.g. when he speaks of 'Intention auf den Namen'. This intention has as its goal to restore the identity relation of word and thing through and in the name, which is believed to have an ontological relation to that which it names.
52. How deep these notions go in Celan's thinking can be gleaned from remarks such as '[d]ie Sünde am Wort' — a vocabulary entirely absent in du Bouchet (Huppert, p. 320). For other aspects of the mystical in Celan's poetry, see, amongst others: Schulze; Irene Fußl, *'Geschenke an Aufmerksame': Hebräische Intertextualität und mystische Weltauffassung in der Lyrik Paul Celans* (Tübingen: Niemeyer, 2008). Fußl analyses in particular the Kabbalistic motifs of Shevirat ha'Kelim in Celan's poetry as articulating the loss of an originary state (Fußl, pp. 55–67).
53. My interpretation of the multiplicity of languages in Celan differs from that of Derrida who seems to see (multilingual) difference as integral to Celan's poetry when he states that '[c]haque poème a sa propre langue' and speaks of the 'valeur différentielle' as a 'condition [...] du poème' (Jacques Derrida, *Shibboleth: Pour Paul Celan* (Paris: Éditions Galilée, 1986), p. 56).
54. De Rijcke, 'Entretiens avec André du Bouchet', p. 295.
55. Cf. also: 'Gespräch mit André du Bouchet', in *Aussichten des Denkens*, ed. by Jakob, pp. 63, 69.
56. Elke de Rijcke 'Sur la traduction: Compost de langue retourné en fleurs et en fruits, un entretien', *L'Étrangère*, 16–17–18 (2007), 269–76 (p. 274).

57. Alain Mascarou, *Les Cahiers de 'l'Éphémère' 1967–1972: Tracés interrompus* (Paris: L'Harmattan, 1998), pp. 192–93. Layet also points to du Bouchet's lack of historical reference in his poetry and his lack of a Jewish identity as demarcating the poetry of du Bouchet from that of Celan: Layet, 'La Survie insensée' (esp. pp. 179–80).
58. Much of this is also echoed in Celan's translation of Bazaine (see also the analysis of 'Halbzerfressener'); cf. Bazaine, pp. 35–36.
59. Huppert, p. 321.
60. Cf. also Bogumil, '"Ortswechsel bei den Substanzen"', p. 133. Celan's note, in turn, is also reminiscent of a sentence in Émile Bréhier's introduction to his French translation of Plotinus' *The Enneads* (in which Celan had particularly underlined explanations relating to the image): '[l]a vision, d'après la thèse platonicienne, se fait par un contact entre la lumière intérieure à l'œil et la lumière extérieure' (Celan, *La Bibliothèque philosophique*, p. 68).
61. 'Als das Unübertragbare, selbst nicht leicht zu Tragende und oft Unerträgliche — unerträglich Schwere — haßt man das Gedicht. Wer das Gedicht nicht [...] mit-tragen will, überträgt und spricht gern von Metaphern' (*M*, 158, also pp. 69, 121, 128). Celan's use of the word *übertragen* implies both translating and metaphorizing — a double meaning comparable to *translatio* in Latin. It is worth remembering that some critics' descriptions of Celan's poetry as figurative and metaphoric ('Traumbilde[r]') seemed to betray a deliberate attempt at ignoring the poems' underlying history (see Emmerich, pp. 94–95). Some of Celan's notes for the 'Meridian' speech appear to have been made specifically to reject such a reception of his poetry (cf. *M*, 158).
62. Metaphor gets a similarly dismissive treatment in Celan's poetry; cf. the 'Metapherngestöber' in his poem 'Ein Dröhnen' (*KG*, 206), which is reminiscent of the all-destructive 'Partikelgestöber' in his poem 'Engführung' (*KG*, 115).
63. Cf. the context of this mention of 'Bild' and 'Metapher': just before, Celan had declared that '[d]as absolute Gedicht — nein, das gibt es nicht, das kann es nicht geben!' (*M*, 10).
64. Olschner, *Der feste Buchstab*.
65. Among others: Harbusch; Goßens, *Paul Celans Ungaretti-Übersetzung*; *Stationen: Kontinuität und Entwicklung in Paul Celans Übersetzungswerk*, ed. by Jürgen Lehmann and Christine Ivanović (Heidelberg: Winter, 1997); Gellhaus; Pennone.
66. For instance, many of the translations in the third and fourth volumes of C. H. Beck's anthology of French poetry are Celan's. *Französische Dichtung: Eine zweisprachige Anthologie in vier Bänden*, ed. by Friedhelm Kemp and others, 2nd edn, 4 vols (Munich: Beck, 2010).
67. Cf. 'Gespräch mit André du Bouchet', in *Aussichten des Denkens*, ed. by Jakob, pp. 80–81. However, Celan apparently had not given much advice beyond a 'mot à mot' translation, so du Bouchet had no idea that e.g. the 'Hütte' referred to in Celan's poem 'Todtnauberg' was Martin Heidegger's (de Rijcke, 'Sur la traduction', p. 282).
68. Cf. Olschner, *Der feste Buchstab*, p. 304; Bernhard Böschenstein, 'Supervielle in Celans Fügung', in *Paul Celan*, ed. by Werner Hamacher and Winfried Menninghaus (Frankfurt a. M.: Suhrkamp, 1988), pp. 222–39.
69. Cf. Olschner, *Der feste Buchstab*, pp. 303–18; Cf. also Pennone, p. 402.
70. Bogumil, '"Ortswechsel bei den Substanzen"', pp. 182–84.
71. Hence, Pennone corrects Bogumil's assumptions (Pennone, pp. 403–04).
72. Paul Celan, *Strette*, trans. by André du Bouchet and others (Paris: Mercure de France, 1971).
73. Paul Celan, *Poèmes*, trans. by André du Bouchet (Paris: Clivages, 1978).
74. Paul Celan, *Poèmes*, trans. by André du Bouchet (Paris: Mercure de France, 1986). Du Bouchet also gave two speeches in which he touched on Celan. Together with Celan, just a month before Celan's suicide, he participated in the conference celebrating Hölderlin's 200th anniversary, where he gave his speech 'Hölderlin aujourd'hui'. André du Bouchet, 'Hölderlin aujourd'hui', in *L'Incohérence* (Paris: Hachette, 1979), n.p. In his second speech on Hölderlin, du Bouchet returns to his first speech from 1970 and also touches on Celan: André du Bouchet, 'Tübingen, le 22 mai 1986'.
75. Cf. Victor Martinez's bibliography in *Étrangère*, 16/17/18 (2007), 477–78.
76. Bernhard Böschenstein, 'André du Bouchet traducteur de Hölderlin et de Celan', in *Autour d'André du Bouchet: Rencontres sur la poésie moderne*, ed. by Collot, pp. 169–78 (p. 174).

77. Böschenstein, 'André du Bouchet traducteur de Hölderlin et de Celan', p. 178.
78. Henri Meschonnic, 'On appelle cela traduire Celan', in *Pour La Poétique II: Épistémologie de l'écriture. Poétique de la traduction*, 3 vols (Paris: Gallimard, 1973), II, 398–99.
79. Meschonnic, II, p. 372.
80. Badiou, p. 211.
81. Cf. the letter to Hans Bender of 18 May 1960 (*CW* III, 177). Cf. also the frequently used greeting '[j]e vous serre la main' in the correspondence between the two authors (Badiou, pp. 215–16).
82. Cf. ibid., pp. 226–28.
83. Ibid., pp. 216, 225.
84. Ibid., p. 219, also 231.
85. Ibid., p. 219.

CHAPTER 8

The Image in Celan's and Du Bouchet's Reciprocal Translations

Before we analyse Celan's and du Bouchet's translation practice, let us recapitulate the original contexts in which the reciprocal translations of Celan and du Bouchet occurred. Their mutual friendship would have created a sense of obligation that would also have prevented any overt appropriation of the other in one's own style. This seems to be particularly the case with du Bouchet, who was certainly aware of Celan's sensibilities and the historical atrocities underlying his texts. Additionally, du Bouchet's translational licence will have been reduced by his lack of command of German combined with the opportunity to approach Celan at any time during the translations to resolve potential difficulties. For Celan, in turn, the du Bouchet translations fall into the period of his later poetics of translation which exhibits more fidelity regarding the original text.[1] Indeed, Celan's friendship with his younger contemporary, together with his late translational style, might explain why 'Celan [...] du Bouchet so "gegenständig" übersetzt [hat] wie keinen andern Dichter'.[2]

On this basis we can comprehend the overall fidelity of the translations, and it is against this backdrop that we must consider the differences between the translations and the originals — particularly those divergencies that seem to be of a systematic nature. In the previous chapter, I pointed out the differences between Celan's and du Bouchet's conceptions of the image and translation as well as the fundamental connection between them. Some differences between the two authors' poetics seem to also have been observed by Celan's friends. Thus, Celan's fellow poet and friend Franz Wurm was surprised that Celan had translated du Bouchet, having assumed that Celan would share his own resistance to du Bouchet's poetry.[3] Celan replied that he understood Wurm's 'Einstellung' to du Bouchet.[4] Similarly Jean Daive expressed in conversation with Celan that he is 'critique à l'égard d'André du Bouchet, parfois sévère'.[5] The question this chapter thus addresses is how differences between the authors' poetics inform and shape their reciprocal translations. How, concretely, do these differences become manifest in their translations despite their affinities and friendship?

The Form of Celan's Image in his Translations of Du Bouchet

Some major departures in Celan's translations from du Bouchet's originals have already been pointed out by Bogumil and particularly Florence Pennone in her careful study of Celan's translations. These departures concern terms that are integral to either author's poetics. Thus, Pennone determines that du Bouchet's 'souffle' can mean 'wind' or 'human breath'. Existing in a continuous present, this wind or breath moves horizontally along the surface of du Bouchet's 'terre', which is understood as landscape and page. On the other hand, Pennone believes that Celan's 'Atem' is of human origin — embedded in the Greco-Judaeo-Christian tradition of *pneuma* — and even though the act of breathing takes place in the present it is closely connected with history. History in turn is often represented by vertical dimensions in Celan's poems, for instance, by going into the depth of the earth (see e.g. the preserved 'Atemkristall' in the poem 'Weggebeizt').[6] According to Pennone, this notion of verticality and the idea of a history that can be read and retraced like geological layers explains why Celan translates du Bouchet's 'du fond des terres' with 'aus dem Tiefsten all dieser | Erde'.[7]

Pennone also touches upon other, formal divergences in Celan's translations. She discerns an overall similarity between du Bouchet's *blancs* and Celan's caesurae (regarded as a form of placeholder for silence or otherness to break through and emerge in the text)[8] but is also aware that du Bouchet's *blancs* are motivated by a felt affinity to the art of painting. She does not further pursue the role of the image in du Bouchet's poetics,[9] which may explain her underestimation of the scale and importance of Celan's formal divergences, given that du Bouchet's use of the page directly pertains to his conception of the image and poetry.[10]

Celan's fidelity to the original notwithstanding, his digressions are frequent and show a clear handwriting that is his own. Whether we are concerned with Celan's insertion of superlatives, changes in punctuation, or deviations in syntax, Celan's translation subsumes and compacts syntactical and semantic elements, and creates climaxes not present in the original. Bogumil speaks of an added weight ('Schwere' or 'Gewichtverschiebung') in Celan's translations of du Bouchet,[11] which is perhaps not the most felicitous formulation but essentially aims in the right direction. Celan's translation intensifies, indeed, *stratifies* the original text in all senses of the word — figuratively geologically as well as grammatically. Böschenstein puts it more appositely in regard to the syntax of du Bouchet's translations of Hölderlin and Celan:

> [l]a syntaxe allemande s'efforce de créer l'union totale par la structure de mots composés complémentaires établissant l'unité à travers la dualité. La syntaxe française [...] emprunte des voies qui conduisent de manière analytique à cette totalité.[12]

Whether or not this claim about the two languages as such is fully accurate, it is certainly an acute observation with regard to Celan's German as opposed to du Bouchet's French. In keeping with Celan's notion of the image, his syntax evinces a 'union totale' underlying which is the fundamental poetological quest for a unity 'à travers la dualité'. This archetypal unity is approximated — however tentatively and incompletely — by various means of semantic and syntactical stratification whose basic trajectory is often either inward and upward or inward and downward into a depth.[13] Thus, for instance, in Celan's 'Traum vom Traume', we move into the 'Tiefsee', which is at the same time the 'Innenwelt' where the narrator ultimately envisions the possibility of a new archetypal language (see chapter 1); and in Celan's 'Halbzerfressener' movements into a depth (into the crypt of the eye) are combined with upward movements into the sky or heaven of the 'Schädelinnre' where a 'Mehr-als-Sehen' seems to be achieved, to quote Celan's Bazaine translation.[14] As we will see, Celan's tendency to use a hypotactic syntax in his poetry and translations of du Bouchet suggests, on a formal level, a similar tendency to unification and stratification as Celan's frequent semantic movements inwards and upwards or inwards and downwards.

We have already indicated the poetological implications of this quest for 'l'unité à travers la dualité' inherent to Celan's conception of the image and his conception of translation. As we take a closer look at Celan's translations of du Bouchet, the grammatical and formal implications of this quest for archetypal unity in Celan's poetics will take on increased importance. Formal divergences between original and translation constitute the most frequent translational change in Celan and du Bouchet. Let us now take a closer look at Celan's stylistic use of grammar to help us understand how he transforms the image of du Bouchet according to his own conception.

Celan's striving towards an archetypal union is particularly eminent in his compounding of words, which allows him to unite two or more different words or parts of words, such as suffixes and prefixes. We discover one such compound in the title of the poem 'Halbzerfressener'. But Celan does not only condense morphology. Frequently, Celan also uses syntactical subordination to create a unity that may otherwise be missing from his often enigmatic semantics and fragmented arrangement of phrases. Thus, as Pennone has astutely discerned, Celan frequently employs syntactical constructions in which a determiner and its referent, the noun, frame a series of participles, adverbial, and adjectival modifiers. Determiner and modifiers all ultimately, directly or indirectly, modify the noun which is often placed climactically at the end of the sentence or phrase[15] — for instance:

> Aus den nahen
> Wasserschächten
> mit unerweckten
> Händen heraufgeschaufeltes Graugrün (*KG*, 231)

or

> Aschendurchfadmet
> stundaus, stundein,
> von den Lidschatten zu-
> gefallener Augen (*KG*, 243)[16]

As Pennone believes, these types of phrases and sentences 'vermitteln nicht das Gefühl einer zusammenhanglosen Welt. Vielmehr sind sie innerlich hierarchisch gegliedert und wirken *kompakt* und *in sich geschlossen*'.[17] Extreme examples of this hierarchical ordering in Celan's own poetry can be found in the poems 'Über drei' and 'Dein vom Wachen'.¹⁸ For instance, the titular preposition and determiner of 'Über drei' refer to the 'Brustwarzensteine' which close the first stanza. In between the determiner and the complementary noun, we find compacted a prepositional phrase containing another noun ('im meertrunkenen Schlaf') and another prepositional phrase with yet another noun that is further modified by a participle ('mit Braunalgenblut bezifferte'). All of these inserted phrases ultimately modify the 'Brustwarzensteine', so that the first stanza reads:

> Über drei im meer-
> trunkenen Schlaf
> mit Braunalgenblut
> bezifferte Brust-
> warzensteine.¹⁹

This form of subordinating phrases under a noun emphatically placed last in the sentence is complemented by Celan's frequent use of the colon in his poetry, which performs a similar subordinative function, but in reverse order: that which succeeds the colon modifies and is often subsumed under that which precedes it.²⁰ A few poems in which Celan uses the colon have already been discussed in this book, notably 'Bei Wein und Verlorenheit' where the colon demarcates the rest of the poem from the first titular lines of the poem. In both cases, whether regarding the compacted syntax or the use of colons, we encounter a unifying force under which the differences and fragments are subsumed, without their being glossed over or obliterated.

A further, subtler and more versatile type of modification is Celan's dash which tends to function as an emphatic or climactic link between grammatically incomplete phrases (rather than marking a specification as in the common usage of the dash), as can be seen here:

> Nun ging er und trank einen seltsamen Tropfen:
> das Meer.
> Die Fische —
> stießen die Fische zu ihm? ('Kenotaph', *KG*, 84)

The 'Tropfen' is specified by the colon to be the 'Meer' — an almost ironic inversion of the conventional quantitative order of droplet and sea — whereas the dash emphatically marks the beginning of the last line and also links two phrases that could otherwise not be grammatically connected in their given word order in German (noun phrase and interrogative phrase). Similarly in 'Bei Wein und Verlorenheit', Celan's dash joins two juxtaposed notions: 'ich ritt Gott in die Ferne — die Nähe.'²¹

One last characteristic of Celan's grammar and punctuation we need to discuss here is his use of enjambment and hyphenation. Although on the surface especially mid-word enjambments seem to break up the poem, the very sign that seems to embody the separation can also be the strongest possible conjunction of two lines, which creates a unity that is yet mindful of the separation. Rather than creating little islands of words and phrases, as du Bouchet often does with his use of the paginal space (even more so in his later poetry after *Dans la chaleur vacante*), Celan's hyphenation often establishes a connection between distinct parts. Thus, midword enjambment through hyphenation can be used for climactic effect at the end of a stanza or a poem, deliberately creating a tension whose resolution the reader knows by virtue of the hyphen will arrive in the next line. This temporary deferral of a conclusion hence works like an emphasis, while it also reminds us of the fragile nature of poetic language: even when a poem concludes, its tension is not — at least for Holocaust survivor Celan — entirely resolved.[22] One example of this climactic use of a concluding enjambment are the 'Königs- | geburten' in the poem 'Wortaufschüttung'. In the last stanza of this poem more generally we find several instances of enjambment — 'hinaus- | schleuderst' and 'herz- | förmige' in addition to 'Königs- | geburten' — whose regular occurrence in the first, fourth, and seventh line of the stanza create an impression of symmetry.[23]

Before we turn to close analysis, we should summarize the formal peculiarities in Celan outlined above, which we will find again in his translations of du Bouchet. All of these forms of modification often perform the function of linking, condensing, and compounding semantic and syntactical elements. At times, they are the only thing holding together the disparate elements in Celan's poems. All of them share a tendency to emphatically culminate in or foreground a word or a small group of words. With the exception of Celan's use of hyphenation, they also frequently subordinate semantic and syntactical elements. Therefore, Celan's overall tendency is to create a hierarchical syntactical and semantic structure.[24] Unsurprisingly, such a structure is closely related to Celan's conception of the image and quest for an archetypal unity underlying his poetry. This is a unity achieved or at least conceivable in the inward turning of his poetry, potentially leading to a meeting or conjoining of that which is fragmented in intimate and inmost depths. The formally expressed compounding and condensing of language are not merely a poetic reflex on Celan's part but are actively reflected upon in his 'Meridian' speech. Here Celan had rejected Mercier's imperative '*Elargissez l'Art!*' in favour of another, opposed imperative: 'geh mit der Kunst in deine allereigenste Enge' (*M*, 10). This 'Enge' is not conceived as narrowness in the sense of 'constriction' or 'limitedness'. The meaning of 'Enge' Celan had in mind can be gleaned from his notes on and drafts of his speech, where the word 'Involution' plays a central role, later to be replaced by 'in deine allereigenste Enge' (*M*, 124). 'Involution', according to Celan, is 'das in den Keim Zurückgekehrte'. For him, it seems to constitute the core of poems: '[d]as Gedicht ist bei sich selber [...] → Faltung → Involution' (*M*, 124; cf. also Celan's poem 'Engführung', *KG* 113).

Pennone directly links a perceived 'compacité' in du Bouchet's poetry with Celan's tendencies to condense. Furthermore, she perceives Celan's changes in syntax, his compounding of words, and his use of hyphenation as an intensification of what seems to be already present in du Bouchet.[25] I, however, reject this conclusion. Not only are the compounding of words and hypotaxis very rare in du Bouchet's *Dans la chaleur vacante* and even more so in his later poetry, their frequent use in Celan's translation is also not grammatically necessitated.[26] Further compounding of words and hypotaxis and their implications of densification and hierarchization are not an established part of du Bouchet's poetics, patently or latently expressed.

Celan's own hand is visible early on in his translation. Already the original title *Dans la chaleur vacante* is stripped of article and preposition and condensed into *Vakante Glut*, thereby enacting the vacancy of which the title already speaks. But Celan's condensation does not necessarily entail that words are dropped. Thus du Bouchet's '[j]'anime le lien des routes' becomes '[i]ch beseele das die Straßen verknüpfende Band' (*CW* IV, 171). Celan has inserted the participle 'verknüpfende', which does not exist in the French original. Even though he thereby expands the sentence, the semantics of the word 'verknüpfend[-]' emphasize the tying qualities of the ribbon. Celan also made another significant change: he altered the syntax. In the translation, the definite article 'das' creates the expectation of a noun to follow, to which it refers. This noun arrives three words later after the participle ('verknüpfende') and its nominal complement ('die Straßen'), both of which modify the head noun 'Band'. Hence, both syntax and the added word underline the conjointness brought about by the ribbon, implying that the different 'Straßen' are not necessarily to be thought of as one but need the 'Band' to be connected.

The French original, on the other hand, does not regard 'lien' and 'routes' as disparate elements in need of a 'Verknüpfung'. The succession of the noun phrases by a prepositional phrase rather suggests an interpretation of the roads *as* ribbon ('lien *des* routes'; my emphasis). What du Bouchet emphasizes with this metaphor is less the fact that ribbons are of woven material, tying strings (or, figuratively, roads) together, but the fact that they are linear. The linearity of the streets and ribbon hence underline the linearity of the line which the sentence constitutes, in keeping with du Bouchet's awareness of the pictorialness of his poetry.

Another instance of subtle changes with significant consequences for the meaning is Celan's translation of '[à] la déchirure dans le ciel, l'épaisseur du sol' with '[d]em Himmelsriß die Mächtigkeit des Bodens' in his rendition of the poem 'Du bord de la faux' (*CW* IV, 170–71). The 'Himmelsriß' condenses the noun phrase 'la déchirure dans le ciel' into one compound word. Consequently, the progression of dative case to genitive case (from 'dem' to 'des') enabled by the compounding of 'Himmelsriß' emphasizes the verblessness of the sentence fragment, in which the reader jumps from one noun phrase to the next guided by the succession of articles 'dem', 'die', 'des'. Celan's almost maximal omission of functional words, such as prepositions, not only binds the lexemes closer together, his syntactical and grammatical changes also create a hierarchical order not present in du Bouchet. Du Bouchet's 'à' can very much be read as a locative preposition, indeed, this may be the dominant reading. The grammatical relations in Celan's translation are locative relations in du Bouchet's formulation that can be read not only to pertain to semantic relations of the words but also to their location on the page. Thus, the cleft that is the 'déchirure dans le ciel' seems to be syntactically indicated by the fact that 'l'épaisseur du sol' is postpositioned to 'à la déchirure dans le ciel', grammatically recreating the rupture that is verbally expressed. The 'épaisseur du sol' is precisely not at or by the cleft in the sky ('à la déchirure dans le ciel'). Therefore, on the one hand, the fragmented syntax could be read as an embodiment of the gap in the sky. However, another equally valid reading is possible in which du Bouchet's syntactical fragmentation in fact destabilizes the meaning of the cleft. If the 'épaisseur du sol' is not syntactically located at the cleft in the sky, then this syntactical cleft separates the semantic cleft in the sky ('la déchirure dans le ciel') from 'l'épaisseur du sol', contrary to what the semantics indicate which claims that the 'l'épaisseur du sol' is, in fact, located 'à la déchirure dans le ciel'. In du Bouchet's line we are not only faced with semantic and syntactical clefts, but also with a gulf that divides different readings. Celan's translation completely transforms this passage. The fact that he condenses du Bouchet's 'à' and 'dans' into articles and a compound noun turns the impasses of du Bouchet's clefts into a more clear-cut passage. The reason why the reader is so conveniently guided through the phrase by the articles — 'dem', 'die', 'des' — is that Celan's omission of 'à' and 'dans' has created a clear grammatical coherence by creating dependence relations. The 'Boden', as indicated by the genitive case, pertains to the 'Mächtigkeit' which, in turn, becomes an attribute to 'Himmelsriß' by means of the dative. Instead of the various clefts in du Bouchet's phrase, Celan has condensed the phrase to an extreme extent, a way of bridging the gap in the 'Himmelsriß'. Celan's condensation therefore creates 'Brücken | von Sprache zu Sprache, aber — Brücken über | Abgründe'.[27]

The difference between Celan's involution and densification and du Bouchet's syntax and use of *blancs* becomes even clearer when we look at Celan's translation of the third section of 'Le glacier' (*CW* IV, 194–95). The different paragraph format is apparent even at a brief glance. Du Bouchet's left-aligned text faces Celan's justified text. Du Bouchet's original, whose open right margins seem to indicate that it is fluid and not fixed or finished, is turned into a compact block of text in Celan's translation.

> Sur la terre compacte où je continue de brûler,
> l'air nous serrant à mourir, nous ne reconnaissons
> plus le mur. J'occupe soudain ce vide en avant
> de toi.

> Auf der kompakten Erde, wo ich zu brennen fortfahre, erkennen
> wir, da die Luft uns sterbemäßig umdrängt, die Mauer nicht wieder. Plötzlich habe ich die Leere inne, die dir vorausliegt.

Celan's alterations to the text are subtle but in conjunction with his use of spacing bring to bear a different meaning on the text. Du Bouchet's discourse of compactness in the text — 'compacte', 'nous serrant' — is intensified by Celan's more compact textual layout as well as his translation of 'occuper' with 'innehaben' and his insertion of the conjunction 'da' into the second subclause of the first sentence. Unlike *occuper*, which implies a coming together of two entities that are not necessarily compatible and which can even be hostile, Celan's *innehaben* quite unambiguously denotes an internalization. The conjunction 'da' commonly signals a causal relationship, but 'da' could also indicate a temporal simultaneity, a function fulfilled by the present participle 'serrant' in du Bouchet which Celan does not adopt. The conjunction foregrounds the grammatical dependency of the subclause much more strongly than du Bouchet's present participle, and its causal connotation semantically underscores the grammatical relations. Hence, even though du Bouchet's asyndetic subclause is strictly speaking just as much grammatically subordinated as Celan's syndetic one, du Bouchet's passage reads much more paratactically, whereas Celan's is clearly hypotactic. Celan's more stratified syntactical order ties the phrases more closely together, and it is in this sense that Celan's spatial alteration of the last two lines is significant.

The left-justified and enjambed last sentence in du Bouchet's poem explicitly places the 'vide en avant', followed by a line break, ahead of its conclusion. The 'vide' is thereby included in du Bouchet's text, and yet its semantic pronouncement ('vide') is in clear juxtaposition to the actual white gap (number 3 in our model; see chapter 5). The 'vide' is integrated into the text not only *as* text but also as white gap which effectively resists this integration. The enjambment after 'vide en avant' and the void it creates have further implications. Since 'ce vide' is 'en avant | de toi', the question has to be raised as to which void is actually meant: is the 'vide en avant' simply the paginal space following 'avant'? But if this were so, the poem could end here. Instead the void is 'en avant | *de toi*' (my emphasis). Thus we have to ask ourselves whether this void 'en avant' should be read as lying *between* 'avant' and 'toi' — a reading made possible by the line break — or whether the void ahead of the 'toi' is the paginal space following the end of this section of the poem after 'toi'. It is this uncertainty about the 'vide' as space and the clear contrast between a pictorial 'vide' as opposed to the semantically pronounced 'vide' which upholds the tension in du Bouchet's poem.

Celan's translation, on the other hand, erases du Bouchet's pictorial 'vide'. The void is internalized semantically by his translation of *occuper* with *innehaben*. The void is also internalized grammatically by the increased hypotactic stratification. The pictorial dimension of the 'vide' in du Bouchet and its interaction with the semantics of the text are purged from Celan's text. The typographical and spatial arrangement of Celan's text prevents any irruption of paginal space into the semantically described void. Celan excludes what is exterior to the text itself and further underscores the internalizing movement expressed in the text. There is no enjambment indicating that the 'Leere' could also have pictorial characteristics.

Celan's treatment of du Bouchet's line breaks in general betrays a different approach to the conception of the paginal space. For Celan the page seems to be merely the space on which words are inscribed. The page is thus just a means which allows Celan to write words and plays only a passive or negative role. The page's visuality is not significant in its own right in Celan, whereas the opposite is the case in du Bouchet. Its visuality facilitates the creation of meanings which the semantics of his words could not bring about alone (see chapter 5).

Celan's different interpretation of the role of paginal space compared to du Bouchet explains why Celan translates du Bouchet's '[r]ien ne nous sépare de la | chaleur' with '[n]ichts trennt uns von der Glut' in the poem 'Laps' from the first cycle of *Chaleur vacante* (*CW* IV, 198–99). The different tensions created between black ink and white page (number 2, see chapter 5), activated by the tension between the semantically stated absence of a separation ('sépare') and the irruption of the white space into the phrase as non-semantic separation (number 3), are absent in Celan's translation. As we know, Celan does not necessarily seek to seamlessly conjoin what was once separated, but to bridge gaps without obliterating traces of the gaps: 'Brücken über | Abgründe'.[28] His hyphens seek to achieve such a bridging across a separation. In doing this, Celan may have thought of the meaning of the German *Bindestrich* (which is close that of 'hyphen' in Greek),[29] which implies a tying together across the spatial separation. Du Bouchet's separations and *blancs*, as we have seen in chapter 5, are 'passages' and 'séparations' at once, without prioritizing one over the other. A passage from Celan's translation of du Bouchet's 'Sur le pas' showcases Celan's tendency to conjoin words across the space — a space which for Celan is merely there to be crossed — , where du Bouchet's spaces actively participate in the creation of meaning through their interaction with the text:

> Devant cette paroi qui s'ouvre, front traversé
> par le vent qui devance le visage et s'approfondit,
> un arbre comme un mur sans fenêtre
>
> Vor dieser Wand, die sich öffnet, eine vom Wind durch-
> querte Stirn, die dem Gesicht vorauseilt und sich ver-
> tieft: ein Baum wie eine fensterlose Mauer (*CW* IV, 332–33)

The act of traversing in du Bouchet's first line is amplified and the Latin origin *transversus* taken literally in Celan's translation, because here the verse turns with and inside the word: 'durch- | querte'. Celan also gives the syntax more density and coherence. Du Bouchet's 'front traversé' has no determiner and does not need complementarity, grammatically speaking. Yet Celan's 'eine vom Wind durch-' not only makes more specific the nature of the 'Stirn' in the second line by means of the article 'eine' in the first, but this phrase ending on a hyphen in the first line also calls for complementation by the second line. Hyphenation and syntax in Celan's translation thus both call for bridging the gap between the lines. Similarly, in the second line, Celan's hyphenation of 'ver- | tieft' not only ties lines two and three together inside the word which is spread across two lines. The hyphenation also enacts what the word pronounces: the word is deepened, so to speak, by means of placing 'tieft' in the line below 'ver-'. The depth into which we plunge in the line break culminates in the colon, emphatically subsuming the preceding two lines under what immediately follows it: 'ein Baum'. Although it is unlikely that du Bouchet regarded Celan's approach as a misunderstanding of his poetry, Celan's own hand is clearly visible in his translations of du Bouchet. The lines are closely tied together and continuously wind themselves down the page.

Depth and 'bloße Malerei' in Celan's Translation

We have pointed out before that Celan's dense syntax, his use of colons and his hyphenation is closely connected to his conception of a secular *archetypos* that is — its secularity and worldliness terrestrialness notwithstanding (*M*, 12) — embedded in a Neoplatonic Christian and Jewish traditions. But his conception of the image in his translations also becomes manifest in a less subtle manner. Celan's opposition to merely visually perceived *typos*-images, deluding the eye and making it a 'Bilderknecht',[30] becomes clear in his most conspicuous translational divergence, found in the second section of du Bouchet's poem 'Rudiments':

> Rester au niveau, à quelques pouces du front,
> dans le feu infirme.
>
> Comme un arbre dans le froid, le mur franchi se
> perd aussi, vraie peinture.
>
> Auf gleicher Höhe bleiben, ein paar Zoll von der Stirn,
> im bresthaften Feuer.
>
> Wie ein Baum in der Kälte, verliert sich auch die über-
> kletterte Mauer — bloße Malerei. (*CW* IV, 176–77)

In the French original, 'vraie peinture' is unambiguously positively connoted and there is no sense of irony in du Bouchet's words. The syntactical separation by comma makes 'vraie peinture' an apposition to the preceding sentence, but it is difficult to locate it exactly in the context of the section as a whole. Is the painting referred to a figurative painting, bestowing properties of picturesque beauty upon the described poetic landscape? Or is it an 'actual' painting and the poetic landscape described previously is part of the picture? Or are only parts of the landscape, such as the 'mur franchi', depicted in the painting?

To an extent, du Bouchet's 'peinture' is all of these. His view of poetry certainly regards the distribution of ink on the page as a form of abstract modernist painting. At the same time the vertical surface of the wall could be considered a form of natural canvas upon which we see 'vraie peinture'. But several other motives in the previous lines let the reader suspect that 'peinture' does not merely relate to two lines. The third line of the cited text, which initiates the sentence speaking of 'vraie peinture', starts with the comparative adverb 'comme'. It is unclear which is the object of comparison, but 'front' and 'mur' are semantically associated — both being a vertical surface — and since du Bouchet does not strictly distinguish between his poetic voice and landscape-text, both could be referred to by 'vraie peinture'.

This 'peinture' is yet more than that. As the context makes clear, it appears to take up elements of the early version of du Bouchet's 'Image à terme'. The paradoxical combination of 'feu' and 'froid', the uncertainty and elusiveness of the 'feu infirme', and the ultimate lack of a mental presence in the act of *perdre* are strongly reminiscent of similarly paradoxical interactions in his 'Image à terme'. There we encounter 'le froid auquel ce feu a donné son sens', the evanescence of the 'image [...] éteinte' and the uncertainty of the 'feu qui ne tient pas en place', and our apparent 'inattention' to all of this (*AB*, 86).[31] Thus, the above-cited 'feu infirme' and 'froid' from du Bouchet's poem 'Rudiments' gain an almost programmatic dimension in light of the resonances with his 'Image à terme'. They express du Bouchet's '[i]mage parvenue à son terme inquiet', an image that can only assert its presence in the fraction of an instant (see chapter 7). The presence of the image ('vraie peinture') also paradoxically implies the 'feu infirme' being lost or forgotten ('se | perd').[32] In this light, the proclamation of the painting's truthfulness, although a positive ascription seemingly rendering the image definitive and giving it a sense of permanence, has to be taken with a grain of salt. If 'vraie peinture' is to be related to all the preceding lines, the true painting is constituted by the 'feu infirme' and the 'mur franchi' which 'se perd'. Hence the true painting is constituted by momentary characteristics which have already vanished by the time they are declared to be 'vraie peinture'. Significantly, what du Bouchet says of the image in his early 'Image à terme' now seems to be attributed to painting in his poem 'Rudiments', perhaps already revealing du Bouchet's later path to increasingly conceive of the image less as an abstract entity and more in the form of painterly concretion.

Celan makes something entirely different of this passage. His translation of the four lines concludes in a dash — one of a mere handful he places in the entire volume — followed by the sobering 'bloße Malerei'. The dash streamlines the whole preceding section which culminates in its being depicted as mere painting. In Celan's copy of du Bouchet's *Dans la chaleur vacante*, into which Celan had noted his first translations of the poems, we find that Celan had initially translated this passage with 'wahres Gemälde'.[33] Thus Celan's choice of 'bloße Malerei' is a deliberate and most pronounced deviation from du Bouchet's 'vraie peinture'. The negative valuation, 'bloß', associates the painting with an illusion, as something that is not real or truthful in the sense of being constitutive of the (poetic) world. The image painted here by Celan's 'Malerei' is a *typos*-image. The uncertainty and loss pronounced in the preceding lines — the 'bresthaft[e] Feuer'; the 'Mauer' which 'verliert sich' — climactically result in the terse 'bloße Malerei'. These moments of loss and forgetting in Celan's translation are not considered positive and truthful ('vraie') as they are in du Bouchet.[34] Instead, Celan turns du Bouchet on his head and compresses his own, different conception of the image into the two words 'bloße Malerei'. Painting is made out as something that is to be left behind, perhaps to be similarly *überklettert* as the canvas-like 'Mauer' in the poem. Whereas for du Bouchet the act of losing is also, paradoxically, an act of gaining, as we know, the movement of surmounting something in Celan becomes an act of transcending it by means of a negative detachment from the untruthful and painterly.

In a similar spirit, Celan increases the depth of du Bouchet's 'fond' in his translation of the eponymous section of the cycle 'Sur le pas':

> Je reviens,
> sans être sorti,
> du fond des terres
> à ces confins
>
> Ich komme,
> ohne heraus zu sein,
> aus dem Tiefsten all dieser
> Erde an diese Grenzen zurück (*CW* IV, 330–31)

Celan's translation fundamentally changes the meaning of space in du Bouchet's text.

'[F]ond' has turned into 'Tiefsten', which is more akin to the French 'profondeur' or 'tréfonds'. Celan's immaterial but worldly conception of language in his 'Meridian' speech (cf. *M*, 12) and the notions of truth and depth in 'Traum vom Traume' (cf. chapter 1)[35] seem to resonate in his translated lines 'aus dem Tiefsten all dieser | Erde'. Pennone corroborates our analysis when she remarks about this passage that: '[k]ombiniert mit "Erde" im Singular (gegenüber einem Plural im Original [...]) [...] das substantivierte Adjektiv eine *vertikale* Ausdehnung des Raumes nach unten [suggeriert], die für *Dans la Chaleur vacante* untypisch ist, in Celans Werk aber ein wichtiges Motiv bildet'.[36]

Celan has treated the participle 'sorti' in a similar manner as 'fond' by translating it with the adverb 'heraus'. The French verb can simply mean 'exit', which has nothing to do with notions of depth, or it can signify 'coming out of something'. Celan's adverb delimits the ambiguity of 'sorti' and stipulates its association with depth. Celan's almost unnoticeable change of the preposition in the third line, rendering 'de' with 'aus', adds to this reading of du Bouchet's poem. The return *out of* the deepest depth to boundaries in Celan's translation, as opposed to du Bouchet's return *from* depth, clearly underscores the verticality of the movement. The superlative of 'Tiefsten', further amplified by the depth-emphasizing preposition and adverb in Celan's translation, thus echoes the idea of depth in his notion of the image (see also our discussion of 'Traum vom Traume' in chapter 1).

The return from 'fond' to 'confins' in du Bouchet, on the other hand, traverses a smaller space. The greater proximity of 'fond' and 'confins' in the poem's imaginary space emphasizes, rather, the 'tension qui ne fléchit pas' between 'fond' and 'confins'.[37] We hence reach the 'confins' about which du Bouchet says in the context of his discussion of Baudelaire that they reconsign us to the 'fond' of a 'présent réel', rather than giving us a glimpse into a beyond outside of our experiential bounds (*AB*, 288; see also chapter 2).

Although Celan takes less conspicuous translational liberties in his translations in the later sixties, when he does use poetic license, his changes are not less deliberate with respect to du Bouchet than the changes during the time of his 'Gegenübersetzungen'.[38] A brief look at one last passage from Celan's du Bouchet translation corroborates his tendency to spatially recodify du Bouchet's poetic space in a way which is more conducive to Celan's conception of language and the poetic image rather than du Bouchet's. Du Bouchet writes in 'Accidents' from the cycle 'Sol de la montagne': 'de l'autre côté de ce | mur' (lines 3–4) and '[d]e l'autre côte du mur' (line 6), which Celan respectively translates by 'jenseits dieser Mauer' and '[j]enseits der Mauer' (*CW* IV, 228–29). The French 'côté' suggests proximity, in turn making the locality to which it refers seem familiar and thereby identifiable. Celan's '[j]enseits', however, only indicates a rough direction that leads into an immeasurable distance not without spiritual connotations (we may also think of Celan's 'jenseits der Menschen' in the poem 'Fadensonnen'; *KG*, 179).

Du Bouchet's Translations of Celan as 'Autre en Je'

Du Bouchet's translations of Celan are more difficult to parse for differences to Celan's original that are intentionally produced and not merely the accidental result of du Bouchet's misunderstanding the German of his contemporary. This problem can be partially addressed by comparing his earlier with his later translations to see what changes he has made. Thus, we find that in 1971, for instance, du Bouchet initially translated the first lines of Celan's 'Sprachgitter' — 'Augenrund zwischen den Stäben' — with 'Œil — le rond parmi les ferrures'.[39] This translation is very probably a misunderstanding, since Celan could hardly have meant that the eye is amongst the bars, but rather between them. Du Bouchet must have discovered this error and in his republication of the poem in 1986 he corrects the preposition and instead translates: 'Œil-le-rond entre les ferrures'.[40] In this way, we can more surely distinguish accidental deviations in du Bouchet's translations that are changed in later editions from those translational differences to the original which remain unchanged across the different editions of du Bouchet's translations. Consequently, we can presume these latter differences to be poetologically motivated.

Another problem is raised by the more limited grammatical possibilities of French morphology and syntax which make Celan's idiosyncratic German particularly unsuitable for translation into French. Michel Favriaud addresses this problem with respect to the complex forms of syntactical subordination in Celan, which simply cannot be preserved.[41] Celan's word compound neologisms often simply cannot be rendered in one word in French. Celan himself does not attempt to do this in his *mot-à-mot* translations of his poems which he sent in letters to his wife. For example, he translated 'Flugsand' with 'sable volant' and 'Stirnsaum' with 'lisière du front', 'Flügelaug' with 'œil ailé',[42] or 'stern- | durchlässiges Blatt' with 'feuille perméable à l'étoile', and '[s]cherbenversiegelt' with '[s]cellées (de tesson) | d'éclats'.[43] Although these *mot-à-mot* translations were certainly not intended as polished and finished translations ready for publication, Celan's handling of his own poetic language in his translations of and by himself is a sure indicator of the translational difficulties faced when trying to express his poetry in French.

In contrast to Celan's syntactical changes of du Bouchet, du Bouchet tries to remain as close as possible to Celan's original syntax, despite the syntactical limitations of French. For instance, he translates the first two stanzas of Celan's poem 'Über drei' — which is almost entirely composed of Celan's heavily subordinated syntax — in the following way:

> ÜBER DREI im meer-
> trunkenen Schlaf
> mit Braunalgenblut
> bezifferte Brust-
> warzensteine
>
> stülp deinen sich
> von der letzten
> Regenschnur los-
> reißenden Himmel.

> Sur les trois — à même le somme
> ivre de mer
> par le sang brun du varech
> à la poitrine chiffrés —
> les trois pierreux mamelons
>
> renverse — comme à la dernière
> corde de pluie, lui, va
> s'arrachant — ton ciel.[44]

Although du Bouchet's attempts at recreating Celan's syntax in French are grammatical,[45] they seem even more contorted than Celan's German.[46] In order to fit in all the modifiers between determiners and the determined nouns, he has to resort to inserting the modifying subclauses between dashes and presumably makes use of repetition (he uses 'les trois' twice, once before and once after the inserted subordinate clause) or additional pronouns and even inserted comparative particles to clarify the syntactical and semantic relationships ('comme à la dernière | corde de pluie, *lui*, va s'arrachant'; my emphasis). Johanna Dueck hence finds that these additional insertions of words and punctuation marks create an interrupted reading, 'accentu[ant] les coupures présentes dans les poèmes celaniens', even if the grammatical, modifying relationships 'rest[ent] (le plus possible) fidèle à l'ordre des mots allemands'.[47] The extent of du Bouchet's syntactical contortions becomes most apparent when we look at how Jean-Pierre Lefebvre renders this passage:

> Sur trois oursins fossiles
> à tétons chiffrés
> de sang d'algue brune
> dans le sommeil
> de mer
>
> pose la cloche de ton
> ciel qui s'arrache
> à la dernière
> corde de pluie.[48]

Lefebvre, unlike Celan and du Bouchet, gives us the object of the sentence in the first line ('oursins') and turns the subsequent lines into a chain of dependencies relating to the noun. Lefebvre's French translation seems to flow more easily compared to du Bouchet's, and yet Celan's friend remains syntactically closer to the original. Du Bouchet's syntactical contortions arguably render Celan's syntactical complexities more apparent, while the foreignized character of the translation marks it as translation.[49]

Du Bouchet's translations of Celan's neologisms follow a similar line, stretching French morphology even beyond the point of correctness. Favriaud already noted that du Bouchet's translations of some neologisms create more enigmas than the original: '[d]u Bouchet traduit "Sprachgitter" (titre de poème) par *"Parler-La-Grille"*: *"Augenrund"* (v. 1) par "Œil-le-rond" (pp. 47/16). Que l'on pourrait traduire par: "grille de parole" (ou "grille de parloir"), "rond des yeux", "nuit de l'aile".'[50] Such constructions are highly unusual in French and, like du Bouchet's translational syntax, mark the translation as such. In line with Dueck's observation that du Bouchet 'accentu[e] les coupures présentes dans les poèmes celaniens', Favriaud holds with respect to du Bouchet's translations of poetry: '[d]ans le poème, à l'inverse de ce qu'il faisait — jeune — avec Faulkner et Shakespeare, Du Bouchet traduit le rythme, sans élucidation ni réduction, hanté par l'Autre en Je.'[51] Thus, the French with which du Bouchet confronts us in his translations of poetry in a sense seems to be 'le français [qu']il me reste encore à traduire du français', as du Bouchet says in his 'Notes sur la traduction'.[52] This translation into a French that is a French in need of translation, 'l'Autre en Je' as Favriaud says, hence seems to put du Bouchet's conception of translation into practice.[53] This method of translating Celan is also reminiscent of Celan's own conception of translation as 'Brücken | von Sprache zu Sprache' in which one has to retain the 'Anders- und Verschiedensei[n]' of the original text.[54]

However, du Bouchet departs from Celan in that there is no meridian-like return to the self, there is no 'über die beiden Pole in sich selbst Zurückkehrendes' (*M*, 12). The consequences du Bouchet draws from the retained Other of the original in the translation differ from those of Celan, because for du Bouchet there is no return to the self and to one's own language. 'Je traduis parce que j'entretiens un rapport de difficulté avec ma propre langue: il s'agit d'abord de me traduire moi-même en français.'[55] While Celan's relationship with the German language is without doubt fraught with difficulties, the figure of the meridian implies a returning full circle. To du Bouchet, this return does not seem possible in the wake of the Rimbauldian heritage of 'Je est un autre'[56] and his own conception of the image. Du Bouchet does envision a unity between the 'je' and the 'tu': '[l]a relation avec la langue implique deux personnes qui n'en sont une, "un" qui se dédouble' (see also chapter 6).[57] This unity, however, is perennially evasive, projected into a future that is never reached: 'je rejoins un autre a l'infini. [...] Le sens d'un mot est toujours au futur, mobile, mouvant à l'infini.'[58]

The 'je' as a perennial Other to itself in du Bouchet is, if only to a certain extent, reminiscent of the 'Du' in Celan's poetics which is so essential for establishing the poetic dialogue through which the first-person poetic voice can express itself. Yet unlike du Bouchet's 'je', Celan's 'ich' is still at the centre of the 'Raum [des] Gesprächs' and in speaking constitutes 'das Angesprochene' (*M*, 9; see also chapter 6). In du Bouchet, on the other hand, the relation between 'je' and 'tu' is fragmented and lacks a stable conception of the 'je' which could function as the centre for his poetry. Du Bouchet writes in his 'Notes sur la traduction': 'traduire, je ne peux pas: je serai traduit.'[59] The translation of the 'je' that — other to itself — cannot express itself is projected into the future ('serai'). Indeed, parts of this citation return later in the 'Notes': 'traduire, je ne peux pas. || sur l'occurrence d'un mot qui, dans l'autre langue — c'est la mienne — sera perdu, faire halte à nouveau.'[60] Once again the 'je' fails to find an adequate means of expressing itself in its own language that is at the same time 'l'autre langue'. If we still continue to wait for the moment in which 'je serai traduit', we are waiting in vain. As the 'Notes' conclude that 'il me reste encore à traduire du français', it also becomes clear that for lack of a proper language it can call its own, the 'je' remains untranslated.[61]

The different assumptions by Celan and du Bouchet about the first-person subject which organizes the poetic dialogue have implications for their respective conception of translation. For du Bouchet the moment of fusion between translation and original will always also remain a moment of separation.[62] Celan's 'ich' which centres his poetry and is constitutive of 'das Angesprochene' perhaps explains why Celan transforms du Bouchet's poems in his own image in translating them. On the other hand, du Bouchet's translations of Celan quite overtly retain the foreign spirit of the text,[63] revealing the 'autre' that is the French language and the 'je' yet awaiting its translation.[64]

Du Bouchet's method of translation is not exclusively a foreignizing one which remains as close as possible to the original text. There are some significant changes he makes in his translations which must be attributed to a poetological difference to Celan. Philippe Lacoue-Labarthe touches upon a significant divergence when he asks '[w]hy did du Bouchet systematically eliminate "Ladies and Gentlemen" from "The Meridian"' but leaves this question unanswered.[65] In his translation of Celan's 'Meridian' speech, du Bouchet removes the dialogical Other from the speech. Celan's repeatedly addressing the audience present during the speech underlines the importance of the communicative engagement in Celan's poetics. The dialogical form of Celan's speech is almost entirely absent in du Bouchet's translation. Whereas dialogue is not only the object of the verbal discourse in Celan's speech but also constitutes it in its seeking out and continuously addressing the audience, in du Bouchet's translation the closest we get to implying an inclusion of the reader into the text is when he utilizes interjections and imperatives such as 'voici'[66] or impersonal pronouns like 'cela'.[67]

The fact that du Bouchet translates a speech is only clear from the small note preceding the text which states 'Prononcé à l'occasion de la remise du prix de Georg Büchner, le 22 octobre, à Darmstadt'.[68] From the text itself we can at best only infer that it is a speech when at the end it culminates in a repeated address to the audience and its character as speech is most clear (*M*, 12–13). Only du Bouchet's use of the second person plural pronoun and the mention of the location 'Hesse' insinuate an addressee's concrete presence in time and space characteristic of a speech and thereby betray traces of Celan's presence of the Other.[69] But even here, where the repeated address to the audience almost imposes the dialogical character of the speech on du Bouchet's translation, du Bouchet makes a decisive change. As Celan ends '[m]it Ihnen und Georg Büchner und dem Lande Hessen' (*M*, 12), du Bouchet translates '[a]uprès de vous et de Georg Büchner et du pays de Hesse'.[70] This is the conclusion of the speech in which Celan asserts he believes to have come full circle, to have touched the meridian, and to have bridged the communicative divide between 'ich' and 'Du'. This is not merely a constative statement but also a performative one: '[m]it Ihnen [...] habe ich ihn [den Meridian] soeben wieder zu berühren geglaubt' (my emphasis).[71] We touch the meridian in the very act with which Celan evokes *and* enacts the togetherness of 'ich' and 'Du' by his use of the preposition 'mit'. Although du Bouchet's rendition of this last passage betrays the presence of an audience for the first time ('vous'), his translation of '[m]it' with '[a]uprès' testifies to his reluctance to assert a genuine togetherness that would enact the performative character of this statement. Instead of Celan's preposition which ties together the two pronouns in the sentence, the component 'de' of the compounded preposition 'auprès de' suggests a degree of separation that the proximity implied in 'auprès' cannot quite overcome.[72]

Du Bouchet's Translation of Celan's 'Nichts' in 'Erblinde'

Celan's desire to communicate and be understood underpins his seeking out an archetypal language. Celan's poetic style reflects this desire for unification on a micro level. Syntactical density and his proclivity to compound words as well as, for instance, his use of colons reveal Celan's wish to combine what is separate and to subsume it under a unifying expression. Du Bouchet, on the other hand, is sceptical not only of the possibility of such a final unification — which Celan's poetry and poetics do not claim to ever achieve either — but also of the possibility of envisioning such a unifying trajectory in unambiguously positive and non-paradoxical terms. Let us explore these differences by looking at one final translation by du Bouchet of a poem by Celan. His translation of the poem 'Erblinde' (KG, 186) is perhaps the clearest evidence that du Bouchet seeks to transform moments of transcendence in Celan's poetry by returning us to the 'confins' of a 'fond' that is not located in a beyond. In the following, I will be discussing du Bouchet's translation of 1971, which is the translation on which he will have worked most closely together with Celan.[73]

Celan's poem relates to a tradition of thinking and writing for which the moment of true cognition and true seeing — Celan's 'wahrnehmen' — occurs precisely in turning the eye away from the visible world and training it on truths beyond the world of ephemeral phenomena, of *typoi*. In his notes and essays on Hugo, du Bouchet had outlined a similar conception of seeing in the former, because he had once professed a hope to go blind one day like Homer and Milton and thereby become a true poet (cf. AB, 149). However, in his analysis of Baudelaire, du Bouchet had abandoned the conception of a vision through which an archetypal beyond reveals itself (see chapter 2).

Du Bouchet's rejection of such vision contrasts with the archetypal vision in Celan's poem 'Erblinde', even if this vision is only tentatively evoked. The perception of an eternity which is full of eyes does not lend itself to positive description, and the ultimate and elusive vision is expressed *ex negativo* in the very last word of the poem: a substantivized, substantialized 'nothing'. That the 'Nichts' points to the otherworldly seeing of said eternity full of eyes can also be gleaned from the fact that in Hebrew the word 'ajin' means 'nothing' but also 'eye', as Celan will surely have known.[74] Thus, the 'Nichts' which concludes the poem ties together the poem in its entirety and relates back to the eyes of the two opening lines, which seem to initiate but also outline the subsequent poetic development.

In the following analysis we will respond to Wolosky's and Fischer's interpretations of the poem, a discussion of which should help illuminate the poem's meaning and why du Bouchet translated it the way he did. Wolosky believes that eternity and nothing are entirely negatively connoted, not least because she pursues a very secular and worldly reading of Celan. She is right in asserting that for Celan 'significance must be temporal and worldly and cannot be abstracted into a metaphysical realm'.[75] But in the poem it is precisely because we speak after Babel that we eventually envision leaving the realm of language and using a more intimate, gestural way of communicating with the 'du' in the poem ('was auch dich aus der Sprache | fortnahm mit einer Geste, | die du geschehn ließt'). This communicative gestural engagement between poetic voice and 'du' lets us arrive at the 'nothing' that closes the poem. Our divesting ourselves of *typos*-images and of language leads us to the nothing at which point our blindness culminates and turns into a form of eternal seeing.[76] The different stages of negation through which we go ('ertrinkt', 'erlischt', 'fortnahm') are emphatically tied back — through the reiterated, solitary lines with 'darin' — to the first two lines in which the act of going blind seems to lead to an eternity full of eyes.[77]

Certainly, the nothing at which we ultimately arrive is still described in words and thus rooted in the language which we thought the 'du' had left behind a few lines before. The tentativeness of what happens to language and in language here is clear from the comparative particle 'wie' on which hinge the last two lines of the poem. As Markus Fischer says: '[d]ie Entzogenheit, der unwillkürliche Charakter dieses Ereignisses [d.h. der das Du aus der Sprache fortnehmenden Geste] wird jedoch [...] durch den Vergleich ins Gedicht gebannt.'[78] Thus, the tentativeness expressed by the comparative particle, the imperative of 'Erblinde schon heut' on whose fulfilment the entire poem hinges, and the confinement to negative enunciation all indicate only a possibility rather than an actuality. Even the climactic 'Nichts' — as negative expression and as part of the comparison initiated by the comparative particle — is not the realization of the imperative impelling us to go blind. It only outlines the very boundaries of what is expressible. The 'Nichts' is as close as we can get to a positive enunciation of the eternity full of eyes. We are reminded of a similarly positively connotated 'Nichts' in Celan's poem 'Mandorla' where 'Nichts' is equated with God as king (*KG*, 142, see also Wiedemann's commentary, 690).[79]

Wolosky is right in her emphasis on the terrestrial trajectory to which Celan confines his poetry. But her equation of 'eternity' with 'blindness' overlooks the unfulfilled imperative of the first line, which nonetheless projects a desire to achieve an eternity of eyes.[80] The 'Nichts' as the poem's point of culmination does not and cannot positively constitute an absolute 'metaphysical realm', since Celan holds that the absolute poem is impossible (cf. *M*, 10). However, a trajectory towards the absolute is nonetheless inscribed in every real poem (*M*, 10), and this is precisely the route which the poem 'Erblinde' describes.[81] The 'Nichts' at which we arrive is akin to the *locus* wherein this calling of the absolute is realized and at the same time reduced to absurdity, marked as impossible in the *u-topos*.[82] Fischer thus concludes appositely: '[d]och diese utopische Gegenwart [...] steht noch aus. Das "schon heut" und der Imperativ "erblinde" verweisen auf einen Raum außerhalb des Gedichts, in dem das angesprochene Du die im Gedicht intendierte Bewegung nachvollziehen vermöchte.'[83]

For du Bouchet, on the other hand, even such a cautiously projected trajectory toward an eternal 'Nichts' is inconceivable. Therefore, his translation of the poem departs most significantly from Celan's original when it comes to translating 'Nichts'. Even though Celan's 'Nichts' does not positively constitute a metaphysical realm of eternity and archetypal vision, the fact that it is substantivized indicates that it is substantial. It is a nothing that is not merely the privation of the earthly, equivalent to the logical operator '¬' which merely negates the attribution of a predicate to an object (¬P). Rather the 'Nichts' is itself a substance which turns away from the terrestrial but toward an unspecified elsewhere. Du Bouchet does not translate and adopt Celan's 'Nichts' and instead opts for a relative 'rien' that is a negation rather than a substantial nothing. Although the poem is virtually rewritten between the editions of 1971 and 1986,[84] and even though du Bouchet could just as easily have translated 'Nichts' into French with 'néant' and maintained much greater fidelity to the original, as Jean-Pierre Lefebvre's translation shows,[85] du Bouchet maintains his 'rien' even in his revised versions.

Du Bouchet's 'rien' implies the rejection of evoking and approximating 'l'éternité', even if it does so apophatically. Rather than 'Nichts' as a substantial negation, du Bouchet negates the negation, as it were, and refuses the notion of an archetypal 'Nichts'. Du Bouchet's reading is very close to Wolosky's interpretation of the poem in her resolute insistence on the terrestrial in Celan and on Celan's rejection of the eternal or metaphysical. It is in this spirit that the successive stripping away of the images and of language in du Bouchet's translation is much more negatively connoted than in Celan. The insertion of 's'abîme' which doubles the effect of 'se noie' conveys a plunging motion, whereas the departure from the worldly images and language in Celan was more reminiscent of climbing the steps of a ladder to reach the goal predetermined in the imperative '[e]rblinde'. The plunging motions in 'noyer' and the 'abîme', which is echoed in 's'abîmer', resolutely entrench us in this world, given that du Bouchet's poem does not conclude in pointing to an eternal nothing. They convey the ineluctable experience of the 'présent réel' in confrontation with the 'inimaginable' which du Bouchet had discovered in Baudelaire.

The reciprocal translations by Celan and du Bouchet show that both transformed the other in translation. These translational divergences from the respective original testify to an underlying difference in their conceptions of the image. Thus, whereas Celan, for instance, endows du Bouchet with a certain measure of transcendence when he translates 'fond' with 'Tiefsten' and '[d]e l'autre côté' with 'jenseits', du Bouchet does the opposite by negating Celan's 'absolute' nothing in his turning it into a relative 'rien'. In a way, du Bouchet's staunch insistence that there is no conclusive finality to translation — indeed, that even the French into which the poem is translated remains to be translated — manifests itself in the ultimate refusal to allow his French translation the transcendent resolution of Celan's poem.

Notes to Chapter 8

1. I use the word 'fidelity' here not in any specific theoretical sense, but following the work of Olschner, who first perceived a turn to more 'Wörtlichkeit' in Celan's translations from about 1964 onward (Leonard Olschner, *Der feste Buchstab*). See also Böschenstein's essay 'Supervielle in Celans Fügung' for a more detailed analysis of this turn to fidelity in Celan's translations.
2. Böschenstein, 'André du Bouchet im Gespräch mit Paul Celan', p. 227.
3. 'Ich habe, seit ich diese Gedichte kenne, einen solchen Widerstand — gegen sie, daß ich, ohne mirs auch nur zu überlegen, in Ihnen [Celan] einen gleichen erwartet hätte'; Wurm to Celan, letter of 23 August 1967 (Paul Celan and Franz Wurm, *Paul Celan — Franz Wurm: Briefwechsel*, ed. by Barbara Wiedemann (Frankfurt a. M.: Suhrkamp, 2003), p. 91.
4. Ibid., p. 93.
5. Jean Daive, *La Condition d'infini* 5 (Paris: P.O.L, 1996), p. 133.
6. Pennone, pp. 447–57; cf. also Böschenstein, 'André du Bouchet im Gespräch mit Paul Celan', pp. 226–27.
7. Cf. Pennone, pp. 450–51.
8. Ibid., p. 559.
9. Bogumil also does not pursue this further, even though she has recognized Celan's crass divergence — in the context of his overall fidelity — from du Bouchet's original text when Celan translates 'vraie peinture' as 'bloße Malerei' (*CW* IV, 176) (Bogumil, '"Ortswechsel bei den Substanzen"', p. 185).
10. Given the role of the image in French poetics in general — whether the image in Breton's surrealism, Reverdy's conception of the image, or the image's role in Bonnefoy (see introduction) — Pennone's conclusion that Celan believed German poetry had to go 'andere Wege als die französische' leaves much open to question (Pennone quotes Celan's answer to a question by the Librarie Finker here, cf. p. 465).
11. Bogumil, '"Ortswechsel bei den Substanzen"', p. 185.
12. Böschenstein, 'André du Bouchet traducteur de Hölderlin et de Celan', p. 171.
13. Celan's tendencies to alter, add, or intensify these directions in his translations of du Bouchet have not escaped Bogumil's eye. She perceives in Celan's alterations of du Bouchet's original texts Celan's very own 'historisch-poetische Gestalt', for which 'das weite Draußen zugleich ein tiefes Innen ist' (Bogumil, '"Ortswechsel bei den Substanzen"', p. 185). The overall envisioned trajectory of movement in Celan's poems and, at times, even the diction of his quest for unity is reminiscent of Christian and Jewish mysticism or Neoplatonism, e.g. in Meister Eckhart: '[u]nd wenn sich daher der Mensch in Liebe ganz zu Gott fügt, so wird er entbildet und eingebildet und überbildet in der göttlichen Einförmigkeit, in der er mit dem Gott eins ist. Dies alles besitzt der Mensch im *Innebleiben*'" (my emphasis) (Meister Eckhart, *Predigten: Deutsche Werke I*, ed. by Niklaus Largier, trans. by Josef Quint, 2 vols (Frankfurt a. M.: Deutscher Klassiker Verlag, 2008), I, 433. Similarly, Eckhart's notion of the 'Grund' has locative connotations and connotations of depth and shares characteristics of Celan's tendency to move into depths in his poetry: '[d]ie Stätte des Wesens der Liebe ist allein im Willen; wer mehr Willen hat, der hat auch mehr Liebe. Aber wer davon mehr habe, das weiß niemand vom andern; das liegt verborgen in der Seele, dieweil Gott verborgen liegt im Grunde der Seele' (Meister Eckhart, *Predigten und Traktate: Deutsche Werke II. Lateinische Werke*, ed. by Niklaus Largier, trans. by Ernst Benz and others, 2 vols (Frankfurt a. M.: Deutscher Klassiker Verlag, 2008), II, 363.
14. Bazaine, p. 35.
15. She calls these phrases 'komplexe Satzglieder' (see Pennone, p. 440). According to Hubert Haider's discussion of these aspects of German syntax, we should distinguish between adjectival and participial complementation. In the first case, the adjective takes a nominal complement, in the second case the participle becomes an adnominal attribute (Hubert Haider, *The Syntax of German* (Cambridge: Cambridge University Press, 2010), pp. 243–44).
16. A further example is analysed more closely here below.
17. Pennone, p. 440.
18. Cf. *KG* 185 and 178, respectively.

19. Du Bouchet's translation of this poem is briefly discussed below.
20. However, as noted below, the colon can also be used as culmination at the end of a poem, climactically subsuming what came before the colon in one last word or phrase after the colon.
21. Du Bouchet will make extensive use of the dash in the collections published after *Chaleur vacante*. His later use of the dash, however, is very different to that of Celan, as it operates 'neither to open a parenthesis nor to qualify an idea; it operates above all as an intrusion' (Wagstaff, *Provisionality and the Poem*, p. 41).
22. There are different categories of hyphenation in Celan: in prefixed adjectives, adverbs, verbs, and nouns the prefix is sometimes separated from the root via hyphenation. Another type of hyphenation is Celan's frequent mid-word enjambments in compound words containing two independent substantives. In some cases, Celan even compounds two nouns through hyphenation, as is common in English, rather than agglutinating the nouns by means of inserting a genitive suffix between the compounded nouns, as is more common in German. See e.g. the 'Blutklumpen-Botin' in the poem 'Schieferäugige' (*KG*, 210–11).
23. We should not forget a prominent counterexample to Celan's use of enjambments outlined above. We discussed in our analysis of 'Bei Wein und Verlorenheit' that Celan combines the syntactical parallelism between the noun phrases 'sie | schrieben' and 'sie | logen' with enjambments which in turn break up grammatical dependencies within the noun phrase. These enjambments, on the other hand, were the marked feature of the parallelism (see also chapter 4).
24. These hierarchical structures are reminiscent of the verbally evoked vertical structures in Celan's poetic geology (cf. Pennone, p. 444).
25. Cf. Pennone, pp. 427–43. (She borrows the word 'compacité' from Depreux's work on du Bouchet).
26. Colons: *CW* IV, 205, 215, 323, 331 & 333; syntactical subordinations of the kind described above: *CW* IV, 171, 183, 207; dash: *CW* IV, 207, 251, 295, 325, 339.
27. Sanmann, pp. 388–89.
28. Sanmann, pp. 388–89.
29. 'Hyphen, n.', *OED*.
30. Cf. 'Wohin mir das Wort' (*KG*, 155).
31. Cf. also chapter 5, where this passage is analysed.
32. Cf. '[N]ous essayons de *revenir*: cette voie à laquelle nous voudrions avoir accès sans disparaître, que la poésie donne de façon inopinée, et que nous voulons parcourir à notre gré sans le moindre risque. [...] Que nous voulons jalonner. Mais on ne peut jalonner que ce qui a été déjà parcouru, et ce n'est pas la même route que l'on parcourt. La critique ne s'exerce pas sur l'avenir. [...] [L]a perte de l'{image} créée, déjà existante: c'est la perte, *un appel des chasseurs perdus dans les grands bois* [du Bouchet quotes Baudelaire here, J. K.], l'image acquise s'efface au bord de l'éternité' (*AB*, 298).
33. Cf. Celan's copy of du Bouchet's *Dans la chaleur vacante* (Paris: Mercure de France, 1961) containing Celan's handwritten initial translations and notes, which is preserved in the Bibliothèque littéraire Jacques Doucet, Paris. Du Bouchet's estate, held by the same library, allows us to observe the different writing processes of Celan and du Bouchet. As evinced by the historical critical editions of Celan's works and as can be seen in Celan's notes toward a translation of du Bouchet's *Chaleur vacante*, Celan had an almost surprising surety in finding his words before he consigned them to the page. Major revisions of his own poems or translations of du Bouchet are relatively rare. On the other hand, du Bouchet's documents and manuscripts show that du Bouchet constantly reworked notebook entries, reassembled snippets of paper with short texts and notes, almost as if he were hesitant to assign finality to his writings. A particularly conspicuous example are his manuscripts of the poem 'Sur le pas' where a large number of notes are solely preoccupied with whether or not the poem should say 'hier, je respirais' or 'hier, j'ai respiré' and alternate between the two numerous times (document numbers: Ms 25457–62).
34. Cf. also Pennone's remarks about the 'Gedächtnistiefe' in Celan's poetics which is closely related to the frequent evocations of geological substrata in his poetry. She believes that du Bouchet's 'Zeitauffassung' completely lacks this 'Dimension der Gedächtnistiefe' (Pennone, p. 453).
35. Cf. also footnote 13 on the relation between *archetypos* and inner utmost depth, utmost height, and inwardness.

36. Pennone, p. 451.
37. De Rijcke, 'Entretiens avec André du Bouchet', p. 288.
38. Cf. the title of Ute Harbusch's study of Celan's translations of French symbolist poets: *Gegenübersetzungen*.
39. Celan, *Strette*, pp. 22–23.
40. Celan, *Poèmes* (1986) pp. 16–17.
41. Michel Favriaud, 'Traduction: Poétique inachevée de la relation', in *André du Bouchet et ses Autres*, ed. by Michel Minard and Philippe Met (Paris-Caen: Lettres modernes Minard, 2003), pp. 175–213 (po. 206–07).
42. Paul Celan and Gisèle Celan-Lestrange, *Correspondance: 1951–1970. Avec un choix de lettres de Paul Celan à son fils Eric*, ed. by Bertrand Badiou and Eric Celan (Paris: Seuil, 2001), pp. 73–74.
43. Ibid., pp. 617–19.
44. Celan, *Strette*, pp. 38–39.
45. Cf. Favriaud, pp. 206–07.
46. About other attempts by du Bouchet at translating such participle constructions, Dueck says that 'le trait caractéristique le plus frappant de cette recherche formelle est le fait qu'elle transgresse très souvent les règles de la syntaxe française' (Dueck, p. 258).
47. Ibid., p. 263.
48. Paul Celan, *Renverse du souffle*, trans. by Jean-Pierre Lefebvre (Paris: Points Poésie, 2006), pp. 68–69.
49. I am using the term 'foreignization' in a more general sense here than Lawrence Venuti who popularized this term (based on Friedrich Schleiermacher's notion of 'paraphrase') and propagates it in conjunction with a linguistic, social, and political translational programme, as it were, that accords more visibility to and appreciation for the translated foreign culture and the translator's vocation. Although I believe du Bouchet would be sympathetic to Venuti's project, my argument that du Bouchet's translations of Celan are foreignizing here rests rather on a more generally conceived idea of foreignized translations as a deliberate preservation of the linguistic alterity of the original in the translation. Cf. Lawrence Venuti, *The Translator's Invisibility: A History of Translation* (London: Routledge, 1995), pp. 19–20; cf. also Friedrich Schleiermacher, 'On the Different Methods of Translating', in *Translation, History, Culture: A Sourcebook*, ed. by André Lefevere (London: Routledge, 1992), pp. 141–65 (p. 148).
50. Favriaud, p. 205.
51. Ibid., pp. 199.
52. Gellhaus, pp. 397–400.
53. Cf. also Martinez, *Poésie, langue, événement*, pp. 51–54.
54. As Celan says in a letter to Werner Weber of 26 March 1960 (Gellhaus, pp. 397–400).
55. De Rijcke, 'Entretiens avec André du Bouchet', p. 277.
56. Rimbaud, p. 340.
57. *Entretiens d'André du Bouchet avec Alain Veinstein*, ed. by Veinstein, p. 43.
58. Ibid., pp. 26–27.
59. André du Bouchet, *Ici en deux*, n.p.
60. Ibid.
61. Ibid. For a further discussion of this passage in du Bouchet's *Ici en deux*, see Koch, 'Translation as Poetics in the Works of André du Bouchet', pp. 40–44; see also Wagstaff, *André du Bouchet*, p. 107.
62. De Rijcke, 'Entretiens avec André du Bouchet', p. 287. Cf. the elaborate discussion of the notion of translation in the poetics of du Bouchet in the previous chapter.
63. Böschenstein had also noted foreignizing tendencies in du Bouchet's translation of Hölderlin's poem 'Der Einzige' ('L'Unique') in which du Bouchet had omitted articles (Böschenstein, 'André du Bouchet traducteur de Hölderlin et de Celan', p. 171).
64. See also what du Bouchet's says elsewhere: 'une parole, à l'envisager, aussitôt je m'interromps, étant moi-même fraction de la langue, également' (André du Bouchet, 'Tübingen, le 22 mai 1986', p. 346).
65. Philippe Lacoue-Labarthe, *Poetry as Experience*, trans. by Andrea Tarnowski (Stanford, CA: Stanford University Press, 1999), p. 105.

66. Celan, *Strette*, p. 185.
67. Ibid., p. 182.
68. Ibid., p. 178.
69. Ibid., p. 197.
70. Ibid., p. 197.
71. J. L. Austin, *How to Do Things with Words*, ed. by Marina Sbisa and J. O. Urmsson, 2nd edn (Oxford: Oxford University Press, 1975). The statement is only of performative *character*, because there are no clearly established 'felicity conditions' for this specific type of poetological speech act (cf. ibid., pp. 12–24).
72. Dueck puts it more strongly, perhaps too crassly: '[u]ne dernière tendance de ces traductions est [...] qu'elles "dépersonnalisent" les poèmes. Selon la poétique de du Bouchet, cette dépersonnalisation résulte du refus poétique de communiquer' (Dueck, p. 285).
73. Celan, *Strette*, p. 41.
74. Leonard Olschner, 'Mandorla', in *Kommentar zu Paul Celans 'Die Niemandsrose'*, ed. by Jürgen Lehmann and Christine Ivanović (Heidelberg: Winter, 1997), pp. 178–82 (p. 180).
75. Shira Wolosky, *Language Mysticism: The Negative Way of Language in Eliot, Beckett, and Celan* (Stanford University Press, 1995), p. 260. She also does not consider that the images' trajectory across and beyond the path only to be ultimately destroyed themselves is very reminiscent of similar transcending movements of the image, which we discussed previously, notably with regard to the poem 'Halbzerfressener' (see chapter 6).
76. Cf. also Markus Fischer's reading of the poem in his *Celan-Lektüren: Reden, Gedichte und Übersetzungen Paul Celans im poetologischen und literarhistorischen Kontext* (Berlin: Frank & Timme, 2014), pp. 39–41.
77. Cf. Fischer, p. 39.
78. Fischer, p. 40.
79. Cf. Olschner, 'Mandorla', pp. 180–81. In 'Mandorla', the perceiving eye is opposite and perhaps even in contradiction to a (divine) nothing. Nonetheless, it is unmistakable that the eye stands for and by the king ('Dein Aug, dem Nichts stehts entgegen. | Es steht zum König.'; KG, 141), despite the potential shortcomings of this visual, bodily act of seeing. The similarities between the two poems 'Mandorla' and 'Erblinde', particularly their notions of seeing as well as the otherworldly dimension ascribed to seeing *ex negativo*, is also apparent in Celan's unusual choice of vocabulary. It is certainly not common to combine 'stehen' with 'Augen'. The use of the word 'stehen' in 'Erblinde' suggests constancy and persistence — perhaps even resistance — and echoes the emphatic use of the verb in 'Mandorla' (Olschner, 'Mandorla', p. 179); cf. also Leonard Olschner, *Im Abgrund Zeit: Paul Celans Poetiksplitter* (Göttingen: Vandenhoeck & Ruprecht, 2007), pp. 103–25.
80. Wolosky, p. 257.
81. Fischer, p. 40.
82. Cf. Celan's evocation of the 'U-topie' in his 'Meridian' speech (*M*, 10).
83. Fischer, p. 41.
84. Celan, *Strette*, pp. 41–42; Celan, *Poèmes* (1986), p. 20, respectively.
85. Celan, *Renverse du souffle*, pp. 72–73.

CONCLUSION

We began our exploration of the conception of the image in Paul Celan and André du Bouchet with their poetic beginnings in the late forties. We traced the image in Celan's poetics until his death in 1970 and compared it with the image in du Bouchet's poetic thought until his late version of 'Image à terme' (1979) and his poem 'Peinture', published in the 1986 poetry volume *Ici en deux*. In 1986, du Bouchet also published his last edition of his translations of Celan.[1] Although du Bouchet continued to write until his death in 2001, the cut-off in our timeline is the late eighties, in order to focus on Celan's and du Bouchet's engagement with each other's poetry and poetic image. This engagement was most intense during the time of their reciprocal translations and collaboration on the poetry and art magazine *L'Éphémère* from the late sixties until Celan's death. We started our comparative study with each author's earlier works before they became more closely acquainted with each other's writing, because both authors had developed their poetry and poetics independently of each other up until 1966, when they would meet regularly and became close friends.[2] Thus, in order to understand what we are comparing and contrasting when we speak of Celan's and du Bouchet's poetic image, we needed to know the genesis of their poetics of the image. Especially in the case of du Bouchet, a further motivation for our elucidating his early poetological developments and engagement with his poetic predecessors was the fact that it is not a well-studied period of his writing, since many of his early essays have only relatively recently become more widely available, thanks to François Tison's and particularly Layet's untiring efforts.

We saw that du Bouchet moved increasingly away from the traditional conception of the image as split between an invisible, intangible, and transcendent *archetypos* and a *typos* that resembles and embodies the *archetypos* while being also fundamentally different to it. Du Bouchet's early essays, which engage with the image in Scève, Hölderlin, Hugo, and Baudelaire, provide ample evidence for his increasingly paradoxical conception of the image. His image moved more and more away from the hierarchically ordered *archetypos–typos* distinction. Rather, his mature conception of the image emphasizes the tension between and interaction of what we termed *absence* (e.g. represented by the word 'défigurer') and *présence* (e.g. 'figurer') in his image. *Absence* and *présence* are conceived as codependent in du Bouchet's image. Beginning with *Dans la chaleur vacante*, but already apparent in even his early *Carnets*, his more mature poetic writing also embraced the visual possibilities of poetic writing. Du Bouchet experimented with the distribution of black ink on the white page. Since, for instance, the word 'vide' cannot simply be conflated with a paginal gap, we studied how the visual dichromaticism of his written page interacts, but does not coincide with, the notions of *absence* and *présence* negotiated on the semantic level. We thus called his image polychotomous, because it evinces an oscillation between several poles: the semantic poles *absence* and *présence* and the visual, dichromatic poles of ink and page.

Similar to du Bouchet, Celan was hesitant to simply affirm the presence of the *archetypos*. However, unlike du Bouchet, Celan never went so far as to abandon the framework of *archetypos* and *typos* altogether. Rather, Celan evokes archetypal poetic speech via *negationis* by, firstly, criticizing the false nature of the *typos* and by, secondly, seeking out a dialogical Other to testify to the *archetypos*. The fundamental struggle in his poetry is to bridge the differences between poetic voice and Other and to achieve a form of archetypal communication which overcomes the confusion of tongues wreaked by Nazism. Nonetheless, archetypal speech never becomes fully manifest in his poetry, because Celan is aware that after the confusion of tongues poetry speaks in *typoi*. Thus, poetry can testify to the *archetypos* only in a language of *typoi* and the possibility of an original and historically unencumbered poetic discourse is lost. No doubt this loss is in large part due to Celan's direct experience of the Holocaust and the irretrievable loss of his parents. This loss is also a linguistic one in more than just abstract terms, given that his mother tongue and his mother's tongue was the German language which Celan loved, but also the language that was spoken by his mother's murderers. The Holocaust is thus at the heart of and a threat to Celan's experiential and linguistic identity, as we have seen perhaps most clearly in his 'Tenebrae', where the lack of an archetypal *imago Dei* almost undermined the poetic voice's subjectivity. Yet, unlike du Bouchet, Celan does not radically undercut traditional notions of subjectivity, even if the Holocaust in many ways poses a threat to his own as well as his poetic voice's identity. Indeed, somewhat paradoxically, precisely because of the incisive experience of the Holocaust, Celan cannot and does not abandon notions of truth (with its deep links to the notion of *archetypos*) and asserts a poetic subject and speaker that is not merely an arbitrary, fragmentary (de-)construction but can give testimony of an *archetypos*. Thus, in discussing 'Bei Wein und Verlorenheit', we realized that even if the poetic voice could not make manifest divine song, we here encounter a confident poetic voice — akin to the traditional poet-horse Pegasus, no less — that contrasts clearly with the untruthful languages of man. Similarly, Celan's poem 'Halbzerfressener' and his speech 'Der Meridian' had ended on the hopeful outlook that in the dialogical engagement with the Other an approximation of the *archetypos* was possible.

It is, of course, speculative whether a direct experience of the Holocaust would have made du Bouchet a different poet. Nevertheless, his only indirect experience of the Holocaust from abroad will have, in a sense, freed him from obligations toward history similar to those Celan felt. Nonetheless, spending his late teenage and early adult years speaking English in his exile in the United States likely influenced du Bouchet's perception of language and his later radical scepticism towards notions of a native tongue.[3] Instead, as we have seen, language for him is inherently relational and translational and thus is possible only in-between the domestic and the foreign.

To some extent, both du Bouchet and Celan pursue unification in their image. However, they do so against the backdrop of a very different conception of language and the image. The ultimate trajectory of Celan's wish to overcome the confusion of tongues is to establish a unified, archetypal communication. This pursuit of truthful poetic speech which somehow bridges the communicative division between poetic voice and Other also informs his conception of translation as a unifying act. Similarly, in du Bouchet's poetry we find ample evidence of coincidence, fusion, and unification between word and reality, between self and Other, or between acts of (poetic) communication in different languages. However, for du Bouchet unification is only conceivable through the notion of separation. Thus, translation for du Bouchet is always the ambiguous 'traduire | la séparation', indefinitely fluctuating between the two meanings of relating language across a linguistic separation or preserving the separation (between languages) in the act of translation. These different conceptions of the image and of translation in du Bouchet and Celan also become apparent in their translation practice when they translate each other's works. Celan structures du Bouchet's fragmented and paratactical syntax into a much more hierarchically organized hypotaxis. This increased hierarchical ordering of grammatical dependency relations compared to du Bouchet's paratactical and fragmented syntax betrays Celan's desire for unification. Du Bouchet, on the other hand, sought to preserve the otherness of Celan's language in his translations: he even used syntax and morphology which bend the rules of the French language and thereby also preserved 'la séparation' between French and German in his translation. However, whenever Celan's poetry evoked an *archetypos* (such as his nominalized 'Nichts' in 'Erblinde schon heut'), du Bouchet's translations deliberately altered and relativized it ('Nichts' became 'rien' in his translation).

The different but nonetheless comparable conceptions of the image in both authors' works were the guiding threads through this book. Yet, as the elaborate conceptual and historical introduction indicated, our aim was also to embed these two authors in a broader context of thinking about the image and, in turn, to read their works for fruitful ways in which we can think about the image. It is not very surprising that Celan's historical awareness and thorough erudition in religion and philosophy also inform his conception of the image. His image, at heart, follows the Neoplatonic *archetypos–typos* distinction, with its privileging of unity, and of that which is (presumed to be) originary, over difference. Du Bouchet, on the other hand, took a unique and more radical path which privileges neither union nor difference, and does not present us with a unifying or absolute point of origin or end. His paradoxical poetic discourse not only extends to semantics but also to his visual configuration of the page, which becomes an active part in the creation of his polychotomous poetic image.

In pursuing the aims summarized above, this study addressed several shortcomings in present research on both authors. As the introduction showed, literary scholars habitually read the word 'image' simply as an extension of or a metaphor for the concept of metaphor. I believe this interpretation of the image short-changes the meaning and usage of the word in two main respects: first, conceiving of the image as metaphor is a fairly recent phenomenon (dating back to roughly the eighteenth century; see introduction) and neglects the millennia of discourse on the image and its cognates in philosophical and religious contexts. Especially in German, the morphological and semantic flexibility of the word 'Bild', being contained in the notions of 'Urbild' and 'Abbild' (and also 'Bildung'), is forgotten in treating the 'image' as more or less synonymous with 'metaphor'. Since we have seen how important the distinction between *archetypos* and *typos* is in Celan's poetry and even du Bouchet's early thinking, I believe we were well-justified in looking beyond metaphor in trying to understand Celan's and du Bouchet's image. Looking beyond metaphor is all the more important, because, second, neither Celan nor du Bouchet understood the image as metaphor. To my knowledge there is not a single positive note or poetic expression of the concept of metaphor in Celan, which he frequently and very explicitly distinguished from the image. Similarly, I am not aware the word metaphor is even part of du Bouchet's poetic vocabulary.[4] Given du Bouchet's admiration for the visual arts and his own frequent collaborations with painters, indeed, given that he hung up pages of his poetry for visual display at his workplace, treating them akin to pieces of visual art,[5] the notion of image in du Bouchet very clearly extends beyond the concept of metaphor.

It is surprising that the notion of the image in Celan had not been explored to any sufficient extent, considering that Celan is a well-studied poet and that the image is an important concept for poetological exploration. Many studies examine the image in terms of metaphor[6] or speak about motifs from the visual arts in Celan's poetry.[7] However, to my knowledge nobody has sought to look at the notion of the image in its more philosophical and religious contexts, focusing on conceptions of *archeytpos* and *typos*. The lack of scholarship engaging with religious and philosophical notions of the image in Celan is surprising because the author's interest and erudition in these fields was extensive, as is well known.[8] Hence my study hopes to complement existing research on Celan and the visual arts by exploring the poetological and theoretical underpinnings of Celan's conception of the image. My book seeks to contribute to research on Celan in more specific ways, too. 'Traum vom Traume', 'Tenebrae', and 'Bei Wein und Verlorenheit' are recognized for their importance to Celan's poetry and poetics, and my new perspective on these poems should contribute to a new understanding of them. In addition to that, I hope that my close reading of the rarely analysed poem 'Halbzerfressener' has demonstrated its importance for understanding Celan's poetics of subjectivity in connection to the image.

Relative to the extent to which du Bouchet's poetry has been studied, there is more research on his concept of the image and his interrelations with the visual arts compared to Celan. This has to do with the fact that the image is arguably the most important poetological term in du Bouchet (at least the du Bouchet of Celan's lifetime). Nonetheless, there are gaps in the research on du Bouchet's conception of the image, which this study addressed. Du Bouchet's poetry has been studied to a lesser extent than Celan's. Unlike Celan's works, his oeuvre still awaits a complete, not to mention a critical or even historical-critical edition. For these reasons, some materials have not yet been accessed or published, let alone researched. Some materials have only been relatively recently published and not extensively studied, among which are the important interviews with Alain Veinstein[9] and Elke de Rijcke[10] as well as du Bouchet's early essays[11] and *Carnets*.[12] Consequently, my study was privileged to be among the first able to draw on the early essays,[13] through which we could gain an idea of the genesis of du Bouchet's thought on the image. The more theoretical approach of this study seeks to supplement the existing range of research on du Bouchet's collaboration with artists[14] and to complement other, more theoretical works on du Bouchet and the image which did not or could not pursue the developments of du Bouchet's poetics in such detail.[15] Among the specific texts by du Bouchet I discussed, I hope that especially my investigation of du Bouchet's 'Image à terme' is illuminating for further research into du Bouchet's conception of the image. Furthermore, I believe that the model of reading du Bouchet's mature poetry and its *blancs* developed in chapter 5 could provide a new avenue for future research focusing on du Bouchet's polychotomies. Any presumed 'dehors', 'réel', or 'au-delà' of du Bouchet's poetry is articulated consciously and exclusively in the interstices and interactions *between* the different poles of his polychotomous image, and hence I expect that investigation of these will prove to be more fruitful than chasing a presumed underlying ontotheology in du Bouchet's poetry.

There is one last contribution this study has aspired to make to scholarship particularly on du Bouchet. The importance of translation to Celan's poetics was recognized very early. Leonard Olschner's book of 1985, published fifteen years after Celan's death, was the start of a wealth of studies on Celan and translation.[16] My study, on the other hand, should have demonstrated how central translation is, also, in du Bouchet's conception of the image, poetry, and language more generally, despite the fact that du Bouchet's corpus of translation is much smaller than Celan's and despite his reputed lack of command of the languages from which he was translating (see esp. chapter 7).

If most of the focus in this study was on the differences between Celan and du Bouchet's poetry, while their affinities and close friendship were discussed only in passing, this is for two main reasons: firstly, by focusing on the image we examined an aspect in their poetics in which they particularly diverge. In fact, I believe it is with regard to this particular aspect that they differ the most. Secondly, the two authors are also, quite simply, very different writers, considering that they otherwise had much in common, e.g. being contemporaries with Jewish ancestry living in Paris. Their poetics differ when it comes to some of the most fundamental characteristics of any poetry. For instance, they disagree sometimes subtly, but often decidedly, in their conception of the poetic voice, their idea of time, what role is accorded to the written word compared to the spoken word, and their notion of the Other. We could not cover all of these aspects to the extent they deserve, yet our initial findings should have pointed out the degree to which these two authors depart from each other.

This focus on their differences should not mask the fact that they also shared interests in some writers important for the poetics of each, especially Hölderlin and Mandelstam, and that their poetics have some fundamental motifs and tropes in common, particularly that of snow. Fortunately, quite many of these commonalities have been aptly researched by Amthor. Even though their collaboration on *L'Éphémère* and their contribution compared to that of the other editors of the journal would merit further examination, our study could not fill this gap. Nonetheless, full-length monographs in three different languages covering a large range of the journal's editors' diverse range of poetics and thought about the arts have already been dedicated to *L'Éphémère*.[17]

There are other challenges this study could not meet and gaps of research which this study could not fill. Whereas much has been written on Celan in English, German, and French, and the weekly *séminaires Celan* have been convened uninterruptedly for more than twenty-five years at the École Normale Supérieure, and conferences on Celan are still a common phenomenon (not least in 2020, the centenary of his birth), his younger French colleague has not been researched at a similar level of depth, yet. While there have been two conferences on du Bouchet so far, resulting in two volumes compiling the contributed papers,[18] there is still a steady stream of unpublished materials being printed, most recently his interviews with Alain Veinstein in 2016.[19] Accounting for the unequal balance of research on both authors and giving both authors a treatment of equal depth was constantly present in my mind when working on this study. Inevitably, it was not possible for me to completely balance out the scales. Yet, I hope that this study has shown why these two very difficult authors are fascinating in equal measure. Much is to be gained for our understanding of Celan's *and* du Bouchet's poetics when they are interpreted alongside and in contrast to each other.

While this study focused on two particular poets, its ambitions go beyond merely seeking to contribute to the respective scholarship on each author. Over the course of this book, I have outlined an extensive background to notions of the image generally. While this was necessary for an informed exegesis of the two poets whose image was influenced by this history, I hope that my having framed their image conceptions in this way will inspire future research to more generally re-evaluate the poetic image beyond notions of the image as figurative language or metaphor.

While Celan's image is, at least in relative terms, more adherent to traditional notions of the image, he provides interesting avenues to rethink these traditional notions in non-absolute ways in an attempt on the one hand to do them historical justice, as it were, but on the other hand to challenge the idea that we could just carry on drawing naively on the idea of an *archetypos* after the Holocaust. Conversely, du Bouchet's radical break from these traditions puts him in a close relationship with W. J. T. Mitchell, who rethinks the traditional distinction between language and images, when he states that 'there is no essential difference between texts and images and thus no gap between the media to be overcome' and that:

> [l]anguage can stand in for depiction and depiction can stand in for language because communicative, expressive acts, narration, argument, description,

exposition and other so-called 'speech acts' are not medium-specific, are not 'proper' to some medium or other. [...] While it's true that Western painting isn't generally used to perform these sorts of speech acts, there is no warrant for concluding that they could never do so.[20]

It seems to me that du Bouchet's polychotomous image achieves a hybrid of visual image and language that — in the reciprocally referring visual *blancs* and linguistic 'écarts' — expresses precisely the mutability of these two media Mitchell speaks about.

Finally, as can be gleaned from my resorting to the Greek terms *archetypos* and *typos* because of a lack of adequate English terminology, the difference between Celan's and du Bouchet's image at least to a degree is also a linguistic one. Unlike in French and English, in German the fault line between *archetypos* and *typos* runs *within* the image: both *Urbild* and *Abbild* are *Bilder*. Thus, at least to an extent, this multilingual study hopes to have provided intriguing moments of linguistic cross-fertilization by thinking about the image in different languages. In so doing, it has also asked the fundamental question to what extent language frames our concepts.[21]

Notes to the Conclusion

1. Celan, *Poèmes* (1986); André du Bouchet, 'Tübingen, le 22 mai 1986'.
2. Cf. Badiou's meticulous notes on their correspondence, p. 209.
3. See Wagstaff, *André du Bouchet*, p. 98.
4. As far as I can determine, the word 'métaphore' is not mentioned in any of the available editions of his *carnets*, nor have I found it in e.g. *Ici en deux* or *Dans la chaleur vacante*.
5. Cf. *Entretiens d'André du Bouchet avec Alain Veinstein*, ed. by Veinstein, p. 48.
6. E.g. Fournanty-Fabre; Ivanović, 'Eine Sprache der Bilder'.
7. E.g. Ivanović; Bahti; Könneker. For a comprehensive bibliography, see Brüder, pp. 284–86.
8. Cf. Paul Celan, *La Bibliothèque philosophique*.
9. Cf. *Entretiens d'André du Bouchet avec Alain Veinstein*, ed. by Veinstein.
10. De Rijcke, 'Entretiens avec André du Bouchet'.
11. André du Bouchet, *Aveuglante ou banale: Essais sur la poésie, 1949–1959*, ed. by François Tison and Clément Layet (Paris: Le Bruit du temps, 2011).
12. Du Bouchet, *Carnets 1949–1955*.
13. That is the edition published by Clément Layet and François Tison: du Bouchet, *Aveuglante ou banale*.
14. Wagstaff, 'Francis Ponge and André du Bouchet on Giacometti' and 'André du Bouchet and Pierre Tal Coat'; Collot, '"D'un trait qui figure et défigure": Du Bouchet et Giacometti'.
15. Esp. Collot, *L'Horizon fabuleux*, pp. 179–211.
16. Olschner, *Der feste Buchstab*; Gellhaus; Goßens, *Paul Celans Ungaretti-Übersetzung*; Harbusch; Pennone.
17. Siobhan Marie La Piana, 'Sovereign Moments: May 1968, *Écriture*, and the French Literary Journal *L'Éphémère* (1967–1972)' (unpublished doctoral thesis, University of Michigan, 1995) <https://search.proquest.com/docview/304224832/citation/ED10D5AD695E41A9PQ/1> [accessed 23 June 2017]; Mascarou; Gabriele Bruckschlegel, *L'Éphémère: Eine französische Literaturzeitschrift und ihr poetisches Credo* (Wilhelmsfeld: Egert, 1990); James Petterson, *Postwar Figures of 'L'Éphémère': Yves Bonnefoy, Louis-René des Forêts, Jacques Dupin, André du Bouchet* (Lewisburg, PA: Bucknell University Press, 2000); Wagstaff, *André du Bouchet*, pp. 34–61 (chapter 2).
18. *Autour d'André du Bouchet: Rencontres sur la poésie moderne*, ed. by Collot; *Présence d'André du Bouchet*, ed. by Michel Collot and Jean-Pascal Léger (Paris: Hermann Editeurs, 2012).
19. *Entretiens d'André du Bouchet avec Alain Veinstein*, ed. by Veinstein.

20. Mitchell, *Picture Theory*, p. 160.
21. In fact, the research for this book was foundational for my own rethinking of eighteenth-century German notions of the imagination as opposed to those present in French or English. See my forthcoming article 'The "Urbild" of "Einbildung": The Archetype in the Imagination in German Eighteenth-Century Aesthetics', in *Journal of the History of Ideas*, 82.4 (2021).

BIBLIOGRAPHY

Primary Sources

CELAN, PAUL, *Atemkristall. Radierungen von Gisèle Celan-Lestrange* (Frankfurt a. M.: Suhrkamp, 1990)
—— *La Bibliothèque philosophique. Die philosophische Bibliothek: Catalogue raisonné des annotations*, ed. by Alexandra Richter, Patrik Alac, and Bertrand Badiou (Paris: Presses de l'École Normale Supérieure, 2004)
—— *Poèmes*, trans. by André du Bouchet (Paris: Clivages, 1978)
—— *Poèmes*, trans. by André du Bouchet (Paris: Mercure de France, 1986)
—— *Renverse du souffle*, trans. by Jean-Pierre Lefebvre (Paris: Points Poésie, 2006)
—— *Schwarzmaut. Radierungen von Gisèle Celan-Lestrange* (Frankfurt a. M.: Suhrkamp, 1990)
—— *Strette*, trans. by André du Bouchet and others (Paris: Mercure de France, 1971)
CELAN, PAUL, and GISÈLE CELAN-LESTRANGE, *Correspondance: 1951–1970. Avec un choix de lettres de Paul Celan à son fils Eric*, ed. by Bertrand Badiou and Eric Celan (Paris: Seuil, 2001)
CELAN, PAUL, and FRANZ WURM, *Paul Celan — Franz Wurm: Briefwechsel*, ed. by Barbara Wiedemann (Frankfurt a. M.: Suhrkamp, 2003)
DE RIJCKE, ELKE, 'Entretiens avec André du Bouchet', *L'Étrangère*, 16/17/18, special issue: *André du Bouchet 2* (2007), 277–300
—— 'Sur la traduction: Compost de langue retourné en fleurs et en fruits, un entretien', *L'Étrangère*, 16-17-18, special issue: *André du Bouchet 2* (2007), 269–76
DU BOUCHET, ANDRÉ, *Annotations sur l'espace non datées* (Fontfroide-le-Haut: Fata Morgana, 2000)
—— *Aveuglante ou banale: Essais sur la poésie, 1949–1959*, ed. by François Tison and Clément Layet (Paris: Le Bruit du temps, 2011)
—— *Carnet 2* (Fontfroide-le-haut: Fata Morgana, 1999)
—— 'L'Écrit à haute voix', in *André du Bouchet*, ed. by Pierre Chappuis (Paris: Seghers, 1979), pp. 90–91
—— *L'Emportement de muet* (Paris: Mercure de France, 2000)
—— 'Hölderlin aujourd'hui', in *L'Incohérence* (Paris: Hachette, 1979), n.p.
—— *Ici en deux* (Paris: Mercure de France, 1986)
—— *Ici en deux*, ed. by Michel Collot (Paris: Gallimard Education, 2011)
—— 'Image à terme', in *L'Incohérence* (Fontfroide-le-Haut: Fata Morgana, 1979), n.p.
—— 'Image parvenue à son terme inquiet', in *Dans la chaleur vacante. Suivi de Ou le soleil* (Paris: Gallimard, 1991), pp. 109–18
—— *Openwork: Poetry and Prose*, trans. by Paul Auster (New Haven: Yale University Press, 2014)
—— *Peinture* (Fontfroide-le-Haut: Fata Morgana, 1983)
—— *Qui n'est pas tourné vers nous* (Paris: Mercure de France, 1974)
—— 'Résolution de la poésie', *Arguments*, 4.19 (1960), 42–44
—— 'Tübingen, le 22 mai 1986', *Hölderlin Jahrbuch*, 26 (1988), 343–59

―― *Une lampe dans la lumière aride: Carnets 1949–1955*, ed. by Clément Layet (Paris: Le Bruit du temps, 2011)
JAKOB, MICHAEL, ed., 'Gespräch mit André du Bouchet', in *Aussichten des Denkens*, trans. by Michael Jakob (Munich: Fink, 1997), pp. 57–85
VEINSTEIN, ALAIN, ed., *Entretiens d'André du Bouchet avec Alain Veinstein* (Strasbourg: Institut National de l'Audiovisuel & L'Atelier Contemporain, 2016)

Secondary Sources

Online

CORRIGAN, KEVIN, and L. MICHAEL HARRINGTON, 'Pseudo-Dionysius the Areopagite', *The Stanford Encyclopedia of Philosophy* (2015) <http://plato.stanford.edu/archives/spr2015/entries/pseudo-dionysius-areopagite/> [accessed 18 April 2016]
'Gesichtig, adj. und adv.', *Wörterbuchnetz — Deutsches Wörterbuch von Jacob Grimm und Wilhelm Grimm* <https://woerterbuchnetz.de/?sigle=DWB&mode=Vernetzung&lemid=GM02008#3> [accessed 16 March 2021]
HOYT, ROGERS, 'Translating André du Bouchet', *The Fortnightly Review* (2015) <http://fortnightlyreview.co.uk/2015/06/translating-andre-du-bouchet/> [accessed 31 May 2016]
'Hyphen, n.', *OED Online* (Oxford University Press, 2017) <https://www.oed.com/view/Entry/90403?rskey=uXraDT&result=1&isAdvanced=false#eid> [accessed 25 March 2021]
'Maske, f.', *Wörterbuchnetz — Deutsches Wörterbuch von Jacob Grimm und Wilhelm Grimm* <http://woerterbuchnetz.de/cgi-bin/WBNetz/wbgui_py?sigle=DWB&mode=Vernetzung&lemid=GM02008#XGM02008> [accessed 12 May 2017]
LA PIANA, SIOBHAN MARIE, 'Sovereign Moments: May 1968, *Écriture*, and the French Literary Journal L'Éphémère (1967–1972)' (unpublished doctoral thesis, University of Michigan, 1995) <https://search.proquest.com/docview/304224832/citation/ED10D5AD695E41A9PQ/1> [accessed 23 June 2017]
'Les Misérables Narrator Point of View', *shmoop* <https://www.shmoop.com/les-miserables/narrator-point-of-view.html> [accessed 18 September 2017]
'Nu, Nue, adj. et subst.', *Le Trésor de la Langue Française informatisé* <http://atilf.atilf.fr/> [accessed 9 March 2021]
'Phosphène, subst. masc.', *Le Trésor de la Langue Française informatisé* <http://atilf.atilf.fr/> [accessed 25 February 2021]
RILEY, PETER, 'The Apophatic Poetry of André du Bouchet', *The Fortnightly Review* (2015) <http://fortnightlyreview.co.uk/2015/04/andre-du-bouchet-riley/> [accessed 4 July 2015]
'Terme, subst. masc.', *Le Trésor de la Langue Française informatisé* <http://atilf.atilf.fr/> [accessed 9 March 2021]
'Traduire, verbe trans.', *Le Trésor de la Langue Française informatisé* <http://atilf.atilf.fr/> [accessed 18 March 2021]
'Vision, f.', *Wörterbuchnetz — Deutsches Wörterbuch von Jacob Grimm und Wilhelm Grimm* <http://woerterbuchnetz.de/cgi-bin/WBNetz/wbgui_py?sigle=DWB&mode=Vernetzung&lemid=GV09255#XGV09255> [accessed 15 April 2019]
'Vision, n.', *OED Online* (Oxford University Press, 2016) <http://www.oed.com/view/Entry/223943> [accessed 31 March 2016]
WEISSMANN, DIRK, 'Poésie, judaïsme, philosophie: Une histoire de la réception de Paul Celan en France, des débuts jusqu'à 199' (unpublished doctoral thesis, Paris 3, 2003) <http://www.theses.fr/2003PA030084> [accessed 24 April 2017]

Print

ADLER, JEREMY D., and ULRICH ERNST, eds, *Text als Figur: Visuelle Poesie von der Antike bis zur Moderne* (Konstanz: VCH, 1988)

ALLOA, EMMANUEL, 'Bildwissenschaft in Byzanz: Ein iconic turn avant la lettre?', in *Philosophie des Bildes: Philosophie de l'image*, ed. by Anton Hügli (Basle: Schwabe, 2010), pp. 11–35

AL-TAIE, YVONNE, *Tropus und Erkenntnis: Sprach- und Bildtheorie der deutschen Frühromantik* (Göttingen: Vandenhoeck & Ruprecht, 2015)

AMTHOR, WIEBKE, *Schneegespräche an gastlichen Tischen: Wechselseitiges Übersetzen bei Paul Celan und André du Bouchet* (Heidelberg: Winter, 2006)

ASMUTH, BERNHARD, 'Seit wann gilt die Metapher als Bild? Zur Geschichte der Begriffe "Bild" und "Bildlichkeit" und ihrer gattungspoetischen Verwendung', in *Rhetorik zwischen den Wissenschaften: Geschichte, System, Praxis als Probleme des 'Historischen Wörterbuchs der Rhetorik'*, ed. by Gert Ueding, Walter Jens, and Joachim Dyck (Tübingen: Niemeyer, 1991), pp. 299–311

AUGUSTINE, *Confessions*, trans. by William Watts, 2 vols (London: Heinemann, 1912)

—— *On the Trinity: Books 8–15*, ed. by Gareth B. Matthews (Cambridge: Cambridge University Press, 2002)

AUSTIN, J. L., *How to Do Things with Words*, ed. by Marina Sbisa and J. O. Urmsson, 2nd edn (Oxford: Oxford University Press, 1975)

AZÉRAD, HUGO, 'Parisian Literary Fields: James Joyce and Pierre Reverdy's Theory of the Image', *The Modern Language Review*, 103.3 (2008), 666–81

BADIOU, BERTRAND, '"...vivant et redevable à la poésie": Le Dialogue entre Paul Celan et André du Bouchet à travers sept lettres écrites au tournant de l'année 1968', *Europe: Revue Littéraire Mensuelle*, 89.986/87, special issue: *André du Bouchet*, ed. by Nikolaï Zabolotski (2011), 208–31

BAHTI, TIMOTHY, 'A Minor Form and its Inversions: The Image, the Poem, the Book in Celan's "Unter ein Bild"', *Modern Language Notes*, 110.3 (1995), 565–78

BAQUEY, STÉPHANE, 'Le Sens du dehors', *Europe: Revue Littéraire Mensuelle*, 89.986/87, special issue: *André du Bouchet*, ed. by Nikolaï Zabolotski (2011), 84–93

BAUCH, KURT, 'Imago', in *Was ist ein Bild?*, ed. by Gottfried Boehm (Munich: Fink, 1994), pp. 11–39

BAUDELAIRE, CHARLES, *Œuvres complètes*, ed. by Alphonse Lemerre, 7 vols (Paris: Lemerre, 1888)

BAZAINE, JEAN, *Notizen zur Malerei der Gegenwart*, trans. by Paul Celan (Frankfurt a. M.: Fischer, 1959)

BEEKES, ROBERT, ed., 'Κρυπτός' [Kruptós], *Etymological Dictionary of Greek* (Leiden: Brill, 2010), 786

BEESE, HENRIETTE, *Nachdichtung als Erinnerung: Allegorische Lektüre einiger Gedichte von Paul Celan* (Darmstadt: Agora, 1976)

BEIERWALTES, WERNER, *Denken des Einen* (Frankfurt a. M.: Klostermann, 1985)

—— *Identität und Differenz* (Frankfurt a. M.: Klostermann, 2011)

BERKELEY, GEORGE, *Principles of Human Knowledge and Three Dialogues*, ed. by Howard Robinson (Oxford: Oxford University Press, 1999)

BERNER, CHRISTIAN, '"Se rendre compte de ce qu'on voit": À propos de *La Jambe* de Giacometti', in *Puissances de l'image*, ed. by Jean-Claude Gens and Pierre Rodrigo (Dijon: Éditions universitaires de Dijon, 2007), pp. 187–99

BIBLE, *King James Version* (Glasgow: Collins, 1991)

BISHOP, MICHAEL, *Altérités d'André du Bouchet: De Hugo, Shakespeare et Poussin à Celan, Mandelstam et Giacometti* (Amsterdam: Rodopi, 2003)

—— 'Longer, sans attache: Neuf remarques pour une ontologie dubouchettienne', in *Présence d'André du Bouchet*, ed. by Michel Collot and Jean-Pascal Léger (Paris: Hermann, 2012), pp. 213–25

—— 'Pierre Reverdy's Conception of the Image', *Forum for Modern Language Studies*, 12.1 (1976), 25–36

BLUM, MATTHIAS, 'Gottesmord', in *Handbuch des Antisemitismus: Judenfeindschaft in Geschichte und Gegenwart. Begriffe, Theorien, Ideologien*, ed. by Wolfgang Benz and others, 8 vols (New York: De Gruyter, 2009–15), III, compiled by Brigitte Mihok (2011), 113–14

BLUM, WILHELM, 'Kleists Marionettentheater und das Drahtpuppengleichnis bei Platon', *Zeitschrift für Religions- und Geistesgeschichte*, 23.1 (1971), 40–49

BLUMENBERG, HANS, 'Paradigmen zu einer Metaphorologie', *Archiv für Begriffsgeschichte*, 6 (1960), 7–143

BOGUMIL, SIEGHILD, 'Geschichte, Sprache und Erkenntnis in der Dichtung Paul Celans', in *Der Glühende Leertext: Annäherungen an Paul Celans Dichtung*, ed. by Christoph Jamme and Otto Pöggeler (Munich: Fink, 1993), pp. 127–42

—— '"Ortswechsel bei den Substanzen": Paul Celan als Übersetzer von André du Bouchet und Jacques Dupin', in *Stationen: Kontinuität und Entwicklung in Paul Celans Übersetzungswerk*, ed. by Jürgen Lehmann and Christine Ivanović (Heidelberg: Winter, 1997), pp. 163–93

BOHN, WILLARD, *The Aesthetics of Visual Poetry, 1914–1928* (Cambridge: Cambridge University Press, 1986)

—— *The Rise of Surrealism: Cubism, Dada, and the Pursuit of the Marvelous* (Albany, NY: SUNY, 2012)

BOLLACK, JEAN, 'Chanson à boire: Über das Gedicht "Bei Wein und Verlorenheit"', *Celan-Jahrbuch*, 3, ed. by Hans-Michael Speier (1989), 23–37

BOLLACK, JEAN, JEAN-MARIE WINKLER, and WERNER WÖGERBAUER, eds, *Sur quatre poèmes de Paul Celan: Une lecture à plusieurs. Analyses et présentation des débats* (Villeneuve d'Ascq: Université de Lille 3, 1991)

BÖSCHENSTEIN, BERNHARD, 'André du Bouchet im Gespräch mit Paul Celan', in *Celan-Jahrbuch*, 8, ed. by Hans-Michael Speier (2001/02), 225–35

—— 'André du Bouchet traducteur de Hölderlin et de Celan', in *Autour d'André du Bouchet: Rencontres sur la poésie moderne. Actes du colloque des 8, 9, 10 décembre 1983*, ed. by Michel Collot (Paris: Presses de l'École Normale Supérieure, 1986), pp. 169–78

—— 'Supervielle in Celans Fügung', in *Paul Celan*, ed. by Werner Hamacher and Winfried Menninghaus (Frankfurt a. M.: Suhrkamp, 1988), pp. 222–39

BREITINGER, JOHANN JAKOB, *Critische Dichtkunst worinnen die poetische Mahlerey in Absicht auf die Erfindung im Grunde untersuchet und mit Beyspielen aus den berühmtesten Alten und Neuern erläutert wird* (Zurich: Orell und Comp., 1740)

BRETON, ANDRÉ, *Manifestes du Surréalisme: Premier Manifeste, Second Manifeste, Prolégomènes à un Troisième Manifeste du Surréalisme ou non, Position politique du Surréalisme, Poisson Soluble, Lettres aux voyantes, Du Surréalisme en ses œuvres vives*, ed. by Jean-Jacques Pauvert (Montreuil: Pauvert, 1962)

BRUCKSCHLEGEL, GABRIELE, *L'Éphémère: Eine französische Literaturzeitschrift und ihr poetisches Credo* (Wilhelmsfeld: Egert, 1990)

BRÜDER, FRANK, 'Kunst', in *Celan-Handbuch: Leben, Werk, Wirkung*, ed. by Markus May, Peter Gossens, and Jürgen Lehmann, 2nd rev. and ext. edn (Stuttgart: Metzler, 2012), pp. 278–85

BUCK, THEO, *Celan schreibt an Jünger*, Celan-Studien, 7 (Aachen: Rimbaud, 2005)

—— *Muttersprache, Mördersprache*, Celan-Studien, 1 (Aachen: Rimbaud, 1993)

BURGER, HERMANN, *Paul Celan: Auf der Suche nach der verlorenen Sprache* (Zürich: Fischer, 1974)

CHAMPEAU, SERGE, *Ontologie et poésie: Trois études sur les limites du langage* (Paris: Vrin, 1995)
CHAPPUIS, PIERRE, ed., *André du Bouchet* (Paris: Seghers, 1979)
CHOL, ISABELLE, *Pierre Reverdy: Poésie plastique. Formes composées et dialogue des arts (1913–1960)* (Geneva: Droz, 2006)
COLLOT, MICHEL, 'Bouchet, André du', in *Dictionnaire de poésie de Baudelaire à nos jours*, ed. by Michel Jarrety (Paris: Presses Universitaires de France, 2001), pp. 85–89
—— *L'Horizon fabuleux* (Paris: Corti, 1988)
—— 'Ici en deux: André du Bouchet, poète et traducteur', in *Génétique & Traduction*, ed. by Serge Bourjea (Paris: L'Harmattan, 1995), pp. 147–67
—— 'La Syntaxe du visible: Reverdy et l'esthétique cubiste', in *Reverdy aujourd'hui: Actes du colloque des 22, 23, 24 juin 1989*, ed. by Michel Collot and Jean-Claude Mathieu (Paris: Presses de l'École Normale Supérieure, 1991), pp. 67–77
—— '"D'un trait qui figure et défigure": Du Bouchet et Giacometti', in *André du Bouchet et ses Autres*, ed. by Michel Minard and Philippe Met (Paris-Caen: Lettres modernes Minard, 2003), pp. 95–107
——, ed., *Autour d'André du Bouchet: Rencontres sur la poésie moderne. Actes du colloque des 8, 9, 10 décembre 1983* (Paris: Presses de l'Ecole normale supérieure, 1986)
COLLOT, MICHEL and JEAN-PASCAL LÉGER, eds, *Présence d'André du Bouchet* (Paris: Hermann, 2012)
COOPER, IAN, *The Near and Distant God: Poetry, Idealism and Religious Thought from Hölderlin to Eliot* (London: Legenda, 2008)
DAIVE, JEAN, *La Condition d'infini 5* (Paris: P.O.L, 1996)
DANTO, ARTHUR, 'The Artworld', *The Journal of Philosophy*, 61.19 (1964), 571–84
DE GOURMONT, REMY, *La Culture des idées* (Paris: Société du Mercure de France, 1900)
—— *Le Problème du style* (Paris: Société du Mercure de France, 1902)
DEPREUX, JACQUES, *André du Bouchet; ou, La Parole traversée* (Seyssel: Champ vallon, 1988)
DERRIDA, JACQUES, 'The Double Session', in *Dissemination*, trans. by Barbara Johnson (London: The Athlone, 1981), pp. 173–287
—— *Limited Inc* (Evanston, IL: Northwestern University Press, 1988)
—— *Le Monolinguisme de l'autre; ou, La Prothèse d'origine* (Paris: Galilée, 1996)
—— *Shibboleth: Pour Paul Celan* (Paris: Éditions Galilée, 1986)
—— *La Voix et le phénomène: Introduction au problème du signe dans la phénoménologie de Husserl*, 2nd edn (Paris: Presses universitaires de France, 1998)
DE STAËL, ANNE, 'Chronologie d'André du Bouchet', in *L'Étrangère*, 14/15, special issue: *André du Bouchet 1* (2007), 355–89
DILLMAN, KARIN J., *The Subject in Rimbaud: From Self to 'Je'* (New York: Lang, 1984)
DIRSCHERL, KLAUS, 'Wirklichkeit und Kunstwirklichkeit: Reverdys Kubismustheorie als Programm für eine a-mimetische Lyrik', in *Lyrik und Malerei der Avantgarde*, ed. by Rainer Warning and Winfried Wehle (Munich: Fink, 1982), pp. 445–80
DRUCKER, JOHANNA, 'Stéphane Mallarmé's *Un Coup de Dés* and the Poem and/as Book as Diagram', *Journal of Philosophy: A Cross-Disciplinary Inquiry*, 7.16 (2011), 1–13
DUECK, EVELYN, *L'Étranger intime: Les Traductions françaises de l'œuvre de Paul Celan* (Berlin: De Gruyter, 2014)
EIGELDINGER, MARC, and ARTHUR RIMBAUD, *Lettres du voyant (13 et 15 mai 1871). Précédées de: La Voyance avant Rimbaud* (Geneva: Droz, 1975)
ELLESTRÖM, LARS, 'Visual Iconicity in Poetry: Replacing the Notion of "Visual Poetry"', *Orbis Litterarum*, 71.6 (2016), 437–72
EMMERICH, WOLFGANG, *Paul Celan*, 6th edn (Reinbek: Rowohlt, 2014)
ENGELL, JAMES, *The Creative Imagination: Enlightenment to Romanticism* (Cambridge, MA: Harvard University Press, 1981)

ERNST, WOLFGANG, 'Absenz', in *Ästhetische Grundbegriffe: Historisches Wörterbuch*, ed. by Karlheinz Barck and others, 7 vols (Stuttgart: Metzler, 2010), I, 1–15

FAVRE, Y.-A., 'Le "Réel absent"', in *Le Centenaire de Pierre Reverdy: Actes du colloque d'Angers*, ed. by Yvan Leclerc and Georges Cesbron (Angers: Presses de l'Université d'Angers, 1990), pp. 25–34

FAVRIAUD, MICHEL, 'Traduction: Poétique inachevée de la relation', in *André du Bouchet et ses Autres*, ed. by Michel Minard and Philippe Met (Paris-Caen: Lettres modernes Minard, 2003), pp. 175–213

FELSTINER, JOHN, *Paul Celan: Poet, Survivor, Jew* (New Haven: Yale University Press, 2001)

FERRAN, BRONAC, '"A Language that No-One Speaks": Celan and the Concrete Poets', in *Celan-Perspektiven 2019*, ed. by Bernd Auerochs, Friederike Felicitas Günther, and Markus May (Heidelberg: Winter, 2019), pp. 107–25

FETZER, GLENN, 'Du Bouchet et la dynamique de l'image', *Dalhousie French Studies*, 111 (2018), 35–41

—— *Palimpsests of the Real in Recent French Poetry* (Amsterdam: Rodopi, 2004)

FEUDO, MICHELA LO, 'Paul Celan and Jacques Dupin in the Journal "L'Éphémère"', trans. by Alexander Booth and Peter Douglas, *Studi Germanici*, 3/4 (2013), 129–54

FIORETOS, ARIS, 'Nothing: History and Materiality in Celan', in *Word Traces: Readings of Paul Celan*, ed. by Aris Fioretos (Baltimore: Johns Hopkins University Press, 1994), pp. 295–341

FISCHER, MARKUS, *Celan-Lektüren: Reden, Gedichte und Übersetzungen Paul Celans im poetologischen und literarhistorischen Kontext* (Berlin: Frank & Timme, 2014)

FØLLESDAL, DAGFINN, 'Husserl's Reductions and the Role They Play in his Phenomenology', in *A Companion to Phenomenology and Existentialism*, ed. by Hubert L. Dreyfus and Mark A. Wrathall (Malden, MA: Blackwell, 2006), pp. 105–15

FOURNANTY-FABRE, CATHERINE, 'Images et réalité dans l'œuvre de Paul Celan' (unpublished doctoral thesis, Paris 4, 1999)

FRANK, MANFRED, *Ansichten der Subjektivität* (Frankfurt a. M.: Suhrkamp, 2012)

—— *Einführung in die frühromantische Ästhetik: Vorlesungen* (Frankfurt a. M.: Suhrkamp, 1989)

—— *Selbstbewusstsein und Selbsterkenntnis: Essays zur analytischen Philosophie der Subjektivität* (Stuttgart: Reclam, 1991)

—— *Was ist Neostrukturalismus?* (Frankfurt a. M.: Suhrkamp, 1984)

FRAZER, RAY, 'The Origin of the Term "Image"', *English Literary History*, 27.2 (1960), 149–61

FURBANK, PHILIP NICHOLAS, *Reflections on the Word 'Image'* (London: Secker & Warburg, 1970)

FUSSL, IRENE, *'Geschenke an Aufmerksame': Hebräische Intertextualität und mystische Weltauffassung in der Lyrik Paul Celans* (Tübingen: Niemeyer, 2008)

GADAMER, HANS G., *Gesammelte Werke*, 6th edn, 10 vols (Tübingen: Mohr Siebeck, 1985–95)

GEINOZ, PHILIPPE, *Relations au travail: Dialogue entre poésie et peinture à l'époque du cubisme. Apollinaire — Picasso — Braque — Gris — Reverdy* (Geneva: Droz, 2014)

GELLER, STEPHEN A., 'Hebrew Prosody and Poetics: Biblical', in *The New Princeton Encyclopedia of Poetry and Poetics*, ed. by Alex Preminger and T. V. F. Brogan (Princeton: Princeton University Press, 1993), pp. 509–11

GELLHAUS, AXEL, ed., *Fremde Nähe: Celan als Übersetzer. Eine Ausstellung des Deutschen Literaturarchivs* (Marbach am Neckar: Deutsche Schillergesellschaft, 1997)

GIACOMETTI, ALBERTO, *Écrits* (Paris: Hermann, 2007)

GOETHE, JOHANN WOLFGANG VON, 'Prometheus', in *Berliner Ausgabe*, ed. by Siegfried Seidel u.a., 23 vols (incl. 1 supplementary vol.) (Berlin: Aufbau, 1960–78)

GOMBRICH, E. H., 'Icones Symbolicae: The Visual Image in Neo-Platonic Thought', *Journal of the Warburg and Courtauld Institutes*, 11 (1948), 163–92

GOODMAN, NELSON, *Languages of Art: An Approach to a Theory of Symbols* (Indianapolis: Hackett, 1976)

GOSSENS, PETER, 'Nachwort', in *'Angefügt, nahtlos, dem Heute'. 'Agglutinati all'oggi': Paul Celan übersetzt Giuseppe Ungaretti. Zweisprachige Ausgabe. Italienisch, deutsch. Handschriften. Erstdruck. Dokumente*, ed. by Peter Goßens (Frankfurt a. M.: Insel, 2006), pp. 185–222

—— *Paul Celans Ungaretti-Übersetzung: Edition und Kommentar* (Heidelberg: Winter, 2000)

GOSSENS, PETER, MARKUS MAY and JÜRGEN LEHMANN, eds, 'Leben und Werk — eine kurze Chronik', in *Celan-Handbuch: Leben, Werk, Wirkung*, 2nd rev. and ext. edn (Stuttgart: Metzler, 2012), pp. 7–15

GRUBE, CHRISTOPH, 'Phänomenologie', in *Celan-Handbuch: Leben, Werk, Wirkung*, ed. by Markus May, Peter Gossens, and Jürgen Lehmann, 2nd rev. and ext. edn (Stuttgart: Metzler, 2012), pp. 250–54

GRUNDMANN, REGINA, *'Rabbi Faibisch, Was auf Hochdeutsch heißt Apollo': Judentum, Dichtertum, Schlemihltum in Heinrich Heines Werk* (Stuttgart: Metzler, 2008)

HAIDER, HUBERT, *The Syntax of German* (Cambridge: Cambridge University Press, 2010)

HAMACHER, WERNER, 'Intensive Languages', trans. by Ira Allen and Steven Tester, *Modern Language Notes*, 127.3 (2012), 485–541

HAMLIN, CYRUS, 'German Classical Poetry', in *The Literature of Weimar Classicism*, ed. by Simon Richter (Rochester, NY: Camden House, 2005), pp. 169–210

HARBUSCH, UTE, *Gegenübersetzungen: Paul Celans Übertragungen französischer Symbolisten* (Göttingen: Wallstein, 2005)

HEIMBÜCHEL, UTE, and VOLKER NEUHAUS, eds, *Briefe an Hans Bender* (Munich: Hanser, 1984)

HENRICH, DIETER, 'Fichtes ursprüngliche Einsicht', *Wissenschaft und Gegenwart*, 34 (1967), 7–48

HORACE, *Satires, Epistles, and Ars Poetica*, trans. by Henry Rushton Fairclough (London: Harvard University Press, 1936)

HUBERT, ETIENNE-ALAIN, 'Autour de la théorie de l'image de Pierre Reverdy', in *Bousquet Jouve Reverdy: Colloques poésie-Cerisy*, ed. by Charles Bachat, Daniel Leuwers, and Etienne-Alain Hubert (Marseille: Sud, 1981), pp. 289–317

HUGO, VICTOR, *Les Contemplations* (Paris: Nelson, 1856)

—— *Les Misérables*, 10 vols (Brussels: Lacroix, Verboeckhoven, et Cie, 1862)

HUPPERT, HUGO, ' "Spirituell": Ein Gespräch mit Paul Celan', in *Paul Celan*, ed. by Werner Hamacher and Winfried Menninghaus (Frankfurt a. M.: Suhrkamp, 1988), pp. 319–25

HUSSERL, EDMUND, *Husserliana*, ed. Stephan Strasser and others (Den Haag: Nijhoff, 1950–), II: *Die Idee der Phänomenologie: Fünf Vorlesungen*, ed. by Walter Biemel (Den Haag: Nijhoff, 1950)

—— *Logische Untersuchungen*, 4th edn, 2 vols in 3 (Tübingen: Niemeyer, 1968)

IVANOVIĆ, CHRISTINE, 'Eine Sprache der Bilder: Notizen zur immanenten Poetik der Lyrik Paul Celans', *Études Germaniques*, 55.3 (2000), 541–59

—— *Das Gedicht im Geheimnis der Begegnung: Dichtung und Poetik Celans im Kontext seiner russischen Lektüren* (Tübingen: Niemeyer, 1996)

—— 'Kunst — der von der Dichtung zurückzulegende Weg: Pablo Picasso und Paul Celan', in *Stationen: Kontinuität und Entwicklung in Paul Celans Übersetzungswerk*, ed. by Jürgen Lehmann and Christine Ivanović (Heidelberg: Winter, 1997), pp. 27–53

—— ' "des menschen farbe ist freiheit": Paul Celans Umweg über den Wiener Surrealismus', in *'Displaced': Paul Celan in Wien 1947–1948*, ed. by Peter Goßens and Marcus Patka (Frankfurt a. M.: Suhrkamp, 2001), pp. 62–70

Jakob, Michael, *Das 'Andere' Paul Celans; oder, von den Paradoxien relationalen Dichtens* (Munich: Fink, 1993)

Janz, Marlies, *Vom Engagement absoluter Poesie: Zur Lyrik und Ästhetik Paul Celans* (Frankfurt a. M.: Syndikat, 1976)

Kemp, Friedhelm, and others, eds, *Französische Dichtung: Eine zweisprachige Anthologie in vier Bänden*, 2nd edn, 4 vols (Munich: Beck, 2010)

Kleist, Heinrich von, *Werke und Briefe in vier Bänden*, ed. by Siegfried Streller, 4 vols (Weimar: Aufbau, 1978)

Koch, Julian Johannes Immanuel, 'The Allegorical Image and Presence in Celan's "Wortaufschüttung"', *Seminar — A Journal of Germanic Studies*, 56.1 (2020), 22–36

—— '"The False Appearance of Totality Is Extinguished": Orson Welles's *The Trial* and Benjamin's Allegorical Image', *Film-Philosophy*, 23.1 (2019), 17–34

—— 'The Image in Celan's Poetics', *German Life and Letters*, 71.4 (2018), 434–51

—— 'Translation as Poetics in the Works of André du Bouchet', *The Modern Language Review*, 114.1 (2019), 35–51

—— 'The "Urbild" of "Einbildung": The Archetype in the Imagination in German Eighteenth-Century Aesthetics, *Journal of the History of Ideas*, 82.4 (2021)

Kohler-Luginbühl, Dorothee, *Poetik im Lichte der Utopie: Paul Celans poetologische Texte* (Berne: Lang, 1986)

König, Frank, *Vertieftes Sein: Wahrnehmung und Körperlichkeit bei Paul Celan und Maurice Merleau-Ponty* (Heidelberg: Winter, 2014)

Könneker, Sabine, *'Sichtbares, Hörbares': Die Beziehung zwischen Sprachkunst und bildender Kunst am Beispiel Paul Celans* (Bielefeld: Aisthesis, 1995)

Kreuzer, Johann, 'Philosophische Hintergründe der Gesänge "Der Einzige" und "Patmos" von Friedrich Hölderlin', in *Geist und Literatur: Modelle in der Weltliteratur von Shakespeare bis Celan*, ed. by Edith Düsing and Hans-Dieter Klein (Würzburg: Königshausen & Neumann, 2008), pp. 107–37 (p. 133)

—— 'Was heißt es, sich als Bild zu verstehen? Von Augustinus zu Eckhart', in *Denken mit dem Bild: Philosophische Einsätze des Bildbegriffs von Platon bis Hegel*, ed. by Arno Schubbach and Johannes Grave (Munich: Fink, 2010), pp. 75–99

Kummer, Irène Elisabeth, *Unlesbarkeit dieser Welt: Spannungsfelder moderner Lyrik und ihr Ausdruck im Werk von Paul Celan* (Frankfurt a. M.: Athenäum, 1987)

Lacoue-Labarthe, Philippe, *Poetry as Experience*, trans by Andrea Tarnowski (Stanford, CA: Stanford University Press, 1999)

Ladner, Gerhart B., 'The Concept of the Image in the Greek Fathers and the Byzantine Iconoclastic Controversy', *Dumbarton Oaks Papers*, 7 (1953), 1–34

Layet, Clément, '"Annuler les images, les casser": L'Image dans la poésie d'André du Bouchet', *French Forum*, 37.1 (2012), 137–47

—— 'Demain diamant', *Europe: Revue Littéraire Mensuelle*, 89.986/87, special issue: *André du Bouchet*, ed. by Nikolaï Zabolotski (2011), 27–39

—— 'La Survie insensée', *Europe*, 94.1049/50 (2016), 176–87

—— 'Temps apparent', in *Présence d'André du Bouchet*, ed. by Michel Collot and Jean-Pascal Léger (Paris: Hermann, 2012), pp. 227–43

Lehmann, Jürgen, 'Bei Wein und Verlorenheit', in *Kommentar zu Paul Celans 'Die Niemandsrose'*, ed. by Christine Ivanović and Jürgen Lehmann (Heidelberg: Winter, 1997), pp. 61–64

Lehmann, Jürgen, and Christine Ivanović, eds, *Stationen: Kontinuität und Entwicklung in Paul Celans Übersetzungswerk* (Heidelberg: Winter, 1997)

Leinkauf, Thomas, 'Der Bild-Begriff bei Cusanus', in *Denken mit dem Bild: Philosophische Einsätze des Bildbegriffs von Platon bis Hegel*, ed. by Arno Schubbach and Johannes Grave (Munich: Fink, 2010), pp. 99–129

LESSING, GOTTHOLD EPHRAIM, *Laokoon; oder, Über die Grenzen der Malerei und Poesie: Studienausgabe*, ed. by Friedrich Vollhardt (Stuttgart: Reclam, 2012)
LEUWERS, DANIEL, 'Le Carnet et ses autres', in *André du Bouchet et ses Autres*, ed. by Michel Minard and Philippe Met (Paris-Caen: Lettres modernes Minard, 2003), pp. 43–53
LINARES, SERGE, 'Quant au blanc', *Poétique*, 160.4 (2009), 471–84
—— 'Reverdy et du Bouchet: Deux poètes en regard', in *Présence d'André du Bouchet*, ed. by Michel Collot and Jean-Pascal Léger (Paris: Hermann, 2012), pp. 41–57
LINDNER, BURKHARDT, 'Allegorie', in *Benjamins Begriffe*, ed. by Michael Opitz and Erdmut Wizisla, 2 vols (Frankfurt a. M.: Suhrkamp, 2000), I, 50–94
LLOYD, LUCY-JEAN, 'Writing and Forgetting: Reading Reverdy through André du Bouchet', *Nottingham French Studies*, 28.2 (1989), 66–74
LÖNKER, FRED, 'Tenebrae', in *Kommentar zu Paul Celans 'Die Niemandsrose'*, ed. by Jürgen Lehmann and Christine Ivanović (Heidelberg: Winter, 1997), pp. 187–96
LORBE, RUTH, 'Paul Celan, "Tenebrae"', in *Über Paul Celan*, ed. by Dietlind Meinecke (Frankfurt a. M.: Suhrkamp, 1970)
LOWTH, ROBERT, *Lectures on the Sacred Poetry of the Hebrews*, trans. by G. Gregory (Boston, MA: Joseph T. Buckingham, 1815)
—— 'Paul Celan and Martin Buber: Poetry as Dialogue', *PMLA*, 86.1 (1971), 110–20
MALDINEY, HENRI, *Art et existence* (Paris: Klincksieck, 2003)
MÂLE, EMILE, *The Gothic Image: Religious Art in France, 13th Century*, trans. by Dora Nussey (New York: Harper, 1958)
MARTINEZ, VICTOR, *André du Bouchet: Poésie, langue, événement* (Amsterdam: Rodopi, 2013)
—— 'La "Phénoménologie de l'inapparent" dans les œuvres de Heidegger et Du Bouchet', in *Figuren der Absenz*, ed. by Anke Grutschus (Berlin: Frank & Timme, 2010), pp. 59–71
MASCAROU, ALAIN, *Les Cahiers de 'l'Éphémère' 1967–1972: Tracés interrompus* (Paris: L'Harmattan, 1998)
MAY, MARKUS, '"Bild-Poetik/-Politik: Anmerkungen zu Paul Celans Hinwendung zur Phänomenologie"', *treibhaus: Jahrbuch für die Literatur der fünfziger Jahre*, 13 (2017), 72–97
MEISTER ECKHART, *Predigten: Deutsche Werke I*, ed. by Niklas Largier, trans. by Josef Quint, 2 vols (Frankfurt a. M.: Deutscher Klassiker Verlag, 2008)
—— *Predigten und Traktate: Deutsche Werke II. Lateinische Werke*, ed. by Niklas Largier, trans. by Ernst Benz and others, 2 vols (Frankfurt a. M.: Deutscher Klassiker Verlag, 2008)
MENNINGHAUS, WINFRIED, *Paul Celan: Magie der Form* (Frankfurt a. M.: Suhrkamp, 1980)
—— *Walter Benjamins Theorie der Sprachmagie* (Frankfurt a. M.: Suhrkamp, 1980)
MERSCH, DIETER, 'Materialität und Formalität: Zur duplizitären Ordnung des Bildlichen', in *Materialität und Bildlichkeit: Visuelle Artefakte zwischen Aisthesis und Semiosis*, ed. by Finke, Marcel and Mark A. Halawa (Berlin: Kadmos, 2012), pp. 21–49
MESCHONNIC, HENRI, 'On appelle cela traduire Celan', in *Pour la poétique II: Épistémologie de l'écriture. Poétique de la traduction*, 3 vols (Paris: Gallimard, 1973), II, 398–99
MICHAUD, GUY, *La Doctrine symboliste: Documents* (Paris: Nizet, 1947)
MITCHELL, W. J. T., *Picture Theory: Essays on Verbal and Visual Representation* (Chicago, IL: University of Chicago Press, 1994)
MÖNIG, KLAUS, *Malerei und Graphik in deutscher Lyrik des 20. Jahrhunderts* (Freiburg i. Br.: Rombach, 2002)
MORAN, DERMOT, and JOSEPH COHEN, '"Eidetic Insight"', in *The Husserl Dictionary* (London: Continuum, 2012), pp. 91–92
NEUMANN, GERHARD, 'Die 'absolute' Metapher: Ein Abgrenzungsversuch am Beispiel Stéphane Mallarmés und Paul Celans', *Poetica*, 3 (1970), 188–225
O'CONNOR, CLÉMENCE, 'Poetry as a Foreign Language in Heather Dohollau and André du Bouchet', *Nottingham French Studies*, 56.2 (2017), 188–200

OLSCHNER, LEONARD, *Der feste Buchstab: Erläuterungen zu Paul Celans Gedichtübertragungen* (Göttingen: Vandenhoeck & Ruprecht, 1985)
—— *Im Abgrund Zeit: Paul Celans Poetiksplitter* (Göttingen: Vandenhoeck & Ruprecht, 2007)
—— 'Mandorla', in *Kommentar zu Paul Celans 'Die Niemandsrose'*, ed. by Jürgen Lehmann and Christine Ivanović (Heidelberg: Winter, 1997), pp. 178–82
OSTROGORSKY, GEORG, *Studien zur Geschichte des Byzantinischen Bilderstreites* (Wrocław: Marcus, 1929)
PANOFSKY, ERWIN, *Idea: Ein Beitrag zur Begriffsgeschichte der älteren Kunsttheorie* (Leipzig: Hessling, 1924)
PENNONE, FLORENCE, *Paul Celans Übersetzungspoetik: Entwicklungslinien in seinen Übertragungen französischer Lyrik* (Tübingen: Niemeyer, 2007)
PETTERSON, JAMES, *Postwar Figures of 'L'Éphémère': Yves Bonnefoy, Louis-René des Forêts, Jacques Dupin, André du Bouchet* (Lewisburg, PA: Bucknell University Press, 2000)
PETUCHOWSKI, ELIZABETH, 'Bilingual and Multilingual "Wortspiele" in the Poetry of Paul Celan', *Deutsche Vierteljahrsschrift für Literaturwissenschaft und Geistesgeschichte*, 52.4 (1978), 635–51
PEYRÉ, YVES, *A hauteur d'oubli: André du Bouchet* (Paris: Galilée, 1999)
—— 'La Coïncidence de temps', in *Autour d'André du Bouchet: Rencontres sur la poésie moderne. Actes du colloque des 8, 9, 10 décembre 1983*, ed. by Michel Collot (Paris: Presses de l'École Normale Supérieure, 1986), pp. 41–53
—— *Peinture et poésie: Le Dialogue par le livre, 1874–2000* (Paris: Gallimard, 2001)
Plato, Aristotle, Horace, Longinus, *Classical Literary Criticism*, trans. by Penelope Murray and T. S. Dorsch (London: Penguin Books, 2000; repr. 2004)
PLATO, *Cratylus. Parmenides. Greater Hippias. Lesser Hippias*, trans. by H. N. Fowler (Cambridge, MA: Harvard University Press, 1939)
PÖGGELER, OTTO, ' "Schwarzmaut": Bildende Kunst in der Lyrik Paul Celans', in *Die Frage nach der Kunst: Von Hegel zu Heidegger*, ed. by Otto Pöggeler (Freiburg i. Br.: Alber, 1984), pp. 281–375
—— 'Schwerpunkt: Wort und Bild. Paul Celan und Gisèle Celan-Lestrange', *Sprache und Literatur*, 33.89 (2002), 3–42
—— 'Symbol und Allegorie', in *Paul Celan, 'Atemwende': Materialien*, ed. by Gerhard Buhr and Roland Reuß (Würzburg: Königshausen & Neumann, 1991), pp. 345–61
RANNOU, FRANÇOIS, 'André du Bouchet, lecteur de Mallarmé', in *Présence d'André du Bouchet*, ed. by Michel Collot and Jean-Pascal Léger (Paris: Hermann, 1986), pp. 28–39
RAY, GORDON NORTON, *The Art of the French Illustrated Book, 1700–1914*, 2 vols (New York: Pierpont Morgan Library, 1982)
REICHERT, KLAUS, 'Hebräische Züge in der Sprache Paul Celans', in *Paul Celan*, ed. by Werner Hamacher and Winfried Menninghaus (Frankfurt a. M.: Suhrkamp, 1988), pp. 156–69
REUß, ROLAND, *Im Zeithof: Celan-Provokationen* (Frankfurt a. M.: Stroemfeld, 2001)
REVERDY, PIERRE, 'L'Image', *Nord-Sud*, 13 (March 1918), n.p.
RIMBAUD, ARTHUR, *Œuvres complètes*, ed. by André Guyaux and Aurélia Cervoni (Paris: Gallimard, 2009)
ROCHE, ISABEL, *Character and Meaning in the Novels of Victor Hugo* (West Lafayette, IN: Purdue University Press, 2007)
RYLAND, CHARLOTTE, *Paul Celan's Encounters with Surrealism: Trauma, Translation and Shared Poetic Space* (London: Legenda, 2010)
SANMANN, ANGELA, *Poetische Interaktion: Französisch-deutsche Lyrikübersetzung bei Friedhelm Kemp, Paul Celan, Ludwig Harig, Volker Braun* (Berlin: De Gruyter, 2013)
SCHELLING, F. W. J., *Sämmtliche Werke*, ed. by K. F. A. Schelling, 14 vols in 2 parts: I [i–x] & II [i–iv] (Stuttgart: Cotta, 1856–61)

SCHLEBRÜGGE, JOHANNES VON, *Geschichtssprünge: Zur Rezeption des französischen Surrealismus in der österreichischen Literatur, Kunst und Kulturpublizistik nach 1945* (Frankfurt a. M.: Lang, 1985)

SCHLEIERMACHER, FRIEDRICH, 'On the Different Methods of Translating', in *Translation, History, Culture: A Sourcebook*, ed. by André Lefevere (London: Routledge, 1992), pp. 141–65

SCHMIDT, ARNO, '"Bei Wein und Verlorenheit ...": Bemerkungen zu einem Dithyrambos von Paul Celan aus der Sammlung *Die Niemandsrose*', *Archiv für Papyrusforschung und verwandte Gebiete*, 57.2 (2011), 345–55

SCHMIDT, JOCHEN, *Die Geschichte des Genie-Gedankens in der deutschen Literatur, Philosophie und Politik, 1750–1945*, 2 vols (Heidelberg: Winter, 2004)

SCHMITZ-EMANS, MONIKA, 'Paul Celan und die schriftmetaphorische Tradition', in *Der Glühende Leertext: Annäherungen an Paul Celans Dichtung*, ed. by Christoph Jamme and Otto Pöggeler (Munich: Fink, 1993), pp. 87–113

—— *Poesie als Dialog: Vergleichende Studien zu Paul Celan und seinem literarischen Umfeld* (Heidelberg: Winter, 1993)

SCHNEIDER, PIERRE, 'La Figure et le fond', in *Autour d'André du Bouchet: Rencontres sur la poésie moderne. Actes du colloque des 8, 9, 10 décembre 1983*, ed. by Michel Collot (Paris: Presses de l'École Normale Supérieure, 1986), pp. 101–09

SCHULZE, JOACHIM, *Celan und die Mystiker: Motivtypologische und quellenkundliche Kommentare* (Bonn: Bouvier, 1976)

SCOTT, DAVID, *Pictorialist Poetics: Poetry and the Visual Arts in Nineteenth-Century France* (Cambridge: Cambridge University Press, 2009)

SEARLE, JOHN R., *The Rediscovery of the Mind* (Cambridge, MA: MIT Press, 1992)

SENG, JOACHIM, *Auf den Kreis-Wegen der Dichtung: Zyklische Komposition bei Paul Celan am Beispiel der Gedichtbände bis 'Sprachgitter'* (Heidelberg: Winter, 1998)

SHAFTESBURY, ANTHONY ASHLEY COOPER, *Characteristics of Men, Manners, Opinions, Times*, ed. by Lawrence Eliot Klein (Cambridge: Cambridge University Press, 1999)

SOHN, MICHAEL, 'In Mallarmé's Harness? André du Bouchet and Stéphane Mallarmé', *French Forum*, 32.1/2 (2007), 117–35

SOWA-BETTECKEN, BEATE, *Sprache der Hinterlassenschaft: Jüdisch-christliche Überlieferung in der Lyrik von Nelly Sachs und Paul Celan* (Frankfurt a. M.: Lang, 1992)

STEINER, GEORGE, *After Babel: Aspects of Language and Translation*, 3rd edn (Oxford: Oxford University Press, 1998)

STEINER, WENDY, *The Colours of Rhetoric: Problems in the Relation between Modern Literature and Painting* (Chicago: University of Chicago Press, 1982)

STIEHLER, HEINRICH, 'Vom Bistilismus zum Zweitsprachengebrauch: Tristan Tzara', in *Horizont-Verschiebungen: Interkulturelles Verstehen und Heterogenität in der Romania. Festschrift für Karsten Garscha zum 60. Geburtstag*, ed. by Karsten Garscha, Claudius Armbruster, and Karin Hopfe (Tübingen: Narr, 1998)

SYROTINSKI, MICHAEL, 'Image', in *Dictionary of Untranslatables: A Philosophical Lexicon*, ed. by Barbara Cassin, Steven Rendall, and Emily S. Apter (Princeton: Princeton University Press, 2014), p. 478

TAIBON, MARKUS, '"Ein Wort nach dem Bild des Schweigens": Zur Sprachmetaphorik im Werk Paul Celans', *Sprachkunst*, 24 (1993), 233–53

TAVI, HENRIIKKA, 'Rezeptionen des deutschen Idealismus in Europa', in *Handbuch Deutscher Idealismus*, ed. by Hans Jörg Sandkühler (Stuttgart: Metzler, 2005), pp. 355–89

TUNKEL, TOBIAS, *Das verlorene Selbe* (Freiburg i. Br.: Rombach, 2001)

VASARI, GIORGIO, *The Lives of the Artists*, ed. by Julia Conaway Bondanella (Oxford: Oxford University Press, 2008)

VENUTI, LAWRENCE, *The Translator's Invisibility: A History of Translation* (London: Routledge, 1995)
VOSWINKEL, KLAUS, *Paul Celan: Verweigerte Poetisierung der Welt. Versuch einer Deutung* (Heidelberg: Stiehm, 1974)
WACKERNAGEL, WOLFGANG, 'Subimaginale Versenkung: Meister Eckharts Ethik der Bildergründenden Entbildung', in *Was ist ein Bild?*, ed. by Gottfried Boehm (Munich: Fink, 1994), pp. 184–207
WAGSTAFF, EMMA, 'André du Bouchet and Pierre Tal Coat: "Sous le linteau en forme de joug"', in *The Dialogue Between Painting and Poetry: Livres d'artistes, 1874–1999*, ed. by Jean Khalfa (Cambridge: Black Apollo, 2001), pp. 105–27
——*André du Bouchet: Poetic Forms of Attention* (Leiden: Brill Rodopi, 2020)
——'Francis Ponge and André du Bouchet on Giacometti: Art Criticism as Testimony', *The Modern Language Review*, 101.1 (2006) 75–89
——*Provisionality and the Poem: Transition in the Work of Du Bouchet, Jaccottet and Noël* (Amsterdam: Rodopi, 2006)
WAHL, JEAN ANDRÉ, *Le Malheur de la conscience dans la philosophie de Hegel* (Paris: Presses Universitaires de France, 1951)
WALDENFELS, BERNHARD, *Phänomenologie in Frankreich* (Frankfurt a. M.: Suhrkamp, 1986)
WEISSENBERGER, KLAUS, *Zwischen Stein und Stern: Mystische Formgebung in der Dichtung von Else Lasker-Schüler, Nelly Sachs und Paul Celan* (Berne: Francke, 1976)
WIEDEMANN, BARBARA, '"Und sie auf meine Art entziffern"', *Jahrbuch des Freien Deutschen Hochstifts* (2001), 263–92
——, ed., *Paul Celan, die Goll-Affäre: Dokumente zu einer 'Infamie'* (Frankfurt a. M.: Suhrkamp, 2000)
WIENOLD, GÖTZ, 'Paul Celans Hölderlin-Widerruf', *Poetica*, 2 (1968), 216–28
WILDE, MAURITIUS, *Das neue Bild vom Gottesbild: Bild und Theologie bei Meister Eckhart* (Freiburg, Switzerland: Freiburg Universitätsverlag, 2000)
WILLEMS, GOTTFRIED, *Anschaulichkeit: Zu Theorie und Geschichte der Wort-Bild-Beziehungen und des literarischen Darstellungsstils* (Tübingen: Niemeyer, 1989)
WOLOSKY, SHIRA, *Language Mysticism: The Negative Way of Language in Eliot, Beckett, and Celan* (Stanford: Stanford University Press, 1995)
YOUNG, JAMES E., *Writing and Rewriting the Holocaust: Narrative and the Consequences of Interpretation* (Bloomington: Indiana University Press, 1988)

INDEX

Amthor, Wiebke 114, 123, 162
Apollinaire, Guillaume 6, 7, 8
   'Lettre–Océan' 6
Archimedes 55
Asse, Geneviève 9
Augustine 3, 60, 106, 110
   De Trinitate 60
   mens humana (concept in Augustine) 60, 64 n. 27
Auschwitz 8
Austria 21

Babel 28, 66, 68, 70, 72–75, 83–84, 124, 151
   see also Bible
Badiou, Bertrand 128, 163
Baroque 38, 74
Baudelaire, Charles 7, 9, 12–13, 30, 34–35, 38, 39, 44–49, 53, 55, 81, 83, 87, 145, 150, 152, 157
   'Le Rêve d'un curieux' 45, 46, 83
   Salons 3, 17
Bazaine, Jean 11, 29, 111, 112, 113, 136
   Notes sur la peinture d'aujourd'hui 11, 29, 111
Benjamin, Walter:
   Ursprung des deutschen Trauerspiels 72–73
   Allegorical image (concept in Benjamin) 72–73
Bible 15, 73
   Genesis 56
   Jeremiah 76 n. 15
   John 61
   Matthew 56, 57, 61
   Old Testament 56, 78
   Psalms 58
Bildung 4, 15, 60, 160
Bishop, Michaël 12, 76, 83
Bogumil, Sieghild 121, 123, 127
Bollack, Jean 74
Bonnefoy, Yves 6, 84, 163
Böschenstein, Bernhard 127, 128, 135
Breton, André 8, 13, 21–23, 81–82
   Manifeste du surréalisme 21–23, 46, 82
Britain 7
Bruno, Giordano 34
Büchner, Georg 149
Bukovina 8

Celan–Lestrange, Gisèle 10, 11, 28
   for her *Schwarzmaut* & *Atemkristall*, see Celan, Paul

Celan, Paul:
   conception of the image:
      image and metaphor 2, 10–11, 23, 75–76, 126–27, 160
      imago Dei 3, 4, 9, 13, 37, 54–55, 60–61, 66, 106, 110, 158
      image and translation 118–27, 134–45
      image and writing 72–77, **114–15**
      influence of surrealism 21–22, 28, 30–31, 47–48
      relation to poetic subject **47–49**, **106–15**
      relation to post-structuralism 11
      terrestrial 28–29, 110, 113, 126–27, 142, 151–52
   poems and other shorter works:
      'Bei Brancusi, zu zweit' 11
      'Bei Wein und Verlorenheit' 4, 13, 28, 59, 63, **66–77**, 83, 99, 105–08, 113, 125–26, 137, 158, 160
      'Blitzgeschreckt' 11
      'Dein vom Wachen' 137
      'Ein Dröhnen' 79 n. 38, 132 n. 62
      'Einkanter, Rembrandt' 11, 71
      'Engführung' 131 n. 47, 132 n. 62, 138; translated as 'Strette' 128
      'Erblinde' 64, 98, **150–52**, 159; translated as 'Sois en ce jour aveugle', **150–52**
      'Halbzerfressener' 4, 14, 28, 48, 50, 59, 70, 83, 99, **105–17**, 126, 136, 158, 160
      'Hüttenfenster' 11
      'Kenotaph' 137
      'Mandorla' 64, 151
      'Meridian' 2, 5, 23, 27–28, 32, 52, 62, 77, 79, 107, 110–11, 113, 116, 118–19, 122, 126, 138, 145, 148–49, 158
      '*Mikrolithen sinds, Steinchen': Die Prosa aus dem Nachlass* 28, 33 nn. 34 & 35 & 39, 65 n. 41, 71, 79 n. 40, 112, 114
      'Sprachgitter' 33 n. 47, 146–47
      'Tenebrae' 3, 9, 13, **53–63**, 66, 68, 70, 83, 105, 106, 107, 110, 126, 158, 160
      'Todesfuge' 22, 65 n. 36, 79 n. 37
      'Traum vom Traume' 5, 8, 13, **21–31**, 47–48, 54, 58, 67, 81–82, 105, 112, 125, 131, 136, 145, 160
      'Über drei' 137, 146; translated as 'sur trois' 147
      'Ungespalten die Rede' 128
      'Unter ein Bild' 11
      'Weggebeizt' 135
      'Weißgrau' 2

poetry volumes:
    Atemkristall (with Gisèle Celan–Lestrange) 10, 28, 135
    Atemwende 71
    Der Sand aus den Urnen 21
    Fadensonnen 70, 113, 145
    Mohn und Gedächtnis 31, 54
    Schwarzmaut (with Gisèle Celan–Lestrange) 10, 28
    Sprachgitter 22, 54
    Von Schwelle zu Schwelle 22, 28, 54

Cendrars, Blaise 6
Centre National de la Recherche Scientifique (CNRS) 8, 9, 11, 13, 37, 39, 41, 44, 48, 83
Chagall, Marc 11
Champeau, Serge 12, 85
Collot, Michel 62, 95
concrete poetry 5, 6
Cusanus, Nicholas 15 n. 12, 49 n. 11, 50 n. 26, 60

Daive, Jean 134, 153
Darmstadt 149
Du Bouchet, André:
    conception of the image:
        absence & présence 39, 46–49, **90–93**, 96, 112, 121, 126, 157–58
        image and metaphor 160
        image and translation 118–27, 146–152
        image and writing **76–77**, 114–15
        paradox 9, 12, 14, 20 n. 94, 35, 37, 40, 42, 47–48, 77, 81, 83–84, 86–90, 96–99, 108, 120–21, 130 n. 25, 143–44, 150, 157–59
        post–structuralism 12–13
        relation to poetic subject **39–49, 106–08, 146–50**
        surrealism 47–48, 81–82
    poems and other shorter works:
        'Ce Balbutiement blanc' 76
        'Du Bord de la faux' 139
        'Image à terme' 30, **87–90**, 143–44, 157, 161
        'L'Écrit à haute voix' 76
        'Notes sur la traduction' 93, 118, 122, 148
        'Peinture' **93–100**, 157
        'Rudiments' 79, 143, 144
        'Sur le pas' 142, 144
    poetry volumes and essay volumes:
        Andains (livre d'artiste with Francis Helgorsky) 9
        Carnets 11, 34, 157, 161, 163
        Dans la chaleur vacante 8, 114, 128, 138, 139, 144, 145, 157, 163; translated as *Vakante Glut* 139
        Dans leur voix les eaux (livre d'artiste with Bram van Velde) 9
        Ici en deux 93, 95, 157, 163; as livre d'artiste with Geneviève Asse 9
        L'Inhabité (livre d'artiste with Giacometti) 9
        Laisses (livre d'artiste with Tal Coat) 9
        Le Surcroît (livre d'artiste with Albert Ràfols–Casamada) 9
        Sous le linteau en forme de joug (livre d'artiste with Tal Coat) 9
        Sur le pas (livre d'artiste with Tal Coat) 9
        Aveuglante ou banale 11, **34–49** 163
            'Baudelaire irrémédiable' 44, 87; 'Envergure de Reverdy' 82, 83; 'Pierre Reverdy, Le Chant des morts' 83; 'Théâtre de la répétition' 44; 'Vision et connaissance' 41, 44; 'Vue et vision chez Victor Hugo' 41

Dedecius, Karl 77, 122
Degas, Edgar 6
Delaunay, Sonia 6
Derrida, Jacques 17, 18, 52, 130, 131
    Dissemination 17 n. 50
    Limited Inc 18 n. 73
    Le Monolinguisme de l'autre 130 n. 34
    Shibboleth 131 n. 53
    La Voix et le phénomène 18 n. 73
Descartes, René 110, 116
Dueck, Evelyn 147, 148

Eckhart von Hochheim (Meister Eckhart) 4, 15 n. 12 & 20, 49 n. 11, 60, 63 n. 5, 65 n. 33, 117 n. 36, 153 n. 13
École Normale Supérieure 162
ekphrasis 11, 23–24
Eriugena, John Scotus 15 n. 12, 65 n. 33

Fall of Man 25–27, 66, 72, 77, 124–25
    see also Bible
Faulkner, William 128, 148
Favriaud, Michel 146–48
Fournanty-Fabre, Catherine 10
France 6–8, 21, 30, 34, 81

Gadamer, Hans Georg 1–2
Germany 67
Giacometti, Alberto 9, 17 n. 58
Goethe, Johann Wolfgang von 60, 64
    'Prometheus' 4, 60
Goll, Claire and the Goll affair 67–68, 77 n. 7, 84
Goll, Ivan 67
Gourmont, Remy de 7

Hegel, Georg Wilhelm Friedrich 12, 34, 50 n. 17, 130 n. 25
Heidegger, Martin 12, 18, 19, 85, 132
Helgorsky, Francis 9
Hesse 149
Hölderlin, Friedrich 9, 12–13, 30, 34–39, 41–43, 46–47, 49, 54, 68–69, 71, 81, 83, 87, 93, 96–97, 128, 135, 157, 162
    'Der Einzige' 49 n. 9, 155 n. 63; translated as 'L'Unique' 9, 155 n. 63

'Brod und Wein' 54, 68, 71
'Hälfte des Lebens' 38
Holocaust 9, 13, 22, 26, 53–59, 62, 67, 68, 70, 75, 76, 83, 124, 125, 138, 158, 162
Holthusen, Hans Egon 67–68
Hugo, Victor 7, 9, 12, 13, 30, 34–35, 39, 40–44, 47, 49–51, 81, 83, 87, 150, 157
    Les Misérables 40, 50
    'À un Poète aveugle' 51 n. 33
    Post–scriptum de ma vie 43
Huppert, Hugo 10
Husserl, Edmund:
    Die Idee der Phänomenologie 33, 113
    Ideen zu einer reinen Phänomenologie und phänomenologischen Philosophie 112
    Logische Untersuchungen 116
    Wesensschau (concept in Husserl) 29, 112, 113

iconoclasm 3, 60
image:
    archetypos & typos (Urbild & Abbild) distinction 3–4, 14
    image and imagination 1, 4, 7, 15, 46, 53, 81, 87
    as metaphor 1–2, 14–15 n. 3
    as natural sign 4–6
introspection 27–28, 105, 109, 111–13
Ivanović, Christine 22, 23

Jakob, Michael 106, 107, 123
Jené, Edgar 5, 10, 13, 21–25, 28, 31
Joyce, James 128

Kleist, Heinrich von
    'Über das Marionettentheater' 23, 26

L'Éphémère 6, 8, 13, 157, 162–63
Lacoue–Labarthe, Philippe 149
Last Supper 56
    see also Bible
Layet, Clément 12, 34, 38, 40, 84, 87, 89, 122, 157
Lefebvre, Jean Pierre 147, 152
Lessing, Gotthold Ephraim 5
Leuwers, Daniel 49
Linares, Serge 85
Livres d'artiste 6, 10, 11, 13, 121
Lönker, Fred 61

Maldiney, Henri 85
Mallarmé, Stéphane 6, 9, 27, 84, 128
    'Un Coup de dés' 6, 9, 84
    'Prose pour des Esseintes' 49
Mandelstam, Osip 114, 123, 162
Martinez, Victor 12, 85
Mascarou, Alain 125, 132
Menninghaus, Winfried 16, 124
Mercier, Louis–Sébastien 138

Meschonnic, Henri 128
metaphor 1, 2, 7–8, 10–11, 14, 21–24, 26, 35, 41, 43, 46, 54, 56, 60, 67, 70, 75–77, 97, 110, 114, 119, 120, 126, 127, 139, 159, 160, 162
Michelangelo 4
Milton, John 1, 43, 150
mirror 23–24, 59, 60–61, 64, 96, 110–11, 130
Mitchell, William John Thomas 101 n. 38, 162–63
modernism 5

Neoplatonism 2, 5, 27, 28, 34, 37, 56, 99, 113, 143, 159

Olschner, Leonard 127, 161

Paris 8–9, 21, 28, 54, 128, 161
Pennone, Florence 135–36, 138, 145
Picasso, Pablo 10, 83
Plato 2, 5, 12, 15, 16, 27, 28, 32 n. 18, 112, 120, 132 n. 60
Plotinus 34, 49 n. 11, 97, 104 n. 74, 132 n. 60
poètes voyants 39
poetic voice 45, 53–63, 74–75, 84, 99, 106–08, 112–13, 143, 148, 151, 158–59, 161
Pseudo–Dionysius the Areopagite 34, 51 n. 30, 65 n. 28

Ràfols–Casamada, Alberto 9
reflection 10, 14, 25, 26, 27, 59, 60, 109, 110, 111, 115 n. 8
Rembrandt 71
Renaissance 3, 8
Reuß, Roland 71
Reverdy, Pierre 6–9, 11, 21, 23, 26, 30–31, 53, 81–85, 98
    'L'Image' 7–8, 81–82
    Le réel (concept in Reverdy) 84–85
Rijcke, Elke de 33, 63, 120, 129–32, 154–55, 161, 163
Rimbaud, Arthur 7, 39, 48
    'Lettres du voyant' 7, 17, 48
Rodgers, Hoyt 97
Romania 21, 127

Scève, Maurice 9, 12, 13, 30, 34, 38, 39, 81, 83, 157
Schelling, Friedrich Wilhelm Joseph:
    System des transzendentalen Idealismus 4
Schlebrügge, Johannes von 22
Schmidt, Arno 74
Seng, Joachim 7, 30, 48, 58, 74, 83, 91, 157
Shakespeare, William 19, 148
Sowa-Bettecken, Beate 57
Steiner, George 5, 66
Steiner, Wendy 5
Supervielle, Jules 127
surrealism 6, 8, 13, 21–22, 28, 30–31, 34, 47, 81–82

Tal Coat 9, 13, 19, 20
Tawada, Yoko 74
Tel Quel 13, 35

Tison, François 34, 157
translation 2, 5, 8, 10–11, 14, 66–68, 73, 75, 77, 87, 98, 106, 108, 111–13, 118–29, 134–36, 138–39, 140–50, 152–53, 157–59, 161
Transnistria 21
Tunkel, Tobias 106
Tzara, Tristan 22, 31
   'La Dialectique de la poésie' 22

Ungaretti, Giuseppe 123
United States 30, 34, 158

Vasari, Giorgio 4
Veinstein, Alain 107, 161, 162, 163

Velde, Bram van 9
Vienna 8, 9, 21, 30

Wagstaff, Emma 76
Wahl, Jean 34
Warhol, Andy 86
Wiedemann, Barbara 67, 151
Wögerbauer, Werner 58, 59, 61
Wolosky, Shira 150–52
World War II 8, 32, 125
Wurm, Franz 134, 153

Yesenin, Sergei 124

www.ingramcontent.com/pod-product-compliance
Lightning Source LLC
Chambersburg PA
CBHW050454110426
42743CB00017B/3353